MICHAEL ROBERTO retired in 2016 from the faculty of North Carolina Agricultural and Technical State University, the largest historically black educational institution in the United States, where he taught contemporary world history. A longtime political activist in Greensboro, NC, he has worked as a journalist and published essays in *Monthly Review, Socialism and Democracy,* and other scholarly journals. Roberto is also a percussionist who has performed with leading jazz and R&B musicians.

The Coming of the American Behemoth

The Genesis of Fascism in the United States, 1920–1940

MICHAEL JOSEPH ROBERTO

MONTHLY REVIEW PRESS

New York

Library of Congress Cataloging-in-Publication Data
available from the publisher

ISBN paper: 978-1-58367-731-5
ISBN cloth: 978-1-58367-732-2

Typeset in Minion Pro and Brown

MONTHLY REVIEW PRESS, NEW YORK
monthlyreview.org

5 4 3 2 1

Contents

To the People of Greensboro, North Carolina

*and to the late Sarah Regis Jeffus whose encouragement
and material support made this work possible*

Preface

SINCE THE ELECTION of Donald J. Trump to the presidency in November 2016, many people have told me how timely it is to be writing a book about fascism in the United States. Trump's presence in the White House has become a nightmare for millions of Americans who cannot understand how someone who thinks and acts like a Mussolini or a Hitler could have been elected to the nation's highest office. Whenever I mentioned that my work was focused on the origins of American fascism in the 1920s and 1930s, many would say they wished I were writing about the current fascist threat. Yet when I provided examples from my research, they immediately recognized how familiar it all sounded in these times of Trump.

This is unsettling because it reveals how little most Americans know about fascism. What is most familiar to them is its infamous European legacy, specifically, that Mussolini took over Italy in the early 1920s and then a decade later in Germany Hitler catapulted to power. Absent is a vital piece of history recorded by American writers—either Marxists of some type or those influenced by Marxism—who in the 1930s and early 1940s believed that fascism was also possible in the United States but warned that it would not look the same as it did in Europe. Their astute observations revealed the peril of a distinct U.S. form of fascism, which was often proclaimed in the name of anti-fascism. For these observers, the real American fascists were those who wrapped themselves in the Stars and Stripes, pronounced themselves as guardians of the Constitution and democracy, and promoted the ideology of 100 percent Americanism. More important, much of it was peddled by reactionaries from the middling ranks of society but propagated by ruling-class elites who gained the most from it. Here was the masquerade these writers believed was the great peril of fascism in the United States. For reasons I hope will become evident in this book, the discourse that emerged during an earlier moment of crisis—the Great Depression—was omitted or marginalized by later historians whose fundamental assumptions about the exceptional role played by the United States, the most democratic of all modern societies, made it immune from fascism.

My ultimate objective in this book is to unmask those who so cleverly and deceitfully clothed themselves in true Americanism so they might conceal their own nefarious ends. From the 1920s, a time of unprecedented capitalist modernization heralded by an incessant ballyhoo of prosperity, the people most responsible for creating the embryo of American fascism stood atop the pyramid of capitalist wealth. Here among the rich and privileged few, whose fortunes were determined by the continued and necessary expansion of capitalist production and exchange, we can detect the germ of American fascism, not only in the mechanisms of repression the rich established to safeguard their interests, but also in the deeper capitalist imperatives that drove them to turn the United States into the world's banker and rising imperial hegemon.

To unveil this masquerade and grasp its more sophisticated guise in the present begins with the recovery of the works of these earlier writers. Their contributions are seminal to our understanding of the fascist threat today. Regardless of their differences, all pointed to the ruling capitalist class, or at least most of it, as the driving force of American fascism while dismissing the overt and often over-the-top small-fry fascisti as fringe groups of little or no significance. Nor did these contemporary writers put much stock in populist demagogues like Senator Huey Long of Louisiana and the Catholic radio priest Charles Coughlin as anything more than forerunners of a full-blown American fascism. Also missing in writings about the political landscape of the United States was a distinctive feature of European fascism—the mass movement. Instead, it was Big Business, Big Finance, Big Industry, Big Ownership, and all the other big entities associated with monopoly and finance capital—with two critics calling Wall Street the "fountainhead" of American fascism. In simplest terms, what was uniquely fascist in their view was the desire of the ruling class to establish a capitalist dictatorship within the framework of liberal democracy.

By relying on these earlier works of the 1930s and early 1940s as core sources, I have attempted to capture their political verve in the hope that it will register in the present. In some chapters of the book, I give considerable space to their texts because the thinking and language is often more vivid and direct than the shades of gray we find in contemporary histories and commentaries. But the recovery of the content is my main concern, because it is crucial to our understanding of the current moment as citizens and students of history. For the public, it provides an alternative to mainstream historical accounts taught in our public schools—as required by the sanitized pedagogy of capitalist schooling. To historians, it beckons further inquiry that will weigh the evidence presented here as the basis for future studies that can contribute to a fuller understanding of the history of American fascism. To both, however, it is my hope that what they discover will enable them to recognize how fascism today is really nothing new, but only its latest and most dangerous manifestation.

I have many people to thank for their unswerving support for my work. Among them is Mark Solomon, who was enthusiastic and encouraging from the moment I began talking about this project. His knowledge and counsel were indispensable. I am also indebted to my editor at Monthly Review Press, Michael Yates, who saw the merit of my ideas from the start and provided valuable criticisms and suggestions at pivotal moments of the project. Paul Breines, Al Brilliant, Joseph Louzonis, Larry Morse, and my son, Nate Roberto, offered invaluable insight and advice. Nate also provided an illustration for the book cover. I also thank Gregory Meyerson: the earliest work for this book was done in collaborative scholarship, publication and friendship. I acknowledge as well the long-standing intellectual and political support of Barbara Foley, Bertell Ollman, James Wood, and Chester Dunning. There are many others whose intelligence and enduring friendship were instrumental to keeping me together when the task seemed too daunting, especially Frank Fasano, Robin Roberto Horgan, Joy Perkal, Stuart Hunt, Randall Harris, Justin Harmon, Claire Morse, and Gayle Nantz, as well as my daughter, Ana Roberto. Still others in a long line of family and friends who supported me include Ernest Hooker, Galen Foresman, Sarah Beale, Jeff Jones, Travis Byrd, Susan and Spencer Andrews, Dean Finocchi, Cathy Fasano, Ed and Delores Freda, Peter Khoury, Kevin Tringale, Bev and Mike Conter, Josie Kite, Keith Tager, Kent Tager, Mike Bowen, Ellie Alinaghi, Roger Webster, David Knoche, and Anthony Bono.

My mother, Ethel Roberto, still sharp as a tack at eighty-nine despite her frail health, always managed short but pithy remarks to my often exhaustive—and exhausting—explanation of the book's contents.

Above all, I owe the greatest debt to my wife, Sharon Weber, whose intelligence, compassion, and keen eye for the written word constantly affirmed for me what I had tried to teach students for many years—that clear writing can only come from clear thinking.

Introduction: Fascism as the Dictatorship of Capital

THIS BOOK EXAMINES the origins of American fascism between the two world wars. My analysis is based on a consensus of writers—historians, political scientists, social critics, Marxists and non-Marxists alike—who saw its rise within the growing powers of monopoly and finance capital during the booming 1920s and the general crisis of the following decade, which we call the Great Depression. For these writers, Big Business, as it was commonly known, was the main source of embryonic fascism in the United States. On the basis of their findings and observations, I identify processes inherent in capitalist production and sociopolitical relations throughout the period as *fascist* because they extended and deepened the hold of capital over American political institutions and mass consciousness. Though these processes never merged to create a distinct fascist trajectory, all contributed to the totalizing powers of capital that made the United States the rising epicenter and hegemon of the world capitalist system—and the coming of the American Behemoth.

My argument is grounded in the principles of Marxist political economy set within the epoch of contemporary world history.

Fascist processes inhered in production and exchange at a pivotal moment in the ascendance of U.S. capitalism after the First World War. America became the world's industrial leader and banker during the 1920s, requiring ever-greater levels of capitalist accumulation necessary for the cycle of investment, production, and exchange—a cycle repeated exponentially for continued economic growth and profits. We see this during the Great Boom of the twenties. The drive to increase the productivity of social labor by means of technological innovation fueled the concentration of economic power—monopoly—and its centralization in Big Business, quickly becoming a system of power, one in which the government was a willing partner. But unprecedented economic growth and the centralization of economic and political power also heightened the contradictions always present in monopoly capitalism: each new cycle of production sharpened the divide between capital and labor. Why? The greater the drive to increase productivity with use of more machines, the more human labor was displaced from production, creating the paradox of growing poverty within an ever-rising sea of plenty. Then the bust! The Wall Street crash in 1929 ushered in a general crisis of American capitalism during the Depression decade of the 1930s.

It is within this historical framework that we find the efficient cause of American fascism: from the growth of state power in the service of the capitalist ruling class to the reactionary politics of the middle class, to the manipulation of the public by advertisers and public relations experts whose sole aim was to commodify everything. All were fascist processes because they aimed at the domination of capital over society. What emerges from this approach is a dynamic definition of fascism as an inherent function of monopoly-capitalist production and relations whose telos was and remains the totalitarian rule of capitalist dictatorship.

Of course, the intellectual and political origins of fascism predate its actual coming to power in Europe after the First World War. Fascist ideas had emerged from the turmoil of European political culture at the end of the nineteenth century and gradually became a force in sectarian politics. Some sects ultimately grew into movements; in Italy they coalesced rather quickly to become the world's first fascist regime under Benito Mussolini and the Partito Nazionale Fascista (National Fascist Party) in 1922. The global capitalist crisis that commenced in 1929 and deepened the following decade fueled the growth of fascism worldwide and the seizure of power by Hitler and the National Socialists in Germany. No wonder, then, that the Italian and German examples are rarely absent in any study of fascism, since anything considered fascist must always pass the litmus test of both in some manner or degree. Writing in 1952 under a pseudonym, the Marxist political economist Paul Baran put it succinctly:

> For a political system to "qualify" as fascist, it has to display the German or Italian characteristics of fascism. It must be based on a fascist mass movement anchored primarily in para-military formations of brown shirts or black shirts. It must be a one-party regime, with the party headed by a Führer or a Duce symbolizing the principle of authoritarian leadership. It must be violently nationalist, racist, anti-Semitic. It must be frankly illiberal, intolerant of opposition, hostile to civil liberties and human rights.[1]

Baran saw this approach as indicative of a sterile paradigm in the study of fascism. Taking his cue, I make a conscious effort to move in another direction by recovering a long forgotten consensus held by many U.S. writers during the 1930s and early 1940s that Big Business or the business system was primarily responsible for the genesis of fascism in the United States. In the process, I discovered a most striking feature about American fascism—its utterly disguised character. This was clear to Dwight Macdonald in his introduction to Daniel Guerin's *Fascism and Big Business* (1939): "Our fascists," Macdonald wrote, "not only don't (yet) wear brown shirts; they proclaim themselves 'anti-fascist' as well as 'anti-communist' and march under the banner of 'liberty' and even 'democracy.'" For Macdonald, here was the real danger:

By spot-lighting the secondary characteristics of European fascism, such as Jew-baiting and book-burning, without exposing its class roots, the false impression is built up that such manifestations are something unparalleled in the history of "civilized nations." This makes it easy to divert the energy of the American working class and its liberal supporters into a crusade against overseas fascism, while our own ruling class is left in power, undisturbed, biding its time to introduce fascism over here when the situation demands it.[2]

Macdonald's was one of many voices warning that fascism would come in the name of anti-fascism; that is, it would be presented as True Americanism. At the same time, he affirmed what his contemporary, the eminent Marxist philosopher and social theorist, Max Horkheimer, said when he declared that "whoever is not prepared to talk about capitalism should also remain silent about fascism."[3]

Fascism and the World Economy: The United States as Capitalist Epicenter

This book builds on the seminal contribution of the sociologist Walter Goldfrank, who employed in 1978 the perspective of world-system theory to argue that fascism was caused primarily by the global economic contraction during the interwar period that accelerated a shift in international relations. Goldfrank reminded his readers that fascism was a unique product of contemporary world history. A global economic crisis had damaged the international order and especially Great Britain, whose domination over the world market was by then nearly eclipsed. What made the capitalist world system less stable was the war of positioning between three rising and competing world powers that challenged Britain's declining imperial reach: a semi-isolationist United States that had already surpassed Britain as the new hegemon; the Soviet Union, the leader of a global revolutionary-socialist alternative to capitalism and imperialism; and Nazi Germany with its sudden rise and horrific hegemonic designs of its own.[4]

According to Goldfrank, fascism emerged in the three zones of the world capitalist system—core, semi-periphery, and periphery— in the first half of the twentieth century. Each zone was determined by the level of capital formation, from the highest form in the core nations, to those in the semi-periphery where capitalism was less developed and therefore at times dependent on the core for capital, to poorer countries and colonies in the periphery, which had no capital of their own and depended entirely on the core and semi-periphery. Fascism had emerged for the first time in Italy, which Goldfrank considered part of the European semi-periphery because its capital formation was lower than the dominant core powers of Great Britain and France, its European allies during the First World War. Soon after the war ended, a postwar economic crisis developed in Italy that threatened the political position of its ruling classes, not all of them fully capitalist. For Goldfrank, Mussolini's coming to power was something of an experiment, the same position taken by a leading communist writer and theorist in the mid-1930s, R. Palme Dutt, who asserted that Italian fascism had "developed only in an experimental stage in a secondary capitalist country."[5] What both said about Italy was striking because it provided another way of thinking about the first fascist regime in history. Italy's semi-peripheral status in the world capitalist system, which reflected that country's weak capital formation, certainly played a huge role in determining fascist forms and processes. For one thing, Mussolini and the primarily middle-class movement he led came to power without protracted struggle, in part because Italy's ruling classes were weak and quickly fell into line. The impotence of the Italian state corresponded to the weakness of Italian capital in relation to the more entrenched landowning class and other traditional elites in the army and the Catholic Church. Capital's weak hold on Italy explained why the driving force of fascism came from a movement led by a fiery demagogue whose political rise subsumed the power of the ruling classes quickly.

Could the same be said of Germany? Here again, the actual developments during the 1920s confirmed Goldfrank's assertions. The political turmoil of a fragile economy made shakier by the French occupation of the Ruhr in 1923 and the passive resistance of German industrialists and workers to it, fueled one of the worst inflationary runs in history. Only massive loans by American bankers the following year stabilized the Weimar Republic. For the next few years, American investors provided huge loans to German public credit institutions, local governments, and large corporations.[6] As a result, the dependence of German capital on American bankers made it semi-peripheral to the United States. When the Wall Street crash signaled the global crisis, the dependency of German capital on U.S. bankers permanently destabilized the economy and opened the door to a rising middle-class movement, primarily the lower-middle class, led by Hitler. For Germany, the historical circumstances differed from Italy's only in scale. Capital formation in Germany was far greater than in Italy, thus its fascist development was more advanced. From Goldfrank and Dutt, we understand that fascism came to power in Germany because it had arisen in a dominant capitalist country as a result of the global crisis. Given its greater capitalist strength, parliamentary rule lasted longer in resisting fascism. Once American capital was withdrawn after 1930, Germany's capitalists could not sustain their class rule without Hitler, who saved them in 1933 when he came to power.

Goldfrank's approach to fascism established two criteria for comparing different forms of fascism on the world stage in the 1920s and 1930s: first among its various forms in the core, semi-periphery, and periphery, and then within each zone. Here was a way to determine similarities and differences of fascist and non-fascist responses to acute crisis conditions developing in the world capitalist system. The specific forms of fascism that emerged in Italy and Germany reflected their respective levels of capital formation, and how existing conditions and circumstances determined their standing in the capitalist core. What Goldfrank failed to do on the basis of the same logic was to show how the world crisis that began in the United States, the new epicenter of the world system, determined its particular form of fascism.

Goldfrank's world-system approach provides us with insights into the origins of American fascism. Did the absence of a mass movement in the United States on the level of Germany's mean there were no fascist processes? Or did they take other forms? Given its position as the epicenter of world capitalism, where the concentration of capital was the greatest, did fascist processes emerge from the needs of U.S. capitalists themselves? To answer these questions required an inquiry beyond descriptive comparisons. Having theorized that fascism in all its forms were products of the world capitalist crisis, Goldfrank omitted the United States, where a number of writers during the 1930s and early 1940s had already made the connection. Having argued that every manifestation of fascism should be examined in relation to the world capitalist system, however, he made no effort to examine how many observers saw its particular form developing in the United States.

Failing to do this, Goldfrank simply submitted to the reigning paradigm that Baran had criticized nearly thirty years earlier, concluding, "If no serious fascist movement had arisen in the twenties, the effects of the Depression were not by themselves so severe as to generate more than echoes and imitations" of those that had developed in Italy and Germany.[7] Yet his analysis of fascism as a world-system theorist suggested otherwise.   Based on its dominant position in the world-capitalist system, American fascism would differ from Italian and German forms because its level of capital formation was the most advanced, the highest in the world-capitalist system. As my study shows, this was indeed the case. Whatever the shortcomings, Goldfrank's analysis still validated Horkheimer's claim in a stimulating and profound way, and confirmed the approach Gregory Meyerson and I would take in 2008 about the plausibility of fascism in the United States.[8]

A crisis in the world-capitalist system was indeed the efficient cause for the global development of fascism during the interwar period—and beyond.[9] Based on what American observers were saying at the time, fascism was definitely in the works during the interwar period, though the record shows that all attempts to create a distinct fascist movement never got very far. Still, these same observers provided palpable evidence of other fascist processes that indicated characteristics of a generic fascism in the United States, the most advanced of all capitalist core countries. This was revelatory. For one thing, Paul Sweezy's assessment in 1942 that "every capitalist nation, in the period of imperialism, carries within it the seeds of fascism," seemed to make even greater sense. This didn't make fascism inevitable. But Sweezy made clear that it "arises only out of a situation in which the structure of capitalism has been severely injured and yet not overthrown."[10]

THE FORGOTTEN VOICES OF THE 1930S AND EARLY 1940S

Much of my work stems from the recovery of what I consider a "lost" discourse on fascism in the 1930s and early 1940s. Recognizing fascism's embryonic forms in the interwar period provides a foundation and perspective for understanding American fascism in the present, now more fully developed with the election of Donald J. Trump to the presidency in 2016.

Two communist writers in 1938, A. B. Magil and Henry Stevens, in writing the only comprehensive treatment of U.S. fascism to date, argued that "the germ of fascism was inherent within American monopoly capitalism; but it was not until the economic crisis of 1929 that it developed into a definite political force of ominous proportions."[11] Their view echoed that of leftist journalist Mauritz Hallgren, who five years earlier asserted that the growth of monopoly capitalism is "the principal element in the making of fascism." Hallgren viewed fascism as "a political philosophy based upon the need of capitalism to employ the power of the State to protect the institution of production for private profit."[12] Both works substantiated what Georgi Dimitroff said when he defined fascism as "the power of finance capital itself" in his report to the Seventh World Congress of the Communist International in 1935.[13]

In this study, I use these and other writers to identify and analyze a wide range of fascist processes that inhered in U.S. monopoly-finance capitalism in the 1920s and 1930s. As such, they are not archival sources but rather written accounts—secondary sources, as historians call them—that have been buried, marginalized, or trivialized, a story itself that needs telling. Among the most significant are the works already mentioned, as well as those by Lewis Corey, Carmen Haider, Robert Brady, and others. Indeed, much of my understanding of conditions that led to the emergence and intensification of fascist processes is derived from the extraordinary analysis by Lewis Corey in his indispensable 1934 work, *The Decline of American Capitalism*. Despite their differences, all these writers shared common ground in viewing monopoly-finance capitalism as the seedbed for American fascism. All of their writings have become the basis for deeper inquiry. Although they emphasized the coercive and often violent practices that capitalists used to extend and secure their hold over the mass of working people, we must also consider how they shaped mass consciousness through manipulation and persuasion. Along with the terrorism came a politics of acquiescence and accommodation to capitalist imperatives essentially non-terrorist in character. To develop this position, I borrow and modify a theoretical tenet from Herbert Marcuse who, in the opening pages of *One-Dimensional Man*, views contemporary industrial society as essentially totalitarian in two forms: "a terroristic political coordination of society, but also non-terroristic economic-technical coordination which operates through the manipulation of needs by vested interests."[14]

Plan of the Book and Its Main Arguments

The book is divided into two parts. In the first six chapters that make up Part 1, I discuss how the seeds of American fascism were sown in the Great Boom of the 1920s, a time of unprecedented capitalist growth and a dazzling spectacle of prosperity that concealed its contradictions and ultimately resulted in the worst economic crisis in the history of capitalism. This may strike the reader as counterintuitive since fascism is generally associated with crisis rather than prosperity. Nevertheless, I argue that this is precisely how fascism develops in the epicenter of the world capitalist system. When understood properly, American fascism is the product of capitalist modernization, which inevitably leads to the domination of finance capital over the rest of society.

In chapter 1, I introduce the reader to the sweeping changes in American economic, political, and cultural life brought by the capitalist ruling class in the 1920s, which transformed the means of production and social relations and widened the gap between wealth and poverty. Chapter 2 builds on what Magil and Stevens meant when they stated that the "germ" of fascism was inherent in American monopoly capitalism. I explain how the contradictions in capitalist accumulation displaced labor and made it increasingly subject to capital. To support their claim and for the benefit of readers unfamiliar with political economy, I examine Karl Marx's analysis of the processes of capitalist accumulation as explained in his great work, *Capital*. I then discuss how Lewis Corey applied Marx's analysis to the U.S. economy in the 1920s and 1930s. By doing so, the reader comes to an understanding of how the Great Depression was the result of contradictions in the so-called Great Boom of the previous decade.

In chapter 3, I describe the material abundance achieved between 1922 and 1929 that created a spectacle of prosperity, which could only be sustained by a corresponding rise in the rate of consumption. Here I introduce the reader to non-terrorist fascist processes in the form of advertising, public relations, and propaganda, all aimed at the increasing commodification of society. In chapter 4 I offer a detailed description of an evolving ideology within the business system as it developed its political arm. In chapter 5, I discuss how the spectacle and ballyhoo of material abundance and its attendant New Era ideology masked the growing divide between those who enjoyed some level of prosperity and the majority of Americans who were left behind. This general condition in U.S. society of growing poverty in a sea of plenty generated a political reaction that fueled the rise of the second Ku Klux Klan during the early and mid-1920s. I close the chapter with a discussion of how the ruling class intensified fascist processes by strengthening their hold over American society as well as other nations and peoples by its expanding global reach—Pax Americana on the rise.

I begin chapter 6 with Corey's detailed and still unrivaled analysis of the origins of the era's general crisis. More than any other economist of the 1930s, he brilliantly explains how overproduction in capital goods caused a halt to further productive investment throughout the entire economy, resulting in rampant speculation, culminating in the Wall Street crash. I summarize Corey's explanation of the "bust in the boom" that set in motion the intensification of fascist processes during the Great Depression.

Part 2 focuses on the general crisis of the 1930s and the extent to which many believed that fascist rule was possible in the United States. These six chapters cover the period from the stock market crash to 1940 when Franklin Delano Roosevelt won his third term in the White House.

Chapter 7 describes the worst years of the crisis between 1929 and 1932 and the toll it took on millions of people. I focus on the rising political instability of the federal government and its failure under President Herbert Hoover to end the crisis. The increasing paralysis caused many business leaders and politicians to call for the suspension of the Constitution and agree to emergency measures that amounted to an American counterpart to Mussolini. Chapter 8 recovers a remarkable discussion of 1934 and 1935, virtually absent in recent historiography and political commentary, about whether the New Deal was fascist or a transition to fascism. It is here where we grasp the vital connection between liberalism and fascism in the transition to state monopoly capitalism in the United States, which for many resembled the corporatist state in fascist Italy. Chapter 9 examines the plethora of fringe groups that made up what many considered to be relatively insignificant in the making of American fascism—what one left-liberal journalist famously called "small-fry fascisti."[15] I also discuss the political trajectories of the two most reactionary populist demagogues of the times, the Catholic radio priest Charles Coughlin and Senator Huey Long of Louisiana, both of whom failed to build mass movements.

This leads to my discussion in chapter 10 of writers in 1934 and 1935 whose class analyses determined that the middle class would not play the primary role in the making of American fascism. In chapter 11, I focus on President Roosevelt's assertion that the business system was "fascist." I examine the background to his use of the word when, in the spring of 1938, he called for an inquiry into the growing power of monopolies and financial institutions that he deemed fascist. I discuss how Roosevelt's position illustrates the "good vs. bad capitalism" dynamic in American politics, which persists today. Chapter 12 closes out the second part of the book with a discussion of Robert Brady's detailed analysis of the business system and the progress it had made since the early 1920s in synchronizing capitalist domination over the marketplace while extending its political influence in government.

I consider this book an introduction rather than a detailed and comprehensive account. I leave the latter to U.S. historians and other social scientists whose knowledge of American history is greater than mine. I wrote this book from the perspective of a world historian who deemed it necessary to consider fascism as a product of capitalist development, specifically in the particular form that fascism took in the United States in the interwar period.

There are aspects of the making of American fascism that will not be found in the following pages. I do not treat the major personalities of the period who are rightly considered its usual fascist suspects—Henry Ford, Charles Lindbergh, and William Randolph Hearst to name a few. Their activities have been covered by many other historians and writers. Nor do I focus on race, gender, religion, or other cultural forms of differentiation, recognizing that the entire history of American fascism in this period requires that these aspects receive full treatment. Instead, I have chosen to emphasize the *capital-labor relationship* and the various ways it was understood by my predecessors in the 1930s and early 1940s. Their findings were central and foundational to my work. I have also chosen not to discuss the man who was considered to be the leading American fascist intellectual of the day, Lawrence Dennis. This is because his peculiar worldview and politics were tangential to those who were the real architects of American fascism: the ruling class and its various attendants in government; trade associations like the National Association of Manufacturers and the U.S. Chamber of Commerce; and the media outlets that knowingly or unknowingly supported fascist ideas and processes.

My hope is that this brief study will convince others that there is much work to be done. Even though this book reflects my training as an historian, what I have done here also reflects my work as a journalist, with the object being to tell a story grounded in the evidence and made readable for the public. To that end, I have endeavored to make the most compelling case possible about the coming of the American Behemoth, to its now mature and frightening presence as a capitalist empire in utter decline and decay leaping from the carcass of liberal capitalist democracy into fascism.

IN 1942, FRANZ NEUMANN published his historic analysis of National Socialism, *Behemoth*, as much of the world fought against the fascist Axis of Germany, Italy, and Japan. Neumann justified his choice of the title by comparing it to Thomas Hobbes's use of the same word for the title of his book on the Long Parliament, which Hobbes called a time of "complete lawlessness" in England, between 1640 and 1660, and which he described politically as a "non-state."[16] This condition, Neumann said, applied to Germany under National Socialism. Moreover, fascist ideology virtually defied theorizing within the boundaries of existing political theory. Though it contained elements of every conceivable philosophy—idealism, pragmatism, positivism, vitalism, etc.—these were not integrated to form a whole. In short, Neumann wrote, National Socialism was "incompatible with any rational political philosophy," and the reason for it could be found in the structure of National Socialist society itself. "There exists," he wrote, "a fundamental antagonism between the productivity of German industry, its capacity for promoting the welfare of the people and its actual achievements, and this antagonism is steadily deepening." Neumann noted that the huge and continuous industrial machinery had been geared toward war while the regime broke one sweet promise after another.[17]

At the same time, National Socialism had grown stronger because it had acted "according to a most rational plan, that each and every pronouncement by its leaders is calculated, and its effect on the masses and the surrounding world is carefully weighed in advance."[18] For Neumann, what made National Socialism a distinct political phenomenon was its appeal to the people. This was the main reason it came to power. It had incorporated into its own ideology the very thing it had wrecked: large-scale democracy under the Weimar Republic. But the appeal of the former lived on in the latter and was essential to it. "National Socialism has transformed institutional democracy of the Weimar Republic into a ceremonial and a magic democracy, a development made necessary by the requirements of totalitarian war, in which the distinctions between civilians and soldiers are annihilated and in which the civilian suffers even more than the soldiers." Neumann referred to the American political scientist Harold Lasswell, who described this situation as "the socialization of danger," which more than ever required "full control over the whole mass of the people and over each aspect of their individual lives."[19] In order to manipulate the masses, to control them, to atomize them, to terrorize them, they had to be captured ideologically. This, Neumann said, was the essence of the fascist dictatorship.

But fascism did not end capitalism and that was central to Neumann's critical analysis of the structure of National Socialism.

No deep antagonisms among the German ruling classes existed, but neither were there common loyalties. "The cement that binds them together is profit, power, and, above all, fear of the oppressed masses," Neumann wrote. But he also recognized that the widening contradictions between the rulers and the ruled held out the possibility that the Nazi regime would not survive, that the German masses would ultimately act on the understanding many had of the whole fraudulent and fictitious character of the regime's ideological front—that it was all just "bunk."[20] Sooner or later, all the contradictions between those who understood the realities beneath the paradox of National Socialist ideology and its anti-capitalist and anti-state propagandas would unwittingly further genuine socialist trends. Unfortunately, the history of National Socialism tragically proved otherwise.

As for the United States, fascism never came to power in the interwar period, though it is marching toward it in the present. For sure, its path is less clear than it was in Italy or Germany. Nevertheless, fascist processes in the United States have now coalesced into a clear fascist trajectory. As we go to press, it is especially evident that the ruling class has taken a decisive step in its dance with a president whose crude pragmatism is at the root of his fascist ideology. In this respect, Trump is no different than was Hitler, who railed against the ruling class and then embraced it at a crucial moment in the consolidation of his power.

To know the American Behemoth as Neumann knew its German predecessor is the condition required to bring it down. This is why I have chosen to study its origins.

PART 1

The Germ of Fascism in the Prosperous 1920s

1—The Wonders of American Capitalism in the New Era

MILLIONS OF AMERICANS weary of conflict abroad and turmoil at home went to the polls in November 1920 and elected Warren Gamaliel Harding as their president. Harding received 60.2 percent of the vote, an unprecedented landslide that stood until Lyndon Baines Johnson achieved a greater victory in 1964.[1] Almost from the start of his campaign, Harding promised a return to "normalcy." But what did that mean? What could be normal for a nation so utterly transformed by its role in a world war and now on its way to becoming the preeminent leader of the postwar global order?

The Great War, as it was then called, had catapulted the United States into a rising global hegemon. But this would not have surprised those who had observed its rise decades earlier, especially Karl Marx and Frederick Engels, the founders of scientific socialism. In *Capital* (1867), Marx wrote that the Civil War had established conditions that put the United States on a path toward world economic and political leadership. British investment had been central to construction of the Transcontinental Railroad, connecting east and west, between 1863 and 1873. Its completion spurred the growth of the mining and steel industries that became the basis of the modern American industrial economy, most of it financed by U.S., not British, capital. It was Marx who recognized the U.S. economy as "a new, dynamic model of capital accumulation."[2] By the early 1880s, he and Engels had determined that America's untapped natural resources and vast internal market would become the basis for its eventual leadership of the world capitalist economy. The combination of its "gigantic agricultural production" and simultaneous exploitation of "its tremendous industrial resources," would soon bring an end to "the monopoly of Western Europe, and especially of England." These were seminal developments not only for the United States but for the rest of the world. As small landowners lost ground to the "competition of giant farms," Marx and Engels wrote, "a numerous proletariat and a fabulous concentration of capital" were "developing for the first time in the industrial regions."[3] Though economic expansion within "the protected home market" also carried the possibility of a crisis of overproduction, the latter would "serve to hasten the time when America becomes capable of exporting and of entering the world market as England's most dangerous competitor."[4]

The pace of these developments quickened dramatically in the 1880s and 1890s as the rise of industrial monopolies established a platform for the emergence of finance capital and U.S. imperialism. In 1936, the Marxist economist and historian Anna Rochester described how the foundation for finance capital in the 1890s had been established twenty years earlier when bankers took advantage of "the whole top-heavy structure of public debt" by financing government and municipal bonds. As the economy expanded in the 1880s, so did the need for a wider range of banking operations in both commerce and investment. While routine business operations relied increasingly on the need for short-term credit, corporations with large aggregations of capital turned to investment bankers to underwrite additional stock and issue bonds. The latter played major roles in the reproduction of capital by underwriting new securities. No one was more successful at this than J. P.

Morgan, whose stealth in the art of the deal became evident when he decided to buy new stock for the New York Central Railroad in 1879. Establishing even greater control over much of the nation's railroads following the crisis of 1893, Morgan had also turned to financing and organizing the great industrial trusts of the General Electric Company in 1892, the U.S. Steel Corporation in 1901, and the International Harvester Company in 1902.[5]

A year before he led the Bolsheviks to revolution in 1917, Lenin cited statistics to argue that the United States had become the world's leader in the concentration of production and its ownership. By 1909, 3,060 industrial enterprises out of 268,491—1.1 percent of the total—employed 2 million of the 6.6 million workers who made up the total workforce and produced an output valued at $9 billion, almost half of the $20.7 billion in total output. Moreover, these giant enterprises covered 258 branches of industry. Industrial cartels and trusts were now determining the course of U.S. industry. By 1909, U.S. corporations constituted 25.9 percent of the total number of business enterprises but employed 75.6 percent of the total wage earners in America. These corporations generated enormous profits, much of it going to dividends for shareholders. Increasing monopolization led to mergers with banking, giving rise to the hegemonic power of finance capital in the hands of a small financial oligarchy. This in turn contributed to further concentration and hierarchical ownership in the form of holding companies. The latter, among other things, pioneered a corrupt system of balance-sheet jugglery between the mother company and its "daughter companies" that could have concealed "doubtful undertakings from the ordinary shareholder," while enriching those who controlled the accounting. Lenin also noted that these fraudulent and corrupt methods bred a business ethics forged principally by American capitalists. He saw the pernicious reach of concentrated wealth and power. "A monopoly," Lenin wrote, "once it is formed and controls the thousands of millions, inevitably penetrates into *every* sphere of public life, regardless of the form of government."[6]

As Anna Rochester argued, the emergence of these great trusts marked the beginning of America's industrial leadership in the world economy. Industrial production soared, displacing raw materials and agricultural products as America's chief exports in 1894; four years later, the United States was exporting more of these goods than importing. The United States no longer depended on foreign investment for further growth. Flush from huge profits, U.S. capitalists sought new outlets for productive investment abroad while opening a market for the sale of foreign government bonds at home. Once again, J. P. Morgan led the way by funding Mexican debt in 1899 and financing Great Britain's South African War in 1900–1901.

All told, these developments had put the country on the road to empire. With the closing of its own frontier and monopoly-finance capital in ascendance, American political leaders pursued the same expansionist policies as their European counterparts, and with greater might. As Rochester concluded, the United States looked to colonize non-capitalist areas and expand its general influence abroad. Victory over Spain in 1900 had delivered the Philippines to permanent U.S. occupation, cementing America's imperial presence across the Pacific and strengthening its grip over the Caribbean and Central America. By then, the architects of a global empire with nascent powers in the Atlantic and Pacific were guided by a vision of unprecedented global power. To that end, the United States began building naval bases wherever it could and started work on the Panama Canal. The canal was finished in 1914, the year the First World War broke out in Europe.[7]

America in the Great War: Economic Supremacy and Political Repression

The European war had raged for three years before the United States finally joined the Allies (Great Britain, France, Italy, and Russia) as a combatant in April 1917, against the Central Powers (Germany, Austro-Hungary, and the Ottoman Empire). American troops were slow to arrive in Europe, and only half of the million men of the American Expeditionary Force actually fought on the Western Front. But their presence alone marked new challenges and responsibilities for the United States as soon as the Armistice was signed in November 1918. Though it had risen quickly on the world stage, U.S. leadership stumbled into the postwar world, now in shambles. The socialist revolution in Russia shocked and frightened the architects of the world capitalist order in Europe and the United States. American diplomacy under an ailing president, Woodrow Wilson, had reached a crossroads. Despite an immediate isolationist impulse to avoid future European entanglements, there was no avoiding the imperatives that came with being the world's industrial leader and new banker. From the latter standpoint, America's leading capitalists agreed that European recovery was vital to U.S. economic interests at home and abroad.

World war had catapulted the United States into the world's mightiest economic powerhouse. Even before it entered the conflict, America's support for the Allied war effort had accelerated the concentration of wealth and the supremacy of monopoly-finance capital over the U.S. economy. Indeed, the war had been good for America's industrial giants and its biggest banks. Capital loaned to the Allies to buy U.S. goods had pumped at least $5 billion of purchasing power, a substantial part of the total national income, into the domestic economy.[8] Returns on investment, especially in munitions, were stunning. Corporate profits soared. Wealthy owners and managers got richer. Better yet, there was enough to go around. Workers made more money and lived better. Farmers reaping the rewards of booming agricultural prices borrowed from local banks to buy new machinery and cultivate more land. The pace of these developments quickened when the United States entered the war. As American soldiers fell on the Western Front, a select few of their countrymen made big killings in the marketplace. By 1919, a year after the war ended, America's corporations were producing 87 percent of all manufactured goods in the domestic economy.[9] Eighteen of the largest two hundred corporations saw net earnings rise to $337 billion during the war. Profits in the steel and iron industries were three times more than original investments. Earnings in the electrical and appliance industries were even better, rising almost two hundred times above their initial investments. Meanwhile, more Americans were adding to their personal wealth. According to income tax returns, the number of millionaires had almost quadrupled.[10]

Then the war ended, and so did the prosperity. Wartime contracts worth billions were canceled immediately, sending industry and agriculture into an uncertain and threatening future. Quickly the boom turned into its opposite. Ruinous inflation, unemployment, and labor unrest shook the economic and political order. The cost of living skyrocketed, but wages and salaries failed to keep pace. Disgusted with their inability to gain any advantages with employers, more than four million workers in various states went out on strike or merely walked off their jobs in 1919. From a general strike in Seattle to striking steel workers in Pittsburgh and coal miners in West Virginia, America's working class challenged the power of the bosses.

Government, in tandem with Big Business, responded decisively to the worker insurgency. As Bruce Minton and John Stuart wrote in *The Fat Years and the Lean* (1940), "The true role of the state became clear." It had become "the weapon … of the industrialists, the financiers, the small minority in Wall Street," who had taken "almost complete possession of the governing agencies." The state became "the hired policeman of the employers." On their behalf, government launched a crusade to rid the nation of all public enemies, especially the communists and anarchists who were blamed for infecting workers with radical ideas. Attorney General A. Mitchell Palmer set out to eradicate these "termites of revolution," who, he claimed, were fed by Lenin and the "Red hordes." Justice Department agents "careened through America, violating every principle of the Bill of Rights." The most significant of the "Palmer Raids" occurred on January 2, 1920, and resulted in the arrest of more than 2,700 men and women, many of whom were jailed for months without being charged. According to Minton and Stuart, 556 were held for deportation, with many deported without proper hearings. The combined arrests included 1,400 members of the Industrial Workers of the World (IWW); 300 were convicted for violating laws against criminal syndicalism and anarchy.[11]

Big Business stood squarely behind Palmer. "The recent action of the Government in the deportation of undesirables is to be commended," wrote Stephen C. Mason, then president of the National Association of Manufacturers (NAM). "It is the only punishment that fits the crime of anarchy, sedition, or revolution by force, and the Government should comb the country with a fine-tooth comb and not let up until the last one of these pests is sent back to the country from which he came."[12] Businessmen blamed the same public enemies but singled out immigrants for infecting American workers—old-stock, Anglo-Saxon—with alien thinking and uppity Negroes who forgot their place in white society. "There is only one way to treat this disease," wrote U.S. Steel chairman Elbert H. Gary whose own workers had struck hard, "and that is to stamp it out, to meet it boldly wherever it can be found, to expose it and to give it no chance for development."[13] The NAM waged concerted economic and political warfare on labor organizations. In the midst of the 1919 strike wave, it established an Open Shop Department designated to promote another of its creations, the American Plan, which took aim at the union movement and the closed shop. Its premise was as political and ideological as it was economic by assuming that "all law abiding citizens have the right to work when they please, for whom they please, and whatever terms are mutually agreed on between employee and employer and without interference or discrimination upon the part of others." Throughout the 1920s, the American Plan was used to promote company unions where workers were deprived of any bargaining powers. It pushed successfully for greater use of the "yellow-dog contract" that forced workers to agree not to join a union and, in some cases, to pledge not to strike. Meanwhile, it promoted the doctrine of "True Americanism" that aimed to define the difference between the old-stock citizens considered the backbone of the nation and alien forces that threatened them. Big Business and state power came together effectively in court-ordered injunctions that made it illegal for workers to strike or even engage in collective bargaining. Despite minor concessions to some workers, the combined power of the state and Big Business proved too much for the working class.[14]

As business and government joined hands, organized labor sought a seat at the table. During the Great War, prosperity had seeped downward to select parts of the working class. This was especially true for workers who were directly involved in wartime production, and earned higher wages and lived more comfortably. But even before peace came in 1918, organized labor struck a deal with Big Business that held up until the 1929 crash. The unions in the American Federation of Labor (AFL), long committed to a reformist and limited agenda in their dealings with employers, had argued that labor's fulfillment of wartime production demands had earned it a rightful place in decision making with government and business. Samuel Gompers and other AFL leaders had demonstrated loyalty to American capitalism by their hard line against the IWW and other radicals who had tried to convince American workers not to support an imperialist war against their brethren in Europe. At the same time, the AFL kept rank-and-file workers in line by winning concessions for higher wages and better working conditions. But the ideological disposition of the AFL was far deeper than its routine activities. In its deliberate aim to reject any hint of socialism and promote what it considered a viable alternative to it, the AFL under Gompers's leadership sought harmonious relations with capital in the hope that it would lead American workers into a corporate-capitalist economic partnership with Big Business.[15]

Government repression and the support it got from business leaders certainly helped to promote other sources of political reaction in the immediate postwar period. The American Legion, counterpart of European para-military groups whose members helped to build the ranks of fascist organizations, declared war against all suspected insurrectionists, and directed its members to attack socialists and other radicals, especially the IWW.[16] After a decades-long crusade led by Protestant fundamentalists and some Progressive Era reformers, Prohibition became the law of the land in January 1920. Anxiety and fear over changing economic conditions gripped much of rural society left behind in the great urban surge. Nativism defined the political landscape throughout small-town and rural existence. White America deemed all others as alien and thus potential targets. Violence unconnected to labor struggles increased. By 1920, the reactionary tide in America was growing in strength and fury.

The greatest force of this reaction and extremism rising up from the middle classes was the so-called second Ku Klux Klan. Established in 1915, its membership remained small until early 1920 when its ranks suddenly swelled. From its birth on Stone Mountain just outside Atlanta, the Klan had spread beyond the South to cities and towns across the United States. According to historian Nancy MacLean, "The North Central and Southwestern states enrolled the most members, followed by the Southeast, the Midwest and Far West, and, finally, the North Atlantic states. By mid-decade, the total reached perhaps as high as five million, distributed through nearly four thousand local chapters."[17] Its mass consciousness, which was deeply rooted in the ideological outlook of its white middle-class members, reflected the anxiety caused by the march of Big Business's growth on the one hand and their fear of the masses, especially people of color, on the other. There were so many to hate—Catholics, Jews, Mexicans, Asians, Italians, and the Reds. Still, the Klan remained at heart the guardian of white supremacy and reserved its most terrorist treatment for blacks. Lynchings and massacres of African Americans rose dramatically in 1919; more than seventy black veterans of the Great War were lynched or burned alive.[18] Many more went unreported. At least a dozen blacks were lynched in a fifty-mile radius of Sparta, Georgia, in a three-month period. Always, African Americans courageously fought back. Across the South, sharecroppers rebelled against debt peonage and the murderous response of white landowners, who feared the loss of black labor from the Great Migration to the cities of the North. Meanwhile, those who had migrated stood their ground against the growing abuse and violence of white supremacy. Urban riots struck more than forty cities, which prompted some black residents to arm themselves and defend their neighborhoods.[19]

WARREN G. HARDING: A SIMPLETON AND CAPITALIST MODERNIZER DECLARES "AMERICA FIRST"

Such was the state of the nation in June 1920 when the Republican Party chose Warren Harding as their candidate for president. Harding was destined for a "troubled presidency" when he entered the White House in 1921 amid crises at home and abroad: a general economic nosedive, the great collapse of agricultural prices, widespread labor unrest, an increase of lynchings in the South, and, of course, the Red Scare.[20] Harding's clear intent as a candidate and incoming president was to lead the country in a return to "normalcy." "By 'normalcy' I don't mean the old order," he declared, "but a regular steady order of things."[21] Normalcy for Harding did not mean "a retreat into the past but an orderly system for progress."[22] As an experienced politician, Harding knew what he was doing. When he told Americans that what they wanted was "not nostrums, but normalcy; not revolution, but restoration," Harding was expressing the desire of the mainstream to move on from the political maelstrom of 1919. To do that required a new vibrancy in American life conducive to business success and the road toward progress. His personal charm and gregariousness enabled him to slap the back of anyone who mattered at the moment. For historian Sean Dennis Cashman, Harding was nothing more than an "amiable simpleton manipulated by sinister forces."[23] But he was more than that. Harding was the first of three Republican presidents during the prosperous 1920s, whose idea of normalcy served as an ideological cover for the titans of American capitalism to expand their powers at home and abroad. Although not the first president to swear that he would make "America First," the slogan carried new weight as the Republican Party made it central to Harding's campaign. This made Harding the perfect front man for capitalist modernization on the grandest scale ever because he actually understood his role in facilitating it.

We see this clearly in Harding's speech to Congress when he aspired to be what the *Saturday Evening Post* wanted most in a president when it declared that America needed "a businessman" in the White House.[24] On April 12, 1921, the new president reminded lawmakers that he had said as much during his campaign:

> I have said to the people we meant to have less of Government in business as well as more business in Government. It is well to have it understood that business has a right to pursue its normal, legitimate, and righteous way unimpeded, and it ought have no call to meet Government competition where all risk is borne by the Public Treasury. There is no challenge to honest and lawful business success.[25]

Harding explained that the federal government would take the lead by becoming more like a business, which meant its own bottom line was to cut government spending to fall "within the limits of national income." To achieve this, he heartily endorsed a "national budget system" on the basis of "business methods so essential to the minimum of expenditure." This would also be crucial to holding down the public debt, which was already "staggering" from the wartime economy. Dire consequences were in store if such steps were not taken. "The unrestrained tendency to heedless expenditure and the attending growth of public indebtedness, extending from federal authority to that of state and municipality and including the smallest political subdivision, constitute the dangerous phase of government today," Harding told Congress. Admitting in his typical jumbled English that government had been "illy prepared" for the transition to a peacetime economy, he was confident that the American people "had appraised the situation, and with that tolerance and patience which go with understanding, they will give us the influence of deliberate public opinion which ultimately becomes the edict of any popular government." What?

To that end, he called upon Congress to work urgently to achieve two critical objectives. First, it should consider a "readjustment of internal taxes," especially the removal of those deemed "unproductive." This is how government could help to revive business activity. At the same time, he sought to allay fears of any shift in the tax burden by emphasizing that cutting government costs would eliminate any necessity for creating new taxes that would impede the free movement of business. The other urgent matter was to protect American business from foreign competition with "an instant tariff enactment." As Harding professed:

> I believe in the protection of American industry, and it is our purpose to prosper America first. The privileges of the American market to the foreign producer are offered so cheaply today, and the effect on much of our own productivity is the destruction of our self-reliance, which is the foundation of the independence and good fortune of our people.

As a proponent of capitalist modernization, Harding emphasized the need to build up communications networks, especially radio and cable and stressed the importance of new investments in commercial aviation beyond government funding.

Some historians have captured the modernizing bent in Harding's presidency. "His background as a businessman from a small town not only shaped his political views but also gave him the important political advantage of seeming to represent both big business and the rural past." As a longtime businessman in Marion, Ohio, and the publisher of its daily newspaper, Harding had learned how vital it was to channel the aspirations of merchants and family farmers in small-town and rural America to the imperial visions of corporate owners and big bankers, and to do so by justifying it on moral and religious grounds. Private enterprise was the "regular order of things" and would save America from decay, he said. "American business was not a monster but the expression of a God-given power to create." [26]

For one of Harding's contemporaries, Richard Franklin Pettigrew, American business was a beast and Harding was chosen by Republican elites to ride it. Pettigrew, one of the strongest and most respected anti-imperialist voices in the country and a longtime leader of middle-class, progressive radicalism in the midwestern states, and the first elected senator from South Dakota in 1899, easily recognized who wanted Harding to be the Republican nominee for president and why. They were all "men who put the United States into the European war … [and] are out for empire," as Pettigrew put it in his 1923 book, *Imperial Washington*. Though the party powerbrokers and imperialists had preferred other candidates, they had finally settled on Harding because he was "the man least objectionable and most certain to stand right on their plans to exploit the rest of the world." Citing a record of Harding's accomplishments, Pettigrew wrote that "on every important test between capital and labor, he voted with capital." [27]

Indeed, Harding did the bidding of capital as a skillful politician highly conscious of the need to represent the whole spectrum of capitalist society while serving party elites who were confident he would promote their interests. His administration quickly initiated legislation aimed at advancing the interests of monopoly and finance capital, among them: lowering taxes, especially on corporations and wealthy individuals; cutting the size of federal bureaucracy; and imposing stronger tariffs to protect U.S. corporations, whose rising exports now drove the world economy. He chose some of the most qualified, wealthy, and powerful capitalist elites to fill key cabinet positions: Andrew Mellon as Treasury secretary, Charles Hughes to lead the State Department, and Herbert Hoover as Secretary of Commerce. All proved highly capable in making Washington subservient to the dictates of Wall

Street.[28] Mellon, one of the five richest men in the world, promptly drafted legislation that Congress made into law with passage of the Revenue Act of 1921. Taxes on the wealthy were reduced significantly as lawmakers shifted the burden of making up for shortfalls with several indirect taxes, doubling the stamp tax on documents and introducing a federal license tax on cars. According to Sean Dennis Cashman, the Revenue Act amounted to nothing more than a "specious justification for the relief of the rich" so they would be freed from burdensome taxation that would prohibit them from further creative and productive investment.[29] Under Harding, trickle-down economics was born.

At the same time, Harding was also a petty-bourgeois reactionary and white supremacist whose leadership in restricting immigration was central to the doctrine of 100 percent Americanism. Defending segregation in his April 12 speech to Congress, he made a lame attempt to address the spike in racist violence and the number of African Americans lynched. He called on Congress "to wipe out the stain of barbaric lynching from the banners of a free and orderly representative democracy." As a white supremacist, however, Harding called this a "condition which cannot be removed" but alluded to the possibility "that some of its difficulties might be ameliorated by a humane and enlightened consideration of it," or as he also put it, "at least, a national attitude of mind calculated to bring about the most satisfactory possible adjustment of relations between the races, and of each race to the national life."

Harding did not last a full term in the White House. A sickly man who drank and ate excessively while relying on a regimen of drugs served up by his quack physician, he died of a likely heart attack on August 2, 1923, in the presidential suite of a San Francisco hotel while on the last leg of a tour dubbed "The Voyage of Understanding." But his relatively brief run is perhaps more significant than even his defenders have argued. His petty-bourgeois ways served as an effective cover for a political agenda that served the capitalist ruling class. As an ardent nationalist, Harding promoted the expansion of American business at home and greater imperial reach abroad with his mantra of "America First." His politics amounted to a *contradictio in terminis*: rooted in a petty-capitalist faith in business, Harding quickly became his opposite once in the White House, a champion of monopoly-finance capital. His presidency indicated a new dynamic in ruling-class politics in the United States, a president posing as a true representative of democratic capitalism, which was considered peculiarly American, but whose policies fueled the centralization and concentration of Big Business itself.

ROARING INTO THE 1920S

Within a year of Harding's entry into the White House, the Great Boom was on. From 1922 to 1929, technological innovation on a massive scale raised the productive capacity of American industry to historic levels which, in turn, made the United States the world's first, true consumer society. Tectonic shifts altered the social and political landscape. Consumerism replaced citizenship. The desire for individual fulfillment pushed aside earlier Progressive Era concerns about collective needs. Wages for some workers rose while the middle class grew in numbers. Those with enough income and credit bought cars, appliances, radios, clothes, cosmetics, and more. The luckiest managed to buy homes, which sparked increased residential construction. A rising segment of the population, mostly white, urban, and employed in various commercial activities and professions, became obsessed with fashion, movies, cigarettes, speakeasies, and other newfound pleasures.

Cultural norms were being uprooted. Women smoked openly. Jazz clubs stretched leisure time into the wee hours. And like never before people talked openly about sex. The petting party, wrote magazine writer-editor Frederick Lewis Allen in 1931, had become "widely established as an indoor sport."[30] In ways generally foreign to other peoples, Americans had proved themselves the quickest learners in the ways of self-indulgence. Those who entered the ranks of the new middle class, among them professionals and mid-level managers, attained levels of social comfort unimaginable only a few years earlier. With the rising self-indulgence came the advocates, practitioners, and propagandists of the "new psychology." There was much talk about Sigmund Freud, though few really understood what he had claimed to have discovered about people. Most important, however, the coming of material abundance—or at least the promise of it—had raised the bar for American individualism to a much greater height.

As for business leaders, politicians, academics, and others, the whirlwind of new ideas, attitudes, and behaviors was indicative of capitalism's long-standing promise of endless prosperity and uninterrupted progress. Some called it a "New Era" or the "New Capitalism," others the "New Economy." Regardless of the terminology, all indicated that a capitalist revolution was underway. How startling! After all, wasn't it Lenin and the Bolsheviks who were claiming that their revolutionary turn to socialism had changed the course of human history? No! shouted the creators and propagandists of the New Era. The real revolution was a capitalist one, and since it was only happening in America it seemed reasonable that the next best thing to do was to sell the idea to the public. By the middle of the decade, the marketing of the New Era, or whatever it was called, made up what people understood as the "ballyhoo" of the times, all that noisy, frenzied barking about what struck them in the moment. From the allure of shiny cars and short skirts, to a new Charlie Chaplin movie, or the stories of famous people being murdered, swindled, divorced, or lionized in the daily tabloids, the clamor of those engaged in selling anything or any idea through advertising, publicity and propaganda was constant.

For all its exuberant promise of an even brighter future, the Great Boom also challenged the capitalist class in equally unprecedented ways. New cracks were opening in the political landscape, adding to longtime spatial and cultural divides. None was more significant than the sudden, widening chasm between urban workers earning higher wages and small farmers in the countryside burdened by declining prices in agricultural products. Rapid industrialization and urbanization were breaking down the old order of agrarian and small-town America. Expenditures for public education rose dramatically. College enrollments soared though millions of Americans were left behind and consigned to ignorance and backwardness. New and often jarring perspectives became part of everyday life, which increasingly divided Americans along many lines. Science challenged religion. Protestants sneered at Catholics. Both despised Jews. Protestantism itself, the dominant form of American Christianity, became a battleground between modernists and fundamentalists. Women were challenging patriarchy at home and in the workplace. African Americans migrated to the North and Midwest to escape the legacy of slavery in the South.

The rapid pace of change also compelled the captains of industry and their partners in finance to create new methods in capitalist production aimed at keeping the American economy moving. To that end, the Great Boom they engineered and the effort to sell it as a capitalist revolution only reaffirmed what Marx and Engels had written seventy years earlier about the revolutionary powers of the bourgeoisie. The U.S. ruling class was now the principal and driving force of global capitalism. While revolutionary communists were attempting to build a socialist road in the newly created Soviet Union, America's capitalist oligarchy was fulfilling its own historic mission, according to criteria formulated by Marx and Engels:

> The bourgeoisie cannot exist without constantly revolutionising the instruments of production, and thereby the relations of production, and with them the whole relations of society. . . . Constant revolutionising of production, uninterrupted disturbance of all social conditions, everlasting uncertainty and agitation distinguish the bourgeois epoch from all earlier ones. All fixed, fast-frozen relations . . . are swept away . . . All that is solid melts into air.[31]

Such was the whirlwind the Great Boom brought to America during much of the 1920s. As the ruling class of a growing empire and epicenter of the world capitalist system, America's leading capitalists and their allies in politics and the media transformed the United States by further revolutionizing the means of production and bringing the consciousness of monopoly-finance capitalism into its most advanced state. The core and the outer limits of a coming Pax Americana were developing quickly. With the exception of two minor downturns in 1924 and 1927, Big Business amassed historic profits by investing in new technology, molding a disciplined workforce through efficient, "scientific" management, paying higher wages to some workers, and extending credit to any eligible borrower who sought it. Corporations, big banks, and Wall Street brokers raked in profits as never before. The boom fueled the growth of a new middle class of doctors, lawyers, scientists, engineers, bureaucrats, educators, and all the medium-level and higher-ups in the world of business. The result was a wondrous spectacle of new things for sale and people with cash or credit clamoring for them in the department stores that lined the crowded streets of big cities and thriving towns. Here was a historic marker for all subsequent trumpeting about the endless promise of the good life that was becoming possible for anyone living under American capitalism.

For Big Business, the continued growth of the U.S. economy meant that it would rely increasingly on its ability to influence the course and content of public life. Businessmen endeavored to create a set of interlocking structures and networks aimed at determining what was required in policies and their implementation. In a short period of time, all of this coalesced into a singular force that made business a *system of power* in its own right. Assisted by their chief executives and managers, salesmen and ad men, trade associations, and the sorcery of public relations experts and social psychologists, the architects of capitalist prosperity made it possible for rank-and-file Americans to consume as never before while going deeper into debt and being made to think that it was normal to do so. If monopoly-finance capitalism thrived on its capacity to create a more acquisitive society, America's capitalists broke new ground to facilitate it.

Unprecedented prosperity brought equally daunting challenges. Even more than their immediate predecessors who had elevated America to the status of a world power, the captains of industry and finance could not rest on their laurels. Simply put, the tremendous leap in production during the 1920s raised the bar on its mandate to sustain profitability. To that end, capitalists needed to find new outlets for productive investment by making more of the same goods for expanding markets, or newer goods to replace older ones in existing markets—or both, ideally. Every goal reached in the production and sale of goods became a new starting point, and failure to reach beyond it would bring overproduction, declining wages, underconsumption, and, consequently, declining profits. This was the sine qua non of monopoly-finance capitalist enterprise: do whatever is necessary to drive further capital accumulation or face the onset of a crisis.

Consequently, all the nation's leading industrialists agreed that the public had to keep buying. But not all recognized the new market imperatives that accompanied the success of expansive and profitable production. Though the Ford Motor Company had mastered production methods and processes from start to finish, Henry Ford was adamant that most of it go into the making of a single car, the Model T, so he could sell it for the lowest possible price. In 1908, its first year in production, the car sold for $845. When Ford himself drove home the last of the line in May 1927, more than 15 million had been made and the selling price had dropped to less than $300.[32] Ford had built the world's greatest integrated production plant, on the Rouge River in Dearborn, Michigan. To make cars, he had bought up whole forests for wood and coal fields for the power he needed. He also built a steel plant as part of the Rouge River complex. Ford's success was astounding. The company produced 1,250,000 cars in 1920, one every 60 seconds. Five years later on a single day, one Model T rolled off the assembly line every 10 seconds.[33] To ensure continued success, Ford did everything possible to increase production and lower costs. He hired experts in scientific management to determine how much movement to allow workers on the assembly lines and rammed cars down the throats of dealers regardless of their inventories. Ford even paid his workers higher wages in the belief that they would buy products like his for the cheapest possible price. By 1927, there were more Model T's on the roads than all other cars combined.

But for all his success, Ford had resisted two key requirements for sustaining profit in the booming 1920s—installment credit and customer satisfaction. According to historian Geoffrey Perrett, Ford opposed the first because he hated debt of any kind, the second because the puritan in him could not see beyond simple utility. Fiercely independent and ever the mechanic he had been in his youth, Ford's actions in the face of rising competition seemed like those of a man who believed he could solve all the challenges of capitalist production and exchange in his own head. Eventually, he would lose ground to General Motors, which had created its own financing company in 1919 and committed itself to making improvements and variations that consumers came to demand during the 1920s. Only in 1927, when sales dropped significantly, did Ford give up on the Model T by shutting down operations in the spring, laying off 40,000 workers until the new Model A was ready for marketing by the end of the year. Then, quite uncharacteristically for Henry Ford, the new car was unveiled amid great clamor in Madison Square Garden on December 1.[34]

Ironically, the man who had pioneered mass production of the decade's most important durable commodity came late to an understanding of the market conditions of the New Era. The imperatives of capitalist enterprise were expanding in relation to the volatility of the market. The war had created unprecedented growth and contributed to greater concentration of wealth and political power. Now, given the challenge of adjusting to peacetime, competition among leading capitalists compelled them to go beyond their predecessors and develop even greater control over the market. Their approach to this challenge took two distinct forms that marked the onset of fascist processes in the U.S. epicenter of the world capitalist system.

TERRORIST AND NON-TERRORIST FASCIST PROCESSES

In a qualitatively new way, state power defended the capitalist class from the surge of working-class upheaval in 1919 and 1920. By 1922, the Harding administration had finished the job of taming American labor. Business-friendly Republicans in government at all levels had done this by often resorting to violence, sometimes paying vigilante citizens' groups to do their dirty work against strikers, union organizers, and radicals. The combination of brute force, use of the legal system, and the ideological push by the NAM, the Chamber of Commerce, and other trade associations crippled labor for much of the decade, though periodically powerful strikes did occur. These were among the mechanisms of repression or terrorist processes created by monopoly-finance capitalism between 1919 and 1929.

It was also during the seven-year period of the Great Boom that the U.S. bourgeoisie advanced capital's control over society through persuasion and manipulation. These were the non-terrorist processes that were most advanced in the capitalist epicenter.[35] Mass production and consumption on a hitherto massive scale required more than the political coercion of labor. Capitalist rule over the market and society, which depended on the circuit of capital operating at successively higher levels of investment, distribution, profit, and reinvestment, could no longer rest on the use of force alone. Though the means of deploying the latter was always present to capitalists and their managers of state power, the need to do so once the boom got underway was minimal. More important, the drive for capital accumulation and profit expanded the properties of commodity production and exchange, in accordance with the explosive growth of the market and demands to maintain it. Mass production on a level never before attained now required mass consumption to follow.

Clearly, the spectacle of abundance created in the boom helped to make this possible. The appearance of so many new and tantalizing consumer goods, and the belief that they could be acquired and enjoyed by everyone, constituted the material basis for an ideological justification that was crucial to the success of the boom. A revolution was occurring in capitalism, its ideological proponents declared, but only in the United States where they convinced millions of Americans to believe that the great promise of universal prosperity was at hand because the boom-bust cycles were a thing of the past. This went along with the creed of 100 percent Americanism whereby everyone who worked hard to fulfill his God-ordained mission on earth could become a capitalist. The main task of the capitalist class and their able assistants was to convince enough Americans that the New Era would eventually create universal wealth. All their efforts had one thing in common: to remove all resistance to the drive for capitalist accumulation. This made their objective the total domination of capital over society and the individual.

For these reasons, American capitalists turned to advertising, "the sword arm of business," as it became known in the 1920s. "Thanks to advertising," wrote the journalist and author Silas Bent in 1927, "a penny's worth of germicidal value in a nationally known antiseptic is marketed for $95; flimsy wood is sold as good furniture; and six-dollar shoes are sold at twelve dollars." But the sword itself was double-edged, especially in newspapers where there were two kinds of news, one that disseminated useful information about events or circumstances on the basis of a "natural demand" for it, the other the result of sheer salesmanship.[36] For Bent, the gathering and packaging of 90 percent of the news by the ever-growing centralized ownership of newspapers and magazines was based on its "pecuniary advantage" in some form or another.[37] Thus the mission of the newspaper business was above all to advance readership on the basis of understanding how to package and sell news. Moreover, it relied on public opinion experts like Walter Lippmann, who argued that it was necessary for elites to "manufacture consent" for a public that could neither see nor understand the world clearly.[38] As a result, news stories increasingly came to depend on ways to hold the reader's attention. The need to captivate, entertain, sensationalize, and titillate the reader was similar to the approach used by advertisers to promote their commodities. As Bent explained, "The merchandiser of manufactured commodities uses methods quite similar to the merchandiser of news."[39] Here was one kind of ballyhoo that made capitalism functional and kept the Great Boom alive, at least for now.

Soon enough, psychologists plumbed the minds of what it considered the "irrational public" to determine ways to assemble and manage public opinion in the service of Big Business. The most notable among them, Henry C. Link, manufactured popularized versions of Freudian psychology that were delivered to order to Big Business. In 1923, Link helped to organize other academics to create and then direct the American Psychological Corporation, whose objective was to provide businessmen with the knowledge of how to use methods of behavioral psychology to the advance of marketing. The "new psychology" of the 1920s served the needs of capitalists in their efforts to sustain the Great Boom and was a crucial means in recognizing social impulses that triggered desire and want, especially if the commodity in question was not needed.[40]

CAPITALIST PROGRESS AND ITS CONTRADICTIONS

Such were the efforts by America's rulers who played a pivotal role in transforming the class struggle at home and abroad in the 1920s. Marx and Engels had grasped its dynamic throughout world-historical development: "uninterrupted" but always a "hidden" or "open fight" from one epoch or era to another depending on the material conditions of society and their ideological products.[41] In 1920s America, the owners and managers of capital were playing out their revolutionary role at a pivotal moment in the transition to the hegemonic rule of American finance capital in the world capitalist system. As its epicenter, the United States was reconfiguring the international order and transforming the social relations of production toward greater abundance. Warren Harding, the compromise Republican Party candidate from Ohio who saw beyond his petty-bourgeois midwestern roots, had recognized that the United States needed a foreign policy to empower its businessmen to rebuild Europe and reap enormous profits. In the process, the United States quickly recognized that support for Benito Mussolini and his fascist regime in Italy was the basis upon which to establish American hegemony in Europe.

At the same time, the very processes that created Pax Americana carried the seeds of a future crisis. The expansion of U.S. imperial interests, secured at times by the use of military force in Central America and the Caribbean, exacerbated existing contradictions of class and race. This was also true in the Philippines where U.S. imperial rule had been brutal. At home, the ruling class and its state apparatus had crushed the alleged Bolshevik conspiracy in 1920 and quickly moved to quell other forms of opposition. Their defeat of alien forces then made it possible to claim that it was all the work of good, old-stock people who stood for the ideas, images, and proper behaviors of True Americanism. Fearing that white America would be overrun, Congress passed the Emergency Quota Act in 1921, limiting immigration from countries in Europe, the Near East, Africa, and even Australia and New Zealand, though committed white supremacists were disappointed that too many immigrants from southern and eastern Europe were entering the country to poison the ranks of Anglo Saxons. The draconian National Origins Act of 1924 cut quotas even more and was designed to keep out East Asians, especially the Japanese.[42] The "adhesive" of white supremacy at home and abroad was the glue that held together the rising American imperium.[43] And all the while, the gurus of advertising, public relations, and propaganda advanced new and more sophisticated means of capitalist power to propagate a politics of accommodation in society, at times doing so in the most surreptitious and manipulative ways. The class struggle in the United States during the years of the Great Boom remained hidden, though the contradictions operating within it would intensify quickly when the crisis came in 1929.

It is within all of these developments that we find the genesis of fascist processes, terrorist and non-terrorist alike, in the expansion and euphoria of unprecedented capitalist expansion. In the United States, the objective to totalize the powers of capital over all aspects of material life and consciousness marked the onset of fascism—the terrorist and non-terrorist rule of Big Business—in its particular American form. Simply put, these processes fueled the coming of the American Behemoth, a living example of what Marx saw in *Capital*—"a live monster that is fruitful and multiplies."[44]

2—Fascist Processes in Capitalist Accumulation

"THE GERM OF FASCISM," wrote A. B. Magil and Henry Stevens in 1938, in *The Peril of Fascism*, "was inherent within American monopoly capitalism; but it was not until the economic crisis of 1929 that it developed into a definite political force of ominous proportions."[1]

Today, their long-forgotten book remains the only comprehensive account of the rise of U.S. fascism in its specific, national form. Readers will find great resonance in the warning issued by Magil and Stevens. Fascism already had destroyed democratic governments in Italy and Germany, and a similar outcome was plausible in the United States. A decade earlier, the Wall Street crash had ushered in what they called a *general crisis* of U.S. capitalism that "provided the conditions necessary for the speedy growth of embryonic fascism."[2] There was no time to lose in creating a united front against fascism at home and abroad.

Magil and Stevens were American communists who understood how fascism had come to power in Italy and Germany and how the road to fascism in the United States looked different. In line with the position of the Communist International, they certainly had Italy and Germany in mind when they defined fascism as "the open terrorist dictatorship of the most predatory sections of the capitalist class."[3] In both cases, nationalist, racist, and terrorist mass movements rising primarily out of the lower middle class catapulted Mussolini and Hitler toward dictatorship—once they had secured the allegiance of the ruling classes in their respective countries. In the United States, however, embryonic fascism had emerged in a different form. Homegrown U.S. fascism lacked the visceral movements of its European counterparts, which in the case of Germany delivered the spectacle of Hitlerism. To dwell on analyzing American resemblances in relation to distinctive European forms was a mistake. "The national peculiarities of each country, its specific economic and social position, its historical traditions," they wrote, "all play a part in shaping the form that fascist movements and fascism take." Americans should not be looking for "a Man on Horseback riding down Pennsylvania Avenue, or a megalomaniac with a little mustache, making speeches in a big voice." Rather than adhering to some "stereotyped formulae" to explain why fascism arose anywhere in the world, it was better to recognize its "diverse, and frequently subtle, forms" from one place to another.[4] Still, to locate the germ of fascism in monopoly capitalism implied something common to all of them, and for communists like Magil and Stevens it could not be clearer what this meant. "Judged by its works, and not by its professions of faith, fascism stands forth as a form of rule by finance capital."[5] This was especially true for the United States. "The scattered streams and trickles of developing American fascism," they wrote, "have a common source: Wall Street." Big Business was the "fountainhead" of American fascism.[6]

A historic partnership between government and business during the First World War had created what Magil and Stevens called an "entire mechanism of repression" with an array of new agencies and legislation, including the War Industries Board in 1917 and passage of the Sedition Act a year later.[7] All were designed to maximize cooperation between the two sectors in order to produce for the war and quash dissent or opposition to America's involvement in it. This partnership, a leap in the advance of U.S. state monopoly capitalism, delivered profits never before seen to the largest capitalist enterprises during the war and in the decade that followed. As Magil and Stevens wrote:

> The steady concentration of power in the hands of executive officials and the corresponding diminution in the power of legislative bodies . . . was encouraged by big business in the Harding, Coolidge and Hoover administrations, which used their enhanced powers in the interest of the monopolies. Commissions, executive officials and judges, appointed by the President and by state governors, and not elected by the people, were vested with unprecedented authority.[8]

As they make clear, the difference between capitalist states and those that went fascist was not a matter of "class content," but in their respective "methods of rule." In fascist states such as Hitler's dictatorship, fascism

> still represents the rule of finance capital, but in an open terrorist form, involving the complete destruction of democracy, the most brutal suppression of the people, the restoration of feudal relationships on the farms, the destruction of culture, the revival of medieval racial beliefs, the organization of all society for war. It means rule by the most ruthless and predatory sectors of finance capital; by dark reactionaries and fanatics who seek to impose upon modern capitalist society the primitive practices and beliefs of barbarism.[9]

When the crisis of capitalist rule in Germany became acute in January 1933 and the threat of communist revolution or a complete breakdown of the existing capitalist system seemed imminent, German elites, never champions of democracy, turned to Hitler as their only resort to protect, preserve, and further their class interests.[10] As Magil and Stevens rightly observed, the transition from democracy to fascism in Germany had not occurred in a "single leap" but rather was the result of "a long process of whittling down democratic rights." As for the United States, the transition from liberal capitalist democracy to fascism was still in its "preliminary" stage.[11]

As Marxists, Magil and Stevens described the historic origins of fascism in the most general terms. It had emerged in the twentieth century from contradictions in monopoly-finance capitalism, primarily "between the enormous forces of production . . . and the system of private appropriation—the profit system."[12] In this respect, they saw how repression inhered in capitalist growth itself as the result of a growing divide between the ruling class—which had become richer, fewer in number, and more powerful during the prosperous 1920s—and everyone below them in the pyramid of capitalist wealth. They knew that wages represented only a small part of what workers produced, leaving them unable to purchase the products of their labor at sufficient levels to gain a decent standard of living. Still, on this basis, the United States had achieved a "degree of temporary stabilization" in the national economy, but only in the short term. Basic capitalist contradictions had been "glaringly revealed" to those who paid attention. Even in the midst of prosperity, a widening gulf between mass production and consumption caused by "a technical revolution" had become historic by "dooming a large proportion of the productive system and millions of workers to permanent idleness." Then the crisis came in 1929, and "the flimsy props" that had gone into the making of the Great Boom collapsed in a heap.[13]

But why did this happen? Since their primary motive in writing *The Peril of Fascism* was to educate Americans about fascism's immediate threat to U.S. democracy, Magil and Stevens did not provide a more complex analysis of American fascism from the standpoint of political economy. For sure, they detected the germ of fascism in the United States in the myriad processes that created a spectacle of unprecedented capitalist economic growth during the Great Boom of the 1920s; then fascism became an ominous political force during the crisis years of the Great Depression.[14] As Marxists, they surely knew that the "entire mechanism of repression" created by Big Business and the Republican Party had been necessary for the further accumulation of capital and profits. Given the main tasks at hand, however, Magil and Stevens went no further in examining the relationship between capitalism and fascism. Yet their seminal contribution to our understanding of the origins of American fascism remains vital.

Given our greater knowledge in the present, we can move beyond their historical and theoretical position in 1938. Fascist processes in the United States inhered in the drive for capitalist accumulation during the 1920s, a moment of unprecedented economic growth anywhere in the world-capitalist system. The inherent tendency in capitalist accumulation to create greater wealth fueled the simultaneous advance in the centralization of capital and capitalist ownership while displacing working people from the processes of production through technological innovation, thereby fueling a reserve army of labor of the unemployed and underemployed and a general population that became increasingly superfluous to existing methods of production, and thus to the needs of the capitalists. The germ of fascism inheres in the division of labor in the epoch of monopoly-finance capitalism and imperialism. In the end, this is what makes fascism the dictatorial rule of capital over American society.

To grasp how this occurred in the 1920s requires a brief look at one of the most important discoveries of Karl Marx, in *Capital*, his masterwork published in 1867.

Marx on Capitalist Accumulation: The Inherent Subjugation of Labor to Capital

Geographer David Harvey, who has spent many years teaching and writing about capitalism, says that "Marx's aim in *Capital* is to understand how capitalism works by way of a critique of political economy."[15] In the course of examining the anatomy of capitalist production, Marx demonstrates how the system it creates is contradictory to the core. In its constant and necessary drive to accumulate more capital, its movement increasingly subjects society to its imperatives. Owners and workers alike are bound to processes that give rise to a unique feature of the capitalist mode of production, the paradox of growing poverty in an ever-rising sea of plenty.

As Harvey says, Marx makes his case in *Capital* on the basis of concepts that appear to be *a priori*, or even arbitrary, but are in fact historical. This is because his "method of inquiry starts with everything that exists—with reality as it's experienced, as well as with all available descriptions of that experience by political economists, philosophers, novelists and the like." Marx then subjects this material to "rigorous criticism" from which he forms "simple but powerful concepts that illuminate the way reality works." This method, which became central to Marx's work in the mid-1840s when he began his studies in political economy, involved two main steps: conceptualizing empirical evidence and then using those concepts as the basis for discovering the myriad deceptions that abound in the capitalist world. In the first volume of *Capital*, Marx began with the concepts, especially those he believed made sense of capitalist realities and the historical forces that created them.[16] Marx's conceptual arguments about production were derived from his knowledge of Great Britain in the 1850s and 1860s, then the most advanced capitalist nation, as well as in other parts of Europe and North America where similar conditions existed but were not as highly developed.[17]

Marx's masterwork is a detailed and complex treatise that reveals how capital as accumulated wealth in many forms—most importantly as money—must always expand, thereby enlarging the mode of production, which raises the magnitude of the total product. This is how growth and prosperity are sustained across the capitalist system, and it must occur to offset what Marx viewed as a tendency toward stagnation and an eventual crisis. This would become a general condition of capitalism with the further development of technology operating on the basis of monopoly and finance capital. Marx had expounded this tendency in *Capital*. What concerns us here, however, is how he explains that sustained growth depends on the ability of capitalists to produce and sell commodities as efficiently as possible in order to maximize profits—and to do this exponentially. This is their sole purpose as capitalists. Their success always comes at the expense of the workers, whose labor-power is the one thing workers own and, therefore, must sell to the capitalists to survive. For Marx, this contradiction between capital and labor, between the capitalist and the worker, was evident in certain laws of motion peculiar to industrial capitalist production, revealing why economic growth created wealth and poverty together, and how the capitalist assumed even greater control and domination over the worker.

Capitalist Accumulation and the Permanent Divide of Capital and Labor

One of Marx's most important laws of motion, "The General Law of Capitalist Accumulation," is the title of a chapter in *Capital*. Here Marx explicates why the sole purpose of accumulation is forever to raise the value of capital. This involves the drive to increase productivity—the rate of output per hour—by replacing human labor with machines, making production more efficient and thereby sustaining the rate of profit required for further capital investment. The consequence of this is not only the growth of output but the chaining of the vast majority of society, the working class, to the systemic imperatives and dictatorial powers of capital. As capital expands, so does the power of those who own and control it. Two major contradictions occur. Accumulation, which generates fierce competition between capitalist enterprises, drives the less efficient and profitable out of the market, resulting in the greater concentration of capital. This then widens and deepens the gap between fewer and wealthier capitalists and a growing mass of impoverished workers. The labor-power that the capitalist buys from the worker at the lowest price, the so-called minimum or subsistence wage, is the ultimate source of the capitalist's wealth. Marx shows that each step in the process of creating more wealth among fewer and fewer capitalists is accompanied by the increasing diminution of workers and their disposability in capitalist production. Simply put, the march of capital tramples those who initially create it, the working class.

Marx begins the chapter by recognizing how the growth of capital impacts the working class as the result of processes that govern capitalist accumulation and determine the composition of capital, which is always determined by the ratio between *constant* capital—buildings, machinery, land, raw materials, etc.—and *variable* capital, human labor-power. Once capitalism enters its industrial stage, the drive for greater efficiency in production always causes constant capital to grow—with greater reliance on technological innovation—relative to variable capital. Marx posits the relation between these two variants as the *organic composition of capital*. Simply put, as greater wealth is produced on the basis of more machines employed throughout production, an increase in constant capital, the more that living labor, or variable capital, is diminished in production. Every technological advance aimed at greater efficiency in production to maximize profits also disposes more workers who thereby become impoverished.[18]

At the risk of reducing complex formulations to simplest terms, we can say that Marx aims at a scientifically based argument that demonstrates how the value of capital at any moment is based on the amount of labor-power extracted from workers by capitalists in the course of expanding production. It can be extracted because the capitalists own what the workers must have access to, the non-human means of production. This fundamental inequality is what allows employers to take from workers more than what they are paid in wages. Put simply, workers produce all of the output but, in effect, get only part of it back, just enough to sustain their lives. For the capitalist, the appropriation of labor-power from the worker translates into *surplus-value*, or unpaid labor, which is the basis of capitalist profit. Human labor, therefore, is the dynamic force in production that creates more capital through its appropriation by those who already own it. As the political economist Harry Braverman wrote, "The working class is the animate part of capital, the part which will set in motion the process that yields to the total capital its increment of surplus-value."[19]

Marx argues that all growth in capital is based on the productiveness of labor, specifically, the necessary levels of productivity supplied by the labor-power of workers. For capital to accumulate within the framework and mechanisms of industrial production requires that part of the surplus-value generated by it must be "re-transformed" into additional labor-power.[20] When this occurs, capitalists must employ more workers to accumulate more capital. On the surface, this seems like a good thing for workers since their numbers rise. Given the degree to which the requirements of accumulation may exceed the supply of labor, wages might even rise. But the "favourable circumstances in which the wage-working class supports and multiplies itself, in no way alter the fundamental character of capitalist production."[21]

Why is this so?

As stated above, Marx explains that the enlarged scale of production requires capitalists to employ more workers. Yet the increase of employed workers must always benefit the owners of capital since their sole aim is to raise productivity by whatever means and methods necessary to maximize profits. Marx emphasizes that the bottom line for every capitalist is the "augmentation" of his capital. This means ensuring that the production of a commodity contains more labor-power than is paid to the worker in wages. For the capitalist, this is the source of surplus-value; in other words, the amount of unpaid labor-power that is realized as profit when the commodity is sold. On this basis, Marx concludes that the "production of surplus-value is the absolute law" of the capitalist mode of production.[22]

At any given moment, the capitalist must acquire as much surplus-value as necessary to offset the wage he pays the worker. This will vary depending on specific conditions and circumstances in production and exchange. For example, a burst of accumulation and growth dictates a corresponding need for additional labor. Capitalists suddenly need more workers to boost production. It could even lead to higher wages, so long as the cost does not impede the rate of surplus-value required to sustain accumulation and more profits. This is beneficial to workers but only in the short term. As Marx says, an immediate reaction sets in as soon as the amount of paid labor impedes the production of surplus-value. This means there is less profit that can be invested in furthering the means of production. The bottom line is that any rise in wages diminishes surplus-value and impedes accumulation, which is why capitalists must check rising wages at some point.

This is why Marx says that "the rise of wages therefore is confined within limits that not only leave intact the foundations of the capitalistic system, but also secure its reproduction on a progressive scale." Wages can never rise beyond the limits required for the progressive reproduction of capital. Put another way, capitalists can never allow wages to undercut the rate of surplus-value, to the extent that it impedes or halts the reproduction of capital needed at any moment. Conversely, Marx says, this is why labor becomes increasingly subject to capital. In the period of early industrial capitalism, the requirements for accumulation often took the form of lengthening the working day without increasing wages, thereby extracting an even greater amount of surplus-value from the worker in absolute human terms. This is why trade unionism in the second half of the nineteenth century in England fought for and succeeded in reducing the legal limit of the working day from twelve to ten hours. Despite these victories, however, there were limits to what labor could achieve. For Marx, the great and unique irony about the capitalist mode of production was "man . . . governed by the products of his own hand."[23] What does this mean? Simply this: workers set in motion the greater reliance on the machinery they themselves produce, which ultimately removes them from the processes of production.

These processes became more intense as a result of competition between capitalists. Winners succeed in great part because the surplus-value they appropriate from their workers enables them to sell their commodities at the cheapest price. As winners, they vanquish small businesses and larger competitors as well, either drawing in the capital of those they have overcome, or destroying it completely. Either way, the result is a greater centralization of capital, which pulls together scattered sources of money across the marketplace, helping to fund a credit system that facilitates the further expansion of capital. Marx says that centralization and credit become the "two most powerful levers" in the further development of capitalist production and accumulation.[24]

On this basis, the joint-stock company, forerunner of the modern corporation, accelerates accumulation "in the twinkling of an eye."[25] Empowered by credit, revolutionary advances in the technical composition of capital—in a word, machinery—continue to raise the proportion of constant capital in relation to variable capital. This is how the value of capital increases. Existing production must always be re-transformed to a higher degree of technical perfection, requiring a smaller quantity of labor to set in motion a larger quantity of machinery and raw materials.

Marx proceeds to argue how capitalist accumulation creates a "disposable industrial reserve army" of labor that exists solely for the benefit of the capitalists. With the advance of technological innovation, workers are set free into a growing population of the unemployed. Some do find work in other capitalist enterprises, usually older companies that lag behind in new machinery and pay lower wages. Accumulation determines at any given time those employed at various wage levels as well as the unemployed, all who make up what Marx calls "the social capital in its totality." But this totality is always rocked by fluctuations caused by the changing composition of constant and variable capital, that is, more machines, less human labor. Sometimes these fluctuations are what Marx calls "violent." When production expands, so does the need for variable capital, though this is temporary. Because growth is based on constant technological innovation in the most advanced industries, fewer workers are required for production over the long haul. This results in the striking and outright loss of jobs in those industries and makes the absorption of labor in the older capitalist enterprises more difficult. The very expansion of production and all that it unleashes is set in motion by a mass of workers whose own productiveness leads to their removal from it. What the laboring population produces on top of accumulated capital is the means by which it itself is made relatively superfluous, is turned into a relative surplus-population; and it does this to an always increasing extent.[26]

For Marx, a surplus laboring population is a necessary product of accumulation and the development of wealth on a capitalist basis. Regardless of its varying rate at any time in the various phases of production, the outcome is always the same. The rise in constant capital and the diminution of variable capital mean that "with the greater breadth and fullness of all sources of wealth, there is also an extension of the scale on which greater attraction of labourers by capital is accompanied by their greater repulsion." As Marx concludes, "This is a law of population peculiar to the capitalist mode of production."[27] It also is the cause of a disposable industrial reserve army, which is always available to be exploited by capital. Labor ultimately loses out as some workers wind up in lower-paying jobs in lesser industries while others are entirely thrown out of employment. But the one continuous factor is the growth of the reserve army of labor. As Marx says, "The course characteristic of modern industry . . . depends on the constant formation, the greater or lesser absorption, and the re-formation of the industrial reserve army or surplus-population. In their turn, the varying phases of the industrial cycle recruit the surplus-population, and become one of the most energetic agents of its reproduction."[28]

Marx goes to great lengths to explain how work performed by an increasing reserve army of labor takes various forms. At each stage in accumulation, the capitalist can utilize whatever labor he employs to set into motion more production by increased use of machinery, which then allows him to replace skilled laborers with the less skilled, male with female, and adults with children. Nevertheless, the supply of available labor is always greater than the demand for it. Moreover, those who are employed are often forced "to submit to over-work and to subjugation under the dictates of capital."[29]

Marx identifies various forms of superfluous labor subject to the worst of conditions. An example of what he calls "floating" employment are young boys—he likely had in mind the doffers who crawled into industrial machinery to clean it, then perhaps mangled or killed because they could not finish before the bell rang to restart the machine—and who became unemployed if they reached manhood. For Marx, this was a glaring contradiction of the needs of accumulation and its impact on labor, particularly when capitalists complained that they needed more of these young hands while many thousands of men were out of work. Another example was in agriculture, where capitalist innovation caused demand for agricultural labor to fall. Here the contradiction was more extreme compared with industry, where the advance of one phase of production might call for additional labor from an existing surplus pool that could be channeled into secondary capitalist enterprises. This was not the case in agriculture, where machines did away entirely with the need for agricultural labor. The workers might find their way to the city, but they would only augment the industrial reserve army there. For Marx, those left behind in the countryside made up a "latent" surplus population that only grew larger. "The agricultural labourer is therefore reduced to the minimum of wages, and always stands with one foot already in the swamp of pauperism."[30]

The third example, which made up "the broad basis of special branches of capitalist exploitation," was that part of the active labor army that faced extremely irregular employment. "Hence," Marx said, "it furnishes to capital an inexhaustible reservoir of disposable labour-power" whose "conditions of life sink below the average normal level of the working class." Apart from the "dangerous classes" that consist of criminals, prostitutes, etc., paupers fall into three categories: those able to work, orphans and pauper children, and the demoralized and ragged. As Marx writes, "pauperism is the hospital of the active labour army and the dead weight of the industrial reserve army."[31]

From this he concludes:

> The greater the social wealth, the functioning capital, the extent and energy of its growth, and, therefore, also the absolute mass of the proletariat and the productiveness of its labour, the greater is the industrial reserve army. The same causes which develop the expansive power of capital, develop also the labour-power at its disposal. The relative mass of the industrial reserve army increases therefore with the potential energy of wealth. But the greater this reserve army in proportion to the active labour-army, the greater is the mass of a consolidated surplus-population, whose misery is in inverse ratio to its torment of labour. The more extensive, finally, the lazarus-layers of the working class, and the industrial reserve army, the greater is official pauperism. *This is the absolute general law of capitalist accumulation.*[32]

For Marx, the increasing subjugation of labor by capital is characterized by the growth of a relative surplus population and a reserve army of labor always at the ready to be exploited by capitalists. This is the most important dynamic in capitalist accumulation. At the same time, the growth of a reserve army of labor establishes the basis of a coming crisis of the entire system.

Capitalist Accumulation and Its Contradictions in the Great Boom

Marx discovered the general law of capitalist accumulation in the actual conditions of modern production in England in the 1860s, then the center of capitalist industry in the world economy.

The sudden emergence of the United States as the new industrial leader in the 1920s created conditions and processes that developed on much greater levels and degrees of complexity. But the result was still the same. In a rising sea of plenty, more and more working Americans found themselves unemployed or displaced in ways that consigned them to poverty and pauperism. Meanwhile, the rich got richer until their speculative excesses created the bust.

In 1934, Lewis Corey applied Marx's law of capitalist accumulation to explain the root causes of the Great Depression. With a thorough analysis of statistical evidence in *The Decline of American Capitalism*, Corey explained why the unprecedented buildup of the means of production raised the profits for capitalists to new heights but at the expense of workers who were increasingly displaced from production. "Precisely because it is the most highly developed," Corey wrote, "American industry offers the fullest confirmation of the analysis Karl Marx made of the laws of capitalist production."[33]

Corey revealed that the value of constant capital rose more than wages and the output of manufactured goods during the 1920s. Between 1923 and 1929, constant capital in goods had increased by more than four times that of variable capital. Affirming one of Marx's principal arguments about capitalist accumulation, Corey showed that the average American worker in 1929, the year of the Wall Street crash, was earning about the same in wages as in 1923. But during that same period, workers set in motion nearly one-third more constant capital, one-sixth more materials, and one-fifth more output. As the capitalist mode of production expanded to new heights, profits rose and wages fell. "As wages are the price of labor-power, of the worker's skill and muscle and nerves," Corey wrote, "the fall in wages involves displacement of labor and unemployment."[34]

Corey also showed that a qualitative advance in the numbers of displaced workers had occurred between 1923 and 1929, the most prosperous years of the Great Boom. Relative displacement—the number of workers set free from the most mechanized areas of production who found work in less-developed industries or in other areas of the economy—had become a trend. In every year of the period, the number of workers in manufactures was lower than it was in 1919. As capital investment rose 19.1 percent, the absolute displacement of a little more than a million workers contributed to the number of about two million unemployed workers annually in that six-year period.

These major developments defined the U.S. economy during the prosperous 1920s. Productivity rose dramatically because of a massive transformation in constant capital resulting from mechanization. Although this presented the potential of plenty for workers—and was trumpeted by capitalist apologists as the key to universal prosperity—it had the opposite effect. As Corey observed, rising constant capital intensity was an "expression of economic progress" that concealed the contradiction of rising displacement and impoverishment for the majority of the U.S. population. As Corey argued, the growth in capitalist production based on greater use of machines, "simultaneously and antagonistically," had an adverse effect on employment, thus driving down the purchasing power of the workers. As wages fell relative to output, the growing disproportions between wages and profits set "in motion the forces of cyclical crisis and breakdown."[35] As Corey explained:

> The decrease of variable capital (wages) in favor of constant capital (equipment and materials) limits the production of surplus value in proportion to the total invested capital; while the increase in the output of goods and the restriction of mass purchasing power and consumption saturate markets and lower prices to unprofitable levels, thereby limiting the realization of surplus value in the form of profits. The *mass* of profits rises, but the *rate* of profit on the total invested capital tends to fall.
>
> Thus the higher composition of capital [the growth of constant capital and diminution of its variable counterpart] is the

basic objective factor in the contradictions of accumulation and of capitalist production and prosperity.[36]

This contradiction is crucial to Corey's argument about the rising displacement of labor during the Great Boom of the 1920s. Corey used statistical evidence from several sources to argue why the Depression emerged in the midst of "flourishing prosperity" between 1923 and 1929. The main reason was due to the "violent expansion" of production based on higher productivity that compelled even higher rates of efficiency. This created a downward push on what was then the level of "normal unemployment," which he defined as the way "capitalist industry is so organized and managed that there must *always* be a reserve of unemployed workers, even in the most prosperous times, to provide labor for new enterprises and as a means of forcing down wages." Given the "greater and more violent expansion" of American capitalism historically and relative to all other countries, unemployment in the United States always exceeded that in other countries. This was clear during the previous boom of 1900–1913 (excluding the Depression years 1907–1909) when unemployment averaged 7.8 percent of available workers, but it was far worse between 1923 and 1929 given the even greater and "unusual prosperity" generated.[37]

Carefully following Marx, Corey explained how unprecedented capitalist prosperity during those years generated a corresponding higher rate of unemployment than what was normal.

Unemployment is essentially an aspect of the higher productivity of labor under the social relations of capitalist production. Normal unemployment grows when the productivity of labor rises disproportionately to output. Cyclical unemployment prevails in depressions, brought about primarily by forces identified with the higher productivity of labor (which is not matched by higher employment and wages). And the increasingly greater unemployment of capitalist decline is a result of industry having become so highly productive that it is unprofitable to use all its capacity: hence millions of workers are thrown out of work. The increasing efficiency of American industry in 1920–29 considerably raised the total of "normally" unemployed workers. For while the higher productivity of labor *may* mean higher wages, it *always* means a displacement of labor because fewer workers are required to produce a larger output. Thus labor is penalized by its own efficiency.[38]

The basis for the rise in the productivity of labor, in output per worker, was set in motion at the beginning of the decade. Corey uses examples to make his case. Of thirty-five plants surveyed in 1927, output per worker was 75 percent higher than in 1919 and 39 percent higher than in 1924. Labor productivity in automobile production rose 98 percent between 1919 and 1927; it was even higher, 198 percent, for rubber tires. After temporarily shutting down in 1922 to improve machinery, Ford Motor Company resumed production on a new level of productive capacity that reduced the workforce from 57,000 to 40,000. The operation of blast furnaces had become almost completely automated by 1929, raising productivity 135 percent higher than in 1919. Productivity in steel mills and rolling mills rose 43 percent, and there was an increase of 44 percent in petroleum refining. In 1925, something as simple as the adoption of the Owens automatic bottle machine drove man-hour productivity to rise 4,100 times. The invention of the dial telephone displaced more than half the number of operators. Generally, productivity of labor occurred unevenly across U.S. industries, though it rose substantially in all.[39]

Significantly, rising productivity between 1919 and 1929 caused an absolute, or permanent, displacement of labor for the first time in U.S. history. Large numbers of workers were displaced between 1919 and 1927, in manufactures, where productivity rose 42.5 percent, 40.5 percent in mining, 12.5 percent in railroads, and 29.5 percent in agriculture. By 1929, it had displaced 2,832,000 workers, of whom 2,416,000 found employment elsewhere; thus 416,000 workers were permanently displaced. In both mining and railroads, lower output due to technological innovations increased the rate of displacement to 171,000 and 345,000 workers respectively. The improvements in trucking "competed more effectively" with railroad transport, while "electricity increasingly cut into the demand for coal." Steam power plants used less coal by turning to more efficient energy sources, such as hydroelectric plants. But nowhere else in the U.S. economy was there greater permanent displacement than in agriculture. It was the first time this had occurred in U.S. history, a historic development given that so much economic growth throughout the nineteenth century was based on the claiming of the frontier, opening new and massive agricultural production. Between 1919 and 1929, farms gave work to 540,000 fewer persons, as the number of farms fell over the same period. But the actual displacement was much greater, since the overall farm population dropped by about a million, of which many had to find employment elsewhere.[40]

For Corey, the total or "*absolute* displacement of directly productive workers," during the greatest period of capitalist prosperity in the contemporary epoch was an indication of something more general about monopoly capitalism. Compared with earlier economic growth and its adverse impact on labor between 1889 and 1919, the level of labor displacement between 1919 and 1929 was even greater, which, for Corey, marked an "unprecedented development, of profound significance." Considering the increase of 7,180,000 persons to the workforce, plus the 1,155,000 workers who were displaced in manufactures, mining, railroads, and agriculture, Corey reasoned that 8,335,000 workers had to find employment in occupations other than where the displacements had occurred. This would have required these other occupations to be more than three times the size they had been in the earlier twenty-year period. While some ground was gained in distribution services, motor transport, and other areas of trade, absorption in strictly productive enterprises such as construction was limited. As a result, displacement and the absorption rate over the decade of the 1920s revealed that "normal unemployment" increased at least as much as a million, resulting in about 2.5 million unemployed in the year of the crash. As Corey wrote, "This great increase in the reserve army of the unemployed took place in the midst of the most flourishing prosperity."[41]

Indeed, the economy did function on this basis, but only for a short time before it became necessary to divert profits from further investment in actual production to non-productive sectors. These investments were essentially speculative. In this Corey saw a fundamental contradiction in U.S. monopoly capitalism that ushered in its decline. Although the economy seemingly performed spectacularly until the 1929 crash, enabling newly elected President Herbert Hoover to declare that American prosperity would continue indefinitely, nothing could be further from the truth. The seeds of the 1929 bust were already evident only a short time after the Great Boom had begun. Though it is generally agreed that the great upswing in the economy had occurred by 1922, the rate of profit in the productive sectors of the economy began to fall two years later and continued to do so until the stock market collapsed five years later. As the rate of profit declined in productive sectors, capitalists diverted their investments to non-productive areas, primarily in finance. Thus profits in the financial sector increased 177 percent between 1923 and 1929. While investments in new facilities and machinery remained constant during that period, new shares and bonds issued for speculative investments tripled.[42]

But the move toward speculation was itself the product of the higher productivity of labor. Saturated markets for consumer goods meant less investment in capital goods—goods that are produced to make other goods, such as machines used in the production of automobiles—which affected the production of consumer goods and ultimately fueled the displacement of labor. This naturally affected consumption. As American workers who could get credit went into debt, capitalists diverted profits toward more speculative enterprises to make up for the declining rate of profit in productive enterprises. Prosperity became increasingly based on greater speculation until the Great Boom turned into its opposite, the Great Depression. Nevertheless, the underlying cause for this later development inhered in the fundamental divide between capital and labor created by capitalist accumulation. The law that Marx discovered in 1867 to explain how modern industrial growth in England created greater poverty in an ever-rising sea of plenty, was applied by Corey in 1934 to explain how the prosperity of the 1920s caused the greatest economic crisis in contemporary world history.

IN 1938, MAGIL AND STEVENS argued that the germ of American fascism was present in monopoly capitalism in the 1920s when Big Business and the Republican Party created an "entire mechanism of repression" to subject the working and middle classes to its control and domination. For much of the Depression decade that followed, the U.S. ruling class was split on how to end the economic crisis. This was abundantly clear in the battles between Roosevelt and his New Dealers who sought to save capitalism through direct government intervention, and those who remained wedded to the laissez-faire doctrine and ruling-class politics of Roosevelt's three Republican predecessors. Through it all, however, the power of monopoly-finance capital remained superior despite the labor insurgency of 1934 that required the reformist Roosevelt and his administration to usher in Social Security, the National Labor Relations Board, and other components of what we know as the welfare state.

Nevertheless, the power of capital over American society continued to grow throughout the New Deal as the final phase in the transition to state monopoly capitalism. As the epicenter of the world capitalist system—Pax Americana in the making—the United States was the one advanced capitalist nation that could save its own version of liberal capitalist democracy from collapse. As the world's banker and leading creditor to other nations, it prevailed through boom and bust, prosperity and depression, while the myriad and pervasive powers of capital became ever more totalizing at home and abroad. From a Marxist standpoint, it was a course irreversibly determined by the imperatives of monopoly and finance capital—the laws of motion governing its movement and social character—to accumulate exponentially in order to sustain profitability at the highest levels throughout the system. Those who profited most by it then forged new policies aimed at enhancing the executive power of government over the legislative branches and the judiciary, all aimed at preventing a revolutionary socialist alternative, real or perceived, to rise up against it. Simply put, capitalist progress meant the increasing subjugation of labor. Here was the root of the violence, deception, and manipulation that Magil and Stevens recognized as "the entire mechanism of repression." The advance of such power to create and destroy at ever higher levels was a sure indicator of fascism as a result of the decline and decay of American capitalism. The centralization of wealth and power, monopoly, had mandated the increasing anti-democratic politics of the ruling class.

Lewis Corey explained this in 1934 in *The Decline of American Capitalism* by demonstrating how capitalist accumulation and economic growth exacerbated fundamental and irreconcilable contradictions between capital and labor, now at a much higher stage of capitalist development than those Marx observed in nineteenth-century England. Still, Corey affirmed what Marx had discovered as one of many laws governing the motion of capital. The constant and necessary drive for capitalist accumulation during the booming 1920s had subjected American labor to even greater control by capitalists. Just as the seeds of the bust were evident in the boom, so were fascist processes aimed at the domination of capital over society. In the epicenter of world capitalism, fascism neither required an economic collapse, a strong working-class challenge to capitalist rule, nor the fiery rise of its most immediate antagonist, middle-class reaction.

American fascism came to life in the midst of prosperity as a property of capital, specifically in its constant quest to reproduce itself. This was what Magil and Stevens implied by terming Big Business and Wall Street as the "fountainhead" of American fascism and what they surely meant when they defined it as "the rule by finance capital." As Corey noted, modern capitalism was in transition from its industrial stage to a higher form, monopoly-finance capital and imperialism, when Marx's *Capital* was published in 1867. But nothing in this movement to a higher stage of development had fundamentally altered the general law of capitalist accumulation. Corey ably demonstrated that American capitalists were driven to do what Marx saw in their English predecessors: "To accumulate, is to conquer the world of social wealth, to increase the mass of human beings exploited by him, and thus to extend both the direct and the indirect sway of the capitalist."[43]

In the decline and decay of monopoly-finance capitalism and imperialism, the highest and final stage of capitalism, as Lenin had argued, is where we find the germ of fascism in American capitalism during the period between the two world wars. From the standpoint of the present crisis of American and world capitalism, it is now evident that fascist processes aimed at the domination of capital over labor were embedded in capitalist production, in what Corey observed as "the perpetual struggle between the forces of expansion and decline." As Corey says, "Accumulation tends to outstrip itself and limit the means of profitably investing capital, which results in a periodical overproduction of capital goods."[44] Since profits depend on the ability of capitalists to enlarge their markets to absorb the rising output of consumption goods, the failure to sustain this movement eventually compels capitalists to cut back on the production of capital goods.

Overproduction of capital goods reveals why capitalism is utterly contradictory at its core and inherently prone to crisis. This, Corey states, is "the real element" of capitalist decline:

> Capitalist production tends to exhaust the long-time factors of expansion and to limit, at first relatively, then absolutely, the possibilities of economic advance. Capitalist production *must* yield profits and these profits *must* be converted into capital by

means of an increasing output and absorption of capital goods. This is the accumulation of capital.[45]

The contradiction of supply outstripping demand is only made greater with economic growth and the concomitant advance of concentrated wealth and power—monopoly—which ultimately gives way to breakdown, crisis, and the threat of declining profits. "Monopoly answers the threat with control of markets, higher prices, limitation of output, and relative or absolute restriction of progress in technological efficiency." For Corey, "this is an element of decline, as it emphasizes the incapacity to develop fully all the forces of production and consumption." Instead of fluidity in the movement of capital required for further accumulation, monopoly instead becomes more rigid in the face of mounting contradictions in production and exchange, imposing greater controls over the domestic economy while seeking to counter the forces of decline with the export of capital abroad—in a word, imperialism.[46] Throughout, capital strives to exercise greater control over all aspects of social and political life. These efforts, which are ultimately grounded in the fundamental contradiction between capital and labor, generate fascist processes aimed at the domination of the former over the latter.

From its very beginning, American fascism reveals in embryo the basic contradiction between capital and labor in the context of an unprecedented empire that defined the epoch of monopoly-finance capitalism and the contemporary world experience. In the U.S. epicenter during the 1920s, fascist processes inhered in the expansion and complexities of production and exchange, creating greater wealth and poverty at once and thus at every turn requiring mechanisms of repression at home and the ability to deliver militaristic clout whenever necessary in its imperial designs. To that end, the expansion of the means of production in the domestic economy also brought growing displacement of labor. This required capitalists to rely on the powers of government to defend their interests by disciplining and punishing the political forces of labor by whatever means necessary, while pioneering ways to persuade and manipulate mass consciousness through advertising, public relations, and propaganda.

Indeed, the global crisis of the 1930s brought fascism to power in its most brutal form in Germany. But political economy reveals fascist processes deep in U.S. capitalism a decade before Hitler's rise, in the intensification of irreconcilable contradictions between capital and labor that also signaled the coming of the American Behemoth now fully upon us today. Fascism inheres in the processes of monopoly-finance capitalism that inevitably create a general crisis of the system, and from it the plausibility for a crisis of class rule that ends in a revolutionary reconstitution of society, socialism, or the savagery that is fascism, which leads to the common ruin of the whole society. This is a tragic hallmark of capitalism in the contemporary world.

3—The Spectacle of Prosperity and Necessity of Spin

THE GREAT BOOM of the 1920s created a spectacle of prosperity based on America's extraordinary capacities as the epicenter of the world capitalist system. Economic growth between 1922 and 1929 was unprecedented, at times breathtaking, and incessantly transformative. Much of what remained of traditional nineteenth-century American society was swept aside in a whirlwind of change. The once vital role of the petty-bourgeois merchant and small family farmer was fading into history. Capitalist innovation in the means of production seemed to ensure the promise of endless prosperity in the New Era. Mass production, urbanization, and the impact of the automobile and the radio were redoing the physical and mental landscape. Socially mobile Americans, especially those in the rising boomtowns, found pleasure in the swirl of products that seemingly made life more exciting and vivid. The dazzle of it all was reflected in a new obsession with fashions, sports, movies, music, and booze. The businessman was the new American hero, even Christ-like. There was so much ado in the constant movement of things and people that one could be easily lured by the mysterious powers of the commodity. As Marx and Engels first described the sweeping powers of industrial capitalism:

> Modern bourgeois society with its relations of production, of exchange and of property, a society that had conjured up such gigantic means of production and of exchange, is like the sorcerer, who is no longer able to control the powers of the nether world whom he has called up by his spells.[1]

In 1920s America, the capitalist spell had become so intoxicating that millions of Americans believed they were living as individuals never had before. Many more held out the hope that their turn would come. Indeed, a new, more enjoyable lifestyle was enough to convince some that capitalism had changed in a revolutionary way by becoming what it was always supposed to be: democratic.

But to sustain the boom required just the opposite. The First World War had turned the capitalist road into a highway. The partnership of government, business, and labor required for wartime production had expanded the force field within which capital could accumulate. State intervention into the private economy was welcomed by Big Business, making both even stronger in the postwar decade as a more powerful form of capitalist rule emerged. The requirements of capitalist accumulation only furthered the concentration of wealth and centralization of Big Business, its power expanding over the rest of society in ever-totalizing forms. From a capitalist state compelled to raise production and productivity to construct the war machine while still providing maximum profits to capitalists, the U.S. government became the manager for plutocracy that was making business all-powerful in its own right. The conscious aim of three Republican presidents was to promote a policy of laissez-faire in domestic and foreign policies that belied the potential might of a capitalist empire on the rise.

The Great Boom established the basis for a belief in the possibility of abundance, endless prosperity, and the promise of a qualitative advance in material comfort for all Americans. Delivering it was another matter. The extraordinary development of technology and innovation in management caused the fixed component of constant capital, machinery, to rise at the expense of its variable constituent, labor. This meant that production would inevitably deliver far more goods than the mass of people could consume. Without any consideration of this and other contradictions, capitalist leadership quickly became convinced that prosperity required the selling of ideas as well as things. In the marketplace of the New Era, it became as important to constantly remind the consumer that he or she needed a new car, radio, household appliance, or mouthwash as it was to *make* any of them. While the creation of material abundance on a hitherto unknown scale was indeed a remarkable feat, the more enduring achievement of the American capitalists was the genesis of marketing as an industry unto itself. For the first time, capitalist development came to depend on the means and methods of persuasion and manipulation to sustain capitalist accumulation. In the American epicenter of world capitalism where abundance was the greatest and living standards were envied by the rest of the world, the mission of capital was not only to subject labor to its command but to extend its domination in the realm of mass consciousness. It is here where the market mentality prevailed, where consumerism triumphed over citizenship, and where non-terrorist fascist processes based on persuasion, deception, and manipulation aimed at the domination of capital itself were forged.

When war erupted in Europe in 1914, America was considered a backward society by haughty Europeans of high culture. Jonathan Norton Leonard, a writer whose 1939 book *Three Years Down* offered a highly readable account of the worst years of the Great Depression, described the United States in 1914 as "large and rich" but "a provincial country and none too sure of itself." Americans in pursuit of quality higher education and who wanted to become doctors, scientists, or philosophers went to German universities. "Paris ruled the elegancies," while "'the latest thing' in every field was usually of European origin." Before the First World

War, Leonard wrote, Americans "were definitely importers of culture, not exporters of our own." He added:

> Our technical progress was not much considered. Our movies, comic strips, popular music and fashions had not yet begun to Americanize the leisure moments of the world. Our financiers, except when they wanted to borrow money abroad, were completely wrapped up in domestic affairs. Our foreign policy, except for a habit of absent-minded felony toward Latin America, did not exist. Our navy was an expensive gesture and our army a small, hairy-chested farce.[2]

The coming of the Great War changed all that as the United States became a global leader whose many powers seemed magical.

THE FIRST WORLD WAR AND THE ORIGINS OF THE GREAT BOOM

Of all the changes in the international capitalist order following the First World War, the most significant was the emergence of the United States as "the great creditor nation of the world."[3] This underscores what William Leuchtenburg, a highly respected American historian of the 1920s and 1930s, meant when he declared that America's postwar global role was one "of those great shifts in power that occurs but rarely in the history of nations, a transition with formidable consequences."[4] Even before it entered the conflict in 1917, its massive economic potential, tapped by the needs of total war in Europe, had put it on that path. From 1914 to 1916, U.S. trade with the Allies rose from $825 million to $3.2 billion.[5] By the time American troops arrived on the Western Front, total exports of U.S. merchandise to the Allies had reached $6.2 billion, about 11 percent of GNP.[6] The more strategically placed enterprises reeled in the biggest catches; for example, United States Steel's profits rose from $76 million in 1914 to $478 million in 1917.[7] National income nearly doubled from 1914 to 1918, as living standards improved dramatically for millions of Americans employed in wartime production and services. The war also made America the world's leading energy producer. By 1920, its 60 million tons of oil production was two-thirds of the world's total.[8]

Globally, America took a decisive step in ascending to the level of a preponderant economic power, making real President Woodrow Wilson's desire for an active and engaging postwar U.S. foreign policy that would facilitate an "open door" for American goods around the world. The Marxist economist Lewis Corey in 1934 emphasized that the most important result of the war was America's ascendance at the expense of its competitors. In 1919–1920, U.S. exports reached $16.1 billion, the highest to date; exports exceeded imports by almost $7 billion.[9] Moreover, the United States, as the world's new banker, exported more capital than ever before. By 1919, foreigners owed American investors almost $3 billion, not including the more than $10 billion the United States had lent foreign countries, mainly the Allies, to remain in the war.[10] Indeed, when the fighting stopped, America was positioned to exert tremendous economic and political power throughout the world, though the "reluctant giant" failed to do so in the coming decades, at least to the degree required given its new global role.[11]

All this startling growth was the result of a historic partnership joined by Big Business and the U.S. government that was designed to produce whatever the Allies needed. At President Wilson's urging, Congress passed the Military Appropriations Act in August 1916, from which came a Council of National Defense. Cabinet members sat on the council, but its main work was done by business leaders. America's entry into the war the following year led to the creation of the War Industries Board. Other new agencies quickly followed, for example, the Food, Fuel and Railway Administrations, the Shipping Board, the War Trade Board, and the Selective Service Administration. All were needed by the federal government to coordinate production, prices, and labor for the purpose of establishing an effective wartime economy. The waging of imperialist war had made planning a necessity in the workings of capitalist production and exchange. Of course, none of this hurt Big Business. For the first time in the history of capitalism, the state became a highly conscious and informed manager of business interests. Some other wartime European governments had moved in this direction but none as far as the United States in achieving a new benchmark for state power.

Meanwhile, organized labor argued that its commitment to wartime production had earned it a rightful place at the decision-making table with employers and politicians. The AFL contended that business and government needed to take stock of its longtime commitment to reformism and also recognize the hard line it had taken against the IWW. Moreover, its ability to keep workers in line with concessions for higher wages and better working conditions had helped to dampen sentiments for strikes and walkouts. The fact that wartime prosperity had found its way downward to parts of the working class, especially those engaged in war-related production, had raised wages and levels of comfort and security. Nevertheless, whatever gains workers received were undermined by the deepening compromise struck between Samuel Gompers and other AFL leadership with Big Business. The ideological disposition of the AFL could not be clearer. In its deliberate aim to reject any hint of socialism, it sought harmonious relations with capital in the hope that it would lead American workers to become partners with business.[12]

Here were the combined forces at home—government, business, and labor—that turned the United States into a preponderant global power by war's end. This required a foreign policy to open doors for the export of American capital and goods, though the main intent of economic planners and strategists was for the door to swing outward. As mentioned, exports exceeded imports in the billions. The export of American capital also soared to new heights as leading businessmen saw profitable opportunities to invest their capital reserves in underdeveloped areas of the world economy, especially in Latin America. The creation of the American International Corporation in 1915, which included some of the largest U.S. companies and banks, facilitated such investment.[13] By 1918, U.S. banks had established branches in sixteen European and Latin American countries, and the rise of their leadership of the capitalist world coincided with New York replacing London as the world's financial center. That the war had qualitatively advanced the global reach of the American empire at the expense of European capitalist countries was clear to capitalists and communists alike. Even as early as 1915, Thomas W. Lamont of J. P. Morgan and Company gleefully noted that the increase in war business had greatly swung America's trade balance in its favor, enabling American capitalists to buy back U.S. securities from foreign concerns, which eliminated the drain on foreign exchange. Instead of paying interest and dividends to foreigners, American investors were now the recipients. Nine years later, the Soviet economist E. A. Preobrazhensky saw this even more clearly by connecting America's imperial rise to the dollar as the new, dominant currency in the global capitalist system.[14]

Nevertheless, the contradictions of wartime capitalist enterprise ushered in a sharp recession not long after the Armistice was signed in November 1918. Government subsidies had resulted in a combination of huge surpluses in agricultural and manufacturing goods, highly profitable investments, and price inflation. But the coming of peace brought their abrupt end. As the War Department quickly canceled nearly half of its $6 billion in outstanding contracts, the federal government drastically cut overall spending in fiscal year 1919 from $18 billion to $6 billion. Domestic markets already saturated with product were additionally burdened by the relatively quick recovery throughout much of Europe, which only added to the excess. The result was an immediate slowdown in American production across the board. Total industrial output fell by one-third. As inventories piled up, prices nosedived. By 1921, wholesale prices had dropped by 37 percent, with key farm products the lowest. Investments in new factories and machinery declined precipitously, causing unemployment to rise sharply as the decline in demand for industrial workers was made worse with the decommissioning of nearly four million servicemen returning home in search of work.[15] As great as war had been for American capitalism, the coming of peace brought just the opposite.

THE GREAT BOOM

The postwar downturn did not last long. As Lewis Corey would explain, a normal process of general liquidation of prices, wages, and accumulated goods quickly wiped out fixed capital. Eliminating the disproportionate accumulations of capital and goods that had caused the downturn then made possible a new phase of accumulation based on rising demand for consumer goods. Corey likened the process to "the blood-letting of medieval medicine." The point at which the bleeding weakened the patient, who then required the first of several transfusions to regain his vigor, resembled the beginning of recovery as consumer demand rose again. But here, Corey argued, was the real challenge for leading capitalists. To satisfy rising demand for consumer goods required renewed investment in capital goods to replace equipment in old industries or for use in new industries. As Corey said, "The speed of revival and the scope of recovery and prosperity depend upon an *increasing* output of capital goods and the opportunities it provides for capital investment and accumulation." On this basis industry revived and wages rose, giving workers more purchasing power. The recovery that began in 1922 set the stage for the New Era of prosperity to come, though it never would deliver its promise of uninterrupted prosperity and universal wealth.[16]

Yet, the aggregate numbers gave full force to those who were trumpeting its arrival. GNP climbed from $74 billion to $104 billion from the beginning of the recovery in 1921 to the stock market crash in October 1929.[17] In the same period, the output of all manufactures rose 64 percent, though there were wide variations of growth within the industrial complex; for example, the petroleum and coal products industry topped all other producers with a gain of 156 percent.[18] Electric motors rapidly replaced steam engines; by 1927, 70 percent of American industry was electrified.[19] Automobiles and electrification, the twin pillars of growth and prosperity, fueled tremendous expansion beyond the cities with new highways that connected urban centers with new areas of concentric growth, the suburbs. By 1929, there were 26.7 million autos in use, one for every 4.6 Americans. As the automobile revolutionized transportation and redefined social existence, a range of new household appliances rolled off the assembly lines in record numbers.[20] Inside the home, life became more manageable, comfortable, and leisurely. The percentage of households with flush lavatories more than doubled between 1920 and 1930, while the number of homes with radios went from zero to 40 percent. Cheap electricity facilitated new appliances that made cooking and cleaning less burdensome.[21] From this remarkable surge in economic growth emerged a culture of mass consumption based on increasing purchasing power. Total U.S. income rose from $67.9 billion in 1923 to $82.4 billion in 1929, an increase of 21 percent.[22]

By any measure, overall economic growth between 1922 and 1929 was phenomenal. But what was behind it? Writing from the vantage point of the Depression in 1934, Corey explained that the prosperity during those years depended on rising opportunities for capital accumulation, which ultimately depended on sustaining investment and output of capital goods. This, in turn, required that the goods produced for consumers would continue selling at profitable levels. But there was a caveat. As long as sales of consumer goods kept pace with the investment and output of capital goods, capitalist accumulation would proceed on a generally upward path. On this basis, new construction (mainly commercial and industrial building) played a major role in fueling the boom, rising 31 percent. Equally important, the wholesale value of automobile output averaged over $3 billion yearly. Then again, integral to the expansion of capital goods was increasing productivity that provided more impetus for capitalists to invest in new industrial machinery and electrification. Investment in electric machinery more than doubled. Large amounts of capital were also absorbed in investment aimed at technological innovation, such as radios, motion pictures, rayon, chemicals, aviation, mechanical refrigeration, and the power laundry. All this activity came full circle to more construction of industrial and commercial structures, from factories to movie palaces to service stations. As Corey noted, the expansion of new or relatively new industries was especially significant because it required greater levels of capital investment than similar expansion in older industries.[23]

Driving all this was the capitalist imperative to continuously expand production, increase productivity, and create a standard of wages based on factory discipline that turned workers into consumers. Two ways to achieve these ends lay in the systematic organization of mass production and a "scientific" approach to industrial management. The first, known as Fordism because it flowed from the pioneering approach to auto production by Henry Ford, involved the division of assembly-line processes performed by workers engaged in successive stages of the manufacturing process. Based on the rational use of labor operating in systemic cohesion, production became as interchangeable as the different parts of the commodities produced, and like the parts just as easy to replace.[24] But Fordism established more than a new organization of work. It was also, as the historian Michel Beaud succinctly described it,

> a *new model for producing the capitalist commodity* (with relatively high wages for a fraction of the working class, and a strong increase in productivity due to mass production and rationalization), *and a new model for realizing the value thus created* (with development of mass consumption, which spread to part of the working class, whose conditions of living approached those of the middle strata).

No one saw this more clearly than Ford himself, whose managers systematized production by stationing workers on the assembly line, because, as Ford noted, "walking is not a remunerative activity" and because even the "most stupid man" could learn his one defined task in a couple of days. In 1926, 79 percent of the workers in all of Ford's factories went through less than a week of training. But for this level of skill, Ford began paying his workers $5 per day and lowered the working day from nine to eight hours. The daily wage continued to go up, to $6 in 1919 and $7 in 1929.[25]

As Fordism became the norm in mass production, industrialists recognized the need for a more disciplined worker who had a better grasp of the job and therefore was more capable of adhering to the dictates of "scientific management." This approach, according to the historian Tom Kemp, was implicit in the ideas of "Taylorism," which sought to give management undisputed control over the workplace and consequently the leverage it believed it needed to mitigate the influence of unions and the tendency of workers to control their own labor processes. According to Kemp, these efforts did not entirely succeed. "Workers did not give up trying to enforce their concept of work."[26]

The benefits derived from these rational approaches to production made U.S. corporations like Ford, DuPont, and General Electric global models of capitalist enterprise. Turning the least skilled worker into a highly efficient cog in the wheels of production was no mean accomplishment, especially if it justified paying higher wages just so the worker could buy what he made. In the end, however, industrial capitalist ownership reaped the benefits of rising productivity. According to George Soule, output per man-hour in industrial production grew 32 percent from 1923 to 1929, which resulted in lower labor costs but not higher wages. Instead, for much of the decade, the biggest rise in income from productivity increases went to stockholders, whose dividends rose to 65 percent by 1929.[27] The rich got richer. But the disparity carried ominous consequences for the future, though hardly anyone cared.

Meanwhile, U.S. capitalism pumped out capital and consumer goods at unprecedented levels. Rising exports created a big trade surplus. U.S foreign investment rose dramatically. By 1929, U.S.

industry was producing one-quarter of the world's goods and 40 percent of all manufactured items.[28] Exports increased from $3.9 billion to almost $5.4 billion from 1922 to 1929, as U.S. companies went beyond their traditional European markets to Africa and South America where the increase was roughly 130 percent. Imports also grew from $3.2 billion to $4.5 billion. By and large, the figures show an impressive trade surplus and balance of payments.[29]

SALESMANSHIP AND ADVERTISING IN THE SPECTACLE OF ABUNDANCE

If the volume of goods produced by American capitalists between 1922 and 1929 was unprecedented, so was the means by which it was marketed. No longer was it sufficient to present an item for sale, promote its usefulness, and then take the order. Salesmen going door to door needed thinkers back in the office, whose mission was to determine how to persuade the consumer to buy even if the item was not needed just so the bosses could stay ahead of the constant worry of too much product in backroom storage or the large warehouse. Market imperatives to sustain profits required a qualitatively new approach. As never before, wrote journalist Frederick Lewis Allen in 1931, business in the 1920s had recognized that continuous prosperity depended on the consumer "to buy and buy lavishly":

> The whole stream of six-cylinder cars, super-heterodynes, cigarettes, rouge compacts, and electric ice-boxes would be dammed at its outlet. The salesman and the advertising man held the key to this outlet. As competition increased their methods became more strenuous. No longer was it considered enough to recommend one's goods in modest and explicit terms and to place them on the counter in the hope that the ultimate consumer would make up his mind to purchase. The advertiser must plan elaborate national campaigns, consult with psychologists, and employ

all the eloquence of poets to cajole, exhort, or intimidate the consumer into buying,—"to break down consumer resistance."[30]

For the salesmen—women were conspicuously absent from their growing ranks—this meant big changes. For one thing, salesmanship now depended on a growing arsenal of marketing tools, from neon signs to slick deliveries aimed at manipulating consumer needs. Psychologists took care of that. Salesmen learned to sell themselves more effectively so they could sell more product. Gadgets and mind-altering messages aimed at convincing the consumer to buy things that made his or her life easier, or to make them more personally appealing, or to make an ordinary man feel like a millionaire altered the mind of the salesman as well. To sell the commodity by selling himself made him a model citizen whose thinking and existence, his self-identity, was supposed to mirror the ideal market he lived for and sustained.

Such was the world of George F. Babbitt, the eponymous protagonist of Sinclair Lewis's 1922 satirical novel whose daily existence as the consummate salesman was as packaged as the world of commodities surrounding him. A real-estate broker who lived and worked in the fictitious midwestern city of Zenith—the literary counterpart to Warren Harding's hometown of Marion, Ohio—Babbitt awoke each morning at precisely 7:20 to "the best of nationally advertised and quantitatively produced alarm-clocks, with all modern attachments, including cathedral chime, intermittent alarm, and a phosphorescent dial." As a respected businessman in the city, Babbitt lived up to the virtues of his trade "as the servant of society," finding homes for families and shops for businessmen by demonstrating "steadiness and diligence." He was honest, experienced in the matters of titles and leases, and had "an excellent memory for prices." For Babbitt, this was the bottom line. No matter if "his eventual importance to mankind was perhaps lessened by his large and complacent ignorance of all architecture save the types of houses turned out by speculative builders."[31] For Babbitt serenely believed that the one purpose of the real-estate business was to make money for George F. Babbitt. True, it was a good advertisement at Boosters' Club lunches, and all the varieties of Annual Banquets to which Good Fellows were invited, to speak sonorously of Unselfish Public Service, the Broker's Obligation to Keep Inviolate the Trust of His Clients, and a thing called Ethics, whose nature was confusing but if you had it you were a High-Class Realtor and if you hadn't you were a shyster, a piker, and a fly-by-night. These virtues awakened Confidence, and enabled you to handle Bigger Propositions. But they didn't imply that you were to be impractical and refuse to take twice the value of a house if a buyer was such an idiot that he didn't jew you down on the asking-price.[32]

For Stuart Ewen, who has written masterfully on the history of public relations in the United States, George Babbitt was the ultimate foot-soldier of the New Capitalism.[33] But he was also its product, as Sinclair Lewis recognized at the time:

Just as he was an Elk, a Booster, and a member of the Chamber of Commerce, just as the priests of the Presbyterian Church determined his every religious belief and the senators who controlled the Republican Party decided in little smoky rooms in Washington what he should think about disarmament, tariff, and Germany, so did the large national advertisers fix the surface of his life, fix what he believed to be his individuality. These standard advertised wares—toothpastes, socks, tires, cameras, instantaneous hot-water heaters—were his symbols and proofs of excellence; at first the signs, then the substitutes, for joy and passion and wisdom.[34]

Babbitt's character was molded in a totalizing marketplace that took root at a time when business trumped politics, businessmen replaced statesmen, and the consumer replaced the citizen. "Business itself was regarded with a new veneration," observed the writer and longtime *Harper's* magazine editor Frederick Lewis Allen. While the public's interest in politics at all levels vanished, the growth of the Rotary, Kiwanis, and Lions clubs in cities and towns across the country was astounding. In their weekly meetings, members never ceased to praise the "redemptive and regenerative influence of business." The businessman was idolized as "a builder, a doer of great things, yes, and a dreamer whose imagination was ever seeking out new ways of serving humanity."[35] Salesmen and advertisers were the "agents and evangels" of capitalist enterprise.[36]

If it took a novelist like Sinclair Lewis to make Babbitt the archetypal salesman, it was the ad writer and executive Bruce Barton who made Jesus the conqueror of the business world. In his 1925 book *The Man Nobody Knows*, Barton introduced the Nazarene as the creator of modern business enterprise for having "picked up twelve men from the bottom ranks of business and forged them into an organization that conquered the world." To do this required methods that any sound corporate leader would follow. "To create any sort of reception for a new idea or product to-day involves a vast machinery of propaganda and expense," Barton wrote. "Jesus had no funds and no machinery. His organization was a tiny group of uneducated men, one of whom had already abandoned the cause as hopeless, deserting to the enemy."[37] The key to his success was selling the gospel and this, Barton said, showed no offense to the faith:

> Surely no one will consider us lacking in reverence if we say that every one of the "principles of modern salesmanship" on which business men so much pride themselves, are brilliantly exemplified in Jesus' talk and work. The first of these and perhaps the most important is the necessity for "putting yourself in step with your prospect."[38]

To this end, all of Jesus's parables were "the most powerful advertisements of all time" and "show how instantly he won his audiences."[39]

In striking contrast to Christians who pondered the Second Coming as a moment of justice and redemption, Barton claimed that Jesus's presence was ubiquitous in the Great Boom. Look around, he urged his readers, and you will understand who the real Jesus was in his own day, a sociable and unpretentious fellow more likely to be found in the marketplace rather than at Sunday services and, consequently, "the most popular dinner guest in Jerusalem."[40] Make no mistake! He was the Founder of Modern Business and the first modern executive who commanded others through personal magnetism to demonstrate how to handle flawed followers with infinite patience. He lived the life of service, and this was his ultimate message to the businessman. "We are great because of our service," as Barton interpreted the parables. His message to the working man: "We will crawl under your car oftener and get our backs dirtier than any of our competitors." For owners, there was something different. "We put ourselves at your feet and give you everything that you can possibly demand." No matter what they manufactured, all owners made the same pitch. "Service is what we are here for." According to Barton, what business leaders were doing had been done by Jesus almost two thousand years ago. Service was central to the "business philosophy" pioneered by Jesus.[41]

Barton was already a highly successful Madison Avenue executive and a partner in the agency that handled much of the advertising for General Electric and General Motors.[42] *The Man Nobody Knows* instantly became a bestseller. Oddly enough, it placed fourth in total sales for a work of nonfiction in 1925 and first in 1926. Given its eighty-week run on the bestseller list in *Publisher's Weekly*, the book was a bigger seller during those two years than F. Scott Fitzgerald's *The Great Gatsby*, considered a hallmark of American literature.[43] Part of the successful run was due to Barton's own promotion of the book, asking ministers to use it in Sunday school classes and suggesting to employers that they give a copy to each of their ten most valuable employees for Christmas. Some did. Among others, an executive of the National

Mazda Lamp Company in Detroit gave a copy to each of his 125 invited dinner guests. Barton's success further advanced his career in advertising.[44] Perhaps his crowning moment in the business came when he became an adviser to Commerce Secretary Herbert Hoover, who sought Barton's help in his run for the presidency.[45]

In a chapter of his 1938 study of the American capitalist economy, John Blair explained how advertising had become central to what he termed the "distributory function" of the national economy. Blair considered not only the spectacular material contributions advertising had made but also the extent to which its functional role had generated conditions which, in theory, created laws and principles governing its operation. Proof was in the numbers. From 1914 to 1929, money spent on advertising in newspapers and magazines rose from $256 million to $1.1 billion. The spending pace quickened in the late 1920s. Newspaper advertising rose from $220 million in 1925 to $260 million in 1929, an increase of over 18 percent, with about the same rate in magazines. This caused Blair to also consider that the material gain that made advertising integral to capitalist enterprise constituted a "law" or "principle."[46] As he explained:

> In substance the idea embodied in this "law" is merely that as more and more advertising is utilized to sell a certain product to the consumer, the consumer himself becomes more and more immune to that advertising. That is to say, he develops a sort of psychological shell against the forces of advertising. To break through this shell more and more advertising must be utilized, which, in turn, means that the shell becomes all the harder to crack. And so it goes; more and more advertising means a tougher shell which brings forth more and more advertising which means an even tougher shell … *ad infinitum*.

As Blair saw it, every ad aimed at selling a product might lead to a successful sale but in the process the consumer becomes jaded, which then calls for a more appealing ad for further sales of that product. While the objective of selling the product was met, the jaded consumer posed a greater challenge because his "psychological shell" had been hardened. In this sense, the "law" or "principle" of advertising reflected the general law of capitalist accumulation. Every new gain or victory set a new benchmark for further success.[47]

Behind the power of advertising was an even more formidable bulwark of corporate capitalism: the rising complex of public relations and its experts, whose practices and planned propaganda campaigns, writes Stuart Ewen, "grew exponentially" during the 1920s and generated "foundational changes in the American social fabric." Among others, Ewen cites the work of Harold Laswell, a political scientist and leading expert on the subject who noted that propaganda had quickly become "one of the most powerful instrumentalities in the modern world" aimed at controlling public opinion by means of conscious manipulation. Relying on various forms of social communication—symbols, stories, rumors, reports, pictures, etc.—public relations had given rise to what Laswell termed "a dictatorial habit of mind" in the public domain. This, Ewen writes, was cultivated further by means of an "increasingly sophisticated opinion-molding apparatus" that included the use of polling.[48] "By the end of the decade," Ewen says, "the study of public attitudes was moving beyond the concerns of advertising and marketing per se, to inform a more comprehensive approach to corporate thinking."[49] For Ewen, public relations experts who gathered information by means of conscious, steady polling served to transform the public itself into a "commodity" by packaging and selling its opinions to "the highest bidder."[50]

Here perhaps were the true revolutionaries of the New Era. Decades before Pax Americana established its hegemony over the world market, American capitalists were using material abundance as the basis for colonizing the minds of their citizens. The monumental altering and transforming of consciousness required to sustain mass consumption had created a spectacle of abundance that radiated through the magic of advertising. John Blair saw this in the revolutionary power of the advertiser to seize control of the senses. "At night," he wrote, "we find the streets of any metropolitan area alive with ingenious electrical signs of one type or another, evolving pictures of wheels turning around, small automobiles flashing continuously across the facade of a building, arrows pointing at something or other."[51] But as Blair believed, the dazzling and mesmerizing spectacle had always to be enhanced in order to penetrate the consumer's jaded psychological shell.

Another observer, from France, who saw the same powers at work was the writer and cultural critic George Duhamel, who toured the United States in the late 1920s and then wrote a scathing attack on America as a civilization constantly being devoured and devalued by advertising and the machinery of publicity. Like Blair, Duhamel saw the flashing lights and incessant movement as a constant assault on the senses. But what Blair soberly theorized as a law or principle at work was for the highly agitated Frenchman the obscenities of a dehumanized and barbarous culture. Reading this European elitist, who was quite taken with his own sense of genius, could exhaust one's patience. "In the daytime," he wrote of these monstrous creations of the publicity machine,

> the sun makes them powerless, but the night is their own. They have divided among themselves the Kingdom of Darkness. Now here, now there, they begin to awake with the twilight. With the serene persistence of machines, they resume their work of propaganda, of intimidation, in a *charivari* of light, a riot, a battle, a triumph of disharmony and disorder. . . . It is the jungle, with all its savagery.[52]

Beneath the hyperbole was a seminal grasp of the publicity machine's psychological and sociological impact. "It treats man as if he were the most stupid of the inferior animals," Duhamel wrote. Moreover, the "flashes, repetitions, and explosions" were the inventions of those who were themselves "apes, who know not what fresh acrobatics to invent to catch the bewildered gaze of the passer-by" and are thus responsible for "titillations" and "burlesque" that resulted in the constant "masturbation of the eye."[53] In the company of his American guide and companion, Duhamel described a visit to a movie theater where people were pushed in and out as part of a continuously moving queue. Even the theater itself, whose "Gargantuan maw," "imitations of thick Oriental rugs," and statues on pedestals made of "some plastic and translucent material that seemed intended to remind one of Greek sculpture," exhibited "the luxury of some big, bourgeois brothel—and industrialized luxury, made by soulless machines for a crowd whose own soul seems to be disappearing." Everything about the theater and the film struck Duhamel as an imitation of life, to the point where he wondered whether this applied to the moviegoers themselves, a "human multitude that seemed to dream what it saw, and that sometimes stirred unconsciously like a man asleep." It struck Duhamel that everything around him and including him was false. "I myself was perhaps no longer anything but a simulacrum of a man, an imitation Duhamel."[54]

Duhamel was deeply agitated by the false universe that advertising had created in the United States but was even more disturbed by what it held for others. America was a grand social "experiment" that showed the rest of the world its future in paradoxical terms, a complex of social interiority increasingly presented in elemental and seductive imagery. Its "supreme virtue" lay in the powers of a "new truth ... [that] delights the single-minded and enchants children." Assessing the American experiment: "All the children whom I know, reason like Americans when it is a question of money, of pleasure, of glory, of power, and of work."[55] Duhamel's harsh treatment of Americans surely stems in part from an old-world European snobbery that generally reads as parody. He titled his book *America the Menace* because its unthinking, brutish and utterly false existence was beckoning the rest of the world to follow. But he was little inclined to examine the subtle methods that made it possible, the power to persuade and manipulate the public.

DEMOCRACY IN THE MARKETPLACE

As prosperity depended increasingly on rising mass consumption, advertising became more consciously duplicitous. One genre of print ads that flourished during the late 1920s and early 1930s was based on parables intended to convey practical and moral lessons in everyday life. These parables, Roland Marchand tells us, resembled those employed in the Old and New Testaments that aimed to dramatize a central message by means of stark contrasts and exaggeration. But there were basic and consequential differences between the two. For example, Jesus sought to stimulate in his listener the need to rethink decisions and behavior that adversely impacted others and act in a manner that might bring him or her closer to salvation. On the other hand, the parables used by advertisers stressed comfort mainly by conveying that the product was indispensable and could easily be incorporated into one's daily life. While the former focused on the need for restraint, the latter urged that anything was possible. Here were two fundamentally different ideas about human perfection and how to attain it. When Jesus spoke in parables, the core message was that individual existence amounted to nothing without a deep and abiding concern for the welfare of others. In contrast, advertising came up with parables designed to convince each individual that there were no limits to his or her pleasures.[56]

One of the most effective ads was the parable of the "Democracy of Goods." Intended as *tableaux vivants* (living pictures) that highlighted the wonders of mass production and distribution, they aimed to encourage every person to believe that he or she could enjoy society's most significant pleasure, convenience, or benefit regardless of social standing. In his comprehensive study of American advertising during the interwar period, Marchand discusses one such ad that appeared in the September 1929 issue of the *Ladies' Home Journal*. The dominant image is a young lad, Livingston Ludlow Biddle, who is identified as the scion of the wealthy and well-known Biddle family of Philadelphia. With the family coat-of-arms visible in one corner of the ad, the future heir to the family fortune is sitting atop a tricycle with an inquiring and endearing look on his face. Below his image are words carefully chosen by the Cream of Wheat Corporation that focus on the importance of diet in the boy's daily care, as prescribed by "famous specialists." But the central message of the ad goes further by emphasizing in the clearest terms that this efficacious product need not be enjoyed by the rich alone. As Marchand writes of the ad, "Every mother can give her youngsters the fun and benefits of a Cream of Wheat breakfast just as do the parents of these boys and girls who have the best that wealth can command."[57]

Regardless of the particular product and its benefit, the parable genre remained a fixture of advertising throughout the period. All ads of this type proclaiming that "any woman can" or "every home can afford" were bent on publicizing the idea that fine products in the marketplace were not the sole pleasures of the wealthy and privileged. Quite the contrary, they were constant reminders that life in America was truly democratic because everything was available to all in the marketplace. Just because a rich family used a particular product did not mean that it could not be used by others beneath them. "By implicitly defining 'democracy' in terms of equal access to consumer products," Marchand says, "and then by depicting the everyday functioning of that 'democracy' with regard to one product at a time, these tableaux offered Americans an inviting vision of their society as one of incontestable equality."[58]

Here perhaps were the powers of persuasion and manipulation at their most sublime. By focusing on one product at a time, advertisers sought to divert attention from the realities of class, power and privilege. The rich and powerful enjoyed any of these products at any time, but this is what the parable was designed to obfuscate. For example, an elegant butler serving Chase and Sanborn Coffee to a wealthy family in a dining room with a high ceiling was intended to remind all who saw it that "compared with the riches of the more fortunate, your way of life may seem modest indeed, yet no one—king, prince, statesman, or capitalist" has any more power to enjoy such fine coffee than a commoner. Another ad for the C. F. Church Manufacturing Company promoted a toilet seat that was "a bathroom luxury everyone can afford." As the ad stated: "If you lived in one of those palatial apartments on Park Avenue, in New York City, where you have to pay $2,000.00 to $7,500.00 a year rent, you still couldn't have a better toilet seat in your bathroom than they have—the Church Sani-White Toilet Seat which you can afford to have right now." As Marchand concluded from both examples, "No discrepancies in wealth could prevent the humblest citizens, provided they chose their purchases wisely, from retiring to a setting in which they could contemplate their essential equality, through possession of an identical product, with the nation's millionaires."[59]

For Marchand, the parable of the Democracy of Goods was not a "concerted conspiracy" by advertisers "to impose a social ideology on the American people." True, it sought to convince the public that "antagonistic envy of the rich was unseemly; programs to redistribute wealth were unnecessary" because "the best things in life were already available to all at reasonable prices." As such, the most attractive aspect of the parable for advertisers was that it preached "the coming of an equalizing democracy." Yet the fundamental assumptions of the advertisers themselves were necessarily divisive, and it came out in the parable. On one hand, frequently used terms like "everyone," "anyone," "any home," and the like were aimed at "consumer-citizens" ranked economically by advertisers in the top half of the nation's population, which amounted to 4 million as opposed to 120 million people. The connection now was between the 400 top families and the 4 million beneath them, the upper echelon of the rising middle class. As Marchand tells us, "The standard antitheses of the Democracy of Goods parables were 'mansion' and 'bungalow.'" But on the other hand, advertising generally ignored anyone who did not live in the cozy confines of the latter. "These millions," Marchand wrote, "might overhear the promises of consumer democracy in the newspapers or magazines, but advertising leaders felt no obligation to show how their promises to 'everyone' would bring equality to those who lived in the nation's apartment houses and farmhouses without plumbing, let alone those who lived in rural shacks and urban tenements."[60]

THE BALLYHOO OF CAPITALISTS AND PRESIDENTS

The parable of the Democracy of Goods in advertising was reinforced by powerful sources in American society, even by its presidents. In an address to the American Association of Advertising Agencies in the fall of 1926, Calvin Coolidge asserted that in educating consumers on everything from toothpaste to beautiful clothing, advertisers were cultivating the mind and social graces of consumers in ways that "were harnessing America's modern industrial system to the uplift of its citizenry." Coolidge believed this was "molding the human mind" while "ennobling the commercial world." Bruce Barton's Jesus called on those around him "to stand upright and look at God face to face" so he could defend family, community, and country. No wonder then that Coolidge defined the work of ad men as nothing short of facilitating "the regeneration and redemption of mankind."[61]

The belief that capitalism was finally delivering its long-standing promise of universal prosperity, and that it was occurring only in democratic America, was deepened by its leading capitalists, who were convinced of their own ballyhoo—a word used to describe the promotion of anything that took on a life bigger than its own through the constant barking and subterfuge of advertising. Prosperity and progress, they claimed, was changing capitalism itself. New principles and laws of capitalist development were now at work. Charles E. Mitchell, president of the National City Bank of New York, declared that "a revolution in industry has been taking place that is raising all classes of the population to a more equal participation in the fruits of industry, and thus, by the natural operation of economic law, bringing to a nearer realization the dreams of those utopians who looked to the day when poverty would be banished." E. A. Filene, the Boston-based tycoon who pioneered bargain-basement department stores, was ebullient in his praise for the new capitalism making possible "the ever-present human desire for greater total profits [that] will lead to the adoption of new principles." Andrew Mellon, one of the world's richest men and treasury secretary for Presidents Harding, Coolidge, and Hoover, was certain that a new set of economic laws had been established as a result of modern industrial organization governed by efficiency and the "greater diffusion of prosperity among all classes." Such was the bandwagon of rhapsodies about endless prosperity that rose in a crescendo right up until the crash in October 1929. Only months before that fateful event, two more prophets of capitalist progress had written in another widely read book that "the real industrial leaders of present-day America" had realized that their goal was nothing less than "to make everybody rich." By recognizing the necessity of paying high wages, industrialists were not only generating prosperity but also signaling that the time was coming when "the rule of class will for the first time in human history utterly disappear."[62]

These were weighty pronouncements, made even more influential by the political imprimatur of the Republican Party. As the unrivaled champions of private enterprise and laissez-faire government, Republican leaders promoted the arrival of a New Era of American capitalism, which, they claimed, would benefit everyone, while crafting a political agenda that would make the rich even richer. Certainly, Warren Harding played a leading role. Sailing to victory in 1920 from an electoral landslide and the highest popular vote to date, Harding represented everything big business and finance capital required of its leading New Era front man. According to the historian Michael Parrish, Harding

bore a striking resemblance to Sinclair Lewis's fictional real estate salesman of 1922, George Babbitt. Like Babbitt, Warren Harding always tried to fit in. He was a swell guy. At the Elks Lodge or Rotary Club in Marion, the state capitol in Columbus, or the Senate cloakroom in Washington, Harding spent his time cultivating friendships, not making enemies. He had slapped many a back, played innumerable games of stud poker, and hoisted his share of cocktails. . . . He was handsome, charming, convivial, and given to the type of florid oratory— he called it "bloviating"—heard throughout the Midwest on the Fourth of July.[63]

As Harding's successor in the White House, Calvin Coolidge well understood the role of effective advertising as the consummate promotion of American business. But he lacked Harding's personality—it was arguable that he even had one—and seemed doomed when he stepped into the White House. While Harding's drunkenness, infidelities, and other improprieties earned him a pass among Republican elites, Coolidge was considered a boob. Ferdinand Lundberg recalled one story that typified his general ignorance. According to a Washington correspondent for the *New York Evening Post*, Clinton W. Gilbert, Coolidge had confided to his advisers just before entering the White House that he had thought all international trade was paid directly by gold bullion—"so much gold for so much merchandise."[64] Immortalized by his chief biographer, William Allen White, as the "Puritan in Babylon," Coolidge's other claim to fame according to critics was his ability to be "silent in five languages."[65]

But steeped in his austere and frugal small-town New England ways, Silent Cal, as he was called, surpassed Harding to become "the procurator of capitalist prosperity."[66] Oddly enough, this made the seemingly boorish Coolidge one of the great admirers of "advertising ballyhoo," wrote Silas Bent in 1927, who revealed that Coolidge could communicate his message with the best of experts. Bent recalled a statement Coolidge made that revealed his positive view of it:

It informs the readers of the existence and nature of commodities by explaining the advantages to be derived from their use, and creates for them a wider demand. It is the most potent influence in adopting (adapting?) and changing the habits and modes of life, affecting what we eat, what we wear, and the work and play of the whole nation. . . . It is not enough that the goods are made; a demand for them must also be made.[67]

Silent Cal well understood the power of ballyhoo. According to Stuart Ewen, Coolidge's laissez-faire approach to the operations of the government often "rhapsodized on ways that tax cuts and unencumbered assistance to business enterprises" promoted "a state of well-being that reached, without exception, throughout American society." As Coolidge put it: "This policy has encouraged enterprise, made possible the highest rate of wages which has ever existed, returned large profits, brought to the homes of the people the greatest economic benefits they ever enjoyed, and given to the country as a whole an unexampled era of prosperity." It was a most concise statement in unqualified support for the idea that American capitalism in the New Era would deliver all the goods to everyone. And it was a message he never tired of repeating, even in his last State of the Union address in December 1928, less than a year from the great crash:

> The great wealth created by our enterprise and industry, and saved by our economy, has had the widest distribution among our own people, and has gone out in a steady stream to serve the charity and the business of the world. The requirements of existence have passed beyond the standard of necessity into the region of luxury. Enlarging production is consumed by an increasing demand at home and an expanding commerce abroad. The country can regard the present with satisfaction and anticipate the future with optimism.[68]

For Coolidge, the New Capitalism had brought America to the point of universal abundance. He gladly embraced the ballyhoo that made him the most appropriate servant of big capital at the height of prosperity. "In short," the historian Michael Parrish writes, "Coolidge was an ideal leader for many Americans who wished to explore the new land of materialism and self-indulgence, but who also feared the loss of traditional values." He served monopoly-capitalist interests just as Harding had but with the greater proficiency required by continued economic expansion. Whatever Coolidge lacked in personality he made up for in the officious way he tended to business. He gave more formal speeches and met reporters more frequently than any president up to that point and proved highly conversant in many topics.[69]

But Republicans had no monopoly on the message. Prosperity was rewarding to corporate leaders who were also leading Democrats. Only months before the crash, *Ladies' Home Journal* published an article by John Jacob Raskob, Democratic Party chairman and head of General Motors, titled "Everybody Ought to Be Rich."[70]

Then again, it was the very aim of advertisers, who generally looked down upon consumers as nothing more than a mob to be manipulated, that familial happiness was not possible without milk from Carnation's "contented cows," that women who denied themselves Woodbury soap would lose out on romantic love, or a man was not a man if he was not willing "to walk a mile for a Camel."[71]

■

4—Every Man a Capitalist? Fascist Ideology of Businessmen in 1920s America

HISTORIANS HAVE LONG RECOGNIZED how the development of advertising helped to sustain the booming economy in the United States during the mid- to late 1920s. Millions of Americans who lived in urban areas now routinely enjoyed the pleasures of a lifestyle that had only existed for a short time. But it took the genius of advertising to continuously rekindle their desire and acquisitiveness. To this end, advertising surely played an increasingly important role, its ballyhoo constantly rising to penetrate and sway the jaded consumer. To meet the challenge, the world of advertising became an intertwined network of businessmen and ad men whose ties to owners and managers aimed to make business the dominant force in American political and social life. As hundreds of prophets in academe and the media trumpeted the promise of uninterrupted prosperity to the masses, the owners of capital and their highly skilled attendants were surreptitiously shaping a political agenda that guaranteed nothing would change their hold on wealth and power—and their growing influence over society.

In the mix of all these proponents of the so-called capitalist revolution of the New Era, or what some called the New Capitalism, are the roots of a national form of fascist ideology. Within its genesis were two main currents that differed profoundly, to the point of being contradictory. One loudly promoted greater democratization of American capitalism; the other, a quiet but more powerful force, aimed to curtail democracy itself. The former represented the aspirations of the growing middle classes; the latter strengthened the political power of anti-democratic forces among business elites who made up America's ruling class. If we concur with those in the 1930s who defined fascism as the power of finance capital, the merger of the two currents—the failed dreams of the aspiring middle classes from below and the cynicism of the ruling-class modernizers from above—generated a particular, national form of fascist ideology in the United States in the 1920s.

We see this clearly in a close reading of three key texts that help us to grasp the similarities and differences between the two currents, but both generating a capitalist ideology that is inherently fascist.

The Capitalist Revolution in America and the Promise of Everlasting Prosperity

In his campaign for the presidency, Warren Harding had promised to put America first. Five years later, Thomas Nixon Carver declared that the United States was already leading the rest of the world. Carver, a Harvard economics professor and author of *The Present Economic Revolution in the United States*, contended that America was unique in the world because a capitalist revolution was turning its laborers into capitalists:

> The only economic revolution now under way is going on in the United States. It is a revolution that is to wipe out the distinction between laborers and capitalists by making laborers their own capitalists and by compelling most capitalists to become laborers

of one kind or another, because not many of them will be able to live on the returns from capital alone. This is something new in the history of the world.[1]

Admonishing capitalists to avoid absentee ownership and European luxuries and even assume some tasks normally done by laborers, Carver gave most of the credit for the economic revolution to the power of the laborers—never calling them workers. He applauded the labor movement for abandoning the "antiquated methods" of its European counterparts, which were still guided "by a psychology … built up in a primitive and fighting stage of social development." Instead, labor leaders in the United States were "beginning to think in constructive terms" by formulating a "higher strategy of labor." Instead of fighting capital, they were now attuned to the "permanent economic forces" that could be used "as an implement for their own improvement."[2]

Carver was certain the future looked even better. As more laborers earned higher wages, saved prudently, and acted responsibly in all their endeavors, they were putting themselves on the path to capitalist ownership. Of course, there would always be some conflict between employers and employees. But in his homespun approach to complex economic questions, Carver said the conflict was like that between husband and wife. In both cases, each needed the other and whatever differences existed between the two there were also "many elements of harmony" not to be forgotten. Carver reduced it all to a simple matter of choice:

Whether they live in peace and harmony or in a state of antagonisms depends upon which aspect of their relationship they permit themselves to think about most frequently. If they permit themselves to forget their need of one another and the many questions on which their interests harmonize, and to think only of the questions on which there is a conflict of interest, they are not likely to live a very harmonious life. But if, on the other hand, those questions on which there is a unity of interests occupy their minds, they may expect nothing but peace and harmony.[3]

For the first time in its long history, capitalism in its distinctively American form had proved why boom/bust cycles were a thing of the past. As more workers became capitalists, so would prosperity continue and the promise of progress under capitalism finally realized:

> Wealth is not only increasing at a rapid rate, but the wages of those we formerly pitied are rising, laborers are becoming capitalists, and prosperity is being more and more widely diffused. We are approaching equality of prosperity more rapidly than most people realize. What is equally important, we are working out this diffusion of prosperity for all classes without surrendering the principle of liberty which is embodied in modern democratic institutions.[4]

Carver regarded the coming of universal wealth and uninterrupted progress as the fulfillment of capitalist utopia. And it would be utterly democratic! Regardless of where one stood on the class ladder, the economic revolution was leveling the pyramid of capitalist wealth. Labor leaders were playing a key role in this process by staying clear of an antiquated European radicalism based on class warfare. Fortunately, American labor leaders understood that the solution to the labor problem was higher wages, which would quell any discontent that might fuel class consciousness. Thanks to their efforts, America could look ahead to a future "when we shall no longer speak of the laboring 'classes.'"[5] With more laborers becoming capitalists, Carver claimed, the latter were finding it more difficult to hire workers and were thus having to do more of the work themselves. This was a sure sign that the "actual blending of the two so-called classes means that there will be no more classes in this country. Fraternity has never been very clearly defined," Carver added, "but this condition, when there is no class consciousness, comes as near being fraternity as we are ever likely to get, if it be not fraternity itself."[6]

Carver devoted a chapter of his book to the growing financial power of laborers, basing his claim on statistics cherry-picked from savings deposits, assets of building and loan associations, and the premiums paid to insurance companies by laborers. He also considered "incomplete but rather striking figures regarding the investment of laboring people in the stocks and bonds of corporations." He brought attention as well to what he called "the new phenomenon of the labor bank." According to figures from the American Bankers Association, Carver said that total savings deposits had more than doubled between 1914 and 1924, and the total number of depositors "had increased more than three-fold." Moreover, a study of life insurance policies in 1924 showed that more than two-thirds were held by wage workers. He also provided statistics that he used to argue that more laborers were investing in the stock market.[7] As for the rise of labor banks, his entire case was made on the basis of the Brotherhood of Locomotive Engineers, which opened its bank in 1920. This case alone, he claimed, proved that the capitalist revolution developing in America was another great example of the prospect of universal wealth and prosperity now in the making.[8] The inequalities that had always been present in capitalism were being eliminated, proving that they "were not essential to the capitalistic system." Instead, the revolutionary advance of American capitalism was proving that free enterprise worked. "In fact," Carver said, "where capitalism is given a chance to develop freely, unhampered by social and political obstacles, it tends to eliminate its own inequalities and secure . . . great abundance for everybody," more than any other system has ever achieved.[9]

On this basis, the economic revolution presented the greatest opportunity ever to achieve what Carver believed was "the most revolutionary idea" in all economic discussion, "that of a balanced economic system . . . in which all factors of production are combined in such proportions as will yield the most satisfactory results, and yield them automatically." Again reducing complex matters to the simplest terms, Carver served up a case for the dietician who can recommend a balanced diet to an individual simply by knowing "all the elements." Businessmen did this as a matter of course. They always had to know when to apply basic principles on a routine basis; they had to put together combinations to create a desirable balance by establishing "satisfactory ratios" among all competing elements. This same approach held true in more complex situations where the primary objective was to achieve equilibrium. Balance was always the key factor. The idea of a balanced economy could be carried out systematically across the entire industrial system, "balancing every industry against every other, and every element or factor in every industry against every other." This, Carver said, should be the common work of the statesman and the economist.[10]

Carver's book, when it was published in 1925, contributed to the ballyhoo about capitalist progress. Although there were still problems to overcome, they were not, he claimed, "essential to the capitalistic system." The worst that could be said about the capitalist system was that it had yet to abolish the inequality of wealth. On this he was defiant. As long as American capitalism continued on its present course free of obstacles or interference, it would eventually "distribute the best things of life more evenly" than any other system in history.[11]

The main obstacle to this progress was the lack of a solid understanding among most people of what capitalism is and what it does. Without this knowledge, it was easy to draw bad conclusions by judging the system superficially on the basis of its "temporary aspects." This was a mistake, as Carver explained in the most direct and startling terms:

> Strictly speaking, capitalism is not a system at all. It is merely a fact that grows out of the suppression of violence. Wherever violence is repressed, capital comes automatically into existence. Where violence is repressed, the man who has made a

thing, or found it before anyone else has gained possession of it, cannot be dispossessed without his consent. No government can repress violence without automatically creating property as a result.[12]

Carver focused on the importance of "rightful possession" and the role of government to protect those who had possessions from those who possessed nothing. This was the danger posed by socialism and class warfare, he argued, that fueled violence in society. So long as the possessor could not be dispossessed and remained free to do what he wanted with his possession, capitalism would continue to thrive. For Carver, the "germ" of the capitalist system based on private property was in the workings of simple exchange between those who possessed and had something to sell. This, Carver insisted, was what made capitalism natural. There was simply no other way to explain the matter. "Exchange, therefore," he wrote, "grows up automatically and unavoidably along with property, whenever and wherever violence is repressed." The purpose of government, therefore, was to make sure that exchange between those who had rightful possession were unhampered by violence. In the process, government protection transformed simple possession into property.[13]

Carver argued that envy threatened prosperity based on the idea of rightful possession. The envious draw sympathizers, or worse, those who "invent apologies and excuses for them." There are consequences. When envy peaks, it is "likely to lead to acts of violence either by individuals or classes." The ensuing "class war," he said, can destroy civilization if it leads to a government that violently dispossesses the possessors.[14] To prevent this from happening in America, government had to restrict immigrant laborers from countries where capitalism was less developed. They arrived seeking better wages and living conditions, but their presence meant a growing number of "thoughtless and thriftless people." The result would be in all probability a rising propertyless class that could grow large and dangerous. The outcome was ominous:

If it should be able to outvote the class of savers and accumu-
lators, it may gain control of the government and use it as an
engine for the dispossession of those who have managed to
accumulate. The safety of modern civilization requires that these
non-accumulating classes shall be kept few in number.[15]

Carver was sure that class struggle in America was a thing of
the past. American laborers were now plotting "a higher strategy"
that corresponded to the great leap forward in production and the
trend he saw to their eventual ownership of it! This higher strategy
was based on peace and harmony with employers, not struggle and
class war. "Labor has got all it can get by violence." It was time to
get things done "by head-work, not fist-work." In a vague reference
to the great strike wave of 1919–1920 and the alleged Red Menace,
Carver declared that labor previously had brought great fear to the
nation. The time had come to impress the country with its wisdom.
Labor had to confidently cultivate its identity as "a preserver and
developer" in order to increase production for greater prosperity.[16]

As a work of capitalist propaganda, Carver's book said all the
things that Big Business would enjoy hearing in public. His main
points resonated without threatening its hold over society. His central message—the revolutionary advance in American capitalism
will eliminate inequality—was a notable contribution to the ballyhoo of endless prosperity during the New Era. Carver's rapturous
view about the great promise of capitalist progress certainly was
music to the ears of the working and middle classes who longed to
be capitalists themselves, as well as to those who already were and
had the most to gain from it. But the latter—Big Business—had
no intention of leveling the capitalist pyramid of wealth. What it
sought was to remain strong and secure at the top.

The Advent of Business Theory

Businessmen, politicians, and pundits like Carver lent a great deal
of weight to the mantra of prosperity that grew in intensity until

the Wall Street crash. But the clamor about endless prosperity and progress for all served as an unwitting foil for the owners and managers of big capital, who now recognized that their responsibilities to sustain growth and prosperity required their active involvement in politics in order to protect and enhance their economic interests. What evolved from their efforts was a loosely defined political theory of American business that pressed forward central tenets, among them: the notion that a business hierarchy was necessary to preserve the basic functions of democracy as opposed to mob rule; the promotion of True Americanism as an ideal from which to formulate principles and policies binding labor to capital; a defense of selfishness as the key to advancing the public good; and encouraging businessmen to serve their communities and their nation by entering the political arena, especially at the local level, to eradicate the pernicious influence of radicals, organized labor, and the mob.

In 1954, historian James Warren Prothro recognized these efforts in his comprehensive study of capitalist elites in the 1920s who generated what he called a "business theory." As an offering "to systematize and analyze the political theory of American business as it unfolded during that most revealing era in American politics," Prothro saw this theory developing within the concerted efforts of leading trade associations and their efforts to represent a unified front in the name of all business.[17] Accordingly, he relied on the National Association of Manufacturers (NAM) and the United States Chamber of Commerce, the two leading business organizations in the United States, which saw their declared purpose to speak for American business as a whole.

Among the business leaders discussed by Prothro is Charles Norman Fay, who made his fortune from the Remington-Scholes typewriter company, a pioneer in that industry, and was a chief executive for public utilities. Fay served as vice president of the NAM and was a prominent member of the Chamber of Commerce. His *Business in Politics* was published in 1926, a year after Carver's work appeared. Carver and Fay saw even greater prosperity ahead as American capitalism soared to new heights. But they differed sharply about how it would be achieved and who would achieve it. Carver believed it was the laborer who was becoming a capitalist; for Fay it was the big businessman. This mattered a great deal. Unlike Carver who proclaimed an open path for ordinary Americans to wealth and equality, Fay offered "suggestions" to established business leaders about their need to secure a greater hold over the market, society, and government. Carver's vision was a capitalist utopia that was truly democratic. Fay was certain that democracy could only survive if governed by business elites.

Fay dedicated his book to Chamber members "and the great Business Associations throughout the United States." In it, he called on them to recognize that the future of democracy now lay in their hands. No others were suited for the challenging work. The "intense individualism" they demonstrated in their personal success in business must now benefit the public good. "The two are absolutely inseparable," he wrote, and this great attribute was what the masses lacked. "I do *not* believe in government by *average men*, any more than in management of any other *big* business by *average men*," Fay wrote. "*Average men are not big enough to govern!*" And since "government is the biggest of all big business" and requires "the *ablest* management," there was no better training for success in these endeavors than what they had learned in business.[18]

History proved this. "Every student knows that representative government, as planned by our New England and Virginia ancestors, *did not contemplate representation by average or underaverage men*, but by the *foremost* men, carefully chosen by free election." Of course, this was done more readily in earlier times when social life operated on a much smaller scale. Things were different now. Vast modern communities made it more difficult to determine who were "the foremost men, and how best to pick them." The fate of modern democracy was now in peril, and Fay sounded the alarm. The principles of local self-government and individual liberty worked earlier, but its "*primitive* machinery" had been breaking down from its own weight more steadily. Present conditions required "better political engineering . . . applied to the reduction and simplification of our mess of governments." Fay implored his readers to take action. "Competent men" were needed to plan and sponsor how to do it. This could only be done by "big-business men and bankers" assisted by their "leading technical associates and advisers."[19]

Here was the political message that successful businessmen needed to embrace:

> *You* are, moreover, the men who personally have most at stake in the general welfare of city, state and nation; and you are of the few whose large means and high standing raise you farthest above that old, old temptation—to govern for your own private profit—which has cursed politics ever since history began. … *It should be, as it seems to me, the legitimate ambition* of every such man to crown his private fortune and career with public service—a consummation which is not only desirable, but practicable, by way of your great business organizations.[20]

Govern for your own profit and save the nation, he implored. This is why successful businessmen were ideally suited for political office. The great corporations they built and served were "like the city, state or nation . . . democratically governed by a few directors, voluntarily chosen" by qualified electors. Those chosen had many attributes, first and foremost, as large owners of their corporation's shares, which ensured the vital interests of the whole business. They could "command the confidence of fellow-owners" and were "generally so well off and prominent that they *cannot afford* to be 'crooked' in their dealings for or with the corporation." Given such exceptional character, there was no question they could be counted on to govern just as efficiently and effectively. They had learned how to determine primary objectives and then simplified and reduced them to the fewest number possible. All had recognized the importance of entrusting success to "a single executive head, usually to one strong man, carefully chosen," giving him "a free hand, and fullest power" to get the desired results. This was the way to increase company profits and earn his "ample share."[21]

All of this was especially critical at a time like theirs. Only the corporate leader could peer through the turmoil of trade union-ism and see "the *human-nature* of a crowd of workers" and then determine how best to handle them. He alone could assess "the temper and skill of workers" just as much as he needed to know the qualities of the materials used in production. He had learned the importance of establishing an effective and efficient routine under the best of conditions in production guided by the most skilled managers. He had the vision to know when the moment had come to extend employee ownership in corporate stock or to induce workers "to buy into the capitalization of their own job" with their own savings, all aimed at unifying labor with capital.[22] Above all, these were the individuals who, says Fay, "first, last and all of the time,

> determine the nature and scope of the company's operation and finance *by the decisive test of profit and loss*—always rating the ability, the success and the reward of the management and all concerned mainly, not without due allowance for the public wel-fare, by the growth of its business and profits. If the corporation earns dividends, and enough more for its own development, it lives and grows great. If not, before long it dies, and is forgotten.[23]

America needed these men. They, not the common man, were fit to govern the nation:

> The great majority of American voters have not, and in the nature of things, *never can have*, enough experience in large and efficient organization, *of any kind*, to compare for them-selves what government does with what it ought to do, or its cost with what it ought to cost. They know neither what they ought to demand of government, nor what they should refuse it—nor

how to go to work with any prospect of success to get what they should for their taxes.[24]

Unlike Carver, Fay's conception of capitalism was strictly hierarchical:

There are but very few of our multimillions of good, patriotic Americans, who are able enough and experienced enough to map out a successful reorganization of the blundering business of our governments, or to plan the least costly and most efficient way to carry it on. How then to convert our own government, *which is itself the most gigantic of our trusts and monopolies*, into not only the least hurtful of our institutions to our liberties, but the most helpful to our needs—this is indeed a problem for the ablest moral, economical and political engineers.[25]

For Fay, inequality also inhered in the workings of nature. He was convinced that even the masses could accept this as fact. "Nature," he wrote, "creates very few men of exceptional brain and energy; men able to do big things in war or government or even in sport; men who do more, deserve more, and invariably get more, of the good things of life, than the rest of us average or common folk." Most people "instinctively recognize big men, and cheerfully take the orders of our betters, seldom grudging them their bigger reward for greater achievement."[26]

Feeling justified in taking these positions, Fay urged his intended readers, the NAM, Chamber of Commerce, and other trade association members, to run for nonpartisan local and state races. There was much at stake:

Would it be at all hard to put one or two trained and successful men, *out of your own number*, into every American state and local legislative body—provided only that *public opinion among yourselves could but make it the fashion* for your strongest men to do such public duty?

These men would have to use the same patience as business leaders in order to appeal to the public in ways that would prevent "a stupid and demagogic majority" from passing "foolish and needless laws, and waste taxes, for political effect."[27] Fay had the answer. Put one good, big man in every race, even in the smallest cities and towns and watch what happens:

> I have no doubt whatever that if leading members of the great business associations throughout the country, men conspicuous each in his own town for wealth, ability, integrity and public spirit, were to offer themselves, as their residence permits, as candidates for city and county councils, state legislatures, etc., against such cheap politicians as now monopolize nomination, they could be elected, *with your help*; if not the first time, then the next time, and thereafter.[28]

Fay recognized there were a limited number of business elites. "First-class men are perhaps too few and far between to constitute standing majorities in such [state and local legislative] bodies." The solution was "plenty of good second-class men," who could "bore from within" the economic and political system to help the elites work their political agenda. This, after all, Fay said, was what the socialists and trade union leaders had done before them and were still trying to do, first in Europe and now in America. The second-class men would be supported by the great trade associations and the public press. Fay saw "a lasting advantage" in the powers of the associations at work in nonpartisan political action. This was all very "natural" given the daily contact that employers and employees had in their towns and cities.[29]

Fay argued that this was necessary to stop the pernicious threat of organized labor and politicians who represented their interests. Organized labor, though it had bended to business, was still a threat. Leaving any election, even at the local level, to politicians in its service was a green light for unions to coerce employers, even to the point of stopping production. Then there were strikes, walkouts, or legal actions that prevented those who wanted to work from working. Who was behind it? After all, hadn't the socialists backed the AFL's attack on the judiciary for its "autocratic power" and "governing by injunction," calling it capitalistic tyranny? For Fay, this was nonsense:

> No one knows better than yourselves that neither autocracy nor tyranny has ever been furthered by use of the injunction in labor disputes. No worker has ever been ordered to work, or has gone to work for fear of punishment by the courts. Nothing has ever been enjoined except *unlawful* union action, such as violence, intimidation, sabotage, boycotting, interfering with free use of public streets, violation of contracts, and contract right, or combination to restrain production and fix prices. *Not one lawful activity* of union labor has been delayed.[30]

Agitators were responsible for these sweeping and groundless accusations. They were troublemakers bent on confusing uneducated voters with lies. Our courts, they claimed, "are *fortresses of individual liberty and property right only for the rich*; and that in the future an unlimited and collective tyranny and monopoly of power and wealth *by the state*, instead of the rich, is the only hope of the poor."[31] The agitators were enemies of democracy. Businessmen in their respective communities knew who they were and it was their responsibility, Fay said, to educate the voters about the evils being perpetrated. Citizens needed to understand the coercive methods used by unions to deny nonunion men the right to work, which went against the interests of workers and employers alike. The public must be protected against organized labor for electing misleaders—their political protectors who once in office would pass legislation responsible for the "*the steady, constant and unnecessary high prices* of goods and service, due to crippling production and slacking work." The latter, Fay insisted, was normal behavior for unions that robbed the public daily of incredible sums.[32]

Fay hoped that businessmen would enter politics and create legislation furthering economic growth while realizing Harding's idea of putting more business in government and more government in business. Just as corporate leaders had reaped success by increasing productivity and efficiency in their businesses, they should now apply the same principles to the operation of government. Reduce costs and then cut taxes! For Fay, there was no mystery about what to do, nor was there any time to waste: "The very simple principle of Least Government, with its companion principle of Least Taxation, seems to me pretty nearly all that this country needs, if put in practice, to make it entirely safe for democracy."[33] Upon entering government successful business leaders would know what to do. Based on their previous success, they understood how

> large expansion of private business compels constant struggle to simplify; the bigger it grows, the harder becomes the struggle, and the greater the burden of "overhead" or unproductive cost. You know that expansion cannot go on indefinitely. A time arrives, in spite of railways, telephones, motors, etc., when efficiency and economy enforce simplification and *decentralization.*[34]

Economic expansion had necessitated a great leap forward in the functions of national, state and local government. The cost of bureaucracy and government services—*"unavoidable public activities"*—had become too vast for any one organization to handle successfully. Even in earlier times, when small and manageable government put too much strain on the individual, businessmen had learned enough to know that a similar mindset was the key to success in larger and more complicated forms of business. Yet they always knew how to handle these matters because businessmen were strong and morally bound to whatever course the nation required:

> It is an old maxim of good engineering *not to put too great a strain on the material employed.* The same rule applies to good

government, whose material is the human being—not to put too great a strain either on the mind or the conscience that governs. The simple and logical way to minimize American discontent with the shortcomings of American government most obviously is to minimize government itself.[35]

Fay boasted about the efficiency of the U.S. Steel Corporation governed by fifteen directors, "the first business men of the country," who were paid *"nothing but a nominal directors fee"* by its 150,000 stockholders for attending monthly meetings. He pitted that against "the desultory work of our 435 congressmen and 96 senators, 533 Solons in all, who play politics before the nation, in almost continuous session, with endless fuss and feathers, sound and fury, devoting most of the two-year term of each Congress *to defeating each other's largely useless bills*." [36] Again, Fay urged his fellow businessmen to grasp the moment. "Everywhere we turn," he reminded them, "we see the same contrast between the small, quiet, efficient, and usually *honest* board of directors of our great corporations . . . and the big, pretentious, noisy and often *dishonest* mobs of time and money wasters, forced by our political system into our local legislative halls."

Fay called his readers to task:

Now, gentlemen, might we not break away, at least in local government, from a political plan that does *not* work very well to a business plan that *does*? Just as we elect, for a great corporation, a very small compact board of directors, of very able men—*and stop right there*—leaving it to the few men chosen to organize and manage everything for the company until next election—might we not elect, for each new consolidated unit of local government, a small compact board of trustees or commissioners (nine would be plenty) chosen at large—*and stop right there, electing no other officers for the unit*, either executive or judicial? Might we not trust those so chosen to make the laws, and to *appoint* a chief executive, with power to carry them out?[37]

Once this happened on the municipal level, it would then be possible to send out the most experienced organizers "to educate the voters to talk politics in terms of consolidated units of (let us say) 25 miles radius instead of 2." To simplify local politics even further and "promote economy," larger municipalities could be governed by a small compact of directors who would do away with all county officers and elections, "and turn over their oldtime functions to proper bureaus of the consolidated municipalities." But that was not all: "In due time, when enough simplified local units are on the map, might we not follow up on like lines with simplification of state government? That is to say,

> might we not plan for eventually a very small and compact single-chambered legislative body, say a senate of but 15 members—which would be large enough—empowered to make laws, to lay taxes and to *appoint* permanent executive and judicial officers, who should carry on the business and administer the justice of the state?

Fay insisted that the "the principles of efficient government" at the local and state level were "precisely the same as for efficient business organization." Here he makes two main points. First, businessmen will be eager to serve once they recognize how important it is to concentrate power in the hands of a few qualified men chosen by the people to "make laws and lay taxes [raise money]" so government would become less costly and more efficient. Second, ending elections of executives and judges by popular vote and instead appointed by the legislature—"safeguarded, of course, by carefully drawn provisions for removal, by impeachment or otherwise, of unworthy appointees"—would free them "from all fear and danger of political pressure brought to bear on either— *as they should be free!*" After all, these men were not in office "to ignore or twist the law at the behest of politicians, but faithfully to be bound by it and the Constitution." And they should not feel threatened. As long as they performed their tasks without fear of consequence, "they should be entirely immune from vengeance of any disgruntled faction at the polls. *Legislators* should there be held responsible, and they alone."[38]

For Fay, it was all very simple. Educated businessmen would eventually control local and state governments and from there begin to change the political landscape of America. Leading businessmen would win elections and transform government by turning it into a business. The whole effort was hierarchical: government by those who knew best from their success in Big Business. If ballyhoo about the common businessman made him something of a hero or even Christ-like, Fay's business executive was elevated to a small number of the elect whom the saintly Calvin Coolidge believed were America's anointed leaders.

PROPAGANDA AND THE "INVISIBLE GOVERNMENT" IN THE MAKING OF AMERICAN FASCISM

The conscious and intelligent manipulation of the organized habits and opinions of the masses is an important element in democratic society. Those who manipulate this unseen mechanism of society constitute an invisible government which is the true ruling power of our country.[39]

This is how Edward Bernays, known as the father of public relations and a mastermind of American propaganda, opened his 1928 book on the subject. Bernays held that modern democracy could only work if shaped and regimented by "the relatively small number of persons—a trifling fraction of our hundred and twenty million—who understand the mental processes and social patterns of the masses."[40] As he wrote:

The minority has discovered a powerful help in influencing majorities. It has been found possible so to mold the mind of the masses that they will throw their newly gained strength in the desired direction. In the present structure of society, this practice is inevitable. Whatever of social importance is done today, whether in politics, finance, manufacture, agriculture, charity, education, or other fields, must be done with the help of propaganda. Propaganda is the executive arm of the invisible government.[41]

Like Charles Norman Fay, Bernays had no use for democracy unless it was directed by the few who understood and learned how to benefit from it. He was convinced that the majority of Americans had squandered great opportunities granted to them by democracy, especially "universal literacy." Once the common man learned how to read and write, he then could have learned how to take control of his environment and become its master. But here is where he stopped, making him nothing more than

> a rubber stamp inked with advertising slogans, with editorials, with published scientific data, with the trivialities of the tab-loids and the platitudes of history, but quite innocent of original thought. Each man's rubber stamps are the duplicates of millions of others, so that when those millions are exposed to the same stimuli, all received identical imprints. It may seem an exaggeration to say that the American public gets most of its ideas in this wholesale fashion. The mechanism by which ideas are disseminated on a large scale is propaganda, in the broad sense of an organized effort to spread a particular belief or doctrine.[42]

The powers of propaganda could then be unleashed in an enduring effort to create or shape events by means of persuasion and manipulation to influence the public—a common practice in American culture. To this end, propaganda aimed at "regimenting the public mind every bit as much as an army regiments the bodies of its soldiers."[43]

His military analogy came perhaps from the huge success of propaganda during the First World War, which opened the eyes of "the intelligent few in all departments of life to the possibilities of

regimenting the public mind." Both the government and patriotic
agencies that supported the war discovered a new technique of
bidding for public acceptance, one that "appealed to the individual
by means of every approach—visual, graphic, and auditory—to
support the national endeavor." The agencies depended on securing the cooperation of key men in fraternal, religious, commercial,
patriotic, social, and local groups, or from the publications much
of the public read and believed. Simultaneously, "the manipulators
of patriotic opinion made use of the mental clichés and the emotional habits of the public to produce mass reactions against the
alleged atrocities, the terror, and the tyranny of the enemy." When
the war ended, it made sense to these "intelligent few" that the
same technique could be applied to peacetime needs.[44]

Thus "new propagandists" emerged in peacetime in a quest to
understand the anatomy of society and to grasp the importance
of recognizing the individual as a cell of the social organism.
According to Bernays, business enterprise showed this better than
any other organized human endeavor. He agreed with business
leaders like Fay that the nation's destiny lay in the hands of a small
number of elites, except they were not leading businessmen but
molders of public opinion. American society had many powerbrokers during the New Era: the president and congressional leaders,
Wall Street financiers, corporate directors, trade association leaders, and organized labor. Nevertheless, it was well known among
them that they themselves were being led by "invisible wirepull-
ers" whose expertise was hidden from the public.[45] For Bernays,
this was the "propaganda specialist" who knew how to manipulate
society through public relations and advertising. He specialized
in learning how to control the opinions and habits of the masses
by active engagement with the public and then interpreting its
actions for the "promulgators of new enterprises and ideas." The
specialist was a "public relations counsel." He and others like him
constituted the real invisible government in America. He alone
could comprehend the mental processes and social habits of the
masses, which were becoming ever more challenging given "the

increasing complexity of modern life and the consequent necessity for making the actions of one part of the public understandable to other sectors of the public."[46]

The public relations counsel had become a partner with business. A successful business needed more than just knowledge of manufacturing and selling a product. It had to know how to sell itself to the public. For Bernays, public relations counsels were becoming the real rulers of America. They alone knew—and were constantly learning—how to control public opinion for the sole purpose of keeping the economy moving:

> Mass production is profitable only if its rhythm can be maintained—that is, if it can continue to sell its product in steady or increasing quantity. The result is that while, under the handicraft of small-unit system of production that was typical a century ago, demand created the supply, today supply must actively seek to create its corresponding demand. A single factory, potentially capable of supplying a whole continent with its particular product, cannot afford to wait until the public asks for its product; it must maintain constant touch, through advertising and propaganda, with the vast public in order to assure itself the continuous demand which alone will make its costly plant profitable. This entails a vastly more complex system of distribution than formerly. To make customers is the new problem. One must understand not only his own business—the manufacture of a particular product—but also the structure, the personality, the prejudices, of a potentially universal public.[47]

Competition among the giants and the growth of the stock market only made Big Business even more dependent on public opinion. Its leaders had to present the existence of their respective corporations in a most favorable light. "It must dramatize its personality and interpret its objectives in every particular in which it comes into contact with the community (or the nation) of which it is a part." The work of the public relations counsel was just as important as someone in charge of production. It was necessary for the public relations counsel to familiarize himself with "the structure, the prejudices, and the whims of the general public." The effective counsel might be able to "modify" these public traits but could not "run counter" to them. "The public is not an amorphous mass which can be molded at will, or dictated to," Bernays wrote. "Both business and the public have their own personalities which must somehow be brought into friendly agreement." Just as the public needed to appreciate the great benefits of mass production that business offers, business must also appreciate the public's "increasingly discriminative" attitudes and tastes. "It is this condition and necessity," he wrote, "which has created the need for a specialized field of public relations. Business now calls in the public relations counsel to advise it, to interpret its purpose to the public, and to suggest those modifications which may make it conform to the public demand."[48]

The capitalist aspects of business propaganda naturally brought Bernays to conclude that the politician needed to become more like a businessman. "The successful businessman today apes the politician. He has adopted the glitter and the ballyhoo of the campaign. He has set up all the sideshows." He attends dinners and gives countless speeches that stand for so much "pseudo-democracy slightly tinged with paternalism." But all these activities are nothing more than a sideshow by which he builds an image of public service. These are the methods by which businessmen project what is necessary to stimulate enthusiasm and loyalty between directors, workers, stockholders, and the consumer public and to which business performs its function of making products and then selling them to the public. "The real work and campaign of business," he says, "consists of intensive study of the public, the manufacture of products based on this study, and exhaustive use of every means of reaching the public."[49]

Bernays also insisted that the successful politician could not do without the public relations counsel, who alone recognized the importance of strategy in building a campaign, devising platforms, or envisaging policies. A politician might understand the public and know what it wanted and what it would accept. But he could not be expected to know how to put it out for mass distribution. Only a public relations counsel, through study and preparation, could do this. Platforms, planks, budgets, and other vital matters needed to be carefully studied before implemented. Studying the public took precedence over all. A public relations counsel knew how to play to the emotions and habits of the public so he could mold consciousness and determine how to exploit them.[50]

LIKE THOMAS NIXON CARVER and Charles Norman Fay, Edward Bernays believed that capitalism represented the natural order of society. The drive to compete and excel in creating a world of winners and losers defined man as an individual whose selfish instinct was to build, defend, and preserve whatever he deemed necessary to satisfy his own interests. While Carver saw this individual as a laborer who was becoming a capitalist, Fay recognized him as a gifted elite whose success in business justified his lofty position over all others. Bernays went further than Fay by conferring seemingly magical powers on an even smaller group, of public relations counsels, whose specialized knowledge enabled them to cast spells over the entire realm. The public relations counsel was the wisest of all capitalist gurus. His capacity as an invisible wirepuller of the great capitalist elites was what made him a penultimate force in the making of American fascism in the 1920s.

Carver, Fay, and Bernays are equally important as prophets of capitalist progress in the New Era. Carver anointed the laborer as a budding capitalist and architect of the economic revolution in the United States. At the same time, he was unwittingly leading his main audience, the aspiring middle classes, toward political reaction since the elites championed by Fay and Bernays were already undermining the economic basis of Carver's rosy forecast for the future. Carver's supreme belief that every "true" American could become a capitalist was, on the basis of class analysis alone, an extension of the "phantasmagoria" of petty-bourgeois ideology rooted in the mid-nineteenth century.[51] For Carver, capitalism was founded on the possession of property open to all who labored hard and sought to reconcile contradictions between capital and labor through voluntary association with one another. The role of the state lay chiefly in protecting the possessors from non-possessors who would dare seize it through violence or other means. This made Carver as much an anti-communist and proponent of state power as Fay or Bernays. All agreed that government should never be controlled by property-less workers or their political representatives who would sweep away the capitalist order in the name of socialism.

For Fay, the future of capitalist progress within the framework of American democracy lay not with the average man or "everyman" but instead in gifted individuals who had already earned their way to the top as businessmen and who now needed to show the same mettle in governing the country. The man who governed best was the one who had made more money than most. He alone knew how to govern his city, state, or the nation. His real service to the rest of America was to safeguard the political system so the greater wealth he continued to amass would create a greater trickle descending to the rest of society. Fay wanted more hierarchy to preserve American democracy. Yet even he could not succeed without Bernays's public relations counsel whose magical powers could penetrate the minds of others and manipulate their thinking. Such abstract powers generated in capitalist society reflected the laws of motion in capitalist accumulation. Here was another element that made the germ of fascism inherent in monopoly-finance capitalism.

In the ideology of these three men, we find that the nativist dimension in the making of American fascism is the most overt in Carver. He was certain that the American worker had to be protected from his European counterpart, whose alien ideas about class warfare posed a constant threat to the capitalist order and the dream of universal prosperity through harmony. The immigrant was as dangerous as the communist—in his thinking, they were one and the same. For Fay, True Americanism was a subtle undercurrent in many of his "suggestions" to elite American businessmen. Nativism was not at all present in Bernays's characterization of the public relations counsel. Yet he alone was the "invisible wirepuller" among all the powerbrokers fueling the rise of the American empire in the 1920s as, surprisingly enough, an architect of non-terrorist fascist processes.

In Carver, Fay, and Bernays we see three currents of fascist ideology: the champion of the middle class; the lust for political power by the hungry capitalist elite; and the architect of persuasion and manipulation—all harbingers of American fascism.

5—The Paradox of Capitalist Progress, 1922–1929

THOMAS NIXON CARVER, a professor of economics at Harvard University, was one of many New Era prophets of the booming 1920s who had touted the achievements of unprecedented economic growth and what he believed was the crowning achievement of American capitalism. Laborers were becoming capitalists, thus ensuring that prosperity and progress would continue without interruption. Carver made these declarations in his 1925 book, *The Present Economic Revolution in the United States.* But the Great Depression proved Carver wrong on all counts. "Blind, as only the scholar become ballyhoo-maker can be," wrote Lewis Corey in 1934. Corey, a Marxist economist and political writer, called the book "a distortion of history." It had become just "another curiosity of economic literature, a fantastic combination of misleading statistics, apologetic economics, slipshod sociology, and rationalized prejudices."[1]

Almost a century ago, Carver was convinced that a revolution in American capitalism would bring an end to inequality, a systemic feature of the world capitalist system for centuries. It would also make the United States the great bulwark of democracy against the rising menace of international communism. Contrary to what the Bolsheviks were claiming about building a new society in Russia—rarely was it called the Soviet Union—Americans were making the real revolution and it was a capitalist one. Nothing the communists envisioned could match what was being created by the diligent efforts of ordinary people who believed in freedom and the right to own property. Everyman a capitalist! It was a stunning vision of democratic capitalism made possible by prosperity the world had never seen. Yet Carver's ideal scenario bore little resemblance to the realities for a majority of Americans. Instead of an economic revolution destined to eliminate inequality and bring uninterrupted social progress, capitalist modernization in the booming 1920s only widened the gap between wealth and poverty.

The combined force of state power and Big Business had initially crushed and then successfully repressed the working class. The massive strike wave that swept much of the nation in the aftermath of the First World War had been pacified by brute force, court-ordered injunctions, and the complicity of organized labor. Following a sharp but brief economic downturn, a surge in production and the coming of Boomtown USA brought the promise of a modern lifestyle defined by comfort and enjoyment. But this only sharpened the divide between the haves and the have-nots. Prosperity mainly padded the fortunes of those already at the top. As the rich got richer and the upper strata of the middle class prospered, the majority of working Americans and the poor remained at or below minimum levels of need and comfort. Throughout a seven-year stretch (1922–1929) of enormous economic growth, wages and salaries remained stagnant for most working people while corporate profits and dividends soared to record highs. The wondrous world of new things mattered little to millions of people who could not buy them. Always looking to maximize productivity and profits, the great lords of production and finance lowered their production costs by replacing workers with machines and rendering human labor increasingly disposable. As capital accumulation advanced at lightning speed, purchasing power of the masses lagged.

Meanwhile, the scale of capitalist modernization generated deep currents of anxiety, fear, and resentment for a majority of 119 million Americans who did not prosper and found life difficult to comprehend or accept. People who stayed back on the farm became even more steadfast in the mindset and behavior of nineteenth-century rural life. Those who dashed to the cities found themselves in the swirl of modern urban life. Seeking security in the whirlwind, their earlier prejudices became more engrained. Even the established small merchant and banker, the rising professional and salaried employee, and some of the best-paid workers, felt both awed and threatened by the features of the big city. Among the middle rungs of the class ladder arose a stream of consciousness between progress and reaction. While clinging to the vision of a true liberal-capitalist democracy, the middle class, unable to comprehend the rising powers of monopoly-finance capital, became the major force of political reaction in America. Finding solace in identifying themselves as old-stock True Americans, their nativist, racist, and anti-communist views provided the seedbed of right-wing extremism and populist demagoguery.

Such were the main contours—and contradictions—of capitalist modernization in the United States during the booming 1920s. Progress, indeed, but at great cost. If the Great Boom of the New Era fueled unprecedented wealth, it also created growing misery. It was a paradox of capitalist progress—growing poverty in an ever-rising sea of plenty. The great advance in production and exchange that fueled the rise of the American empire, Pax Americana, intensified long-standing capitalist contradictions within the heart of the nation. The power of capital had advanced beyond the capacity of the working class, which, except for periodic strikes of some magnitude, remained quiescent throughout the decade. The aspiring middle classes were also held in check. The most dynamic class in American society was the ruling capitalist class, an oligarchy in the making whose imperial architects were extending the global reach of the United States.

Within this capitalist totality, the economic decline of the middle class as a whole relative to the great wealth of the ruling oligarchy turned it toward political reaction and extremism. Its greatest proponent was the "second" Ku Klux Klan, whose growth extended far beyond the South between 1920 and 1925. All of it was the product of a modernizing drive by the capitalist class. As the latter grew more powerful in its control over production and distribution, its gains were protected by state power now bound to the needs of monopoly and financial capital. Under these conditions came the class divide between the two capitalist classes, the oligarchy who owned and controlled the economy and the middle classes who wanted their fair share of it. Both played their respective roles in the making of American fascism.

Prosperity for Whom?

In a landmark study of American workers published in 1960, Irving Bernstein wrote that "the twenties were, indeed, golden, but only for a privileged segment of the population." From his research and analysis, Bernstein knew where the majority of the American people stood in relation to the ruling class and the paradoxical character of the moment:

> Although on the surface American workers appeared to share in the material advantages of the time, the serious maladjustments within the economic system fell upon them with disproportionate weight. This interplay between illusion and reality is a key to the period. In fact, this was a society in imbalance and workers enjoyed few of its benefits.[2]

The economic revolution that Carver claimed was occurring in 1925 had not materialized. Everyday life had, in fact, remained a challenge if not a struggle for the vast majority who had little left after essential expenses—apart from those who had none at all. It was especially bad in large rural areas where villages and small towns dotted the landscape. The economic boom had concealed the rural exodus of some twenty million people that fueled it. The rush to bustling and prosperous urban centers, which included more than a million African Americans who left the South for cities in the Northeast and Midwest, indicated how sharply people understood that wages in town were better than those on the farm. Technical innovation in capitalist farming wreaked havoc on traditional means of cultivation and employment. It had displaced "the horse, the mule, and, most important, the farmer, his wife, and his children," Bernstein wrote.[3] But this was not news. The economist and historian Louis Hacker had said as much in 1938: American agriculture was "permanently depressed" throughout the 1920s. Unlike the industrial takeoff that commenced in 1922, farmers saw their land values and crop prices plunge as their debt climbed. "Put simply," Hacker wrote, "farm prices had been deflated, while farm costs—necessaries for home and field, mortgage debt, taxes—were still highly inflated. The farm account could not be balanced." For Hacker, the Great Depression of the 1930s only made the bleak picture of the American farmer during the Great Boom even darker.[4]

There were other downward economic pressures. A declining birth rate and restrictions on immigration had driven up the price of labor, compelling employers to rely increasingly on machinery to boost efficiency and lower costs. This halted further growth of the labor force and created a general condition of stagnation in the economy. Those employed in the manufacturing sector amounted to little more than ten million workers who had few opportunities for advancement. On the other hand, the number of white-collar and service workers employed in a range of occupations rose significantly. Then, there were the millions of unemployed. The absence of government statistics made it impossible to report the number accurately. Still, a few studies in the late 1920s showed that anywhere between 10 and 13 percent of the available labor force was unemployed between 1924 and 1929. High unemployment was a permanent feature of the New Era.[5]

One of the first writers and journalists to see these realities was Mauritz Hallgren, whose 1933 book, *Seeds of Revolt*, penetrated what he called the "beautifully deceptive myth" of the New Era. Pulling together numbers from scant government sources and private studies, Hallgren admitted that the nation had indeed experienced "fabulously prosperous" times. Still, only 40 percent of the U.S. population was living in comfort or above in 1929.[6] Available statistics on income and unemployment revealed that the majority had not shared in the general prosperity. In the sources he examined, Hallgren saw a mass of Americans who had "no nourishment, no shelter, no medical attention, no opportunity to lay away money against their declining years." For industrial workers, it often depended on what they were producing or mining. Textiles and bituminous coal industries—among the biggest of the older, "sick" industries—paid comparatively lower wages. According to a 1928 study of wage rates by the Bureau of Labor Statistics, bituminous coal miners in some parts of the country had earned as little as $10.34 weekly in 1926, compared to those in motor vehicle manufacturing who a year earlier were already earning $24.02 per week. There were also the large numbers of seasonal workers—carpenters, bricklayers, masons, plumbers, steamfitters, among others, who earned higher wages, but their yearly totals often qualed those of semi-skilled factory workers.[7]

A report compiled by the Labor Bureau, Inc., a private consulting firm, late in 1928 called the "Minimum Health and Decency Budget" focused on the cost of goods and services required by a family of both parents and three children "below which a family cannot go without danger of physical or moral deterioration." The report admitted that the criteria lacked many of the comforts that should be included in an acceptable and proper "American standard of living." Yet workers even in the largest and most prosperous industrial cities came up short. The highest-paid factory workers in New York and Illinois, for example, were not earning enough to attain the minimum standard of living. In Illinois, only the newspaper printers, whose weekly average earnings were $45.84, and construction workers, who averaged $43.80, came close to the minimum of $46.98 set as acceptable income for the city of Chicago.[8] Of course, the worst off were farmers and farm laborers. Farmers' cash income fell 35 percent from 1919 to 1929, while the tax burden and indebtedness on family farms rose substantially. White-collar workers in the bustling cities were not much better off. According to a November 1929 article in *The Nation*, store clerks made as little as $10 a week; even the best paid among them averaged little more than $30. In 1926, $25 was the average weekly earnings of school teachers, though in some parts of the country it was as little as $14. Even men of the cloth were poorly paid. Those who could count themselves lucky among the "rather munificently paid rectors of fashionable metropolitan churches" averaged $35 a week. According to the same *Nation* report and statistics from the 1931 edition of the *American Labor Year Book*, employees in the executive branch of the federal government, which included high-salaried officials, were making about the same as the best paid clergymen.[9]

Hallgren was highly aware of the significance in the plight of the middle class. Indeed, some of the worst hit during the prosperous years were small shopkeepers, manufacturers, and bankers, all of whom had thrived in earlier times. A few got rich by investing in stocks but the majority had failed to improve their economic status. Many were becoming poorer. Citing material in a 1929 article by Stuart Chase in *The Nation*, Hallgren wrote that 750,000 independent storekeepers were doing less than $25,000 a year in business. A survey of one large city found that a third of its retailers were taking in less than $7 in daily business. All shared the same problem while chain stores, department stores, and mail-order houses cut into their sales. Mass-production factories were doing the same thing to their smaller counterparts. Commercial failures of small shopkeepers and manufacturers amounted to 21,500 annually from 1923 to 1929. A similar fate befell small banks: "No fewer than 4,474 banks—an annual average of 639—were forced to close their doors." All these failures "brought in its wake personal tragedy and catastrophe touching many more individuals than the single factory-owner, shopkeeper, or banker concerned."[10] So this is what "Professor Carver meant by the 'equalization of prosperity,'" Hallgren exclaimed. As he saw it, the lower middle class was "struggling to keep up appearances as required by a new and inflated standard of living" because "the installment-buying psychosis" drove the middle class to live beyond its means—completely ignored were the 22 million paupers spread over the country.[11]

As for the number of unemployed, Hallgren attempted to come up with an estimate, made difficult by the dearth of government statistics. Yet according to the U.S. Bureau of Labor Statistics, at no time from 1924 to 1929 did the 10,000 factories and industrial establishments that reported regularly to the government have enough work for all employees on their payrolls. The bureau estimated that about 14 percent of industrial workers who were listed as employed suffered temporary layoffs during that time frame; in July 1924, the number of workers on payrolls but not working climbed to 25 percent. Even at the high point of the stock market boom in 1929, temporary layoffs ran between 7 and 8 percent of the normal amount employed by these factories and establishments. Hallgren rounded out the picture with studies by individual scholars. An average of various estimates in December 1927 showed that the number of unemployed was likely 3.5 million but could exceed 4 million. One study by Horace Taylor of Columbia University in 1928 suggested the latter number. That year, the Bureau of Labor Statistics also found that 1,847,000 men and women who sought work failed to find it. Though far from a complete picture, the evidence was sufficient for Hallgren to conclude that the prosperity of the New Era was not something experienced by most industrial workers. Their true economic status was "obscured by the operation of such uneconomic devices as installment buying, steam-roller salesmanship, and modern advertising."[12]

Hallgren summed up his analysis by citing two important studies to strengthen his case. In 1928, Irving Fisher of Yale University determined that more than 93 million Americans earned about $500 annually. From this he also figured that the vast majority of Americans appeared to be making only a little over their expenses and had little or nothing in reserve. The following year, Paul H. Nystrom of Columbia University published *Economic Principles of Consumption*, which became the basis for a study by the International Chamber of Commerce on commodity distribution problems in the United States. Hallgren noted that even these hardboiled businessmen, who "cannot afford to be deceived by their own ballyhoo," accepted Nystrom's analysis. It showed that the distribution of purchasing power among individuals and families classified in six categories stretching from "public charges" to "minimum comfort," amounted to 72 million people, or 60.5 percent of the total population of 119 million. These Americans did not make enough income to qualify for a decent standard of living. And among them were the poorest 18 percent, the paupers of Boomtown USA.[13]

"Seeds of Revolt" in the Middle Class: Progress or Reaction?

That the prosperity of the Great Boom had not been shared by more than half the population was nothing new in the history of the world capitalist system. As Karl Marx had explained decades earlier, the general law of capitalist accumulation that governed any advance in industrial production and economic growth always generated poverty as well.[14] But at no other time had the paradox of capitalist progress been more evident in the history of modern capitalism than in 1920s America. The rich got richer while the poor remained paupers, finding relief only from private charities and limited efforts by local governments. Big Business had subjugated the working class to its control. "It may seem cruel," Hallgren wrote in 1933, "but it is nevertheless necessary, to point out that the proletarians, who suffered in silence throughout the post-war decade, were relatively little worse off after three years of economic crisis than they had been at any time during the Golden Age."[15]

But this was not the case for the middle class (Hallgren often uses the terms *lower middle class* or *petty bourgeoisie* interchangeably when referring to the whole middle class). Perhaps more than any of his peers, Hallgren showed a keen sense of the middle-class condition before the Wall Street crash. The small businessman, manufacturer, and banker had taken heavy hits from the growing concentration of capital during the economic boom. Many went down completely or were bought out by stronger competitors, usually corporations. According to the aforementioned studies by Chase, Taylor, Fisher, and Nystrom, Hallgren determined that a good number if not most in the ranks of the middle class lived at or below what was considered acceptable levels of comfort. Yet its peculiar outlook as a class—always looking to reach the top while fearing a fall to the bottom—played a big part in its undoing during the 1920s. Given its low income levels, such dreams of upward mobility were driven by an installment-buying psychosis that was created by the capitalists and presented to them at times in the most crooked ways. For example, the suburban home-buying boom of the mid- to late 1920s had kept the lower middle class chasing its dreams by ensnaring them in deals that amounted to a "criminal racket." Schemes like "pay-the-rest-like-rent" enabled landowners to subdivide their properties and entrap "thousands of mechanics, clerks, salesmen and others" who "were given the illusion of security and prosperity." What they were buying, Hallgren said, was not the property itself but only a share of its inflated value. The crash hit them hard. "The factory manager or corner grocer who had scraped together every dime that he could spare to buy a mortgage bond lost his savings. The insurance salesman or automobile mechanic who thought he was buying a home in the suburbs learned that he was not."[16]

Left behind in the Great Boom, the lower middle class accommodated the status quo but remained essentially reactionary in its political and cultural outlook. Hallgren noted that this trajectory affirmed the position taken by Marx and Engels in the *Communist Manifesto* when they wrote that the petty bourgeoisie was always fighting the capitalist bourgeoisie to prevent its extinction, thereby attempting to roll back the wheels of history.[17] But in the 1920s, looking back to an earlier era of small enterprise was even more futile in the face of capitalist modernization led by Big Business. With the exception of a brief moment in 1924 when its "more politically alert" members cast nearly five million votes for the Progressives and their presidential candidate Robert La Follette, the lower middle class did whatever it could to stay afloat by accommodating its capitalist rulers.[18]

At the same time, there were major developments in the consciousness and behavior of the middle class. The industrial takeoff that spawned an urban-based, cosmopolitan culture had introduced a new and vibrant lifestyle to those who eagerly embraced it. But the volatility of urban life fueled a potent reaction among the 20 million migrants from the countryside who had entered the ranks of the lower strata of the urban middle class. Still rooted in a strict code of Protestant moralism, many felt threatened. The world was bearing down on them, pushing millions toward political reaction that was at times extreme. Shopkeepers and clerks, small manufacturers and salesmen, ministers and policemen, all swept up in modernization were often simultaneously repelled by its culture. Illicit use of alcohol, brazen sexuality, the "loose" woman, disrespectful youth, and many other behaviors, were deemed objectionable according to the strict code of evangelical Protestant morality that had governed their consciousness. Obeisance to the necessities of buying and selling put them at odds with the open and dynamic lifestyles it promoted. As a result, the Great Boom had fractured the consciousness of the middle class as never before. The new urban lifestyle defined by greater acquisitiveness and a desire for personal comfort, enjoyment, and mischief also generated its opposite—a sense of anxiety, discomfort and anger about what they saw and heard. The exaltation of the new freedoms of modern life was accompanied by the advance of bigotry and hate.

In this great wave of reaction were the seminal forces of right-wing extremism, especially among the five million people who joined the Ku Klux Klan between 1920 and 1925.

THE KU KLUX KLAN: THE MIDDLE CLASS AS "ENTREPRENEURS OF HATE"

After decades of obscurity following its heyday of racist terror in the South after the Civil War, the so-called second Ku Klux Klan appeared in Georgia in 1915. But it was not until the post-war anxieties of a society fundamentally changed by war, a major strike wave, the Red Scare, and a deep economic downturn that its membership grew dramatically in 1920, the year Warren Harding was elected president. It quickly became the leading organization of political reaction during the first half of the decade. By 1925 its network of local units (Klaverns) stretched well beyond the South into the Midwest and Southwest, and along parts of the Pacific coast. It was strong in the midwest cities of Detroit, Indianapolis, and Chicago, as well as in Atlanta and other large cities across the South. Far from a monolithic structure, wrote the historian Robert Moats Miller in 1968, the Klan "was a many-splintered thing, or, less invidiously, a many-splendored thing." The Knights were all "troubled souls," but their troubles varied from region to region and Knight to Knight. "It was as though an outraged citizenry participated in a giant police line-up to identify the enemies of society, with each 'good' American fingering the suspect."[19]

Of course, white supremacy against the Negro was the Klan's core. "I swear that I will most zealously and valiantly shield and preserve by any and all justifiable means and methods White Supremacy," read the oath each Klansman took.[20] But the list of enemies in the early 1920s, according to Miller, had grown considerably to include the conspiratorial Catholic, avaricious Jew, dirty Mexican, wily Oriental, bloody-handed Bolshevik, scabrous bootlegger, fancy "lady," oily gambler, fuzzy internationalist, grafting politico, Sabbath desecrator, wife-beater, home-breaker, atheistic evolutionist, feckless-faithed Modernist, scoffing professor, arrogant intellectual, subversive socialist, slick urbanite, simpering pacifist, [and] corrupt labor organizer. Of necessity, the line of suspects was endless because the evils threatening America were legion: miscegenation, mongrelization, Romanism, socialism, urbanism, skepticism, secularism, paganism, modernism, radicalism, internationalism, materialism, Freudianism, relativism, surrealism, alcoholism, sexualism.

Given all these variations, it made more sense to consider the Klan of the 1920s as made up of many local units operating on their own. Each unit, Miller said, prioritized the lists of dangers "just as each Knight was motivated (whether consciously or not) by his life experiences."[21]

The second great anchor and glue for Klansmen was Protestant fundamentalism. Membership was restricted to adult-born Protestant males, which was between 15 to 20 percent of the total male population in the nation, and between 25 and 30 percent of all Protestants.[22] Hiram Wesley Evans, who became Imperial Wizard in 1922, described the Klan as "a recruiting agency" for Protestant churches. Baptists, Methodists, and Disciples of Christ dominated membership rolls. At one point Protestant ministers made up two-thirds of the thirty-nine national lecturers working for the Klan. Each Klavern had its own minister. Leadership boasted that the organization included 30,000 in 1924. That year, Klansmen made up three-quarters of the 6,000 delegates to the Southeastern Baptist Convention.[23]

Still, perhaps the most important feature of the Klan that explained its outlook and behavior in the 1920s was its largely middle-class composition. This was vitally important to historian Nancy MacLean. The appeal of the Klan's politics, she writes, "was rooted deep within American society and culture: in the legions of middle-class white men who felt trapped between capital and labor and in the political culture they inherited from their forebears." For MacLean, the Klan was far from the stereotype of white trash. Anxious about current conditions and fearful of what the future might bring, Klan leaders drew from the wellspring of American politics to fashion an ideology based on established values that they believed would help them make sense of rapidly changing social relations and help them meet challenges to their power.[24]

This mindset was certainly true of the Klan's founder, William Joseph Simmons, whom MacLean describes as "the son of a poor Alabama country physician" and "a man chronically on the make." In 1920, Simmons realized that to build an organization he needed help from those more adept at modern sales practices. So he took on two partners, Mary Elizabeth Tyler and Edward Young Clarke, who quickly built the Klan as masters of advertising and propaganda. They, in turn, hired "seasoned organizers," which turned the KKK into a thriving business, also making "a small fortune" for the dynamic duo.[25] Some of the profit trickled down to recruiters (Kleagles) who kept part of the high initiation fee charged every new recruit.[26] Southern manufacturers also did well doing business with the Klan, especially the Gate City Manufacturing Company in Atlanta, which held exclusive rights to produce and sell Klan regalia. Since each member was required to buy a white robe and pointed cap for $6.50, the profits climbed.[27] Moreover, Tyler and Clark had put together an impressive sales package that blended "white supremacy, Christianity, and the male-bonding rituals of fraternalism." This presented the Klan as the country's foremost "militant defender of 'pure Americanism.'" Armed with this promotional material, Kleagles went out to the fraternal orders, especially Masons, Elks, and Odd Fellows whose memberships were made solidly of Baptists, Methodists, and the Disciples of Christ.[28]

The Klan quickly became a moneymaking machine. A recent analysis of membership datasets from different areas and cities by

Roland G. Fryer Jr. and Steven D. Levitt estimates that Klan leadership from top to bottom generated total revenues amounting to at least $25 million in 1924, its peak year of membership. With only a small portion of that amount needed to fund basic operations, the rest went into the pockets of leaders. Indeed, the "true genius" of the Klan was "its remarkable ability to raise revenue." As Fryer and Levitt wrote, "Rather than a terrorist organization, the 1920s Klan is better described as a wildly successful multi-level marketing entity fueled by an army of highly incentivized sales agents and an unprecedented interest in fraternal groups of all kinds." Citing other scholars, they characterized the Klan as a national organization built by "entrepreneurs of hate."[29]

MacLean's case study of the Klan in Athens, Georgia, reveals a middle-class consciousness rooted in "its own distinctive relationship to capital and labor . . . and its own modes of thought." Local and regional prioritizing of enemies and evils only served to mask what she sees more significantly as the "underlying commonalities that justify treating the petty bourgeoisie as a class."[30] Her analysis revealed that it was mainly an organization made up of "middling men" who had experienced some upward mobility during the war years but whose hopes for further advancement were dashed by the political turmoil and economic downturn of 1919–1921. The single most common occupation of the Klan in Athens was owner or manager of a small business or a small family farmer. White-collar employees of the so-called new middle class—salesmen, clerks, agents, and public employees—filled out the rest in the ranks. Absent were the wealthiest in the city, as were unskilled urban workers and poor farmhands. Without the pull from those below them, these middling men identified with the uptown urban population and landowning families and "lined up against mill operatives and landless farmers."[31]

MacLean calls this petty-bourgeois consciousness in Athens "reactionary populism" and argues that it is typical of the Klan elsewhere, whether in large manufacturing cities or in smaller towns.[32] "Although the exact proportions varied, those most likely to belong to the order included white-collar employees, small-business owners, independent professionals, skilled workers, and farmers." But the real significance in understanding the "clustering" of Klan membership was to see it from a "transnational perspective." Highly critical of the tendency among historians and others to confine class analysis to capital and labor alone, MacLean sees the ominous danger "to obscure the very existence of the petit bourgeoisie as a class with its own distinctive relationship to capital and labor, its own internal dynamics, and its own modes of thought." Most of them were occupationally closer to the upper ranks of the working class, while a few made it to the lower ranks of the capitalist class.[33]

All these occupational differences among Klansmen, MacLean writes, "mask the underlying commonalities" that justified considering the petty bourgeoisie as a distinct class. On the basis of her class analysis of the Klan in Athens, which she viewed as representative of the organization nationally, Maclean explains how the class character of the petty bourgeoisie was shaped by its relation to the means of production and the class struggle. Its "structural position," she argues, "helps account for the characteristic ambivalence of the lower middle class vis-à-vis the capitalists above them and the unskilled workers beneath them in the social order." For sure, big capitalists and small proprietors alike were vested in private ownership. Yet, unlike the actual capitalist bourgeoisie, members of the petty bourgeoisie lived and operated mainly as family members. This made them suspicious of big capitalists who employed many more workers and with whom they could not possibly compete. Thus the small proprietor, manufacturer, artisan, or salaried employee always felt vulnerable and subject to the greater resources of large capitalist enterprise. MacLean cautions that the political volatility that inheres in the petty bourgeoisie can at times bring it into an alliance with the working class and make them anti-capitalist. But this is only temporary since complications arise from the fact that supporting the working class undermines its own interests as small owners who

are being threatened by the increasing concentration and centralization of big business.[34]

"In short," MacLean writes, "the very placement of the petit
bourgeoisie means that it is perennially pulled and pushed in two
directions: towards capital and against labor, towards labor and
against capital." But the push and pull and the extent of its magnitude depends on the state of the capitalist system at any moment,
that is, whether or not it is functioning reasonably or in crisis:

> In trying times, this buffeting tends to become particularly pro-
> nounced. Economic crisis and intense struggle between labor
> and capital aggravate the ambivalence imbedded in the struc-
> tural position of petit-bourgeois people. Faced with the prospect
> of disaster, they can feel pushed first from one direction, then the
> next, shuffled back and forth by forces beyond their control.[35]

MacLean follows closely the broader theoretical analysis of
another historian, Arno Mayer, who observed "the vague sense of
negative commonality" of the petty-bourgeois consciousness that
is "neither bourgeois nor worker" and which becomes heightened
when subject to various "economic, social, and cultural identities."
In such times, Mayer said, the petty bourgeoisie "loses self-con-
fidence and becomes prey to anxieties and fears which may well
predispose it to rally to a politics of anger, scapegoating, and ata-
vistic millenarianism." MacLean adds that no one can know for
sure how "this Janus-faced perspective will be resolved in any particular case." But it was clear in the early 1920s as far as labor was
concerned. "Thinly based, internally divided, and sorely defeated
in the postwar contest with employers," she writes, "it had lost the
momentum that might have enabled it to attract those wavering in
the middle."[36]

Still, the Klan's mix of classical liberalism and republicanism
wrapped in a vision of a True American society was grounded in
the class consciousness of the petty bourgeoisie. As such, it did not
contradict Thomas Nixon Carver's idea of a capitalist utopia made

from hardworking laborers becoming capitalists who personified the ideals of 100 percent Americanism. Both visions were implicitly grounded in a petty-bourgeois worldview of nativist and racist thought that contained within it a virulent form of reactionary populism. True to Carver's outlook as well was the Klan's method of recruitment and organization, which in connecting Protestant congregations with fraternal organizations revealed a business approach consistent with petty-bourgeois entrepreneurship.

Meanwhile—and this may be the most important matter yet to be examined—the small proprietor by day must have felt some discomfort and worry for competing with giant corporations to sell commodities that extolled the virtues of a modern cosmopolitanism, knowing that he would condemn them at a meeting of his Klavern that night.

THE MARCH OF EMPIRE

While the plight of the middle class was clear from the start, it was obvious that the ruling capitalist class reaped rewards and riches greater than ever. For one thing, three Republicans in the White House who believed that the business of America was business itself welcomed all the healthy tax cuts to the wealthy. After all, Andrew Mellon, one of the richest men in the world and Treasury secretary for Harding, Coolidge, and Hoover, made it happen. It was Mellon who coined the term "trickle-down economics." Cutting taxes for wealthy Americans and corporations was justified on the claim that it would stimulate further investment in industrial and commercial enterprises, thereby creating more jobs in manufacturing and the growing service economy. The wealth generated at the top would then flow down to small businesses and local economies. That did not happen. By the end of the decade, the Mellon tax policy had helped 60,000 families at the top of the economic ladder to gather assets equal to the 25 million Americans at the bottom. Income from stock dividends rose 65 percent, indicating that the wealth rescued from taxes was not trickling down but being swept up into the stock market and the bank vaults. According to historian Alan Lawson, Mellon became so obsessed with his doctrine that he ordered the Internal Revenue Service to provide him with an expert to determine how he could eliminate his own personal taxes.[37]

As leading capitalists and their partners in government tightened their grip over American society, they also looked to expand their power and influence abroad. Already the leading industrial power in the world capitalist system, the United States had now become its banker. To sustain further growth in industry and finance required an expanding global reach for the U.S. economy. This was not easy given the official isolationist foreign policy during the 1920s. When he became president, Harding appeared willing to play along with the chorus of Old Guard isolationists who had rejected the internationalist agenda of his White House predecessor Woodrow Wilson. But Harding was no isolationist, and all his talk about "normalcy" was geared to giving the industrialists and bankers what they needed. Under Harding, the United States embarked on an imperialist agenda facilitated by able capitalist modernizers in his cabinet, men who understood that continued prosperity in the domestic economy depended on gaining control over natural resources required for industrial output and establishing new markets for the goods it produced.

More important, the modernizers saw the key to all of this in the increasing flow of U.S. capital into foreign markets in the form of direct investment and loans, which often required walking the tightrope between isolationism and engagement. To get around this, Harding, and Coolidge after him, delegated much of the actual policymaking to leading bankers who, with a clear sense of purpose and vigor, defined spheres of influence for the expansion of U.S. interests vital to the health of domestic business. The results were impressive. Foreign investment doubled during the war years and left the nation a net creditor by more than $3 billion.[38] But then it doubled again from 1919 to 1930, when investment in overseas projects rose from $7 billion to

$17.2 billion.[39] During the prosperous 1920s, the United States furnished two-thirds of all new long-term foreign investment, nearly $9 billion since the war ended.[40] From 1919 to 1926, J. P. Morgan & Company alone issued loans totaling $1.5 billion to more than a half-dozen European nations, Australia, Chile, Cuba, and Japan.[41] In all these ventures, government and business acted in concert to establish U.S. financial hegemony over the European and much of the global economy.

As president, Coolidge's support for the expansion of U.S. finance capital abroad was clearly evident in the crucial loan package to Germany put together by New York bankers in 1924. The Dawes Plan, led by Charles Dawes, who would soon become vice president, sent $2.5 billion to Germany for the purpose of ending a crippling inflationary crisis caused by the Weimar government's attempt to make reparation payments to its former enemies.[42] In effect, the injection of U.S. capital turned the caretaker Weimar government from imminent collapse to overseer of a dynamic though short-lived recovery. Coolidge and other political and business leaders had drummed up public support for the plan, while the Federal Reserve did its part by lowering interest rates that made high-yield foreign bonds more attractive. The Dawes initiative was unprecedented, bringing together a nationwide syndicate of 400 banks and 800 bond houses, all of whom saw nothing but green. Of greater significance, the Dawes Plan made German capital peripheral to and dependent on the United States. A rush "to the trough of American capital" by German local governments and corporations stabilized the national economy. Until American bankers called in their loans following the 1929 Wall Street crash, there was no better example of an advanced capitalist country's peripheral dependence on the centrality of American capital. Between 1924 and the onset of the crisis five years later, German public credit institutions got 80 percent of the loans they received from American investors, while the amount given to local governments and large corporations was almost as high, 75 and 56 percent respectively.[43]

American banks opened a large number of branches overseas, penetrating the monopoly British capital had always enjoyed in financing U.S. traders. By 1926, eight American banks had 107 branches or subsidiaries in foreign countries. The stability of the dollar and its acceptance as the currency of exchange was advantageous to U.S. business, since foreign entrepreneurs who stockpiled dollars tended to spend them on American commodities rather than on those of America's rivals. This promoted the expansion of American production beyond U.S. borders. Throughout the 1920s, American companies extended their operations worldwide and with incredible speed. Companies such as General Motors, International Harvester, United Fruit, IT&T, Ford, and General Electric purchased existing plants or built new ones in dozens of countries. "American utilities took over vast chunks of the Latin American market, and American aviation—a new industry—set up a virtual world monopoly." The rate of investment was impressive across the board: in Europe about $5 billion before 1930, $5.6 billion in Latin America, and $4 billion in Canada. By the end of the 1920s, American holdings abroad, which had been only one-sixth of Britain's in 1913, were now nearly equal.[44]

The significance of this postwar surge in American economic power was clear to Louis Hacker in 1938 when he wrote that the United States had embarked on a truly imperialist course during the 1920s. "This new American imperialism," Hacker recalled, "meant an awareness of the fact that the domestic economy of the nation was inextricably tied up with world economy: that our movements and our decisions were being affected, sometimes to a very marked degree, by events taking place in remote corners of the earth."[45] The rate of growth in monopoly-finance capitalist enterprise had raised the bar on it imperatives. America's continued economic success hinged on three great challenges: to secure raw materials not found within its territorial borders or in short supply; to establish new foreign markets to absorb the surpluses of goods manufactured domestically; and to export capital for profitable investment. Consequently, American business needed much more than the Open Door principle articulated by Secretary of State John Hay in 1899 when he warned Europe and Japan that it needed unfettered access to Chinese markets. U.S. capital now depended on open and direct access to the entire world market which, for Hacker, had surely occurred during the 1920s. By the end of the decade, America's private long-term investments were about equally divided between direct investments (ownership of factories, mines, sales agencies, etc.) and portfolio investments (ownership of foreign securities, both public and private).[46] U.S. investors had reaped immense profits at home and abroad—a fifth of direct investment had gone to foreign manufacturing enterprises competing with American industries worked by American labor. For American capitalists, both were win-win scenarios. Whatever they could not make at home they did abroad since direct investments, as Hacker put it, enabled them "to tunnel under the high protective tariff walls" of foreign governments.[47]

In Hacker, we find no better observer of a Pax Americana in the making. As direct foreign investments increased, so did the political and military arm of American power whenever possible. This was well known to others like him who understood the significance of it all. In 1940, two Marxist writers, Bruce Minton and John Stuart, provided a concise overview of an ascendant empire seeking to extend and defend its commercial and banking interests in Europe, Latin America, and the Orient. Harding and Coolidge relied heavily on cabinet officials to carve out imperialist agendas that operated in subtle conformance with the government's explicit policies of non-engagement. Under Secretary of State Charles Hughes, the Harding administration crafted an imperialist foreign policy that, in the words of Minton and Stuart, "methodically and shrewdly set about winning world outlets for the masters—the great exporters and financiers who were looking beyond the borders of the United States for markets to conquer and exploit." Hughes and company got much help from Herbert Hoover, who had turned the Commerce Department into a "sales bureau for American economic aggression." According to Minton and Stuart:

> The monopolists were offered advice and incentive. Throughout the world, American consuls compiled tables of commercial opportunities in the countries where they were stationed, investigating credits and arranging terms of sales advantageous to American firms. Each month the Department of Commerce issued a bulletin on available supplies of raw materials, the trend of prices, the rates of production, the volume of sales.

Business inquiries multiplied as the department became a major vehicle for U.S. imperialist expansion. This made Hoover its "patron saint."[48]

Minton and Stuart pointed to the increased use of military force to protect American business interests directly or, in some cases, to support a political strongman who would willingly do the bidding of U.S. businessmen. This was especially true in the small countries of Central America and the Caribbean where Wall Street financiers held huge investments in oil or mineral deposits, agricultural goods, and other commercial enterprises. When a putsch government in Guatemala guaranteed American capitalists special privileges in 1922, Hughes "precipitously recognized the most reactionary and malodorous regime" in Central America. Here, recognition required armed protection by American troops for the president and his supporters against the majority of the Guatemalans who opposed him. U.S. Marines occupied the Dominican Republic to supervise elections and ensure the election of a government that would be responsible for protecting U.S. interests. They occupied Nicaragua for the same reasons. Haiti, which became a U.S. protectorate in 1916, saw its parliament suspended during Harding's presidency and replaced by a bureaucracy of 250 Americans who directed the so-called republic's finances, public works, police force, health services, legal activities, and agriculture. A U.S. ambassador told Cuba what laws to pass; Puerto Rico was run by a commission in Washington that ruled with an iron hand.[49]

BIG BUSINESS LOVES MUSSOLINI

After some initial apprehensions following Benito Mussolini's famous March on Rome in October 1922, the Harding, Coolidge, and Hoover administrations gave almost unqualified support to Italian fascism throughout the rest of the decade. American business leaders jumped on board, as did many of the leading newspapers like the *New York Times* and popular magazines, especially the *Saturday Evening Post*. For top American businessmen, Mussolini's leadership in a moment of crisis had turned back the threat of socialist revolution. It then charted a course toward a newfound political stability that offered an exemplary model to American capitalists throughout the New Era. Mussolini was a leader they respected and admired. This was crucial to the architects of foreign policy in both nations who recognized their respective and mutual interests as the basis for a sound partnership in U.S-European relations. As Italy sought strong ties with the United States, knowing that it needed capital investment, U.S. bankers deemed it vital to make Italy a partner in consolidating its position in Europe. In an address to the National Association of Manufacturers in 1923, John A. Emery likened Mussolini's conversion from radical socialist to "the lightning stroke of intelligence" that struck "Saul of Tarsus from his horse" and made it possible for the fascist leader to ride through the streets and unite "a great body of citizens who were determined to restore its institutional government."[50] Emery hoped that Americans would see something encouraging and uplifting in Mussolini's ascension.

According to a *New York Times* report on March 9, 1923, two hundred American delegates to the Second Congress of the International Chamber of Commerce had agreed with Emery. As the largest contingent in the 1,000-strong delegation, the Americans joined their peers from other nations to cheer Mussolini when he entered the Congress accompanied by a platoon of Blackshirts. In what might have been a direct message to the Americans, Mussolini seemed to echo President Harding's position on the future of U.S. politics when he said that fascism "offers to the world the best proof that the Italian nation is rapidly regaining normalcy in its political and economic life." For a fascist dictator in the making, Mussolini had other words of assurance to the guardians of American capitalism in the New Era when he talked about the resilience of the free market and the need for individual initiative. Some American business luminaries in the audience returned home convinced that fascism was a good thing for Italy—and perhaps for America as well. Julius Barnes, president of the U.S. Chamber of Commerce, saw "the beginning of a new era in Italy." William Booth, a vice president for the Guaranty Trust Company, praised Mussolini for lifting the country "out of the slough of despair into the bright realm of promise." Lewis Pierson, chairman of the board of the Irving National Bank of New York who represented the American Bankers Association (ABA) at the Congress told the Merchants Association of New York in a speech that Mussolini was restoring "the ideals of individualism" and pledging Italy to respect the "inviolable rights of property and contract." For Pierson, "progress" in Italy under Mussolini would come through "thrift and hard work."[51]

In his excellent study of America and its relations with fascist Italy, historian John Diggins describes how American businessmen congratulated Mussolini for doing what they had already done in the United States by electing Harding. Fascism had established law and order in Italy and revived the economy on the basis of efficient, "private" management in industries. It had ended the strike wave and prevented the communists from gaining political ground. Fascist ideology served to revitalize Italian nationalism and patriotism while holding up the doctrine of hard work. The president of the New York Stock Exchange, E. H. H. Simmons, told Italian bankers that Mussolini's fascist victory over communism,

that "evil disease from the Orient," and the marvelous achievements he was piling up, had captured the imagination of American
businessmen. Business publications such as *Barron's* and *Nation's
Business*, the official organ of the U.S. Chamber of Commerce,
among others, heaped praise on Il Duce and Italian fascism. "The
list of outspoken business admirers reads like a Wall Street 'Who's
Who,'" Diggins wrote. Among the luminaries were Otto Kahn of
Kuhn, Loeb and Company, who touted Mussolini's leadership and
those of his able assistants. Ivy Lee, the public relations genius,
interviewed Mussolini in 1923 and recorded his encouraging ideas
on balanced budgets, stable government, and American investment opportunities. Elbert H. Gary, chairman of the United States
Steel Corporation, exclaimed that the entire world needed strong,
honest men like those in Italy from whom Americans could learn
much. Julius Barnes, president of the U.S. Chamber, referred to
him as "without question a great man."[52] Barnes told the Executive
Council of the ABA:

> Today he is the one real living force, not only in Italy, but in all
> Europe, and the conversion of that man with his strength and
> his following to the principle of the so-called capitalistic system
> that we believe in is the most extraordinary encouragement to
> us who want to see and hear sound and sane economics put into
> play.[53]

But the American business leader who most vigorously patron-
ized the cause of Italian fascism in the mid-1920s was Thomas W.
Lamont, head of the J. P. Morgan banking network, and who served
as a business consultant for Mussolini's government. Lamont's praise
for fascist Italy, Diggins wrote, was "as mundane as a cost analysis,"
because a "'modus vivendi' had been worked out between capital
and labor" that returned industry to private enterprise, reduced the
national debt, and curbed inflation.[54]

Even Mussolini's life story appealed to the New Era's ethos that
success was possible for everyone through hard work and sacrifice.

The son of a blacksmith, Mussolini was living proof of the self-made man who became a pragmatic statesman. Here, Diggins says, "was the 'practical' leader who rejected the unusable democratic dogmas of the past and the unworkable moral principles of the present." For these reasons, the conservative *Commerce and Finance* and the liberal *New Republic* both praised Mussolini for his realism and pragmatism. Conservative American businessmen admired the rationalizing of the Italian economy, which provided moral imperatives for business success.[55] In an editorial titled "That Man Mussolini!" in the *Nation's Business*, Merle Thorpe explained why American businessmen were inspired by the fascist leader:

> I can understand why a business man would admire Mussolini and his methods. They are essentially those of successful business. Executive action; deeds, not words. . . . The impression you get of [Mussolini] is that he is a fine type of business executive. He cuts through. . . . Not fine-spoken theories; not plans; not speeches he is going to make. None of these. Things done! And that is your successful American executive.[56]

Mussolini's popularity in the United States was fueled by the press. While most newspapers, magazines, and literary journals took a critical or skeptical view of fascist developments in Italy, some publications seemed to give full backing to Mussolini's fascist experiment. None was more approving than the most highly respected daily in the country, the *New York Times*. Its regular team of correspondents covering Italy wrote favorably about fascism and Mussolini. One of them, Walter Littlefield, was even decorated by the Italian government. A few other notable publications were even more openly pro-fascist. None topped the *Saturday Evening Post*. One of its regular writers, Isaac F. Marcosson, said Mussolini had saved Italy because he had prevented a "Red terror" and had demonstrated his genius for economics by engineering a "commercial revolution." Some of its contributors joined in the accolades. For example, the celebrated humorist Will Rogers interviewed

Mussolini only to come away with a highly favorable impression and wrote that dictatorship "is the greatest form of government; that is, if you have the right Dictator." [57]

In his fine study published in 1980 but only recently translated into English, Gian Giacomo Migone mentions Andrew Mellon's support for the important role Mussolini played in helping to stabilize the economic and political situation in postwar Europe—and being favorable for U.S. investments. In a campaign speech for Coolidge in October 1924, Mellon recalled how a strong hand had saved Italy from socialist revolution and then established a government that was freeing industry from regulation, lowering corporate taxes, and producing a nearly balanced budget. According to Migone, Mellon considered Mussolini a "principal exemplar" for laissez-faire economics because it was the very thing Mellon was directing at Treasury.[58]

DURING THE 1920s, the success of the U.S. capitalist state in crushing the radical labor movement had established conditions for the dramatic expansion of American capital—perhaps the first economic takeoff in the rise of Pax Americana. From it came a torrent of new consumer goods in an ever-expanding marketplace that promised greater comfort and pleasure. All this fueled the ballyhoo of the Great Boom that drowned out whatever little was said about the fact that most of the population did not partake in the prosperity. Instead, the paradoxical character of capitalist progress made it difficult for enough Americans to recognize the steady widening of class divisions on a national scale. Whatever political legitimacy was required to sustain the Great Boom was supplied by three Republican presidents and their administrations whose domestic and foreign policies put more and more power in the hands of Big Business. For the affable conciliator Warren Harding, it was "normalcy." For the puritanical Calvin Coolidge, it was praising capitalist elites as members of the "elect" whose sole purpose was to make the nation and themselves rich. And to Herbert Hoover, the Great Engineer, it was to constantly call on capitalists to recognize their civic duties and serve others in a great show of voluntarism. All this made possible a cultural milieu fecund with possibilities for capitalist enterprise and a mindset for acquisitiveness that permeated American society, both of which served the drive for capitalist accumulation and profit.

The rise of Pax Americana could not have happened unless the capitalist ruling class had subjugated domestic labor to its imperatives. Migone makes this clear in his study of U.S. relations with fascist Italy. "Right from the beginning," he wrote, "most Americans saw and appreciated the Fascist *coup d'état* for one particular aspect: the Italian version of a return to normalcy" and a model for all other European countries in the turbulent early 1920s. The great desire for a return to order "squashed every other possible concern. One might expect that the destruction of that constitutional order which was supposed to be the hallmark of the liberal democratic order would elicit some reaction in the nation founded on one of the world's great liberal revolutions." As Migone so presciently stated in 1980:

> The nearly unanimous consent to Fascism in the United States provokes serious questions on the nature and the limits of the American ideology and practice of democracy. At the same time it is important to observe that consent was also, if not exclusively, the product of a specific set of historical values, interests, and mindsets that characterized the United States of the Twenties. The desire for a return to normalcy, in a larger sense than merely economic productivity, was particularly strong. . . . The need for economic expansion and therefore for stable and friendly part- ners, was foremost in the minds of American elites, particularly financial elites; and was never more than in this historical period determinative of their political and ideological orientation, as well as that of a larger range of American public opinion.

Migone revealed the key feature in the future of American lib- eral capitalist democracy when he added that "approval of Fascism became a shared position among both isolationists and those who waited impatiently for the right conditions—the rise of stable and capable partners—to recommence internationalist politics."[59]

At home, the ruling class had crushed the power of labor with the brute force of state power in 1919 and 1920 and then relied on its legal arm and the complicity of the AFL and the rest of organized labor. The result, as Mauritz Hallgren said, was a quiescent working class throughout much of the decade. The displacement of the middle class as the driving force of the American economy and progressive political change took an unmistakable direction toward the reverse—political reaction and extremism. All of this was the result of capitalist modernization fueled by Big Business in the name of progress.

But progress for whom? In serving Italian fascism as a linchpin of its economic power and political influence in Europe, liberal capitalist democracy in the United States revealed its own embryonic fascist processes in the epicenter of the world system.

The germ of American fascism lay in the drive for accumulation and thus was bound up with the modernizing processes of industrial and financial expansion that aimed at capitalist domination at all levels of political and social life. Put another way, fascist processes in the United States were primarily a political and ideological by-product of capitalist modernity in the capitalist epicenter of the world system *and not a reaction to it*. The reaction came instead from a middle class that clung to its fantasy of a democratic capitalism. This explains why the driving force for fascism in the United States came from the top of the social order in the 1920s and how the paradox of capitalist progress concealed a general crisis of capitalist society in the making—and with it the intensification of fascist ideas and processes that were peculiarly American. That the architects of capitalist prosperity succeeded so well explains why the onset of the crisis in 1929 shocked them, and why after futile efforts to prevent its deepening caused many in the ruling class to call for a form of American dictatorship just like Mussolini's.

6—Onset of the 1929 Crisis and the Pivot toward Fascism

MUCH HAS BEEN WRITTEN to undo the once widely held view that the prosperous 1920s in the United States ended suddenly and without warning on October 24, 1929, when the Wall Street stock market crash set off a general crisis of American capitalism. Nothing could be further from the truth. By mid-decade, a good part of the U.S. economy was already in trouble, although exuberant cheerleaders in business and government made it difficult for most people to see anything wrong. Such was the paradoxical character of capitalist progress in 1920s America: despite the apparent prosperity, contradictions in American capitalism were creating a widening gap between wealth and poverty, as terrorist and non-terrorist fascist processes emerged to secure the supremacy of capital over society.

The spectacle of prosperity, however, concealed much of this reality. A booming economy and lifestyle defined by the automobile, kitchen appliances, and the sizzling culture of the Jazz Age in full swing was enough to blind millions of Americans who mainly saw, heard, or read what was given to them in the glitter and ballyhoo of Boomtown USA. All of it served to conceal an epic crisis in the making. With easy money driving that great American invention the installment plan, enough consumers were buying whatever Big Business or Wall Street served up. As Jonathan Norton Leonard wrote a decade later:

> The New York Stock Exchange in 1929 was the nation's Fairy Godmother. It was Aladdin's Lamp. Its workings were beyond the grasp of ordinary minds, but under the direction of the Wall Street general staff it turned out money faster than all of the gold-mines, mints and printing presses in the world. Everybody could get his portion by buying a few shares of stock in a company—like Radio Corporation—which was known to have a great future. The theory of this miracle might be a bit obscure, but the practical application was very simple indeed.

The practical side was certainly evident. Leonard caught the pulse of the Exchange, claiming one could stand in front of it on a typical workday and "almost hear the beating of the nation's heart":

> Inside the building itself, on a large littered floor, a thousand brokers struggled in shifting clots like ants on a sprinkle of sugar. They were much more noisy than ants. . . . An elaborate mechanism of clerks, messenger boys and electricity sifted this sound, extracted long trains of figures and sent them out to the eagerly waiting nation and the almost as eager world.

This was the nation's "state of mind" as Leonard interpreted it just months before the crash. People generally believed that prosperity would continue indefinitely because "unregulated and self-seeking businessmen could be trusted as national leaders."[1]

Yet, as labor economist and writer George Soule noted two decades later, one could not wholly blame the man in the street for his ignorance or greed, given the easy access to credit that had empowered him to indulge in the constant flow of new things.

"The delusions that prevailed were shared by the leaders of finance, business, government, and even many academic experts in economics," Soule wrote. "Rarely has a people been so misled by those who were supposed to be its wisest and most seasoned counselors."[2] Even great minds were misled, including the soon-to-be-celebrated British economist John Maynard Keynes, who told his students they would see "no further crash in our lifetime," or Rudolph Hilferding, the social-democratic economist who theorized that "organised capitalism" had removed the anarchic character of the market and thus with it the possibility of future crises.[3]

But they were wrong. A crisis of American capitalism was developing within the Great Boom. The rapid rise in the output of goods in the early and mid-1920s created the basis for a mass consumer society that required greater efficiency of industrial production in order to sustain itself while keeping profits high. But the constant drive to raise productivity in an increasingly ruthless competitive system ultimately undermined it. The rise in the fixed component of constant capital, that is, the new machinery in which technical innovations were embedded, diminished the level of variable capital, that is, the labor-power of workers. Herein lay a fundamental contradiction that spawned the coming crisis: a reserve army of labor grew and wages remained stagnant, while capitalists were compelled to rely increasingly on technological innovation to produce goods more efficiently, thereby further diminishing the role of human labor-power. Most of the gain in productivity went to the owners of capital rather than workers, who experienced greater poverty.

Here was the coming bust in the boom. As the purchasing power of workers declined, capitalists pumped the masses, through advertising, public relations, and propaganda, to keep them buying, while increasing their debt through easy credit schemes. Still, consumption lagged behind production. By 1927, overproduction and saturated markets were bringing matters to a head. As inventories piled up and the real value of commodities declined, capitalists

stopped investing in productive enterprise because it was not profitable. The lag between production and consumption only added
to the burden of industry, which had operated at much lower than
full capacity even in the peak years of the boom. "Excess capacity
was enormous," Lewis Corey wrote. "In 1928–29, in spite of the
sharp upward spurt in production, most American industries were
capable of producing from 25% to 75% more goods than markets
could absorb," and "particularly great in the newer industries" like
automobiles.[4]

The Wall Street crash set in motion events that slowly revealed
to some observers just how far the ruling capitalist class had gone
to bankrupt the nation for the sake of preserving its economic
interests and political power. As for the masses, it is still difficult to
determine from the evidence how much they had mistakenly put
their faith in the virtues and integrity of people who had led them
to ruin. Nevertheless, their political quiescence enabled capitalist owners and managers to behave with impunity for much of
the 1920s. Workers and people in the ranks of the middle classes
perhaps saw little alternative but to go along with the promises of
uninterrupted prosperity in the hope that some of the fabulous
wealth amassed at the top would indeed trickle down. Only the
crash and the economic depression that quickly followed made it
possible for a few writers to begin peeling back the layers of deception and fraud propagated by propaganda in the service of an
oligarchy selfishly entrenched and wholly insensitive to deprivation and suffering. The ruling capitalist class that had pledged to
be guardians of the Republic had wrecked what they were coming
to own and control.

SYSTEMIC CONTRADICTIONS IN THE GREAT BOOM

During much of the growth from 1922 to 1929, overproduction
and underconsumption became the two main currents developing in the American economy. Production had expanded rapidly
as a huge wave of investment spurred technological innovations

and the scientific management of production. American industry became the leader of global capitalism, mass-producing
capital goods and durable consumer goods with fewer workers.
Fierce competition at all levels in the economic system created
winners and losers. This was evident even at the top, where the
incessant drive to make production more efficient furthered the
concentration of capital and the centralization of ownership on
a massive scale in such a short time. At the same time, the steady
deterioration of purchasing power mandated the opening of new
foreign markets for capital investment and exports, none of which
occurred at sufficient levels for an imperial giant on the rise.

The United States had achieved impressive gains in foreign
trade as a result of its role in the First World War, from which
it assumed the mantle of global economic leadership. Its share of
world exports had increased while Europe's declined, creating a
favorable trade balance for the United States during much of the
1920s. Nevertheless, the dramatic increase in exports fell short of
what American capitalism needed—sufficient numbers of new
outlets to absorb domestic goods. By 1929, the United States was
producing 40 percent of all products manufactured by the world's
industrial nations.[5] While overall manufacturing output increased
by 50 percent between 1922 and 1929, exports lagged behind at
38 percent.[6] One finds no better examples than in the auto and
steel industries, both major forces fueling the domestic boom.
Auto production hit excess capacity by mid-decade, but exports
only averaged 15.2 percent of its output between 1924 and 1929.
Steel exports were somewhat better at 20 percent.[7] Political leaders
proved incapable of molding policies that would open the global
market to increased American commerce. President Woodrow
Wilson's postwar vision of an "open-door" foreign policy that
would extend the principle of free trade throughout the global
economy had dissolved with a new, much-espoused isolationism.
Given this shift in foreign policy, the three Republican administrations of the 1920s turned over much of its decision making to
opportunist Wall Street bankers, who dispensed with Wilson's lofty

idealism while extending the global reach of U.S. capital. But it was not enough to absorb all the capital available for new investment, which revealed a major contradiction. Believing that much of the prosperity lay in the domestic market, decision makers rejected the open door and threw up barriers to foreign imports in 1922 and 1924.

As the world's leading creditor nation and banker, the United States needed to import more than it exported in order to reap the benefits of its investment potential abroad. Without access to U.S. markets due to rising protectionism, however, foreign borrowers could not sell their products at levels sufficient to repay the loans and other forms of credit extended to them by American bankers, further inhibiting U.S. capital investment in their economies. Simply put, U.S. protectionism was gumming up trade and capital flow for a capitalist empire that needed to be free of all obstacles between its domestic and foreign markets. Instead, protective tariffs were erected to assuage American businessmen who sought above all to protect what it called "infant industries" from European competitors and cheaper goods. The Fordney-McCumer Tariff of 1922 was just one example of the way U.S. trade policy negated America's new status as the world's great creditor nation.[8]

Barriers constructed in the name of "America first" only intensified an already protracted crisis in domestic agriculture and the plight of rural communities across much of the nation. With one-fifth of the population still working the land, American farmers endured throughout the 1920s what historian David Kennedy calls "a stubborn agricultural depression."[9] In 1914, they had taken full advantage of a historic opportunity to benefit from the misery of others by producing foodstuffs for war-torn European allies, as well as for other markets disrupted by the global conflict. But the great wartime stimulus dissipated quickly after the war ended and European production of primary goods returned to prewar levels. By 1920, U.S. farm prices plummeted as farmers in the South and Midwest stared disaster in the face. The price of cotton dropped from 35 cents to 16 cents per pound, corn from $1.50 to

52 cents per bushel.[10] From 1919 to 1929, wheat prices fell from $2.19 a bushel to $1.04.[11] Farmers who had borrowed heavily to put marginal land in cultivation, purchasing gas-powered tractors and other new farm machinery, in order to reap inflated, wartime prices, now faced the problems of overproduction. The rapid pace of technological innovation during the 1920s, which increased productivity, only added to their burden.

Already carrying considerable debt from wartime borrowing, farmers were squeezed by rising production and declining demand. In 1919, they accounted for 16 percent of the national income; by 1929 it had dropped to 9 percent. Crop acreage decreased for the first time in U.S. history between 1919 and 1924, as "13 million acres were abandoned to brush." Throughout the 1920s, farm income remained below prewar levels.[12] As the historian Alan Lawson has written:

> The average annual income of the 5.8 million farm families at mid-decade was only $240, and, although modern technology and increased money at the top for land speculation had produced an elite of large growers, 54 percent of all farmers earned less than $1000 per year. Steadily, farm mortgage debt rose while commodity prices and land value declined even though the cost of manufactured goods increased and nonfarm land values almost doubled.[13]

Across the board, farmers believed they were hit by a combination of forces. A booming industrial economy had put them at a disadvantage as producers and consumers. By 1929, farming became a more "speculative business enterprise" that departed from the traditions of a productive rural economy.[14]

By mid-decade U.S industry faced similar perils as the nation's productive capacity expanded far beyond the demand of consumers. Well before the debacle on Wall Street, the domestic market spilled over with record numbers of unsold automobiles, appliances, and other consumer goods. Lewis Corey saw this in

1934: the yearly average of production of all goods between 1923 and 1929 was 5.9 percent above its "normal" rate; consumption, reflected in retail sales, was only 1.3 percent above its "normal" rate.[15] According to economic historian Richard DuBoff, business inventories had tripled between late 1928 through mid-1929.[16] David Kennedy also found that inventories nearly quadrupled in value to some $2 billion between late 1928 and the following summer.[17] By mid-decade, it was already clear that the market for new automobile sales and residential construction was saturated. The auto industry, the most dynamic of newer industries, was the first to show signs of a slowdown. Although the number of cars on American roadways increased from 9.3 million in 1921 to 23.1 million in 1929, an analysis of passenger car registrations shows that the percentage rate of increase peaked at 24 percent in 1923 and then steadily slowed until it dropped to 5 percent in 1927, the same year output of new cars decreased by 22 percent. The number of replacement buyers steadily increased, while the rate of first-time buyers declined.[18]

As inventories piled up, banks, corporations and smaller companies used various forms of consumer credit and installment buying to sustain consumer demand for new cars, but to no avail. By the late 1920s, three out of every five cars were bought on installment plans. As one historian of the Depression, Robert McElvaine, has written, "The amount of installment credit outstanding in the United States more than doubled, from $1.38 billion to $3 billion" between 1925 and 1929.[19] The boom in residential construction, which easily surpassed investment in commercial and industrial buildings in the early 1920s, also peaked by mid-decade; for one-family houses in 1925 and for multifamily apartments in 1926.[20] By 1929, Corey says, excess capacity was enormous for most American industries: they were capable of producing anywhere from 25 percent to 75 percent more goods than existing domestic markets could absorb.[21] All these trends demonstrated that the rapid expansion of installment buying still could not keep up with the rising glut of durable goods in the marketplace and warehouses. The general problem was exacerbated by the fast approaching limits of the consumers themselves, and what constituted good-risk borrowers. As Soule wrote, the only way that purchasing power could keep up with the expansion of industrial goods was "through sufficient increases in wages and salaries or through sufficient reduction in retail prices."[22] Neither occurred.

Once again, herein lay the contradictions of capitalist prosperity during the Great Boom. With productivity increases going their way, capitalists enjoyed rising profits at the expense of workers whose wages lagged far behind. Corey reports that profits in manufactures in 1929 were 22.9 percent higher than in 1923, though total wages rose only 6.1 percent. He admits that the economic revival between 1922 and 1929 was partly the result of a substantial rise in real wages due to depressed agricultural prices, which did increase mass purchasing power to some degree. Consumption was 6.5 percent higher in 1923 than it was in 1920, "an unparalleled increase." After 1923, however, the "upward movement in real wages and mass consumption slackened and came practically to a standstill." Corey reports that the yearly average of all wages for 1924 to 1928 was higher than in 1923, but he says this was "not the true measure of wages in relation to corporate profits" because it included "wages of servants and of workers in non-corporate enterprises, whose profits are not included." For Corey, industrial wages (manufactures, mining, construction, and transportation) provided a truer picture. Between 1924 and 1928, the average of industrial wages was only 0.5 percent higher than in 1923.[23]

With wages stagnant after 1925, the income gap widened between those who owned and controlled capital and those who worked for their companies. Between 1923 and 1929, the top 1 percent of Americans saw their share of the national income rise by almost a fifth; by 1929, the richest 5 percent of the population owned a third of the nation's wealth.[24] Robert McElvaine cites a Brookings Institution study, *America's Capacity to Consume*, which showed that "the top 0.1 percent of American families in 1929 had an aggregate income equal to that of the bottom 42 percent." In real numbers, about 24,000 families at the top had a combined income equal to that of 11.5 million working-class and lower-middle-class families. While disposable income per capita for all Americans rose by 9 percent between 1920 and 1929, this figure paled in comparison to the top 1 percent who benefited from a 75 percent increase. The disparity in wealth was even greater; in 1929, nearly 80 percent of America's families (21.5 million households) had no savings, compared to the top 0.1 percent (24,000 families) that held 34 percent of total savings.[25] According to Richard DuBoff, real disposable income per person between 1920 and 1929 showed an incredible disparity. Those in the top 5 percent enjoyed an increase in their share of disposable income from 24 to 34 percent. "By 1929," DuBoff wrote, "the income distribution reached another 'plateau of high inequality.'"[26] That personal debt grew much faster than disposable income after 1922 contributed to this trend.[27] In contrast, capitalists reaped profits 22.9 percent higher that year than in 1923.[28] According to two communist writers, A. B. McGill and Henry Stevens, net corporate profits increased from $7.7 billion in 1923 to $10.9 billion in 1929.[29]

Without doubt, rising wealth in the 1920s flowed disproportionately to the owners of capital. The extraordinary increase in the wealth of American capitalists was greatly due to their ability to benefit from rising productivity levels. According to historian Alan Lawson, capitalist ownership enjoyed a "30 percent rise in productivity per worker from 1921 to 1929."[30] Political scientist Alan Dawley comes up with almost the same statistic (32 percent between 1922 and 1929) and then compares it to the 8 percent increase in wages for the same period. The numbers, which he says were ignored at the time, "harbored a hidden time bomb."[31]

In the final analysis, declining purchasing power added to the economic distress experienced by the mass of working people and undercut the hype about growing prosperity for all. "Almost 8 percent of workers in the industrial sector were unemployed," Alan Lawson says, "a consequence of technological advances and higher worker productivity that the euphoria of progress overshadowed."

Citing the 1934 study by the Brookings Institution, Lawson described the realities of life for millions of Americans in the previous decade: more than 70 million persons in over 60 percent of America's families "subsisted at less than the $2000 per year needed to acquire basic necessities." Only 25 percent of the 21.6 million nonfarm families had enough income for an adequate diet. "Especially ominous for the economy," he wrote, "was the unheeded downslide that most people experienced even before the Great Crash; between 1928 and 1929, the meager overall rise in income since World War I reversed into a 4 percent decline for 93 percent of the nonfarm population."[32]

Income at the top soared as a result of the growing concentration of wealth and centralization of corporate control over the economy. More and more corporate wealth fell into the hands of fewer capitalists. The magnates of industry and finance became an even greater economic and political force through corporate consolidation and mergers. The number of recorded mergers in manufacturing and mining increased from 438 in 1919 to 1,245 in 1929; the total share of net income of the wealthiest 5 percent increased from 76.7 percent to 84 percent.[33] Five years after the stock market crash, Lewis Corey provided a precise breakdown. In 1923, the largest 1,026 corporations, 0.26 percent of all, received 47.9 percent of all net corporate income. Six years later, the largest 1,349 corporations, again 0.26 percent of total, received 60.3 percent of all corporate net income.[34] Meanwhile, 8,000 businesses went down during the same period.[35]

Horizontal mergers pulled together leading companies in the production of steel, chemicals, food products, primary metals, non-electrical machinery, and coal which often led to the emergence of a giant "number two firm." The merger movement traversed the whole spectrum of capitalist enterprises, among them General Motors, Chrysler, B. F. Goodrich, Caterpillar Tractor, United Aircraft, General Mills, and leading petroleum companies. General Foods Corporation was the first diversified food giant.[36] Electric light and power companies led the merger movement. According to William Leuchtenburg, by the end of the decade, the United States was producing more electric power "than all the rest of the world combined." Holding companies merged small firms into "great utility empires" that caused over 3,700 local utilities to disappear between 1919 and 1927. Following the same trend, larger banks swallowed up smaller ones, and then created branches. Between 1920 and 1930, the number of branch banks rose from 1,280 to 3,516. "By 1929, one percent of the financial institutions in the country controlled over 46 percent of the nation's banking resources." The merger movement, Leuchtenburg wrote, "had reached boom proportions. By 1929, the 200 largest non-financial corporations in America owned nearly half the corporate wealth of the nation, and they were growing much faster than smaller businesses." The same processes were at work in banking. The number of bank mergers increased from 80 in 1919 to 259 in 1927.[37]

With wealth more concentrated at the top, it fell to the leading institutions of finance capital to keep the consumer economy buoyant by providing cheap money to those who had enough income to consume. The result was a short-lived recovery in 1928 and the first half of 1929. But the "final spurt," as George Soule put it, was the by-product of increasing speculation rather than further expansion of the productive economy. Thanks to huge cash reserves from productivity increases, large corporations were awash in cash and in no need of commercial credit from banks. This compelled them to engage in speculative lending, especially to individual investors and stockbrokers. Such was the impetus for the Great Bull Market that quickly transformed the purchase of stocks based on their actual value to prices that primarily reflected the inflated value of constant resale for quick profit. As businesses entered recession in 1927, the stock market kept rising. The Federal Reserve added to the speculative mania. In the second half of 1927, the Fed fueled the flow of easy money toward speculation in the stock market by lowering the discount rate from 4 to 3.5 percent, causing loans and investments among its member banks to shoot up by almost $1.8 billion in the same period, although only 7 percent of the increase went toward commercial loans. "Much of the credit," as George Soule wrote, "flowed into stock market speculation, brokers' loans on the New York Stock Exchange rising 24 percent." The whole process of financing speculation by corporations and banks ultimately fell to the control of the speculators themselves. Financiers acquired new status as the chief promoters of economic growth. Meanwhile, the most fortunate sectors of the corporate and business economy benefited in the form of large salaries and dividends. By 1929, dividends amounted to 7.2 percent of total national income.[38]

That everyone was becoming rich from the stock market was just ballyhoo. According to Robert McElvaine, the actual distribution of dividends tells the real story. Just before the crash, stock ownership had become extremely centralized. Only 4 million out of the total U.S. population of approximately 120 million owned stock that year; 1.5 million of those held enough stocks to warrant an account with a broker. In fact, the vast majority of stockholders owned little stock at all. According to McElvaine:

> Almost 74 percent of all 1929 dividends went to the fewer than 600,000 individual stockholders with taxable incomes in excess of $5,000. Just under 25 percent went to the 24,000 taking in over $100,000 for the year, and nearly 6 percent of all dividends went to 513 individuals whose families reported an income more than $1 million for the year.[39]

Perhaps the best explanation of the causes of the Great Depression was provided by Lewis Corey with the 1934 publication of *The Decline of American Capitalism*. From his meticulous use of statistical evidence combed from all available sources, Corey demonstrated that contradictions in capitalist accumulation during the 1920s were the root cause of the general crisis of U.S. capitalism. Applying Karl Marx's approach and method to the study of political economy, Corey was able to show how the unprecedented buildup of the means of production served to raise overall profits to the biggest capitalists at the expense of workers who were displaced or removed from employment.

For Corey, one contradiction was primary: in the economic expansion of the Great Boom between 1923 and 1929, constant capital in manufactures grew significantly more than variable capital. As the number of machines grew, fewer workers were needed. Affirming one of Marx's principal arguments about capitalist accumulation, Corey showed that the average wages for American workers in 1929 was nearly the same as in 1923. As the capitalist mode of production expanded to new heights based on the growth of constant capital, profits soared while wages fell. Here was the contradiction based on Marxist political economy: "Wages *must* decrease as the composition of capital becomes higher: larger capital investment requires larger profits, and more capital is invested in the constant than in the variable form." For Corey, as for Marx, capitalist growth made labor increasingly superfluous.[40] As Corey said:

> The most characteristic expression of the decline of capitalism is the misery of an increasing "surplus population" of unemployed and unemployable workers (including professionals), who barely exist on the "rations" of reluctant charity, meager unemployment insurance, or poor relief.[41]

Corey saw another significant development: the multiplication of stockholders led to "a financial oligarchy" made up of representatives from the largest banks and financial houses. While profits of non-financial corporations between 1923 and 1929 rose 14 percent from $5 billion to $5.6 billion, those of financial corporations (including banks, finance, and holding companies) were much greater, what Corey called "a phenomenal increase" of 177 percent, from $879 million to $2.4 billion. The whole process became even more "frenzied" in the two-year period leading up to the crash, prompting Corey to conclude: "Finance capital, interested more in the speculative production of profits than in the production of goods, dominates industry; the appropriation of surplus value and profits is increasingly separated from their production." Consequently, corporations greatly increased disbursements to investors. Dividends (excluding intercorporate dividends) in the same six-year period rose from $3.3 billion to $5.8 billion and interest payments from $3.3 billion to almost $5 billion. While the average yearly increase in industrial wages was only 0.5 percent, the income for stockholders was significantly greater at 16.4 percent. [42]

In this increasingly speculative economic climate Corey also detected a growing need for the upper classes to sustain consumption by purchasing luxury goods. Despite the clamor about mass consumption and mass markets, economic growth relied on a leap in conspicuous consumption during the 1923–1929 period, primarily by those who could afford to consume the most expensive goods. Although installment buying had pulled in the middle class, the burden of sustainable consumption fell steadily to the wealthier classes. This was evident by mid-decade when the extension of credit and an avalanche of advertising could not bridge the widening gap between excess capacity and slackening demand. As Corey wrote, luxury goods were always important in capitalism because they were ruling-class necessities and desires. However, they were never more central to the history of capitalism than during the 1920s:

> As mass markets are saturated because of the limited conditions of mass consumption, an increase in production, other than capital goods, comes to depend upon "those people who have buying surplus, who buy for style, change, whim, fancy," and whose incomes, particularly the speculative, rise steadily during prosperity. Surplus capital flows into luxury or variety production, where low wages and the lower composition of capital (more variable than constant) yield an exceptionally high rate of profit. This eases the pressure of surplus capital on the rate of

profit in other industries. But the high rate of profit in variety production eventually tends to fall, because of excess capacity and competition and because modern luxury production often requires large fixed capital.[43]

Even as the rich played a growing role in perpetuating prosperity, they only hastened the day when all would face the consequences of a contradictory system on the verge of a profound crisis.

A WORLD-HISTORICAL APPROACH to the study of fascism is critical to understanding why it emerged as a distinct form of politics in the opening decades of the twentieth century. For one thing, it enables us to transcend the myopia that fascism was for the most part a European political form. This was already clear to the Marxist economist Paul Baran in 1952 when, in the midst of anti-communist hysteria fueled by Senator Joseph McCarthy, he warned Americans of "the widely observable complacency" about "the danger of fascism in this country." It had permeated "the political thinking of the so-called general public, of the conformist intellectuals, and of the kept press." To see fascism only from the standpoint of its Italian and German characteristics, Baran said, was "quite misleading." To determine whether something was fascist on the basis of Italian and German examples—extreme and violent mass movements led by men in black or brown shirts, racist and anti-Semitic at their core, "illiberal" and "intolerant of opposition, hostile to civil liberties and human rights"—only reinforced the "complacency" Baran observed in the American public about the threat of a particular form of fascism developing from within.[44]

There were reasons why the majority of Americans were complacent. The myopic tendency to see all things fascist through a European lens put too much focus on the "*forms* of political events" and "insufficient attention to their social content and historical significance." Baran did not discount the importance of knowing all about the forms themselves. But it was more crucial to recognize that they varied "from country to country and from period to period, and that it is only through understanding the economic and social *substance* of the historical process that specific political events can be seen in their proper light." From this standpoint, Baran wrote:

> Fascism is a political system evolved by capitalist societies in the age of imperialism, wars, and social and national revolutions. It is designed to strengthen the state as an instrument of capitalist domination and to adapt it to the requirements of intensified class struggle on the national and/or international scene.[45]

Baran's view of fascism as a global phenomenon rooted in capitalist development, specifically a crisis of the system that intensified the class struggle and required the capitalist class to rely on the greater coercive power of the state, marked the continuation of a budding discourse on fascism that began in the 1930s. At that time, Big Business and Wall Street were seen as the driving forces of fascism in the United States. As A. B. Magil and Henry Stevens wrote in *The Peril of Fascism* (1938), its "germ" inhered within American monopoly capitalism.[46] Magil and Stevens had recognized that the mechanisms of fascist oppression were already emerging in the prosperity of the 1920s but became "a definite political force of ominous proportions" in the Great Depression that followed.[47] Given their main objective as members of the Communist Party in 1938 to forge a democratic, popular front against fascism at home and abroad, the two writers focused on the authoritarian, coercive, and terrorist processes they defined as fascist.

But as we have seen, the germ of American fascism within monopoly capitalism went much deeper than Magil and Stevens thought. Lewis Corey, a more formidable Marxist with detailed knowledge of political economy, had already pointed to this in 1934 in his analysis of the causes of the Great Depression. Corey examined the anatomy of capitalist production and exchange of American capitalism in the 1920s and early 1930s from the standpoint of one of Marx's central tenets in *Capital*, what he called the "general law" of capitalist accumulation. In so doing, Corey showed that economic growth during the Great Boom of 1922–1929 only furthered the unbridgeable divide between capital and labor, owner and worker, class against class. While the capitalist ruling class reaped more wealth and power, the rest of society was consigned to greater unemployment and poverty in the midst of plenty—until the bust that was inevitable.

For Corey in 1934, the general crisis that inhered in the boom was a clear sign of American capitalism in decline and decay, its ruling class driven toward state monopoly capitalism—with fascism as a last resort—to maintain its rule over society by eviscerating liberal democracy while always looking to snuff out working-class radicalism and a socialist alternative. Although a brilliant Marxist autodidact, Corey still fell short of grasping the full potential of the United States to save itself from economic collapse as the world's banker and leading creditor. For Corey, the contradictions seemed too advanced for him to consider what actually did occur: Roosevelt's second New Deal in 1935 and his complete embrace of Keynesianism, or what some of his closest advisers called a compensatory economy based on permanent government intervention in 1938. This was pivotal to recovery and based partly on preparing for war industrially to fight fascism elsewhere in the world.

Still, from the perspective of the present, Corey was accurate in discerning the essential characteristics of U.S. monopoly-finance capitalism and, to some extent, the future course of the American Empire. Throughout the interwar period of boom and bust in the United States, the advance of monopoly-finance capital was palpable and incontrovertible: greater centralization of wealth and power among fewer capitalists with state power falling increasingly into the hands of the executive branches of government. In the process, Big Business and the government built what Magil and Stevens described as an "entire mechanism of repression" to save the capitalist order in the 1920s, clearly fascist in character once the crisis struck. The power of capital to dominate society and the individual in the most advanced capitalist society required methods of persuasion and manipulation as well, which Corey, Magil, and Stevens observed though not fully. Capitalist rule also came to depend on the capacities of advertising, public relations, and propaganda to manufacture consent. It meant the class-conscious effort of its gurus to construct a spectacle of prosperity that dazzled the masses and drove them toward more acquisitiveness. Throughout boom and bust, however, the power of American finance capital and Wall Street—the "fountainhead" of fascism in the United States—prevailed and ultimately became greater in its magnitude and reach.

Contemporary U.S. history clearly reveals two fundamental trends that have long been ignored, marginalized, or trivialized in the liberal historiography of the 1920s and 1930s, past and present alike. While the reproduction of capital furthered the centralization of ownership toward a financial oligarchy, the oligarchs used state power to advance, preserve, and protect ruling-class interests at the expense of democracy. This was true of Republicans and Democrats. After contradictions in capitalist accumulation set off a crisis in 1929, the ruling capitalist class forged new means to keep a Pax Americana intact, the social-democratic welfare state, that is, until the Second World War brought the United States out of the Depression with another round of massive capital accumulation based on the formation of a permanent war economy. This is the history of the interwar period that also reveals the genesis of fascist processes, terrorist and non-terrorist, aimed at the domination of capital over society, the individual, and nature—in the march of monopoly-finance capitalism toward centralization of ownership and authoritarian control of constitutional-democratic government.

From another perspective, fascist processes undermined the concept of citizenship at the heart of liberal capitalist democracy. As capital extended its powers over society and the individual, the citizen was transformed into a consumer who had been convinced by advertising and propaganda that real democracy was in the marketplace and not in the polling place. The quest for greater and greater profits on the part of the ruling class was based on its mantra of making business the compass for all Americans. The businessman was the new hero, who, in serving his community, did so as a True American. Business was becoming a system of power in its own right. Capitalist owners depended less on their guns at home—but certainly not abroad!—following the Red Scare of the early 1920s and relied more on advertising, public relations, and propaganda to persuade and manipulate the public into believing that capitalism in the New Era would fulfill their dreams of wealth, security, and comfort. On top of general repression brought by the steady advance of state power in their hands, the ruling oligarchy sought further success by turning the public into a commodity, adding to the "masquerade" of a coming American fascism in the name of democracy and the "shibboleths of old-fashioned Americanism" that Magil, Stevens, and others saw clearly as imminent and perilous during the Great Depression of the 1930s.[48]

PART 2

The General Crisis and Embryonic Fascism in the 1930s

7—"Years of the Locust" and the Call for a Mussolini

THE WORST PHASE of the Great Depression between the Wall Street crash of 1929 and the beginning of Franklin Roosevelt's presidency in March 1933 cast doubt about the future of the American economy and the ability of the federal government to end the crisis. Mass unemployment and deprivation fueled tremendous anger at Roosevelt's predecessor, Herbert Hoover, who had refused to commit the federal government to intervene directly to end the three-year crisis. It had proven so costly to man and nature that the writer Gilbert Seldes chose *The Years of the Locust* as the title of his 1933 book. Seldes was unsparing in his criticism of business leaders who had insisted throughout the crisis that there was nothing fundamentally wrong with the economy. Nor did he care much for their cheerleaders in the press who used every opportunity to declare the long-awaited turnaround whenever the slightest uptick appeared. Seldes reserved most of his contempt for Hoover himself. The man Americans knew as the Great Engineer and had personified the spirit of rugged individualism now stood truly alone. Scorned by the masses who felt betrayed, his Big Business supporters watched him dangle in the wind of public opinion.

Here was a man whose substantial personal fortune, after all, had been made in stocks. Less than a year after he became president, the stock market collapsed.

As the crisis deepened, Hoover remained adamant that any deviation from core American values of self-sufficiency and resiliency even in such harsh times would be disastrous to the nation's future. By the end of 1932, his insensitivity to the plight of those who sought his understanding and compassion had become legend. For Seldes, there were no limits to Hoover's bungling. He refused to meet with bedraggled Great War veterans who made up the Bonus Expeditionary Forces (BEF)—also known as the Bonus Army—who had found their way to the capital, many with their worn-out wives and hungry children behind them, hoping their president would help them receive the bonus pay promised to them more than a decade earlier. It was so desperately needed by many of these men, who only a few years earlier had been gainfully employed in a range of middle-class enterprises, or who had been well-paid workers. Instead, Hoover ordered his sabre-rattling Army Chief of Staff, Douglas MacArthur, to break up the billets and encampments in parts of the city where the veterans and their families had assembled. Once they were cleared out, Hoover lost no time and spared no effort to justify the action as the necessary removal of communists or those duped by them. Yet Hoover was always quick to invite celebrities to the White House. On one occasion, the popular crooner Rudy Vallee was invited to sing a song Hoover had asked VecyE to write about life being "a bowl of Cherries" and why not to take it "serious" because it's "too mysterious." This was all Seldes needed to call Hoover a "psychologically stupid" man "who stood still and met every shock, lacking the mental agility to dodge."[1]

More than a decade had passed since Warren Harding had entered the White House in 1920 as the middle-class backslapper who immediately became the facilitator-in-chief for capitalist modernization on behalf of the ruling class. Now it was Hoover's turn to be the stolid standard bearer of economic recovery. Hoover felt secure, believing that the force field of bourgeois ideology he had helped to create during the prosperous 1920s could withstand the anger of the masses. Another keen observer at the time, Jonathan Norton Leonard, characterized the smug security of the oligarchs who "except for the financial screw-balls whose 'empires' were cracking under their feet," were not all that worried:

> Money might be scarce—scarce enough to make them lay up the yacht and shutter a couple of country places—but nothing alarming. The rich understood depressions. They believed correctly that they were among the inevitable consequences of "free enterprise" running at large in an industrial country. They did not welcome them wholly for they knew how hard they were on the poor, who had a regrettable tendency to fight back, but they realized that they offered fine chances for a level-headed man with a good lump of capital. All he had to do was sit tight. If hard times lasted long enough, he would be able to pick up all sorts of tidbits dropped by lesser men whose personal requirements had eaten up their reserves.[2]

Even the lowest point of the Great Depression "was no mere rich man's panic." Instead,

> theirs was the complacent panic of prairie dogs skittering down their safe deep holes ahead of a tornado. They knew the storm was coming, but they knew what to do and had the means to do it. Buy bonds. Get rid of half the servants. Whistle the wife and girls back from Palm Beach. Comb out the pay roll and pull your neck in. Such measures will bring you out richer at the other end. It doesn't do any harm, of course, to make a noise as if you were being hurt. It makes those who are really being hurt feel better.[3]

The writer Edmund Wilson observed this mindset in the renegade big-time banker Dwight Morrow who was running for the senate in New Jersey. Wilson's account of Morrow was among many revealing stories about people from all walks of life from October of 1930 to October 1931 that made up the content of his 1933 book *The American Jitters*. Wilson recalled Morrow's speech at his campaign kickoff rally in Newark. Morrow praised Hoover for continuing to talk about the 1920s as "a period of almost unparalleled prosperity" and how it had raised "the standard of living of the great majority of our people in all parts of the country." Morrow admitted that the country was in the throes of a deep economic crisis, but this would end, repeating Hoover's standard litany of calling on the people to remain confident and firm about the bright prospects that lay not far ahead. That's what would "pull them through." He was sure that "every employer who has faith is doing something to end the Depression" and called on workers to do their part. Morrow shared another point uttered by many capitalists: "There is something about too much prosperity that ruins the fibre of the people." Remember, he said, "men and women that built this country . . . were reared in adversity." He advised political leaders in Trenton, the state capital, to follow their predecessors and hold the line themselves. Don't ask the federal government to relieve you of your own difficulties. Recovery and renewed prosperity could only be achieved by those who have "the courage of the men who built the city and by its industrial leaders who maintain their organizations until the turn comes."[4]

By the end of 1932, all talk about confidence, sacrifice, and resilience had run its course. Unemployment had soared to almost a quarter of the working population, and, given the lack of hard data, this was no doubt an underestimate. Banks were failing at record numbers. Farmers heavily in debt who faced foreclosure often put their shotguns in the face of the local sheriff who showed up with eviction papers. Much of the nation was in economic distress to varying degrees. But the middle classes, old and new—the small merchant and businessman, banker, manufacturer, salaried employee—had lost more than anyone since the Wall Street crash. Among them were souls who just could not take it anymore.

Edmund Wilson described the plight of three people on the day of March 25, 1931, all immigrants, in the chapter titled "A Bad Day in Brooklyn." All three had done what they could to stay afloat, then lost hope and tried suicide—and failed to the one. But many others succeeded. According to journalist and author Edward Robb Ellis, one who did see it through dramatically was Gan Kolski, an unemployed artist in New York City. Before leaping to his death from the George Washington Bridge, Kolski wrote a few parting words to those he left behind: "To All: If you cannot hear the cry of starving millions, listen to the dead, brothers. Your economic system is dead."[5]

But was it? And if so, was a revolution at hand?

A Revolutionary Moment?

Recent historians have played down suggestions that the worst years of the Depression presented a moment of revolution in America. One of the most prominent, David Kennedy, has written that the "cries of impending revolution were largely empty rhetorical posturings."[6] Contemporary accounts suggest a more complex condition.

In a compelling book later published as a personal memoir, Matthew Josephson described the "waves of panic" and "panorama of unrest" in the winter and spring of 1932, especially in small towns and rural areas where thousands of banks had closed and low crop prices were ruining farmers. Sifting through his collection of newspaper clippings and notes, Josephson later recalled the stories of rural violence often downplayed or simply ignored by the larger metropolitan papers. Here, he noted, was the unreported or underreported history of the period. Farmers in the Pacific Northwest and upper Mississippi Valley, who once prided themselves as Republican voters and now "thought nothing of breaking the law," picked up their shotguns, barricaded roads, overturned delivery trucks, and often mobbed police officers trying to protect agents of banks and insurance companies from foreclosing on properties. Tax collectors went about their work in constant fear of being beaten or worse. In some midwestern states, governors were forced to call out militias to keep order. Farmers and small-town folk talked of revolution, not the socialist kind for sure, but an action in defense of their land and their homes. For many rural Americans, revolution meant taking up their small arms and putting them to use against the big "eastern bankers" who had saddled them with mountainous debt.[7]

Similar conditions and fears existed in the cities. A widespread sense that the government was doing little to relieve the suffering of the unemployed and underemployed only served to promote a feeling of imminent upheaval. David Kennedy cites the example of Chicago's mayor, Anton Cermak, who told a congressional committee that the federal government had a choice: send relief or troops to his city.[8] Another historian of the Depression, Robert McElvaine, recalls that organized labor feared the same. He cites Edward F. McGrady, vice president of the American Federation of Labor, who declared that a revolution was clearly on the horizon "if nothing is done at once to create work for the unemployed or to meet their needs in some other way."[9]

There was plenty of despair and anger throughout much of society. In the defense of powerful interests in the cities, police treated any protest or rally by the hungry and the homeless as the work of communists. Jonathan Norton Leonard described this reaction in Chicago during the summer of 1931 when unemployment climbed dramatically, especially in the Negro section where half of the men were unemployed and home evictions spiked. Agents sent by landlords started showing up to evict families, but only after they determined the men were not at home. Once the men got wise to this tactic, "a marvelously effective method was discovered." The whole neighborhood gathered to meet the agents the next time they appeared at someone's doorstep. The agents were powerless as police sympathetic to the neighbors stood by. "There was very little disorder," Leonard recalled, "but the Negroes would stay packed tight for hours, sometimes singing hymns, sometimes

with African cheerfulness making a gay party of the occasion."
Meanwhile the bankers who held the mortgages on such homes
were furious and cried that "it threatened all sorts of sacred
American institutions." It didn't take long for the *Chicago Tribune*
to blame it on "Communist devils" because it was "long believed
that Moscow was about to take Chicago over" and now the paper
was "sure of it."[10]

Radicalism was surely in the political wind though most of
the radicals were anything but communists. Seldes saw this in
1933. "The spearhead of an American revolution may be a compact and disciplined Communist Party," he wrote, "but the spirit
of revolution in the conservative farmer and the loyal citizen is
more important."[11] Seldes noted that throughout the worst three
years of the Depression, only one of five "mass movements," as he
called them, was communist inspired, and that one began peacefully and with police permission as 3,000 unemployed workers
marched from downtown Detroit to the Ford Motor Company
plant in nearby Dearborn. The march turned into a riot when the
chief of Ford's private police force drove his car into the marchers
and fired on them. The peaceful and legal march devolved into
a full-scale riot when police and Ford's private cops fired again,
this time using a machine gun. When the crowd broke and ran,
four were dead in the street and many others wounded. The other
four movements consisted of food riots and industrial disputes in
Arkansas, Oklahoma, Pennsylvania, and North Carolina, all the
"work of respectable and even reactionary citizens, farmers, veterans and the dispossessed of the middle class."[12]

Nevertheless, Seldes was not sure if the crisis had generated
conditions sufficient for a systemic revolutionary upheaval in
1932. This was hotly debated by writers who had turned to communism or were influenced by it. Edmund Wilson suggested that
what Karl Marx had deemed essential for any revolution against
capitalism was the necessity of the subjective factor, namely,
class consciousness. "We have not even after two years of depression," Wilson wrote, "seen the general cleavage of society into a

conscious bourgeoisie and a conscious proletariat" nor "a general conflict between these two classes."[13] As for the middle class, Wilson asserted that what made Marx a master economist was his "psychological insight" into the "instinctive workings of human acquisitiveness, selfishness, and self-deception," all of which were present in "liberal-minded bourgeois" such as himself "who at first sight seem to have no real stake in the present order, who in fact would seem to have many reasons for wishing to see it superseded, yet cling to it with such tenacity, remain so obstinately oblivious of what is happening."[14] Examining his own consciousness, Wilson was as unsparing in his self-criticism as he was in his critique of Dwight Morrow:

> For one thing, of course, they are simply lazy, they simply don't want to be disturbed. But for another they depend more than they realize on an assurance of superiority to other people. A bourgeois is brought up with the conviction that he is better than a workingman and though he may be as sensitive and intelligent and liberal-minded as possible, that conviction means a good deal to him. It means much more than people usually admit: we have been told so much about American democracy that we hate to believe this is true. But imagine some of the most amiable bourgeois of your acquaintance in a society which did not allow them special privileges, which did not lend itself to their illusion of superiority. Their self-confidence and self-respect would wilt—some would grow peevish and disagreeable, others would get discouraged and die. And that is one reason, I take it, for the present attitude of many of the American liberals. Why otherwise, in spite of their liberalism, do they fight so—as their extreme skittishness about Russia shows they do—against the idea of a classless society?[15]

In a remarkable self-assessment as a troubled petty-bourgeois intellectual whose combination of family means and modest inheritances enabled him to enjoy classical studies and good liquor and engage in generally irresponsible behavior, Wilson summed up a most enigmatic moment in the middle-class mindset:

> What we have then at the present time is an economic crisis due to capitalist contradictions and beginning to produce actual class conflicts; a general collapse of morale due to the deflation of capitalist ideals; but at the same time a general persistence of what the Communists would call the bourgeois "ideology" which makes people value bourgeois social position. [16]

If America was indeed at the point of revolution as many thought or feared, the Communist Party of the United States of America (CPUSA) had little part in it. Unquestionably, the Party tried hard to play a leading role in unmasking the plight of the millions of unemployed and the underemployed. It created unemployment councils across the country and successfully organized a series of nationwide protests in March 1930. It vigorously supported efforts in Congress to pass a federal comprehensive unemployment insurance bill, which helped pave the way for the Social Security Act in 1935. Party cadre waged relentless struggles against discrimination and succeeded in creating an interracial organization in the North. In the South, it fought tremendous odds to create a mostly black Sharecroppers Union in 1931. And it won widespread support for its role in the Scottsboro Case, helping to save the lives of nine young black men charged with the rape of two white women, which went all the way to the Supreme Court's declaration of a mistrial in November 1932. It was also one of the first organizations to warn Americans about the threat of fascism, internally and abroad, and the global war it would bring.

For all its hard work and courage, the Party failed to turn mass misery into a mass revolutionary movement. Top Party leaders could not devise a program of strategy and tactics that might transform the unemployment councils into a unified organization. Despite a profound crisis that revolutionary theory indicated was ripe for a mass movement, the Party did not grow and the revolution never happened. Much of the blame was due to the Party itself. Party leaders had instructed cadre to build revolutionary fervor among poorly educated workers through internationalism with slogans that called for the "Defense of Chinese Socialists" or the need to wage constant combat against liberals and socialists, who were nothing but "social-fascists."[17] All this flowed from the Party's political line that adhered strictly to political positionS of the Communist International in 1928. All leftist forces to the right of the communists, liberals and socialists alike, had compromised with capitalism and were therefore in a permanent state of decline and decay. For the communists it was either real socialism and progress or fascism and barbarism. For the capitalists, the latter was its last resort. Meetings typically involved long and fruitless discussions on how best to apply the Party's line to existing conditions rather than examine them and then struggle over whether the line furthered or impeded the objectives. At the same time, organizers on the ground often ignored such directives from top leadership, which they considered irrelevant or even antagonistic to the immediate needs of the people they were attempting to organize, and which drove them as communists to press for immediate and sensible demands.

Edmund Wilson grasped the main problem of the Communist Party's inability to connect with the American people when he observed its leader, William Z. Foster. Summoned to a congressional committee investigating the communist movement in the United States, Foster used the occasion as a pretext for "propagandist speeches." This was typical of Party comrades who were first and foremost expected to advance the Party's position on a range of issues. What especially troubled Wilson, who had been drawn to Marxism and its method of engaging society on the ground floor, was Foster's language. Simply put, it was "quite alien to anything which has hitherto been characteristic of even the militant American workman—it is the idiom of Russian Communism." Foster dealt in ideologies rather than ideas. Even more annoying was his talk about "liquidating" things, which communists considered the proper term to simply mean getting rid of something. Wilson wrote:

> In Russia, they liquidated the *kulaks* [rich peasant farmers], they liquidated the Church—and the Soviet prosecutor has recently demanded that the traitorous engineers be liquidated—in other words, shot. The House Committee may well have been puzzled by Foster's continual talk of liquidation applied to everything from the collapse of capitalism to the dispersal of a recent Communist demonstration by the Capitol police.[18]

Despite its many failures and shortcomings, the Party kept trade unionism alive in the early 1930s by abandoning attempts to build its own unions. It learned to do a better job of developing sensible and familiar revolutionary slogans to be used against reaction and the threat of fascism within the existing structure of American bourgeois democracy. At mid-decade it would help lay the foundation for a popular front by correcting the broadly—and poorly—defined line of the Communist International that drew no distinction between fascist and democratic forms of government.

THE ECONOMIC NOSEDIVE AND MASS SUFFERING

Little effort had been made by financiers or government officials to cool down the speculative fever on Wall Street in the months leading up to the 1929 crash, which actually occurred over a span of several days. The Federal Reserve had raised the discount rate in August 1929 in an attempt to increase the cost of call money borrowed to buy stocks on margin. But nothing could halt the mad rush to quick profits. The bull market peaked at the beginning of September and then became increasingly unstable. The plunge began on October 24, Black Thursday, with complete devastation the following Monday and Tuesday when rampant selling erased 21 to 23 percent of the value of all stocks. So began the long and painful slide to the bottom in July 1932, as stock values on average fell 89 percent below the September 1929 peak.[19] Investors who had gorged themselves in the feeding frenzy tried to arrange more loans to cover their losses. But borrowing became more difficult and many went bust. This made matters worse for lenders whose loans went bad.[20]

The result was an unprecedented economic collapse, the worst in the five-hundred-year history of capitalism. During the last quarter of 1930, U.S. industrial production dropped 26 percent below the 1929 average, compared to 13 percent abroad; a year later it dropped by 40 percent at home, 21 percent abroad. By August 1932, the figures were 51 percent and 31 percent respectively.[21] It was indeed a nosedive. From the pinnacle of prosperity in 1929 to the abyss in 1933, GNP fell 29 percent, consumption expenditures 18 percent, construction 78 percent, and investment 98 percent. Construction, which had peaked in 1925, fell 26 percent in 1930, 29 percent in 1931, and 47 percent in 1932.[22] The number of automobiles coming off assembly lines dropped from 440,000 in August 1929 to 92,500 in December. Across the board, corporations cut production to reduce inventories. Sales of durables and other consumer goods fell precipitously as declining demand caused prices to drop.[23] Farm prices fell more than any other category of commodities. As a result, more farmers went into greater debt. By 1931 nearly 40 percent of all farms in America were mortgaged, up from 30.8 percent in 1925.[24]

The deflationary trajectory of the U.S. economy extended to foreign trade, which declined from $9.6 billion in 1929 to $2.9 billion in 1932, or nearly 70 percent.[25] Enormous surplus in exported goods, as well as dollars, piled up with no outlets to absorb them. Foreign issues on the New York Stock Exchange fell from a billion in 1928 to 229 million in 1931, and then to zero in 1932.[26] Charles Kindleberger, one of the foremost economic analysts of the Great Depression, succinctly summed up the impact of the stock market's rise and fall on U.S. foreign trade: "On the rise, the stock market cut off capital movements to the developing countries; in decline, it produced a liquidity crisis that led to rapid reduction in these countries' exports. The process fed back to the United States. By the turn of the year, U.S. exports had turned sharply downward."[27]

Failure by U.S. lenders and policymakers to shoulder the responsibility of the United States as the world's leading creditor nation had resulted in haphazard foreign lending and direct investment. As labor historian Broadus Mitchell pointed out in the late 1940s, loans to Europe and Latin America during the 1920s were "lavish and reckless," while at the same time setting up their borrowers to develop respective national economies on the basis of consumption levels that required a continuing volume of foreign trade. Consequently, if U.S. lenders suddenly changed priorities, the impact on these economies, especially in Latin America and other parts of the developing world, would unleash great instability and only make U.S. interests in those countries more insecure. This is precisely what happened in mid-1928 when U.S. lenders decided to cash in on the quick profits to be made in stocks rather than to continue lending abroad—the immediate trigger for Germany's plunge into fascism a few years later. New issues for foreign accounts, which had amounted to a little over $1 billion in 1928, fell to $415 million in 1929. With the exception of a brief reversal in 1930, the total of new loans made abroad dwindled to a mere $51 million in 1932. The amount of dollars supplied abroad also fell precipitously, from $7.4 billion in 1929 to $2.4 billion in 1932. As the Depression deepened, U.S. imports declined from roughly $4.4 billion in 1929, to a little over $3 billion in 1930, a little over $2 billion in 1931, and then to $1.3 billion in 1932. As a result of all these developments, national income in the United States fell to its lowest point in 1932, and did not recover until the coming of the Second World War.[28]

As economic conditions worsened, unemployment rose from 3.2 percent in 1929 to 24.9 percent in 1933.[29] Counting the number of unemployed Americans was highly problematic due to scant government reporting on unemployment. Consequently, officials had to rely on estimates provided by a half-dozen agencies, public and private. Analysts first arrived at an estimate of the total labor force and then another for those who were employed. Unemployment was then determined roughly by subtracting the second number from the first. In the midst of the worst economic depression in history, arguably the most modern government in the world still could not provide hard-and-fast numbers on employment. While the White House reported 3.1 million out of work in April 1930, the Commerce Department put the figure significantly higher at 4.5 million.[30]

From the existing evidence, certain patterns and trends in employment were evident. Unemployment rates were especially high among workers engaged in the production of durable goods—cars and appliances the most important—and in construction. Generally, unskilled workers were hit hard because production cuts downgraded many skilled workers into their ranks. Much of America's unemployed lived in its most populous cities, but as Broadus Mitchell keenly pointed out, the evidence showed that "the percentage of employable persons unemployed appears to have been largest in small towns and villages." Mitchell also said that no group felt the cruelties of unemployment more than young people.[31] By 1932 two million vagrants, many of them young people, were roaming the country. Two-thirds of Detroit's population was out of work or underemployed, the latter statistic only a rough estimate since the city lacked any precise way of determining it.[32]

Throughout much of the nation, living standards deteriorated steadily, creating a paradox of capitalist crisis—hunger amid abundance. While Americans starved or lacked adequate daily sustenance, farmers and ranchers destroyed their own capital because they saw no profit in it. Untold acres of wheat across Montana were left to rot in the fields, as were apples and peaches in the orchards of California and Oregon and cotton in Texas and Oklahoma. Ranchers killed their cattle and sheep because they could not afford to feed them. To stay warm, farmers in Kansas burned their wheat crops. Nearly thirty states had established barter systems so people could exchange products they needed to survive.[33] Broadus Mitchell reported on the horrific conditions in West Virginia where coal mines were no longer working in the summer of 1932:

> The miners occupied the mine shacks, had coal enough, walked miles to Morgantown for Red Cross flour when issued, started gardens from charity seed, lived to a large extent on blackberries. Some had almost no furniture, and slept on straw ticks on the floor. In one camp with several hundred people, including many babies, there was no soap, the women making a sort of suds from soap weed. The one cow in the settlement was half starved herself, and gave blue milk.[34]

In his 1933 book *Seeds of Revolt*, Mauritz Hallgren estimated that "perhaps as many as ten to eleven million of the sixteen million persons reported unemployed in the spring of 1933 belonged to the lower middle class."[35] But this was merely the result of a long process of dispossession over decades of the advance of monopoly that greatly accelerated during the 1920s. He wrote:

> Not a few of the petit-bourgeois victims of the panic—or rather of modern capitalism—had struggled through the best years of their lives to follow, as they thought, that upward path of individualism which Mr. Hoover, though he did not practice it himself, considered the only truly American way of social and economic progress. They had bought homes, automobiles, radios, furniture, had amassed something in the way of savings, were carrying reasonably large insurance policies, and were by other means they deemed wise and economical spending their earnings present and potential. In the lower reaches of this class, making up the bulk of the petit bourgeoisie, the white-collar workers and skilled artisans, though perhaps on a less extensive scale and certainly with greater dependence on the instalment-buying system, had been similarly inflating their standard of living. Indeed, considering the incomes of most of

these people, they had to inflate their standard of living in order to consume the vast quantities of bathtubs, radios, and automobiles that were being turned out for their special benefit. This trick of making it appear that an entire class was managing to lift itself by its bootstraps was called prosperity.[36]

HOOVER'S RELUCTANT RESPONSE AND THE COMING OF STATE CAPITALISM

From the onset of the crisis, Hoover and the Republicans remained united in their defense of laissez-faire capitalist doctrine while insisting that the economy was fundamentally sound and turning around. Recovering from the Wall Street debacle only required time and patience. But cracks began to appear in 1931 as the crisis deepened. While all remained united in principle to the defense of laissez-faire, it became evident to Hoover that his administration needed to push corporate leaders and big bankers to take bolder steps and put a halt to the economic nosedive. This took the form of limited state intervention, mainly by using public money to extend greater credit to private banks and corporations, as well as providing funds to state and local governments instead of implementing direct federal financing of public works projects and relief for those who could not work. In fortifying the ruling class, Hoover led the way toward state monopoly capitalism. But when his limited measures failed and the crisis deepened, Big Business resisted, some of its stalwarts even calling for an American Mussolini to defend their interests.

Hoover had taken the lead in dampening the panic of the Wall Street collapse but steadily became a man at odds with himself. As early as May 1930 he declared that the country had weathered the worst of the storm and simply urged Americans to work more and harder. For much of that year, rather than describing in real terms the deepening economic and social crisis, Hoover told the American people not to panic, assuring them that conditions would improve substantially in the coming year. Meanwhile,

Americans in distress must help themselves and when necessary rely on private charities or local government to provide immediate relief. As a moral justification, Hoover insisted that government intervention would sap the spirit of self-sufficiency and individual freedom. By the fall, he was convinced that his new instrument of social policy, voluntary social behavior, was working. Prosperity was just around the corner.

And Hoover claimed he had the proof. Investment expenditures of railroads and public utilities in the first eight months of 1930 had increased from $4 billion to $4.5 billion from a year earlier. Public works expenditures had also increased at all levels of government, rising from $2.5 billion in 1929 to $2.9 billion in 1930. Federal spending did increase, by a third, from $155 million to $209 million. But the gains were offset by the $5 billion to $4 billion decline in private non-residential construction and $4 billion to $2.3 billion decline in residential construction. From this and other negative developments, the administration decided that it was necessary to increase public works expenditures for the rest of the fiscal year 1931 (January to June). Accordingly, Hoover asked for emergency public works expenditures of $150 million.[37] All the while, however, things just got worse. Factories and businesses were shutting down. Wages, prices, and industrial output were falling. Banks were crashing. Unemployment climbed dramatically. Yet Hoover remained anchored to his fundamental reliance on voluntarism and the goodwill of business, spurred on by his coterie of loyal administrators and capitalist cronies. As conditions worsened in 1931, Hoover continued to defend the shibboleths of laissez-faire capitalism—the private enterprise system, voluntarism, business self-regulation, and balanced budgets.[38]

At the same time, the president began to part ways with some in his administration whose uncompromising laissez-faire views were more hard-line than his. Among them was Andrew Mellon, his wealthy Treasury secretary who insisted that the federal government should sit idly by while the deflationary spiral liquidated inflated values of commodities and stocks. As their ringleader of sorts, capitalists listened to Mellon when he claimed that the Depression was a good thing because it would rid the economy and society of rottenness and dead wood, encouraging moral virtues like thrift and ensure the survival of the fittest. True to the teachings of Adam Smith, one of the first great economists and advocate of free market capitalism, government should let nature take its course since no federal agency could solve the problem. This spurred Hoover to pursue an independent course. As economist Herbert Stein has written, Hoover understood early in his political career that the era of laissez-faire had passed. The economy could not be left to industrial self-management. Instead, government needed to promote the social application of economic theory in order to maintain constant flows of expenditures and income, which Hoover considered the best preventative to rising unemployment.[39] Convinced that the ongoing commitment of business leaders to free trade and competitive self-interest had culminated in the wholesale financial speculation that brought on the crash and the Depression, Hoover tirelessly promoted the need for a basic adjustment in their thinking and called for voluntary associations among industrial and business leaders to determine how to establish equilibrium between supply and demand. This was the best way to restore purchasing power to the American people and end the Depression. The federal government would play a catalytic role to spark greater voluntarism in the private sector. To his credit, Hoover engaged in ongoing struggles with business leaders and members of his own administration who either believed there was no fundamental structural problem with the American economy or worse, those like Henry Ford, who trumped Andrew Mellon when he said the Depression was a "wholesome thing in general."[40]

Nevertheless, two of Hoover's most notable attempts at relief on a voluntary basis, the Federal Farm Board and the National Credit Corporation, were spectacular failures. The Farm Board, which had been established months before the Wall Street crash in the summer of 1929, had sought to encourage farmers to organize cooperative marketing organizations that would establish self-regulating mechanisms aimed at keeping down surpluses. There would be no fees or taxes imposed on farmers and the government would not become involved in the buying and selling of farm products or attempt to fix prices.[41] It lent money to many of these cooperatives in order to underwrite loans that had been made to individual farmers by local banks, or to purchase surpluses which were taken off the market. To this end, the Farm Board took a hands-off approach to the buying and selling of commodities while insisting that no federal agency had the right to undermine the freedom of the American farmer. The results were disastrous. Spurred on by loans, farmers did exactly what they thought necessary given the steep drop in farm prices, which was to expand crop production to make up for lost profits. This only added to the surplus, which did not stop the slide in commodity prices. By 1931, the Farm Board wound up owning a third of the national wheat supply.[42]

Hoover's last attempt at relief through voluntarism, the National Credit Corporation (NCC), fared no better than the Farm Board. More than 1,300 banks had failed in 1930, and the number kept rising. This prompted Hoover to convene a secret meeting of bankers and insurance company leaders, at which he urged them to form a voluntary association that would restore confidence to the banking system. And so the NCC was created in October 1931 with $500 million of entrepreneurial funds from the country's leading banks. In theory, the strongest banks committed to keeping their weaker counterparts afloat. Instead, the leading bankers generally balked at making loans to those they could easily swallow. Later estimates determined that only around $10 million was actually loaned out. Thus the association did nothing to stem the tide of defaults as American banking continued its nosedive. Depositors lost more confidence as credit became more difficult to secure. As a result, nearly 2,300 more banks failed in the course of 1931.[43]

With farming and banking sliding deeper into the crisis, Congress finally realized that only an unprecedented, peacetime intervention of state power into the private sector could stave off complete collapse. With Hoover's reluctant approval, the Reconstruction Finance Corporation (RFC) was created in January 1932 and chartered by Congress to lend funds to banks, railroads, building and loan associations, and similar institutions. According to Herbert Stein, the RFC provided $500 million of taxpayers' money from the start. Congress authorized the RFC to borrow up to $3.3 billion from the Treasury or elsewhere for emergency loans to troubled institutions. The corporation borrowed almost $1.6 billion from the Treasury in fiscal years 1932 and 1933, though only the initial $500 million appeared as a budgetary expense.[44]

However, the main thrust of the RFC, which was to make credit available to banks and financial institutions in order to loosen credit and move the country toward recovery, failed to achieve its objective. As Robert McElvaine rightly points out, "The fundamental mistake was to think that the credit problem was one of supply. Given the paucity of purchasing power, businesses were not interested in obtaining loans. Expansion was the last thing on the minds of most businessmen in 1932."[45] Nevertheless, the winds were changing, as business leaders, government officials, and economists were coming to recognize amid the deepening economic crisis in 1932. While the old paradigm of laissez-faire prevailed, the RFC represented the seeds of a new political economy based on the necessity of state intervention and deficit spending. Voluntarism, self-help, and altruistic appeals to big business had run their course. Still light-years away from the fiscal revolution that would come in the spring and summer of 1938, the RFC clearly marked a pivotal turn in that direction.

Meanwhile, Hoover continued to blame international events for the Depression and especially singled out Europe as "the great center of the storm" that eventually "burst into a financial hurricane" in 1931.[46] Yet he was only attributing to others what had begun in the epicenter of world capitalism, first as a protracted crisis rooted in the agricultural and then industrial sectors of the U.S. economy, and then ultimately leading to a speculative bubble on Wall Street and the crash. The global crisis that became acute by the end of 1932 was in fact a by-product of a crisis that began in the United States as the world's leading manufacturer and creditor. Blaming Europeans for their demands for remission of reparations and debts of the postwar settlements, as well as Great Britain's abandonment of the gold standard, only gave Hoover another excuse to reject anything more than a limited role by the U.S. government to intervene in the domestic economy. Unfortunately, limited intervention in the name of non-intervention only made things worse. For example, his pledge to farmers to protect their goods from cheap imports caused him to remain wedded to high tariffs. This led to the Hawley-Smoot Tariff Act, the last will and testament of the New Era's claim that individualism was the key to economic success and prosperity, which Hoover signed into law in spring 1930. In response, twenty-five nations raised their tariffs, thus widening the gap between American exports and imports.[47] Hoover's focus on international causes and consequences served as his primary justification for shying away from domestic problems and their own much-needed solutions, the most important of which would require substantial federal intervention. At the same time, his refusal to follow Britain and remove the dollar from the gold standard only reinforced the deflationary spiral of the U.S. domestic economy by negating a major countervailing force that would cause prices to rise.

A rising chorus from some economists and academics called for the federal government to turn away from efforts to balance the budget by raising taxes and instead embark on a deliberate path of deficit spending. All efforts, private and public, to reverse the deflationary spiral had failed. Steadily, Hoover came to see this but then reversed himself after Great Britain departed from the gold standard in 1931, which brought even greater instability to U.S. banks due to renewed runs on their coffers. Asking for a sizable tax increase in the Revenue Act of 1932, Hoover was still left with a federal budget that featured a deficit of $2.7 billion—almost 60 percent of federal expenditures—the largest peacetime deficit in

U.S. history. As David Kennedy points out: "No New Deal deficit would be proportionately larger. Ironically enough, Franklin D. Roosevelt was soon to make the federal budget deficit a center-piece of his attack on Hoover in the presidential election campaign of 1932."[48]

The gradual but steady shift from voluntarism to direct government intervention marked a pivotal moment in the development of state monopoly capitalism in response to a deepening structural crisis. Herbert Stein has argued that Hoover believed the economy needed some increase in the level of federal expenditures. But he refused to commit to more spending beyond mid-1931. Hoover thought that recovery would be well underway by that point. In his defense, Stein insists that Hoover was constrained by realities, chiefly that the federal budget itself was not large enough to facilitate a vast expansion of public works. Still, Stein concludes, the expanded public works programs of 1931 probably pushed Hoover to lay the groundwork for the New Deal. At the same time, his decision to raise taxes at the end of 1931 to balance the budget reveals the other pole of Hoover's mindset. Hoover was now challenged by activists clamoring for vast public works projects in 1932. That required more spending. The crucial steps toward full state monopoly-capitalist development had been taken.[49]

The Endgame: The Battle of Washington, Calls for Dictatorship, and the Fascist Turn

Hoover's last year in office was the worst of the Great Depression and his presidency. Millions of Americans were barely hanging on as American capitalism staggered to a near halt. In the summer of 1932 something happened in Washington that epitomized the deepening crisis and growing authoritarianism of the ruling class—if not the intensifying class struggle—that led to calls for dictatorship as the only solution.

In June, nearly 20,000 veterans and their families from various parts of the country converged on the nation's capital to demand immediate payment of the bonus that had been promised to them as veterans of the Great War. Calling themselves the Bonus Expeditionary Force (BEF), veterans arrived wearing parts of their old uniforms. According to the vivid and detailed account of their March on Washington provided by the writer Jonathan Norton Leonard a few years later, the veterans arrived "ragged and penniless" but conducted themselves like the soldiers they once were during the war. They even created their own military police to ensure that no one begged, made radical speeches, or carried deadly weapons. Communists were shunned and kept from their ranks. In fact, Leonard wrote, "the trouble with the B.E.F. was its irreproachable political background." It was

> not "red"—not even by the most extended meaning of that elastic word. Its members were overwhelmingly white and of native stock. Most of them were married or had been married before the Depression broke up their homes. They were all voters and all in the prime of life. They had all fought for their country a few years ago and had papers to prove it. The songs they sang were the songs of high school picnics and lodge meetings the country over. The words they spoke were familiar. Their faces were familiar.[50]

When the veterans and their families arrived, they became the responsibility of the Superintendent of the Metropolitan Police, General Pelham D. Glassford, who treated them respectfully and earned their devotion in return. Glassford found himself immediately at odds with the White House. While Glassford did all he could to make the veterans feel safe and secure and win their cooperation in return, Hoover and his circle showed nothing but contempt for the vets. When the vets made their way to the Capitol, they did so peacefully and with dignity as they met with political leaders, never intimidating or threatening anyone. As a result of their meetings, the House passed the Bonus Bill. However, the Senate balked. Now, everyone waited for the veterans to turn violent. But they did not, which made the public more sympathetic to their cause. This only enraged Hoover and his truculent advisers, who now realized they had a major public relations nightmare on their hands. Hoover tried to stem the protest by recommending that Congress appropriate $100,000 to pay for the veterans to return home. Many of them accepted and left. But more than 8,000 remained and took up permanent residence in tents and makeshift dwellings on the swampy flats across the Anacostia River from Washington. When about sixty of them marched up Pennsylvania Avenue toward the White House hoping to see Hoover, they were met with closed iron gates and behind them fifty White House police armed with deadly weapons.[51]

People could not fathom why Hoover decided on such a show of force. This was especially true of government workers who observed the whole episode and became more supportive and sympathetic to the plight of the veterans and their families. This forced Hoover to his last resort—label them Red. Relying on the familiar trope of the Red Menace, the administration decided to use the whole affair as a fixture in the coming presidential campaign. "Hoover vs. the Reds." At a White House meeting on July 27 that included cabinet officials and General MacArthur, Hoover decided to take action. Once Glassford was informed that the veterans would be asked to leave voluntarily, he began the orderly evacuation with the greatest care but not without some conflict, which resulted in the shooting deaths of two veterans and the wounding of a third and a bystander. Glassford was not quick enough for MacArthur, who assembled four troops of cavalry, a mounted machine-gun squadron, four companies of infantry, and six tanks on Pennsylvania Avenue. At first, the veterans cheered the soldiers as loyal brothers-in arms when they saw them coming. But then the cavalry began to charge with drawn sabers into packs of veterans and bystanders alike, wreaking havoc, injury, and death upon whomever got in their way. No two accounts could agree on the details because no one was in a position to see the whole thing unfold. Nevertheless, from the various reports, Leonard wrote:

Horsemen dashed back and forth forcing pedestrians to climb on parked automobiles to escape the hoofs and sabers. A great cloud of tear-gas drifted across the entire "affected district." A company of masked infantry charged a dense crowd of civilians, tossing bombs ahead of them. Children fell on the sidewalks in choking convulsions. A legless veteran dragged himself out of one of the buildings almost unconscious from gas. The wives and children of the veterans fled this way and that, while the soldiers set fire to their tents and shanties, refusing to let bedding or clothing be rescued from the flames.

There was little resistance from the veterans. Later that night the final assault was made on the encampment. Those who had lived there peacefully and with the protection of city police gathered whatever they could and stumbled into the night to escape the bayonets and tear-gas. As Leonard wrote, "The Battle of Washington was over."[52]

But it did not end there. The Hoover administration had to prove that communists were behind the whole thing, forcing the arrest of thirty-six of the marchers and claiming they were nothing but hobos and criminals. The press refused to buy Hoover's story, while the Veterans Bureau determined that almost all of those arrested had genuine war records and two-thirds had fought overseas. For Leonard, the great significance of Hoover's anti-communist response was that it doomed his own bid for reelection. Charges of communists responsible for the run on banks fell on deaf ears. So did the statements of retired generals who "were tuning up, getting red in the face," or the fears of "rich old ladies" with flashlights looking for communists under their beds. The "Red-hunt phase" of Hoover's campaign might have worked, Leonard wrote, until Hoover bungled the whole thing by ordering MacArthur to put down what he declared had been "a challenge to the authority of the United States." As Leonard concluded, no one believed that the vets were Reds or that they had launched an assault on the government, and even if that were the case, it did not warrant the deployment of troops, tanks, gas, and machine guns. "The attempt to dramatize Hoover as a bulwark against Revolution had been such a complete political failure that all similar sham-battles with the Reds were doomed to failure in advance."[53]

Hoover's refusal to acknowledge the need for a change in course by the government only further paralyzed the economic system. As the general election neared, so did the fear among ruling-class elites and politicians who served them that all could be lost unless Congress considered suspending the Constitution and creating some form of extraordinary executive committee. In their 1938 study of American fascism, A. B. Magill and Henry Stevens cited numerous examples of these elites who called for some form of dictatorship as the only solution to the crisis. Many were leading businessmen who, since the mid-1920s, had praised Mussolini and Italian fascism for demonstrating how to end a crisis, restore order to society, and create political stability on a new and firmer basis. As early as October 1931, Alfred E. Smith, who had lost the presidential election to Herbert Hoover in 1928 and would soon lose his party's nomination to Franklin Delano Roosevelt, had called for "*a mild form of dictatorship*, honestly operated, honestly intentioned" in order to bring relief to the unemployed. Others jumped on board. A member of a large New York Stock Exchange firm, C. T. Revere, suggested that any European country confronted by the crisis then facing the American people would lead to "a demand for a dictator." Demarest Lloyd, a wealthy businessman who a few years later would take a leading role in the creation of the American Liberty League, a Big Business spearhead against what it feared was a socialist New Deal, wrote that Congress, "like a long line of unfit rulers in the past, should abdicate" and "delegate its powers and functions to a small group, not over a hundred of the most well-informed, intelligent and patriotic men in the country." In a speech to the Chamber of Commerce, Henry I. Harriman called on Congress to give the president the right "to suspend the operation of existing laws and to provide for emergency measures required by the public welfare."[54]

In September 1932, *The New York Times Current History* magazine reported that "certain powerful elements" meeting in New York and Chicago "have been toying with the idea that the way out of our troubles lies through the establishment of some form of economic and political dictatorship." Even an editorial in the *Times* a month before Roosevelt's inauguration suggested the need for some form of dictatorship: "Few Americans," the *Times* stated, "are ready to give up their existing form of government . . . but many are saying, or sighing, that it ought to be supplemented or reinvigorated and directed by some great personality . . . either the President should be given more power to govern by decree or else that some sort of Council of State should have the right and duty to act when Congress fell short." Some members of Congress had gone further. Senator David Reed, a Pennsylvania Republican known for his intimate ties to banker-industrialist and former Treasury secretary Andrew Mellon, declared on the Senate floor that the country "needed a Mussolini."[55]

At this acute point of the crisis of American capitalism, Mauritz Hallgren detected the genesis of fascism in the existing political order. Hallgren was keenly aware of the particular American form it was taking, specifically in the breach between the two main classes in capitalist society. Constrained as anyone by his or her own place in history, Hallgren believed the lower middle class in America was in permanent decline. He quoted Marx and Engels in the *Communist Manifesto*, who defined the lower middle class (or the petty bourgeoisie) as a class in "decay . . . in the face of modern industry" and, therefore, "reactionary" because it tried "to roll back the wheel of history." For Hallgren the lower middle class was the spearhead of reaction during the boom and bust in America during the 1920s and early 1930s. The small capitalist was now an anachronism in the era of monopoly-finance capital. And now the system was locked in an irreversible and permanent crisis. "If the economic crisis of 1929–33 accomplished nothing else," Hallgren wrote, "it measurably advanced the decay and final disappearance of the lower middle class." No other group had suffered as much since the Wall Street crash, "and in no other class did there develop so many signs of spontaneous rebellion."[56] But there was nothing revolutionary about its worldview and politics now that the final crisis of American capitalism was at hand. The oligarchy that drove capitalist modernization now openly considered some form of dictatorship as a solution to the crisis. In response, the lower middle class looked to the fantasy of democratic government that would save it from utter ruin. For Hallgren, the lower middle class would look to Roosevelt as its savior.

Always the good journalist, Hallgren had the statistics that revealed the plight of the lower middle class in simplest terms. Every welfare list in the country contained the names of hundreds, in some cases thousands, of lower-middle-class applicants for relief. "It used to be the wage-earner alone who was on the welfare lists," said the mayor of Detroit in January 1932. "Now it is the skilled artisan and the cultured citizen." The available evidence—and it was scant—showed that between 10 to 11 million of the 16 million persons reported as unemployed in the spring of 1933 were from the ranks of the lower middle class; the other 5.5 million or so Hallgren called the "pre-Depression proletarian class." When all their dependents were added, the total number of people impacted by unemployment could have amounted to as much as 40 million people. The final number had to be far greater, but this was still a conservative estimate. Also to be counted were the more than a million members of the pauper class, as well as sharecroppers and tenant farmers, who were not listed among the unemployed. There were also the millions of suffering small farmers and skilled mechanics who were working on a part-time basis, some whose incomes were cut by more than half. Then, too, Hallgren pointed to the "professional workers who were their own bosses and therefore not grouped with the unemployed, though their incomes had been reduced virtually to nothing." This only made it more difficult to arrive at a definitive number of the total number of unemployed who were once ranked as lower middle class.[57]

Hallgren had his finger on the pulse of a lower middle class now in deep distress as victims of modern capitalism. Its members had struggled through their prime to follow the "upward path of individualism" that Hoover and his ilk had told them was theirs as Americans. Instead, they had been tricked into believing that their inflated lifestyles based on installment buying and other credit schemes had actually put them on the road to lasting prosperity and progress. Yet technological innovation during the 1920s had already reduced the need for skilled mechanics and white-collar workers, shifting those who remained employed to less-skilled jobs and lower wages. The ballyhoo of prosperity had tended to obscure all of this. The extremely wealthy grumbled about their paper losses, knowing, however, that it would not cause them to reduce their comfortable and lavish living standards. But the same could not be said for the lower middle class which "felt the full impact of the Depression."[58]

Though the middle class as a whole had been deceived and undermined by the Republicans throughout the 1920s, it had remained loyal to them until the crash and the onset of the Depression. Some had drifted toward the Progressives, "who clamored loudest for a third party, [and] defeated their own ends by clinging to their high moral perch when they ought to have been down working in the political gutters." Hallgren was ruthless in his criticism of these reformers, who "shuddered at the very thought of getting into politics themselves." They were good at fighting "the good fight at dinner conferences in New York City or by addressing endless formal demands to Mr. Hoover, though the real fight was out among the people, in the factories, on the farms, on the streets." All the while, this class and its self-proclaimed representatives appeared to be moving to the left toward revolution when in fact they were still trying to roll back the wheel of history to an earlier time when they had been the driving force of capitalism. Having nowhere else to go, they would turn *en masse* to the Democratic nominee, Franklin D. Roosevelt, in November 1932, failing to recognize or accept that "the platforms and programs of the two major parties had grown more and more to resemble one another" and that the resemblance "was due to the fact that the ownership and management of both organizations had passed into the hands of big business and high finance."[59]

Hallgren saw in the crisis the political bankruptcy of the lower middle class and its lack of a viable independent program. Its reform-minded representatives took aim at high-profile bankers, industrialists, and politicians but defended the government in principle and the capitalist order it served. For Hallgren the lower middle class was at odds with itself. "They were in rebellion against the capitalist-entrepreneur class and its political servants," he wrote, but understood they could not "halt the advance of monopolization and imperialism." Thus the lower middle class looked to their last line of defense and "surviving symbol of security" and that was the state:

> The State would acquire control of the economic system, would act as the administrator of the major economic functions of the nation, and thus the balance between the classes would be restored and the iniquities in the national economy which had produced the crisis would be eliminated. But the intervention of the State should not go beyond that point; it should not in any way compromise the fundamental principles and purposes of a capitalist society.[60]

As Hallgren saw the moment, this was the "mission that Roosevelt was charged with by the rebellious lower middle class in the election of 1932."[61] But it also revealed something far deeper about the crisis of liberal capitalist democracy:

> The governing class pulled in one direction, the petit bourgeoisie in another. The former wished to preserve the principle of *laissez faire* by defending it against further modification in the form of increased social control; the latter, instinctively perhaps, rather than consciously, understood that only by such

modification could they be helped. The political representatives of the "people" were thrown into a quandary. They hardly dared to rebel openly against the owners and managers of the two major parties, and yet they could not ignore the rising protest of their constituents, for liberal democracy had armed their constituents with the power to vote them out of office.[62]

The capitalists were also held in check by their own limitations and doubts. Knowing that the American people still stood firmly for democracy, whatever its shortcomings, the governing class was neither willing nor prepared to challenge the democratic process. While it was imperative to prevent the lower middle class from pressing for a solution to the economic crisis on the basis of democratic principles and practices, business leaders and their political servants in both the Republican and Democratic parties knew they could not deprive the people of the vote. Outright dictatorship was out of the question. But, as Hallgren determined from his reporting of the events between 1930 and 1933, holding on to power by those at the top—the monopolists—could be achieved by "forming a political coalition subservient to the governing class, thereby nullifying the will of the electorate, or by undermining the confidence of the people in their own political representatives."[63] Indeed, this was the form of ruling-class power that defined most of Hoover's presidency. With this power, capitalist elites and their political representatives in both parties used all of their influence to discredit Congress, fearing that pressure from the majority of its constituents would amount to the enactment of legislation necessary for the relief of the lower middle class, and by extension those below, and result in higher taxes on the capitalists. As all efforts failed to restore prosperity, the breach between the two capitalist classes only widened.

At precisely the moment when the lower middle class looked toward Roosevelt to help it turn back the wheels of history, the capitalist oligarchy looked beyond liberal capitalist democracy toward dictatorship and the fascist alternative. If the oddity of a coming American fascism lay in a reactionary middle class—especially its lower strata—clothed in republicanism, it was even more odd that the modernizing oligarchy should seek to destroy the Republic to preserve its rule over the rest of society.

8—The New Deal as a Transition to Fascism?

MARCH 4, 1933, the day Franklin Delano Roosevelt took the oath as president, marked the lowest point of the Great Depression. Unemployment stood at nearly 25 percent. Almost every bank in the nation had closed. Small and medium-size businesses and farms were failing by the thousands. Major corporations had slashed production and jobs. Life among the majority of working and poor people was one of constant insecurity. It was not much better for a broad swath of the middle class who lost the most in the frightful plunge of business and profits since the Wall Street crash three years earlier. On the morning of the inauguration, every financial institution in the United States was closed. The New York Stock Exchange and the Chicago Board of Trade had suspended trading. "The financial machinery of the world's most powerful capitalism had completely ceased to function," wrote two communist writers, Bruce Minton and John Stuart, in 1940.[1]

Despite great hope that the president-elect would offer Americans a "new deal," the economy had continued to nosedive after the election, adding to growing fears among all quarters of society that only drastic measures could save the nation from impending disaster. As the historian Ira Katznelson reminds us in his recent study of the New Deal, the period between Roosevelt's election and his inauguration was filled with talk about whether the incoming president would require extraordinary powers to end the Depression. "At issue," Katznelson has written, "was not whether the United States would permanently lose its democracy but whether, faced with grave dangers, it would have to undergo a period of emergency rule in which uncommon powers would be delegated from Congress to the president and the executive branch." Even the liberal economist Stuart Chase had called for a "business dictatorship." Walter Lippmann, the nation's most powerful political columnist, proposed that Roosevelt be given extraordinary powers for a year. In one of his widely read op-ed pieces for the *New York Herald Tribune*, Lippmann advised Congress to "suspend temporarily the rule of both houses, to limit drastically the right of amendment and debate, to put the majority in both houses under the decisions of a caucus." Visiting Roosevelt a month before the inauguration, Lippmann told his good friend that there might be "no alternative but to assume dictatorial powers."[2]

Grasping what the nation wanted of him, Roosevelt declared in his inaugural address that he would use all his power to end the crisis. The nation faced an "emergency that has the potential to undermine the democracy itself." As he would do repeatedly during his long presidency, Roosevelt asked Americans not to be overcome by fear. "Our Constitution is so simple and practical that it is possible always to meet extraordinary needs by changes in emphasis and arrangement without loss of essential form." Certainly, he conceded, "the demands of the hour" brought "the risk and cost of violating fundamental principles." Perhaps with Lippmann in mind, as Katznelson suggests, Roosevelt warned that Congress might not act promptly on the legislation he would soon send them, which would require a "temporary departure" from its normal proceedings. But that would bear consequences.

"I shall not evade the clear course of duty that will then confront me," Roosevelt cautioned. "I shall ask the Congress for the one remaining instrument to meet the crisis—broad executive power to wage a war against the emergency, as great as the power that would be given to me if we were in fact invaded by a foreign foe." The American people had given him "a mandate" to take action. "They have asked for discipline and direction under leadership. They have made me the instrument of their wishes. In the spirit of the gift, I take it."[3]

Once in the White House, Roosevelt and his "Brain Trust" of core advisers, who had come together during his campaign, acted swiftly and boldly.[4] The legislative whirlwind during Roosevelt's first hundred days in office saved American capitalism from collapse and the nation from chaos. Remarkably, almost all of it was drafted by key members of his administration and then rushed through Congress with very little debate. In passing each piece of legislation, Congress gave unprecedented power to the executive branch of government to create several new agencies. Thus, the earliest phase of the New Deal marked a decisive step toward a permanent role by the state in the affairs of the private economy. At issue was the need for compensatory spending by the federal government to stimulate economic growth and lift the nation out of the Depression. In this transition to *state capitalism*, or more properly understood as *state monopoly capitalism*,[5] the question for some in the mid-1930s was whether the New Deal was fascist or marked a transition toward the particular national form fascism would take in the United States.

This question is rather jarring. In their popular understanding and dwindling memory of U.S. history, Americans associate the New Deal with a now familiar liberal impulse to reform government to serve the interests of the people. This tendency has reduced complex historical processes to simple constructs in a narrative that glosses over or minimizes fundamental contradictions in the world's foremost capitalist society and in its political order during the 1920s and 1930s. Consequently, the public knows even less about Roosevelt's true motives and the objectives of the New Deal, and how both altered the meaning of liberalism as a political doctrine in the United States. In the name of liberalism, Roosevelt and his New Dealers took aim at the Hoover administration and the monopolists of Big Business for their callous indifference to human suffering. In defense, Hoover and those around him claimed that their policies of limited government intervention into the private economy and reliance on voluntarism by business leaders was a truer expression of liberal-capitalist orthodoxy—the doctrine of classical laissez-faire. Who then was the real liberal, Hoover or Roosevelt, the monopolists or the New Deal reformers? Was it Hoover who claimed to defend the classical liberal position of a free market operating unencumbered by the state that made capitalism and America work? Or was it Roosevelt the reformer who would bind the private economy to state power as never before, allegedly to serve the interests of the majority of Americans, but which in the end only strengthened monopoly and financial capital itself?

Such is the folklore of American liberalism. Certainly Roosevelt and his Brain Trust were sincere in their beliefs that immediate action by the federal government was necessary to save the millions of unemployed and destitute Americans. This has defined them as liberals in the pages of American history and in subsequent American political discourse. Yet, the New Deal required a qualitative leap by the federal government into the workings of the private economy—against the whole tradition of *laissez-faire* and the free market, the core of liberalism itself, which had characterized the history of American business enterprise since its inception.

Rejecting a socialist alternative, Roosevelt's first task was to save the American capitalist system, starting with banking, the main source of economic power. Once the financial sector was stabilized, his administration could turn to halting the deflationary spiral and jump-start the economy toward recovery. To achieve this, however, government and the private economy needed to work in concert to restrict production, in the belief that rising prices would inflate the economy and ultimately lead to higher wages, increased consumption, and renewed prosperity. Herein lay the fundamental contradiction of the New Deal. Saving Big Business, that is, monopoly-finance capital, put it at odds with a genuine concern for the "forgotten man," who, crippled by the Depression, needed government intervention on a massive and unprecedented scale to help him get back on his feet. Simply put, liberal reform in response to the abuses of liberal orthodoxy only made liberalism more corporate and subject to the power of the state. The reformulation of liberalism in the New Deal brought recovery to Wall Street but not enough to Main Street.

A close look at the New Deal from a standpoint of its sharpest critics at the time does much to reveal the chameleon-like character of American liberalism in the service of monopoly-finance capital and the role it plays in the coming of American fascism.

THE MAKING OF THE NEW DEAL

Roosevelt's initial efforts, which historically provide a picture of capitalist leadership at its most effective, cannot be minimized. Within two weeks of Roosevelt's entry into the White House, the new administration pushed legislation through a willing Congress that ended the banking crisis, cut federal expenditures, and raised new revenue. The day he took office every bank in thirty-two states had been shut down either by governors' proclamations or other executive actions, and in several states where banks had remained open depositors could only withdraw 5 percent of their money.[6] Furthermore, demands by depositors that their withdrawals be issued in gold coins instead of paper resulted in a huge and steady outflow of gold from U.S. banks.

As soon as he took office, Roosevelt declared a national bank holiday. Congress then quickly passed the Emergency Banking Act on March 9, enabling 70 percent of banks across the nation to reopen within a week's time under strict government supervision.

The Reconstruction Finance Corporation, which had been established under Hoover to provide federal loans to states and local
governments, was pumped up to provide liquid capital in the form
of loans to troubled banks while the Federal Reserve made loans
to non-member state banks. The turnaround was breathtaking.[7]
In the following three weeks depositors returned $1.2 billion of
currency to reopened banks. Additionally, to stop the drain on
gold, the banking act provided the president with the power to
control the flow of gold in and out of U.S. banks and then in and
out of the nation. This was achieved in two executive orders: the
first required the return of all gold coins or bullion to the Federal
Reserve or member banks, as well as the return of all gold and
gold certificates by member banks to the Federal Reserve itself.
The second took the country off the gold standard by forbidding
gold export unless it could be shown "to promote the public interest."[8] The departure from gold devalued the dollar which, it was
hoped, would loosen credit, stimulate new investment in production, and raise prices that would help pay off debt—all aimed at
raising employment and purchasing power. Ultimately, the Gold
Reserve Act of January 1934 set the price of gold at $35 per ounce.

After restoring stability to the financial system, the administration turned to the immediate relief of the unemployed
and the long-depressed state of agriculture. In short time, it
pushed through Congress numerous initiatives that resulted in
new agencies. Among them was the Federal Emergency Relief
Administration (FERA), which provided millions of dollars to
the states for jobs on various projects and direct relief to those
unable to work. Another agency, the Civilian Conservation Corps
(CCC), created jobs in natural-resource conservation and related
projects to over a quarter-million young men. The Agricultural
Adjustment Administration (AAA) dealt with the long-standing
problem of overproduction in farm goods and disastrously low
prices by creating a domestic allotment plan that asked farmers to
restrict crop cultivation and livestock raised for slaughter. Farmers
received federal subsidies in return. This seemingly forward step,

however, was detrimental for millions of Americans who desperately needed food and other farm products. Indeed, the agrarian history of the United States during the New Deal is replete with stories from farmers and hungry people alike who considered such practices to be utterly mad. It even made some in Roosevelt's liberal circle queasy. Agriculture Secretary Henry Wallace, though horrified at plowing under 10 million acres of cotton and the slaughter of 6 million piglets, could "tolerate it only as a cleaning up of the wreckage from the old days of unbalanced production" and certainly "not acts of idealism in any sane society."[9]

On June 16, 1933, Roosevelt signed the National Industrial Recovery Act (NIRA), which established the National Recovery Administration (NRA), a centerpiece of the New Deal. Charged with creating unified action between government, business, and labor, NRA administrators set out to end the ruthless competition they believed had created the menace of overproduction in the marketplace. Its mission was defined in the principles and structures of its three main components or "titles." Title I aimed primarily to stimulate industrial recovery by establishing federally supervised "codes" on prices of capital and consumer goods to end "unfair competition" in business enterprise. All were subject to presidential approval. It also contained provisions for labor. Section 7(a) stipulated that labor had the right to organize into unions and engage in collective bargaining; Section 7(b) established measures for determining maximum work hours, minimum pay rates, and working conditions in those industries covered by the codes, as well as banning yellow dog contracts. Title II allocated $3.3 billion for public works projects in conservation and natural resource development. To this end, it created the Public Works Administration (PWA) that also provided vast relief efforts. Title III gave the NRA the authority to take over the role of primary agent of reconstruction from the Reconstruction Finance Corporation created under the Hoover administration.[10] In apparent recognition that the era of laissez-faire had run its course, the architects of the NRA—and the whole New Deal at that—believed that it could work on what Ira Katznelson described as a "massive voluntary endeavor, underpinned by public authority."[11]

The goal of the NRA was a planned and managed economy operating on the basis of cooperation between capital and labor. Government would preside over industrial self-management, nothing new in the era of monopoly finance capitalism and, in fact, a cornerstone of corporate and Republican Party thinking throughout the prosperous 1920s. Now, however, the Roosevelt administration sought to legitimate this same idea in a new form. Instead of leaving Big Business to manage its affairs, NIRA made government a viable, though somewhat subservient partner. The administration gave all power to create codes on prices to Big Business, specifically to the trade associations that represented its collective interests. As they understood their charge, their chief task was to determine how to reap profits while avoiding ceaseless competition and, consequently, overproduction. Antitrust laws, which had failed to prevent this from occurring, were suspended in the newfound belief that cooperation would win the day. Labor would also benefit from this arrangement, or so was the claim. In theory, every code would establish maximum work hours and minimum wages in addition to fixing prices. Labor was guaranteed the right to organize and bargain collectively, and child labor was abolished. The NRA cheerfully promoted itself as the honest broker between business and labor. Roosevelt considered it a partnership in planning between government and business.[12]

Before the U.S. Supreme Court ruled the NIRA unconstitutional in May 1935 as an unwarranted invasion by government on commercial rights, more than 700 codes had been approved. Undoubtedly, the codes overwhelmingly favored business interests by facilitating the shift toward planned limitation of output while making sure that profitability was maintained. This was especially crucial in the production of capital goods since it was here that the crisis caused by overproduction in the early and mid-1920s had its roots. Nevertheless, higher rates of profit based on production limits meant that the share going to labor, both in the number of workers employed and the value of their wages, had to fall, which is exactly what happened. A blanket provision on codes governing all industrial workers stipulated an hourly wage for workers and a maximum workweek of 35 hours regardless of the specific conditions in each industry. The historian Alan Lawson, who considers the New Deal an attempt to build a "cooperative commonwealth" from the ruins of the Depression, concluded that NIRA never achieved the much-desired cooperation between government and business. In pursuit of self-interest, business could not hold to voluntary agreements despite what government deemed necessary for the general welfare of society. What ensued was a "race to the bottom" as those business establishments that tried to honor the code agreements were compelled to follow those who transgressed from the start.[13] When that happened, the government could not enforce the codes. What emerged was an ill-coordinated aggregate of protective measures and massive confusion among all parties, except for consumer groups who were virtually absent from the deliberations.

For all its weaknesses, there is little dispute that the NIRA's impact was immediately a positive one. Production and employment increased significantly in July 1933, just as hundreds of codes went into effect. Historian Robert McElvaine viewed this as a "boomlet" that had little to do with the NIRA and was more the product of increased federal spending, Roosevelt's restoration of confidence, and the simple fact that the Depression had already reached its bottom.[14] Apparently unknown to McElvaine was that the Marxist political economist Lewis Corey had already demonstrated this in 1934 in his book *The Decline of American Capitalism*. Corey attributed the upturn more to a "cyclical revival" during the first four months of 1933 which, quite naturally, was energized by the administration's new policies and swift congressional action. Nevertheless, industrial production increased 50 percent as producers built up inventories and hoped for the trend to be sustained by the government's inflation policies.[15] McElvaine suggests that the anxiety about the NRA codes actually spurred manufacturers to build inventories by utilizing cheaper labor prior to the codes on wages going into effect. Consequently, many workers who were hired in the spring were fired in the fall.[16] Profits had shot up in the first and second quarters, as total wages and employment also rose, 20 percent and 10 percent respectively. But the upturn ended in July. By November, half the gains registered in the first two quarters had been wiped out despite all the administration's efforts to create equilibrium between supply and demand and devalue the dollar against gold. By the end of 1933 the inflationary measures had turned into their opposite. Prices rose as did production despite NRA intentions of balanced output. But wages lagged, and workers once again found themselves facing prospects of production cuts and joblessness. Thus the balance sheets came out decisively in favor of business.[17]

"Niraism," as Lewis Corey called it, was Roosevelt's means to establish "fair wages and fair profits" so equilibrium could be restored to a system threatened by the "unfettered" economic action of capitalists.[18] Generally, the formula was based on a long-held conviction that what was considered good about capitalism would only survive by eliminating the bad. The architects of Niraism saw themselves promoting good capitalism by reining in the excesses, abuses, and greediness of laissez-faire during the New Era of the previous decade. To this end, the Roosevelt administration believed that the NRA would spur capitalists to further their own interests by raising wages and limiting profits in order to assure still higher profits. For Corey, Niraism marked two pivotal developments in American capitalism. The first was that the era of laissez-faire had ended. The second, only grasped by Corey and a few others who understood the contradictory forces at work, was that Niraism represented the necessary advance of state monopoly capitalism in response to a profound systemic crisis, which was symptomatic of capitalism's decline and decay.

Some later historians and other writers echoed Corey, though not perhaps as deeply as this thorough Marxist economist. Robert McElvaine, who never consulted Corey's work, wrote forty years later:

By almost any reckoning, the NRA was a colossal failure. Dominated from the start by large-business interests, it served them at the expense of the rest of society. Their first concern was to assure their own incomes so they sought to use the codes to guarantee their margins of profit on the basis of restricted production and higher prices. This was scarcity economics and it meant reduced purchasing power. Businessmen could survive in this way under continuing Depression conditions, but it would simply perpetuate the hard times, not bring recovery or help anyone else. Given its domination by business interests, the NRA offered little hope of bringing about recovery. As long as businesses were permitted to raise prices to coincide with (or exceed) mandated wage increases, there would be no redistribution of income and no stimulation of purchasing power.[19]

THE NEW DEAL FALLS SHORT

The doctrine of free-market capitalism that had guided the Great Boom and resulted in the Great Depression had run its course. Yet the New Deal actually signaled a more profitable era for Big Business even as the nation weathered the difficult years of recovery. Business leaders welcomed the NRA's antitrust measures only because they were given a leading role in determining the content of the codes. Nevertheless, opposition from the Chamber of Commerce, the National Association of Manufacturers, and the American Liberty League mounted steadily. Organized in the fall of 1934 by representatives of the DuPont financial empire and other business titans, the Liberty League cultivated its own version of 100 percent Americanism by accusing Roosevelt and the New Deal for taking the nation toward two alien political doctrines, socialism or fascism. Well before the NRA was ruled unconstitutional, business leaders regularly ignored provisions in the codes as well as subsequent complaints from government officials. Having been saved just as the banks had been with the Emergency Banking

Act, manufacturers took delight in improving business conditions with government as its willing partner, without admitting that any movement in this direction was made possible by rising public expenditures for public works and relief. Still, Roosevelt's desired partnership in planning with business had its limits as far as the monopolists and big bankers were concerned.

Conceived as a means to create common ground between government and industry, the NRA marked a decisive move toward state monopoly capitalism in the United States by extending the federal government's capacity to preserve constitutional democracy. In its devotion to saving capitalism, the Roosevelt administration had no choice—other than a socialist alternative—to leave the real power in the hands of Big Business, which sought at every turn to capitalize on the powers delegated to it in Title I. The result was maximum profits at the expense of labor, which could not stop business from sidestepping Section 7(a) whenever it could, especially when aided by complicit labor leaders. In no way would the Roosevelt administration stand in the way of profit and capitalist accumulation. Historians generally agree that Roosevelt had little concern for the right of collective bargaining when he entered the White House. What he wanted most was for business to finally recognize that the economy needed equilibrium. But in giving practically all the power to Big Business, the New Deal only encouraged its bigger partner to continue down the road to deflation while Roosevelt and his Brain Trust pursued other policies, mainly through currency manipulation—all designed to inflate the economy. The result was a New Deal at odds with itself. Broadus Mitchell, a labor historian and outspoken socialist who ran for governor of Maryland in 1939, called it "planned scarcity." These and other measures, which included domestic price-fixing and reciprocal trade agreements, as well as the more egregious practice of crop and livestock destruction, aimed at saving U.S. capitalism at the expense of mass human need. As Mitchell saw matters, the failure of AAA administrators and their NRA counterparts was startling. "It nowhere seemed to occur to them that an economy which, for its correction and preservation, demanded such violence to reason, had better be abandoned than revived," he wrote in 1947. "Though current thought was not so bold, was there ever a time when avowal of production for use, rather than for private profit, was more appropriate?"[20]

Some writers had said as much soon after the New Deal began. Benjamin Stolberg, an author and labor activist, and Warren Jay Vinton, who worked in the Roosevelt administration on issues of social security and public housing, offered their critique in a short book, *The Economic Consequences of the New Deal*, published in 1935. They criticized Roosevelt's pragmatic approach, which glossed over irreconcilable capitalist contradictions because he and his advisers were bent on saving the capitalist system at all cost. The administration's failure to confront the principal contradiction between capital and labor made any real recovery impossible. Instead of new policies grounded in a scientific and historical understanding of what caused the Depression, Roosevelt led his administration on a bold path of experimentation divorced from any theoretical premises. This sent them moving in all directions at once in an effort to achieve the impossible: restoring equilibrium to an economic system in which disequilibrium was a permanent feature. The American people faced the worst crisis in their history as the result of an "insidious and intricate malady within their economy." That malady, Stolberg and Vinton wrote, was the "irresponsible power of great wealth." The facts revealed an "invariable correlation between the upward concentration of wealth and the progressive crippling of our economy." What could be done to balance an economy in which more than half the nation's wealth was owned by less than half a million people and controlled by a handful of them? Such an effort could be "neither theoretically reconciled nor realistically compromised." For Stolberg and Vinton, the Roosevelt administration had embarked on "crusades of compromise" aimed at a planned recovery without recognizing, or admitting, the necessity of reining in Big Business.[21]

Roosevelt and his Brain Trust laid out legislation based on an "experimental method" of "trial and error" and devoid of any grounding in history, economic science, or social-political theory. The worst offender was the president himself:

> Mr. Roosevelt has the kind of an open mind which accepts with equal hospitality the most contradictory views and the most irreconcilable facts. His whole policy is bent on ignoring the contradictions in our economy … [and] tries to make for a saner economy by strengthening all the opposing forces of the *status quo*, thereby inevitably strengthening the forces already in power.

For Stolberg and Vinton, the architects of New Deal policies had proceeded from a "technique of correlating its own intellectual confusions and liberal gestures with our economic disintegration and social chaos." Here was the bankruptcy of the administration's experimental method. The New Dealers willingly ignored the fact that "science performs no experiments which are not guided ideologically, by the strictest possible theoretical background." They had gone astray from the start in their opportunism, especially in using the word *new*, which Stolberg and Vinton declared "an old subterfuge of the American mind in escaping unpleasant reality." The New Deal "would introduce 'social planning' without changing our property relations." This was no different from the New Era of 1920s prosperity that "sought to make us all rich without disturbing the rich."[22] Despite his declaration of a new deal for the millions who had been leveled by the Depression, Roosevelt could not completely break with the central tenets of laissez-faire capitalism held by Big Ownership during the 1920s that resulted in great wealth and growing inequality at once. If only Roosevelt had recognized that the seeds of the bust were in the boom. Now that the crisis had come, neither the president nor the people around him could abandon their commitment to the monopolies and the big banks. For Stolberg and Vinton, "capitalist recovery, on the classic lines of laissez-faire" had been "arrested" while the "only economic alternative, social planning on socialist lines, had been sedulously avoided."[23]

The Depression, they argued, was hatched in the prosperity of the New Era a decade earlier. Citing statistics that showed the widening income gap between the wealthy capitalists at the top and the rest of the society, Stolberg and Vinton saw clear and ominous signs of a massive, upward redistribution of national income that led to economic collapse. In its quest for profits, Big Ownership farmed out capital to build plants that were not needed, thus leading to overproduction and saturated markets. The lack of productive investment outlets only fueled speculation in credit and stocks that sustained consumption as much as possible until the whole thing collapsed in 1929. During Hoover's term as president, the RFC had pumped nearly $2 billion of public money "in defense of private fortunes." But keeping the banks solvent to support the market at its lowest points only enabled Big Ownership to buy out small enterprises at "bargain prices" during the worst years of the crisis. It was then that Big Ownership got even bigger and, in so doing, increased its percentage of the declining national wealth. Deeming further investment no longer profitable, heavy industry closed its doors. Wages of the consuming classes fell by two-thirds, negatively impacting production of consumer goods. Investment in the production of both capital and consumer goods ceased. Stagnation and paralysis then extended to finance capital itself.[24]

Statistics showed that the New Deal did not halt the upward distribution of national wealth. In 1933, taxpayers who made less than $10,000 a year earned even less than they did a year earlier when the crisis was most acute. But the same could not be said for the top 8,000 with incomes of over $50,000, who increased their takings by 10 percent, the top 2,000 whose incomes rose by 16 percent or, even more astoundingly, those whose annual incomes of $1 million or more increased by almost 50 percent. "Under the New Deal, exactly as in the New Era," they wrote, "Big Ownership profited enormously at the expense of all the rest of us." From October 1933 to October 1934, real weekly wages for industrial workers declined by 2 percent. "Yet the dividends of our great corporations *increased* 17 per cent in the same period. And their industrial profits in the first nine months of 1934 were 76 per cent greater than during the same period in 1933."[25]

Stolberg and Vinton took a dim view of the middle class for failing to recognize what the New Deal meant for them, especially since Roosevelt's promise played a vital role in his election. "The middle class necessarily misreads its hand," they wrote. "It does not know its place in American life, for its psychology infects the whole of it. And it does not understand its function which is manifold, ambiguous, and contradictory. Its interests are so hopelessly confused in its own mind that all it can do is organize its own confusion." It is "a bastard and a mongrel" at once: "It is a bastard class, for it partakes of both capital and labor and yet is neither. And it is a mongrel class because four different and often hostile strains make up its heterogeneous bulk." The bulk included 6.5 million farmers (excluding laborers and sharecroppers), 2.5 million small business entrepreneurs, 1.5 million administrators of business enterprise, and the vast majority of the million professional and pseudo-professional people. Most important, the lines between the middle and working classes were far from clear. "The frayed white-collar worker, though a veritable caricature of the petty bourgeois, is so pathetically wage-dependent that he obviously belongs with labor."[26]

As divided as it was along income and occupational lines, the middle class as a whole was delusional in the belief that its interests were identical to those of Big Business. It looked to the ruling class for security, social status, and, especially, the quest for property. Just like the worker, however, the typical petty bourgeois—farmer, small merchant, salaried employee, skilled artisan, or even the well-paid worker—remained a slave to capital and was forever living on the margins of an economy dominated by Wall Street. The middle class had voted for Roosevelt and his promise of a new deal. Once implemented, however, it did nothing to alter its standing in the economic order. The New Deal did not save their small speculative investments in stocks and securities—only their farms or their homes—and perhaps only for the moment. Limited government action had prevented foreclosures by assuming their mortgages, but it did not scale them down. "The debtors still remained in debt up to their necks."[27]

Having lost so much under Hoover, the middle class found little rebound with Roosevelt. Of all its groupings, the farmer had made out best, though Stolberg and Vinton attributed that to "the ring-around-the-rosy of the scarcity competition which [was] the essence of the whole recovery program." The AAA had set out to organize agricultural scarcity in competition with industrial scarcity. In the end, it was bad for the farmer. While prices on farm goods rose, so did prices on the manufactured goods he needed to buy. Farm exports failed to rise even with the stimulus of a devalued dollar. Raising farm prices while keeping up protective tariffs kept the American farmer from free access to the world market. While the Department of Agriculture determined that 50 million marginal acres of land should be forced out of cultivation, it gave little support to the 2.5 million people who were living on them as mainly subsistence farmers. As for the small retailer caught between the rising prices of the NRA and the impoverishment of his customers, the volume of his business amounted to little more than half of what it was in 1929. "Yet he cannot cut the highest item from his overhead by firing the hired man within himself. . . . The small producer is being messed up by the cartelizing tendencies of the N.R.A." The small storekeeper, the small manufacturer, and even the independent craftsman, faced a shrinking future in an economy driving toward ever greater efficiency through large-scale production. In the long run, government could have reversed the social forces that were liquidating him. Instead, the New Deal did not do for the small capitalist what it had done for big banker and industrialist.[28]

There was something quite revealing about the plight of the middle class:

The New Deal cannot help the worker in him, whom he denies, without attacking his ownership. And it cannot help the owner in him, whom he cherishes, without entrenching the vested interests which exploit him. The truth is that the middle class is hopelessly caught in the deepening struggle between capital and labor and so is the New Deal. Indeed, the more "liberal" its gestures, the more nearly it expresses the doomed liberties of the Forgotten Man.

The tragedy of the New Deal is that the middle class which it politically represents immobilizes it psychologically; and thus demobilizes it as an effective force in combating Big Ownership.[29]

If the middle class held to the fiction that its interests were the same as ownership, stranger still was the "psychological identification" of the American worker with the middle class. This had been building since the late nineteenth century with the coming of mass consumer society. The growth of large-scale industry and monopolies had opposed a trade union movement that had incorporated the spirit of "rugged individualism" molded by the frontier experience. The new frontier was now an industrial one, and its pioneers were just as "imaginative, reckless, able and unscrupulous" as their predecessors. Labor movements were "confused and ineffectual." Under the leadership of the AFL, skilled workers had rolled up their sleeves and fought the bosses for higher wages, shorter hours, and better working conditions. But they had shed all remaining vestiges of socialist thinking and made clear their "hatred of all ideology." Here was the "pure and simple trade unionism" of the AFL. Having no distinct political identity, it succumbed to "the logic of modern capitalism." From the beginning the AFL acknowledged the rights of private ownership of capital, and in so doing "accepted its concept of labor as a commodity," which made work a thing for sale and the employer just another customer. From this point of view "it was an easy step to the property-mindedness of the petty bourgeois." Just like the storekeeper, the skilled craftsman as an "aristocrat" developed an utter contempt for the unskilled workers who flooded into American cities before the Great War in 1914, most of them coming from countries in eastern and south-eastern Europe. "Above all," Stolberg and Vinton noted, the labor aristocrat "kept the Negro out of his unions, thus forcing him into a long and tragic history of strike-breaking."[30] From all this,

> the skilled worker was able to raise his wages till he could live like the petty bourgeois he was. He came to share the outlook of the middle classes politically, socially, and culturally. He bitterly opposed every expression of class consciousness within the ranks of labor. Red-baiting became his favorite sport. He dreaded and fought against the rise of a political labor party. He voted the Republican or Democratic ticket.[31]

In light of these irreconcilable contradictions, the entire New Deal program was for Stolberg and Vinton "in essence nothing but a well-intentioned synthesis of errors." A concerted effort by the government aimed at recovery required greater abundance and consumption, not "scarcity." Strangest of all New Deal illusions was the dream to make Big Ownership accept an economy of abundance. Committed to saving free enterprise and wedded to nothing more than bold experimentation without full knowledge of the facts, the New Dealers sought to go against the very logic of capitalism as "an economy of measured scarcity." As they wrote: "Business is successful to the extent to which it gauges correctly that optimum point of profit at which a maximum price coincides with a maximum demand." It was vitally important for business leaders to prevent an abundance of goods from flooding the market. The same held true in times of boom and bust alike:

> In boom times production is tempted into abundance and scarcity gets out of hand. Capitalist recovery from the ensuing Depression lies in the reorganization of scarcity. During the New Era Big Industry blundered into a disastrous abundance.

And its potential productivity is now so great that it cannot get out of the Depression under its own power. It needed the aid of government to reestablish scarcity and to enforce recovery; and that is exactly what the National Recovery Administration is all about. The codes, avowedly written for the "regulation of competition," are obviously an apparatus for industrial scarcity-mongering.[32]

The New Deal originated and unfolded from a bold experimental method that Roosevelt and his architects believed could bridge the irreparable divide between capital and labor in a time of crisis. Its bottom line was to curtail the excesses of Big Business to prevent overproduction and saturated markets. This meant learning from past errors and planning ahead. The solution was to revitalize the economy by integrating industry and agriculture into a shared program. However, it was a scarcity program that contradicted the immediate needs of the working class and more employment at higher wages. Thus the New Deal flew in the face of the majority of Americans who needed an economy of abundance. This was not the case for the New Dealers who believed their mission was to save the capitalist system. As Stolberg and Vinton noted incisively, the AAA and the NRA were "the first and foremost of the New Deal panaceas" that helped to "render more explicit, through an enormous administrative apparatus, what has always been implicit in the nature of Big Ownership. Under capitalism, scarcity is the life of the trade."[33]

For Stolberg and Vinton, the New Deal created a stalemate between capital and labor. In trying to right the imbalance of economic life, it strengthened all its contradictions. For Big Ownership it was necessary to safeguard profits and to keep intact the instruments of its financial domination. For those in the middle class who could afford to invest in stocks, all efforts to protect their modest investments only served the interests of big bankers and financiers who controlled the market. For labor, the New Deal sought to raise wages, increase employment, and assure some minimum economic security, though it opposed labor's vital need for greater abundance.

All this led Stolberg and Vinton to conclude that there was only one outcome when profits rose and wages lagged. Behind the New Deal's "vivid confusion," the redistribution of the national wealth was "stealthily and fatally progressing *upwards*," while the power of Big Ownership grew steadily larger. "And unless the government succeeds in reversing this disastrous process, Big Ownership is bound to intensify the crisis in the long run."[34]

Was the New Deal Fascist?

The contradictions of American capitalism in the New Era of the 1920s and the subsequent Depression it brought required a qualitative leap in state power to manage the crisis and save the economic system from collapse. But its advance in the guise of the New Deal contained the elements of a crisis all its own. In clinging to existing property relations dominated by monopoly and financial capital within the limits of constitutional democracy, the New Deal did not resolve the fundamental contradictions between capital and labor. It only strengthened them. Its course from 1933 to 1940 marked the final phase in the transition to *state monopoly capitalism* in the United States. Some journalists and political writers even saw the genesis of fascism in American capitalism, comparing Roosevelt's bold steps in a general crisis and national emergency to what fascists had done in Italy and Germany.

Indeed, in the media there was a visible and vigorous discussion about the relationship between fascism and capitalism that began after Roosevelt's inauguration. Must America go fascist? The editor of *Current History* magazine, E. Francis Brown, who knew the history of U.S. ties to fascist Italy and the praise bestowed on Mussolini's corporatist government by American business and political leaders, wrote that "the new America will not be capitalist in the old sense, nor will it be Socialist. If at the moment the trend is toward Fascism, it is an American Fascism embodying the experience, the traditions and the hopes of a great middle-class nation."[35]

Discussion along these lines picked up over the next two years. Most of it went beyond straightforward comparisons of political differences between American liberal democracy and European fascist dictatorship. Instead, many writers employed their knowledge of political economy and class analysis to determine which political and social forces constituted the main fascist threat in the United States. Most deemed fringe organizations such as the Silver Shirts and other groups that emulated Mussolini's black shirts or Hitler's brown shirts as insignificant. None ever came close to creating a mass movement as happened in Italy or Germany. On the other hand, there were definite affinities between the New Deal and Italian fascism. The New Deal bore strong resemblances to the corporatist state established in Italy in its approach to reconciling the antagonism between capital and labor. Both Mussolini and Roosevelt had made clear their commitment to maintain and strengthen capitalism in their respective nations. Consequently, the fascist character of the New Deal could not be easily dismissed, especially given the high praise that American businessmen and politicians had lavished on Mussolini. Three Republican presidents of the 1920s had looked favorably on Mussolini's formula to transform Italy from a crisis-ridden nation in the years immediately following the Great War. Both nations were inextricably linked in the 1920s. American bankers had paved the way for the export of U.S. capital in the form of direct investments and business partnerships in Italy, which made them the most valued of all U.S. partners in Europe. Mussolini always feared losing American capital until conditions in Europe dictated another course for Italian fascism. Roosevelt was no different. In June 1933, he wrote that he was deeply impressed by what Mussolini had "accomplished and by his evidenced honest purpose of restoring Italy and seeking to prevent general European trouble." A short time later, Roosevelt admitted even more: "I don't mind telling you in confidence that I am keeping in fairly close touch with the admirable Italian gentleman."[36]

In the June issue of *Harper's Magazine*, J. B. Matthews and R. E Shallcross argued that the question of whether the United States must go fascist had suddenly become "appropriate and inescapable." As they wrote:

> If an Americanized form of fascism is in the making, now is the time to conduct a free inquiry into the conditions that permit it, the social forces that will be served by it, and the traditional elements in American life that will react sympathetically to a dictatorship of reaction.[37]

What conditions? The New Deal had failed to end the crisis and now called for more "stringent controls." All the experiments tried by the New Dealers had failed to restore employment to a sufficient number. And those who were employed were not earning enough to keep pace with rising prices and the higher cost of living. The "mild measures" of the New Deal had failed, thus preparing the way "for accentuating the tendency toward fascist control." Yet Matthews and Shallcross admitted that no one could predict "the precise point on the political thermometer where the conditions for fascism exist."[38]

Still, a fascist turn was plausible since the crisis was far from over. The New Deal in its failure revealed the paradox of capitalist progress: rising poverty within continued growth and now aimed at recovery. Matthews and Shallcross explained why:

> The productive capacity of capitalist society is matched only by its consumptive inadequacy. Our potential plenty has become most obvious at precisely the moment when poverty is most completely socialized. Our planned recovery is not a planned economy. The fundamental principle of a planned economy is the organization and correlation of the grand aggregate of available resources with a view to higher living standards for the masses. Without this as the dominant and ever-present purpose there is not even a beginning of planned economy.[39]

Rather than a sound plan for recovery, the New Deal presented what they called "planned sabotage," based on a view they attributed to the American economist Thorsten Veblen, as a method he considered "the conscientious withdrawal of efficiency" from production. Americans needed abundance. Instead of increasing production, the New Deal went in the other direction. Its objective was "scarcity profits" to ensure that "price is king." Matthews and Shallcross recognized the basic contradiction rooted in political economy:

> An economy of abundance is implicit in the power age, but the potential abundance has reached such proportions that its actualization would spell disaster for the entire debt structure of finance capital and the disappearance of profits derived from ownership. Capitalism cannot, therefore, accept the implications of the power age and its abundance. It must operate under a natural or an enforced scarcity.[40]

The New Deal's "strictly capitalist" approach to the problem of mass production determined that planned sabotage also included the necessity of currency manipulation. Though an increase in prices diminished the purchasing power of the consumer, it added to the "paying power of the debtor" and, supposedly, would bring "prices and debts into a workable relationship." Give people more money so they can pay their debts! However, the administration had not succeeded in sufficiently inflating the economy to the point where such recovery efforts could gain traction, instead fueling "powerful political forces pulling in opposite directions." While inflationary measures appeared to help the great agricultural sections make their mortgage payments easier, rising prices on farm products amounted to "a concealed tax upon the wages of labor and the salaries of professional groups and also an invisible levy upon the property of creditors." Given their political and financial power, large creditors could "offset" these negative tendencies in the market. But uncontrolled inflation would only ruin middle-class property holders.[41]

For Matthews and Shallcross, the New Deal itself was neither fascist nor revolutionary, although the "spirit of economic orthodoxy" and economic fundamentalism that animated it was the "mainstay of fascism." Its fascist character was evident in the limited recovery:

> Recovery looks backward, not forward. It is not possible to recover a status which has not yet been reached. Even in the so-called days of prosperity in 1929 there were no less than seventy million Americans living below a standard of health and decency. So far as the overwhelming *majority of the people of this country* are concerned, the very suggestion that any past status in American history should be recovered for them is, to put it mildly, extremely cynical when the entire population might now enjoy the abundance made possible through technological progress.[42]

The driving force of American fascism would not be a mass movement from below but would come from the actions taken by the ruling capitalists above. For sure, the lower middle class could be sucked into a movement if conditions worsened. But there were no signs of it on the horizon. "Reliable reports from all sections of the country," Matthews and Shallcross wrote, "indicate a popular willingness to rely upon the conventional political processes of American capitalism to meet the demands of the crisis."[43] Nor did the various shirt groups deserve the publicity they got. The same could not be said for the captains of industry and finance who, fretting over the "mild restrictions of the NRA," yearned once more for the rugged individualism of laissez-faire. "The most extreme characterizations of the New Deal at Washington, whether fascist or socialist, have come from those financial masters of their political servants who desire the resuscitation of prostrate laissez-faire."[44]

These political servants exercised the "extraordinary powers" given to the executive branch under the New Deal. If the crisis deepened, fascist processes would take the capitalist democratic state to its logical extremes of

> complete suppression of civil liberties and placing of all power in the hands of a chief executive. Capitalist parliamentarianism has then given way to fascist rule. When the hundred-day special session of Congress gave extraordinary powers of administration over agriculture, industry, transportation, banking, and the budget to the President, there was an ominous acclaim which overflowed Democratic bounds.[45]

But there was something far greater underlying the growth of executive power itself:

> This tendency toward political dictatorship is accelerated by another factor which is not the product of an economic emergency, but which is itself productive of economic emergencies. This factor is the normal development of monopoly finance capitalism. The logic of advancing capitalism is the concentration of wealth in fewer and fewer hands or, even where there is an actual dispersion of ownership, a concentration of management over fewer and larger aggregates of wealth. This sets up a new tension between the propertied few and the propertyless many, more acute than is the case in earlier stages of capitalism. Inasmuch as the state is the reflection of property relations in society, it follows that there is a corresponding widening of the gap between the many who are reduced by their propertyless state to the category of political ineffectiveness within the capitalist democratic state, and the few who by reason of their enormous property holdings would control, at first covertly, then overtly, the real political power of that state.[46]

Simply put, the increasing concentration of capital required a greater managerial state. Its "sharply rising curve" pointed to the eventual outcome of "complete dictatorship in both the economic and political fields." Matthews and Shallcross defined fascism as the dictatorial rule of monopoly finance capitalism. To support their claim, they cited the landmark 1932 study by Adolf Berle and Gardiner Means, *The Modern Corporation and Private Property*, which showed that two hundred of the nation's largest corporations run by scarcely more than 2,000 directors controlled "the conditions under which the whole of American industry must operate." The powers vested in these corporations and the backing provided to them by the Roosevelt administration guaranteed that fascism was in the making. "Every assault upon labor's right to bargain collectively or the corresponding right to strike is a movement in the direction of fascism," they wrote. NRA leadership had repeatedly made open or implied threats to the basic rights of labor. Even Roosevelt was heard to speak in ways that signaled "compulsory class collaboration."[47]

Matthews and Shallcross took another startling step by connecting the fascist trajectory of monopoly finance capitalism with political liberalism:

The idea of the corporative state is not always expressed with the bluntness that smacks of reaction; it is widely held by liberals who deny the basic fact of the class struggle by expounding a concept of *society* standing above the occupationally divergent groups within it—society whose claims are paramount over those of the classes of which it is composed. Liberals are amused or incensed, according to their individual tempers, at the suggestion that their analysis of capitalist society serves a fascist cause. But their belief that capital and labor may be joined in a wedlock which is productive of some general social welfare leads in a crisis to shotgun weddings such as have been performed in Italy and

Germany with an irate lower middle class brandishing the weapon.[48]

Indeed, the preparation for American fascism clearly revealed the pivotal role played by liberalism, given "its refusal to recognize the class character of capitalist society—a character which involves an absolute irreconcilability of interests between two basic classes."[49] They pointed to Roosevelt's chief architect of the first hundred days, Rexford Tugwell, who "categorically rejects the Marxian concept of the class struggle." Tugwell's own book, *Industrial Discipline*, had revealed

> *his assumption that government* in a capitalist society may be imbued with an essentially social aim that is *inclusive*, and may, therefore, in a grave emergency find it necessary to "compel or persuade a higher co-operation for a national purpose."[50]

From this they concluded of Tugwell's position: "The analysis is *liberal*; the solution is essentially *fascist*." The liberal's road to fascism pointed to another unique characteristic:

> The liberal differs somewhat from the rousing patriot in his nationalism, though not as fundamentally as might appear on the surface. In times of great emergency he joins hands with the *uncritical patriot in demanding* the unqualified loyalty of all to interests that are vital to few.[51]

This was a startling conclusion in a national magazine aimed at a wide middle-class readership. The suggestion that New Deal liberals were fueling the rise of American fascism pointed to a driving force of fascist processes that differed markedly from its Italian and German counterparts. Rather than rabid nationalism, efforts to save monopoly-finance capital from the threat of socialist revolution—perceived more than real—were now engineered by liberal reformers. Still, the coming of American fascism remained an open question. The Roosevelt administration had not "yet taken a decisive stand on the *issue of economic nationalism*," despite the breakdown of the world market which forced other nations toward "an accentuated economic nationalism, or frantic efforts at national economic self-sufficiency."[52] Because this idea was growing in the United States, it pointed to a clear fascist trajectory.

George Sokolsky wrote about America's drift toward fascism in *The American Mercury*, one of the most highly regarded literary magazines in the nation. Sokolsky made no bones that the whole New Deal was fascist. For one thing, it was a vast experiment guided by "no articulate philosophy" to save the capitalist system, but in the process aimed at sweeping aside capitalism itself.[53] The National Recovery Act and its administration was a fascist experiment. In order to save capitalism, Roosevelt moved the United States closer to fascism—but also at the expense of capitalism and the capitalist ethic. This, Sokolsky claimed, was evident in New Deal efforts to transform mass consciousness on the basis of democratic assumptions of equal opportunity and the individualist ethos of Calvinistic Puritanism aimed at capitalist gain. Skillfully, the government joined the spirit of capitalism to the "realism" of the New Deal, which also assumed class war as a constant feature of American society. To move forward democratically required government to intervene "from time to time, on behalf of one class or another."[54] But this ethos, rooted in a romanticized view of democratic, small capitalism was anachronistic in an era in which the crisis of the system and the circumstances it created increased the need for a totalitarian form of government:

The Fascist state intervenes to protect the interests of the whole state when the Dictator, in his personal opinion, believes that such intervention is essential to the "welfare" of the state. The individual has no rights as an individual. He is a cog. . . . But the profit system continues and the individual capitalist might become very rich, if he does not disobey. The worker is given a lollipop or two, but in the main his misery continues as before.[55]

Although Roosevelt and his advisers lacked "a full Fascist philosophy," their experiments aimed at saving the capitalist system were necessarily leading them to fascism.[56] To create a planned economy, especially on the basis of temporary measures, went against the long-held capitalist ethos that everything was grounded in the market. Antitrust laws were suspended so that the NRA had the power to create a balanced economy. But that power, Sokolsky argued, flowed from Roosevelt himself with ominous consequences:

> The "permissive powers" granted the President centralize the planning in him, instead of in Congress, where under the Constitution it belongs. The type of planned economy which has thus far become apparent in Washington is as Fascistic as the planned economy in Italy.[57]

Yet the character of the planning was "not capitalistic," he insisted, "for in capitalism the individual alone must have freedom to determine his activities." Rather, the NRA codes indicated a "Fascistic type of government management." Fascism relied on the "Corporation" rather than the individual "to ensure the success of the managed society, the planned economy," since under fascism "capital and labor function under a strict corporate law (the code) which only the Dictator can change at will." But since American fascism was still embryonic, the "American capitalist"—the very individual who represented Sokolsky's fulfillment of the American ethos—soon "discovered that the N.R.A. was a splendid arrangement for him."[58]

Writing from a Marxist perspective as part of a symposium sponsored by the journal *Modern Monthly* about the possibility of a fascist America, V. F. Calverton opened his contribution by describing fascism as a supreme irony of history:

Built upon the backs and shoulders of the *little* man, better known in America as the *forgotten* man, and supported by that little man through fire and sword, Fascism in every case has proved to be the economic boomerang which has swung back in its course and knocked out that little man before he has been able to catch his breath. In a word the little man has been paid by the big man to serve as an advance pall-bearer at his own funeral.[59]

For Calverton, American capitalist society was divided into three main groups: large-scale business in its corporate-monopoly form, the small businessman or family farmer, and the working man who lived by the wages paid primarily by corporations. While Big Business sought to expand its operations at the expense of small capitalists, workers suffered from starvation wages. The main economic conflict was not between large and small capitalists but between large capitalists and everyone below them. The question of whether or not America went fascist depended on the attitudes of the majority of small capitalists and workers. Since capitalism was surely in decline, it only remained to be seen if its replacement would be fascism led by big businessmen or communism led by workers. The second alternative was only possible if the small capitalist, or the "*little* man" as Calverton called him, who, "psychologically speaking," was in far greater numbers in the United States than any other nation, joined the worker in the fight against fascism, or capitalist dictatorship. All this was evident in the NRA, which, without assuming a fascist guise, was doing the job that European fascism had set out to accomplish, namely the liquidation of the small businessman and dissolution of small business as an economic force. NRA codes were devised especially to aid Big Business in its struggle to dominate the market. In every occupation governed by the codes, Big Business leaders were able to determine the cost calculations and establish the minimum price that governs the operation of the industry, leaving the small businessman incapable of competing with their much greater counterparts. Elected by the forgotten man, Roosevelt was facilitating his extinction as a class and in so doing was achieving the same economic objectives that European fascism had accomplished by "more drastic and desperate methods."[60]

Was There a Transition to Fascism?

If anything, the writers cited here indicated that the New Deal, if not full-blown fascism, indicated a definite trajectory and plausible transition to it. This was the Marxist position taken by Lewis Corey. In his great and still largely forgotten work, *The Decline of American Capitalism*, Corey implied that the New Deal represented the plausibility of a transition to fascism in the United States. His exhaustive analysis of "Niraism," the term he invented to describe the philosophy and practical approach by the Roosevelt administration to reverse the decline and decay of U.S. monopoly state capitalism, could not succeed because it gave greater power only to monopolies, not the rest of society. The NRA marked an unprecedented intervention by the state into the private economy, not to advance technological development aimed at creating a planned economy of abundance, but rather, as Corey wrote, to preserve the decaying old structures through the "*planned limitation of output*." This brought deliberate actions aimed at the repression of production and consumption, the limiting of technological progress, and the wasteful pouring of public money into corporate industry. Moreover, what had begun under the "reactionary" Hoover had advanced qualitatively under the "liberal" Roosevelt. In this respect, Roosevelt's expansion of power in the first months of his presidency represented a tendency of monopoly state capitalism to merge industry and the state more thoroughly in order "to make more direct the control of the state by monopoly capitalism."[61]

In this respect, the NRA made itself master of its own fate by creating "an apparatus for making higher profits," the economic basis by which capital could then wage an even greater assault on the democratic rights of workers, preventing the latter from developing their own path to power. But in doing so, the Roosevelt administration pretentiously proposed a whole series of reforms that were impossible to achieve in full measure. For Corey, the culmination of state capitalism is the same as *state monopoly capitalism*—the New Deal was preparatory to fascism if the crisis intensified. "State capitalism," he wrote, "limits reform to relief, represses the concrete democratic rights of the workers, and prepares their destruction by fascism." Put more simply, without a revolutionary response of the working class toward socialist transition, state monopoly capitalism "becomes a transition to fascism."[62]

> The ruling capitalist class is a small oligarchy. Its rule needs a social base in wider mass support. As the oppressive weight of monopoly state capitalism thrusts the working class on to more aggressive action, other classes are set in motion by their own oppression. The farmers and middle class revolt. *Fascism is an attempt to use the petty-bourgeois masses (including the agrarian) as the upper bourgeoisie has always done, in other forms, to act as a counter-revolutionary mass force.* But these are essentially plebeian masses, the decline of capitalism presses mercilessly upon them, and they are desperate. So fascism masks its purposes with anti-capitalist and radical phrases. But the moment it comes to power fascism reveals itself as the dictatorship of monopoly capitalism.[63]

A year later, R. Palme Dutt, a leading communist writer from India, clearly saw fascism developing in the United States. "The significance of the Roosevelt regime," Dutt wrote in *Fascism and Social Revolution*, "is above all the significance of the transition to Fascist forms, especially in the economic and industrial field." Dutt emphasized that the United States was transitioning toward fascism and in no way was the process complete, but it was definitely moving in that direction:

As the failure of the plans of economic recovery becomes manifest and gives place to new forms of crisis and widespread mass discontent, and above all as the advance to war implicit in the whole Roosevelt policy develops, the demand for corresponding political forms of Fascism will inevitably come to the front in the United States.[64]

The same assessment was provided in the report given by the General Secretary of the Communist International, Georgi Dimitroff, to its Seventh World Congress in 1935. Dimitroff reported that "in a more or less developed form, fascist tendencies and the germs of a fascist movement are to be found almost everywhere."[65] His definition of fascism as "*the open terrorist dictatorship of the most reactionary, most chauvinistic and most imperialist elements of finance capital*" only applied to those capitalist states where fascism had come to power. For Dimitroff, the "*German type*" set the benchmark. The Hitler regime exhibited "bestial chauvinism" and "a government system of political gangsterism." This made it "*the spearhead of international counter-revolution*" and the "*chief instigator of imperialist war.*" Of course, he also made sure to add that this most virulent form of fascism was driven by its "*crusade*" against the Soviet Union, "*the great fatherland of the toilers of the whole world.*" Thus, fascism should be considered neither a form of state power "standing above" the bourgeoisie and the proletariat, nor "the revolt of the petty bourgeoisie which has captured the machinery of state." On the contrary, "fascism is the power of finance capital itself."[66]

As for the United States, Dimitroff said that its people had to consider "*key questions*" in order to do their part in building the fight against fascism at home and abroad. Roosevelt's program for recovery had "collapsed," and Americans were beginning "to abandon the bourgeois parties and are at present at the crossroads." If America went the way of Germany, the world would face an even greater menace than National Socialism:

Embryo American fascism is trying to direct the disillusionment and discontent of these masses into reactionary fascist channels. It is a peculiarity of the development of American fascism that at the present stage this fascism comes forward principally in the guise of an opposition to fascism, which it accuses of being an "un-American" tendency imported from abroad. In contradistinction to German fascism, which acts under anti-constitutional slogans, American fascism tries to portray itself as the custodian of the Constitution and "American democracy." It does not yet represent a directly menacing force. But if it succeeds in penetrating to the wide masses who have become disillusioned with the old bourgeois parties it may become a serious menace in the very near future.

And what would the success of fascism in the United States involve? For the mass of working people it would, of course, involve the unrestrained strengthening of the regime of exploitation and the destruction of the working-class movement. And what would be the international significance of this success of fascism? As we know, the United States is not Hungary, or Finland, or Bulgaria, or Latvia. The success of fascism in the United States would vitally change the whole international situation.[67]

STATE MONOPOLY CAPITALISM, THE NEW DEAL, AND EMBRYONIC FASCISM

The New Deal failed to lift the country out of the Great Depression. Though it saved the banking and financial system from collapse and sought to restrict production in order to push up prices and income to increase consumption, it failed to sustain recovery and solve the problem of unemployment. The New Deal saved Wall Street until wartime production and the waging of war itself finally saved Main Street. The historical record is clear. The volume of real GNP did not reach 1929 levels until 1939. Unemployment, which peaked at almost 25 percent in 1933, averaged nearly 19 percent from 1931 through 1940. As one historian of the U.S. economy concluded, "The anemic nature of the recovery during the 1930s was a direct result of the inadequate increases in government support for the economy . . . [as] the total public-sector deficit averaged only 2.5 percent of the GNP in 1934–37."[68]

American journalists and writers echoed Marxist theoreticians in their belief that the New Deal had definite fascist tendencies. To save capitalism from collapse, the Roosevelt administration had propped up Big Business, which itself had become *a system of power* in its own right. The contradictions of liberal capitalist democracy were also reflected in the warp and woof of liberalism in the 1920s and 1930s that made it inherently contradictory and reduced a once viable political doctrine to folklore. Put another way, these contradictions, which appeared first in a boom and then in the bust, determined the strange and somewhat confusing history of American liberalism. What was unmistakable in the assessments of these writers was that liberalism indeed played a formative role in the making of American fascism.

Lewis Corey presciently saw this in 1934. The attempt to solve the general crisis of the Great Depression required a new round of capitalist accumulation that could only be attained by a resurgent imperialism. Herein lay the inevitable crisis of state monopoly capitalism, which for Corey held the plausibility of American fascism. That it did not come to pass was due to global contingencies that brought fascism to power elsewhere, a menace to the world that America later fought in the name of anti-fascism, which Roosevelt declared in December 1940 as the "Great Arsenal of Democracy."

9—"A Smokescreen over America"

BY THE MID-1930S, some astute observers and analysts saw the origins of American fascism emerging from the crisis of the Great Depression and determined that Big Business was its driving force. Among them were communists and other leftists—socialists, independent Marxists, and progressives of various types. There were others, however, mainly liberals, who believed that America was immune from fascism because it was a distinct European malady. At best, they claimed, any resemblances to European fascism were limited to the thinking and behavior of small hate groups and the demagoguery of reactionary populists. To the extent that it existed at all, fascism in the United States was only present on the margins of mainstream politics, or in the demagogic language of populist leaders whose voices penetrated the masses during the crisis years of the Depression. In short, as many were saying at the time, it couldn't happen here.

George Seldes, a journalist and longtime watchdog for democracy, would have none of this. Instead, Seldes saw the genesis of American fascism in the anti-democratic politics of Big Business. Since the mid-1920s, when his reporting from Italy on Mussolini's regime nearly got him murdered by Il Duce's agents, Seldes had deepened his understanding of the character and features of European fascism throughout the 1930s and early 1940s. His experiences in Europe, in turn, helped him to recognize that fascism was emerging in the United States but in its particular national form. In 1943, Seldes summarized his findings in a book simply titled *Facts and Fascism*. In it, he made common cause with communist writers and those influenced by the Marxist method of class analysis. Big Business was the real fascist threat in the United States. As for the "traitors, seditionists and propagandists" of the fringe hate groups whose activities were eagerly followed by the mainstream press, Seldes simply dismissed them as "small-fry fascisti." Their only success, he wrote, was to raise "a huge smoke-screen over America":

> Behind this artificial redbaiting, anti-Semitic, anti–New Deal fog of confusion and falsehood, however, there was a real Fifth Column of greater importance, the great owners and rulers of America who planned world domination through political and military Fascism, just as surely as Hitler did in Germany, and like groups and like leaders did in other countries. There is no reason to believe that the United States was the one exception to the spread of Fascism.[1]

By the mid-1930s, however, the general thrust of scholarship and political commentary on fascism was moving in a different direction. Liberal writers cultivated a formula for determining whether a group or individual was fascist, quasi-fascist, or just virulently nativist based on a comparison with European fascist movements and the dictators who led them. The first study along these lines was published by political scientist Arthur Steiner in 1935. He described six characteristics that constituted what he termed fascism's "minimum doctrinal standards": rejection of democracy, dictatorial technique, repression of individual freedom, repression of organized labor, intense nationalism, and a reactionary perspective. Contending that certain individuals, organizations, and movements showed some of his six characteristics, Steiner concluded that America lacked a "formal Fascism" because all six were not developing simultaneously on a grand enough scale to make a difference in mainstream American politics.[2]

Steiner and others who took this approach made significant contributions to our knowledge of American fascism. Characteristics of European fascism were certainly apparent in the Ku Klux Klan between 1920 and 1925. During the Depression decade that followed, similar currents of right-wing reaction became stronger and bore a definite likeness to European fascist actions and rhetoric. For writers like Steiner these resemblances were evident in Christian fundamentalist organizations and their respectable preachers, as well as in the leaders of spiritualist or occultist groups who considered themselves oracles of a preordained future. The menace of fascism was visible in various "shirt" groups who meted out old-fashioned American justice to wife-beaters and drunkards, but who reserved greater brutality for labor leaders, communists, Negros, Mexicans, Asians and other nonwhite people, all aliens to their sacred ideal of 100 percent Americanism. Among them were vigilante groups paid by big employers to attack workers, union organizers, and radicals. Then there were the populist demagogues themselves, who sounded as fascist as a Mussolini or Hitler.

Seldes found much common ground with the liberals. But he remained steadfast in his view that fascism, if it did come to power in the United States, would differ from its European counterparts. The small-fry fascisti, he argued, were only diversions from the real source of American fascism—Big Business. Any approach based on the "fascist minimum" was itself a methodological diversion. This view was shared by two communist writers, A. B. Magil and Henry Stevens, who in 1938 urged Americans to unveil the "masquerade" of their own native fascism to see that its "germ" inhered in monopoly capitalism.[3] With fascism imminent, they argued, one had to recognize the menacing and often barbarous political behavior of a ruling class driven by the imperatives of capitalist accumulation and profit, especially in a time of crisis. As for the small-fry fascisti or potent demagogues who might be forerunners of a full-blown American fascism, it was important to see them as parts of a vast yet imperfectly formed wave of reaction to capitalist modernization and as products of social and political upheaval. All exhibited characteristics of anxiety, resentment, and the fear of change. They held either to core Protestant beliefs or bizarre interpretations of Christian spirituality. Some went straight to the lunatic fringe. Most sought to roll back history to an earlier time, to the era of small capitalist enterprise they romanticized, to a life made secure by the knowledge that one's neighbors were old-stock Anglo-Saxons of the Protestant faith, or faithful Catholics who believed they alone possessed true knowledge of the Divine Plan. What they all shared, however, was a belief that they alone were the True Americans, capable of leading the nation just as they led their families and communities.

None of this, however, resulted in the formation of a mass movement. With no workable solution to the Great Depression, the small-fry fascist groups dissolved from their own contradictions and idiosyncrasies or were subsumed by others whose posture made them more acceptable by big employers and politicians. Some became shock troops for reactionary capitalists. The same could not be said for populist demagogues who could become potential partners of the ruling capitalists.

THE BIGGEST SMALL-FRY FASCISTI: PELLEY AND WINROD

The most compelling small-fry were William Dudley Pelley and Gerald B. Winrod. Both emerged from traditionalist Protestantism but from there traveled different roads. While Pelley went deeper into the occult, Winrod remained firmly grounded in fundamentalism. Their trajectories toward fascism make for fascinating reading, especially as described in the detailed and incisive accounts by historian Leo Ribuffo in his classic 1983 study, *The Old Christian Right*.[4]

As Ribuffo tells us, Pelley came from a New England family

"that combined Methodist piety [and a] passion for wealth." His father, a Methodist minister, doubled as a proprietor of small businesses that generated little profit. Pelley admitted that both shared a middle-class trait for "hustle" in the road to success, but he broke with his father's faith early in life upon establishing a philosophically oriented monthly called *Philosopher*. Pelley's writings reveal a craving for the consolation of sentimental religion in spite of his desire to discuss faith in a scientific manner. Both were apparent in his temporary embrace of utopian socialism. Pelley sympathized with the "factory slave" and condemned the ostentatious rich. Jesus was "Comrade Christ," who was "the greatest socialist."[5]

In 1913, Pelley became owner and publisher of the *Deerfield Times* in Wilmington, Vermont. It failed within a year. Fortune smiled on him at last in 1917 when a tribute he wrote to motherhood launched his career as a writer. Over the next decade, Pelley wrote more than 200 stories for leading magazines. The journalist in him ran deep, and in 1918 he bought another Vermont paper, the *Caledonian*. A few months later, he was invited to report on missionary activities in Asia for the Methodist Centenary Movement. He and his wife packed their bags and went to Japan. From August to November 1918, he traveled alone across Siberia, doubling as a correspondent for the American Red Cross and the Associated Press. Returning to Vermont and the *Caledonian*, he wrote what amounted to "fake news" stories about the Russian Revolution and how Bolshevism had reduced Russia to chaos. Now a staunch anti-communist, Pelley jumped aboard the Red Scare bandwagon in 1919. Back at the *Caledonian*, he covered a Senate investigation into Soviet propaganda but ignored the rabid anti-Semitism in its sessions.[6] At this point, Ribuffo says, Pelley's reporting did not yet reveal "a congenital bigot marching inexorably toward the Silver Shirts," the fascist group he would found later. Sympathetic to welfare legislation, labor unions, and Wilson's foreign policy, his occasional "references to Huns, Japs, Chinamen and, once, niggers" showed that he was no more prejudiced than any other reformer of the period.[7]

During most of the 1920s, Pelley fulfilled his petty-bourgeois aspirations—his "Yankee's weakness"—of pursuing "any sort of project that promised a profit."[8] He wrote profitably for leading magazines and other publications. He was also lured to Hollywood. By Pelley's own count, he claimed to have written or supervised twenty-one movie scripts between 1921 and 1928 "at a profit of nearly $100,000."[9] Two were westerns—he knew nothing about cowboys and frontier life—and another became the basis for a Lon Chaney movie. Drained by Hollywood "fleshpots" whom he claimed had ruined his marriage, Pelley sought refuge in the mountains of Southern California where he hoped to get himself straight with God. For several months, he went deep into himself searching for a spiritual breakthrough, which Ribuffo saw as mainly psychological. All changed dramatically with Pelley's conversion experience on the night of May 28, 1928.[10]

For Pelley, it was a critical interruption with the past. His physical appearance changed and he lost his nervous edge. From that point in his life, Ribuffo says, Pelley continued to hear "clairaudient" messages from the other world far beyond established types of mysticism.[11] Moving to New York City, he began publishing his accounts in a series of pamphlets that turned into the *New Liberator*, which Pelley called a journal of "higher verities." Among them was the claim that the "Divine Mind" had created every soul then in the world 28 million years earlier. Another was his theology of the afterlife that was comfortably familiar with his hierarchical view of this world. His petty-bourgeois hustle always made him sound like someone pitching a new sect as a decisive participant in his own oracles of the future.[12]

In 1932, Pelley moved to Asheville, North Carolina, where he established the Foundation for Christian Economics and opened Galahad College. He told followers that he would soon lead a mass movement against anti-Christian conspirators in a Holy War aimed at recasting American society. Pelley believed that "something special was brewing in the universe." Great troubles ahead called for humanity to overcome its softness and greed. He believed that Jesus would return in his lifetime. To that end, he proclaimed himself an officer in the army of reincarnated souls. By 1931, he had become one of the most virulent anti-Semites in the spotlight. "The worst 'demon' spirits inhabited Jewish bodies." Evil was everywhere. In one of his publications, Pelley wrote that President Hoover was manipulated by agents of the "International Shylock," big Jewish bankers responsible for the Depression, while their secretive communist brethren were bent on emasculating Christian principles for "racial profit."[13]

Pelley's admiration for Adolf Hitler led him to create his own fascist legion, the Silver Shirts, on January 30, 1933, the day after Hitler was appointed Germany's chancellor. The Silver Shirts, he declared, would bring "the work of Christ militant into the open."[14] The media pegged him as one of America's aspiring fuehrers. Pelley openly praised Hitler and cooperated with the German American Bund to mold an anti-Semitic program remarkable even by the standards of fellow American bigots. Like other anti-Semites, he insisted that Jesus was not a Jew but had descended from the Gauls, a prominent Germanic group that had swept across Europe during the time of the Roman Empire and became the core of modern-day France. According to Pelley in his read of Exodus, the Jews were responsible for debasing their "pure-blooded" Egyptian masters, which he then claimed was an "ancient version" of the National Recovery Administration—Jews were responsible for the "essence" of communism in Canaan and the Jews running the NRA were now their modern counterparts. Jesus was the "outstanding 'Jew-baiter' of His day." The Jews had defiled the New Testament. Pelley's chief target in both ancient and modern times was the Sanhedrin, the ruling elites who sought world conquest. Pelley was convinced that Christian civilization was under attack by Jewish capitalists and their communist partners, citing familiar though unsubstantiated stories and inaccurate statistics purporting to show that Jews dominated the Soviet Union.[15]

In the United States, Pelley accused Jews of dominating the slave trade and blamed secession on Jewish leadership in the South.

"While whites, imbued with racial 'good sportsmanship,' created productive industries during the late nineteenth century, Jews merely manipulated money." They had created the Federal Reserve in 1913 and held almost complete control of the Wilson administration. Roosevelt's departure from the gold standard in 1933 strengthened Jewish bankers. He attacked the Jewish New Deal bureaucracy and claimed that the president's ancestors included Dutch Jews, which explained Roosevelt's Jewish appointees and his insane hatred for Hitler. In effect, Ribuffo wrote, Pelley equated anti-Semitism with twentieth-century Americanism. As the self-styled premier anti-Semite, he threatened to strike any "kike" who criticized the Silver Shirts.[16]

The class composition and consciousness of the Silver Shirts was typical of other reactionary groups of the 1930s. The bar was set low for its all-white membership. The organization topped 15,000 in 1934 but had shrunk to 5,000 in 1938. Units were active in Cleveland, Toledo, and Youngstown, Ohio; and Minneapolis-St. Paul, San Diego, Los Angeles, Seattle, and Chicago. But recruitment was low in the Northeast and the South. Ribuffo cites the work of historian John Werly, who identified the occupations of 327 members, finding them equally divided between the working class (skilled craftsmen and low-level clerks as well as laborers) and the solid middle class (teachers, clergy, and small businessmen). There were a few farmers but the sample included a fair number of lawyers, physicians, and corporate executives. Pelley erroneously claimed over half of his recruits were Roman Catholic. Ribuffo doubted this since some Silver Shirts doubled as Klansmen, who were virulently anti-Catholic.[17]

According to the political scientist Victor Ferkiss, who wrote an invaluable 1954 doctoral dissertation on American fascism, Pelley sought a Christian Commonwealth that was distinct from Nazism, communism, or capitalism. This was apparent in Pelley's self-published book of 1936, *No More Hunger,* which proposed a Christian alternative to the capitalist profit system as the only solution to the Depression. The nation would be organized into a giant corporation in which all citizens were made stockholders, each receiving a yearly dividend of $1,000 for which he was not required to work. Those who wanted more than mere subsistence could engage in manufacturing and other economic activities that were organized by what Pelley called a civil service. There were no class divisions. All wealth would be owned by the common-wealth except for homes and personal property, which citizens could purchase from their yearly dividends. This eliminated the risk of foreclosures, rent, interest, and the dreaded un-Christian practice of usury. In Pelley, Ferkiss saw the oddball fascist who held to a critique of capitalism grounded in the economic thinking and reactionary worldview of the petty bourgeoisie. Pelley wanted an economic revolution that kept "the small homeowner happy."[18]

Unlike Pelley, whose dive into the occult took him into the realm of the bizarre, Gerald B. Winrod was the stolid though respected Protestant fundamentalist whose increasingly politicized the-ology took him toward fascism. As the leader of evangelical Protestantism in the 1920s, Winrod's reactionary thought was the core of his worldview. His deepening of Dispensationalism, the name given to a particular doctrine that divided history into Seven Ages as proclaimed in the Book of Revelation, turned him into one of America's leading Christian fascists in the 1930s. Winrod feared all forms of modernism, including Protestant denominations that sought to incorporate Darwin's theory of evolution and scientific principles into the faith. Darwinism reduced man's soul and even Christ himself to the "animalistic psychology" found in Sigmund Freud's theories about man.[19] Eventually, this led Winrod to a sys-tematic anti-Semitism in the service of a Protestant theological mindset in which a "World Jewish Conspiracy" bred commu-nism—all a justification for supporting Hitler and the Nazis as the last defense against modernity itself.

As Ribuffo has written, the intense spirituality of Winrod's boy-hood and adolescent years "took precedence over education." From a teenage evangelist to a young minister who supported himself as a bookkeeper, Winrod lived the perfect Christian life of economic stability and godliness. In 1925, he established the Defenders of the Christian Faith in Salina, Kansas, and a year later became owner and publisher of its magazine, the *Defender*. The magazine called all true Christians to return to the Bible. Winrod reached out to other theologically conservative Christians, distancing himself from all theological liberals who, in their acceptance of Darwinism, had reduced Jesus to an "animal ancestry."[20]

As an ardent Dispensationalist, Winrod contended that the world had entered the penultimate age of the Beast or the Antichrist as prophesied in the Book of Revelation. He claimed the Beast would soon restore the Roman Empire and facilitate the return of the Jews to Jerusalem. This signaled Jesus's Second Coming and the defeat of the Antichrist at Armageddon and then a Millennium (or last dispensation) whose end was the "final judgment of all souls."[21] Winrod condemned Darwinism and all its evil offshoots—the communism of Marx, Lenin, and Stalin, the philosophy of Neitzsche, and Freud's psychology. All were components of modernism, with which his divide was unbridgeable. Winrod fought hard to eliminate the teaching of Darwinism in Kansas public schools. His 1932 book, *Christ Within*, denounced the "moral sag" it caused and the depravities it brought to everyday life. He especially condemned Freud's writings, which he refused to even quote in the *Defender*. Its "animalistic psychology" threatened Christian beliefs, principles, and values. Anything less than the return of Jesus required a "nationwide revival of old-fashioned Holy Ghost religion" as "the only alternative to ruin."[22]

Throughout the 1920s, the *Defender* had avoided Jewish stereotypes typical of Christian fundamentalism. Winrod scorned old legends about Jews sacrificing Christian children in their religious rites and regretted the pogroms in Europe they had inflamed. Jews actually fared better in the *Defender* than Roman Catholics and their false theology. In 1928, Winrod even praised orthodox rabbis for fighting modernism within Judaism. But his self-prescribed study of world affairs made him decidedly more radical and ahistorical. Communists in the Soviet Union had dethroned God, he said, but the real diabolical force in the world was the Italian fascist dictator, Benito Mussolini, the world leader who had absorbed the Darwinian idea of the survival of the fittest, from which Nietzsche got his idea of the superman. For Winrod, "Fascism was evolution in fearless action." More important, Mussolini was the best candidate for the Antichrist, or at least paving the way for him by restoring the Roman Empire.[23]

For Winrod, the Great Depression was a clear sign of moral collapse as the whole world awaited Armageddon. He was more troubled, however, by the New Deal's attempt to soften its blows. In the *Defender* and especially in the *Revealer*, another of his publications, Winrod stepped up his political attacks on the Roosevelt administration's programs and personalities. He was particularly critical of the Agricultural Adjustment Administration (AAA) and agriculture secretary Henry Wallace, whom Winrod saw as embracing a political philosophy that was the complete opposite of biblical teachings. Whereas Joseph had prepared for famine by storing crops, Wallace had destroyed food instead of distributing it to starving citizens. The crisis of overproduction was merely a "myth" propagated by Wallace and his fellow New Dealers.[24]

Winrod's middle-class reaction was strong in his opposition to Big Business. As Ribuffo says:

> A successful magazine publisher, Winrod was a small businessman as well as a prophet in politics. Indeed, his social views in their secular aspect were largely congruent with those of other small businessmen opposing the New Deal. Although convinced that the Depression was somehow related to maldistribution of wealth, he proposed neither a comprehensive program nor piecemeal reforms to redistribute the nation's bounty. Unlike Pelley, he never doubted the gospel of success, concluding in 1935: "Any man who will live a good life, work hard, develop his mental faculties and take advantage of his opportunities for self-advancement, can climb without restraint to the topmost rung of human achievement, under the American system of government."[25]

Winrod was shaken by the New Deal and its "sinister" shadow of dictatorship. New Dealers were all enemies of the people. The Tennessee Valley Administration and the NRA were the "first taste" of American fascism. By 1935, however, he had changed his tune. The New Deal was a "Red program" that would carry America toward communism, not fascism. The Depression was "first spiritual, then moral, then economic." America "was cracking up," and liberalism in its secular and theological forms was responsible. There was a style common to liberals, "smart-alecky" arrogance that promoted modernism and mocked the true believers in faith and in the nation.[26] Simultaneously, his politicized theology took him toward lunacy. Anything could be rationalized since the Antichrist could awe mankind by creating an arsenal of mysterious weapons, for example, a world government and a world bank. The Antichrist was no longer Mussolini. He was a Jew. Winrod claimed this discovery only from learning how a "hidden hand" was preparing the way for the Beast. It was the Jewish World Conspiracy. His sources were the forgeries and myths compiled by Russian emigrés and other European anti-Semites in two books, *The Protocols of the Learned Elders of Zion* and *The International Jew*. Both were discussed in fundamentalist magazines during the 1920s. Jews were "Satan's identifiable, semi-autonomous deputies arrayed against God's semi-autonomous prophets."[27] One of the latter was Hitler, whom Winrod considered a "devout Catholic."[28]

In 1938, Winrod ran for the U.S. Senate as a Republican. Even Roosevelt inquired about rumors that an openly fascist man named Winrod was a likely Republican nominee. Finishing third in the primary, his loss was a harbinger of future troubles as he proclaimed himself a native Nazi. From 1939 to 1941, he persisted in crude isolationist arguments to keep America out of the European war, which, combined with his sympathies for Hitler as the bulwark of anti-Semitism, earned him inclusion in a list compiled by Roosevelt administration officials of Americans "to be considered for custodial detention" as native fascists if and when war did come. Winrod was called to testify in 1942 when he and twenty-seven others were indicted for conspiracy to cause insub-ordination in the armed forces. Known initially as *United States v. Winrod*, the case caused turmoil in his life for the next five years.[29] Ultimately, the case was declared a mistrial when the presiding judge died, and another judge later dropped all charges against Winrod and the other defendants.

Shirt Groups and the Black Legion

The liberal historian Arthur Schlesinger Jr., a celebrated if unwit-ting contributor to the *fascist minimum*—the minimum number of characteristics based on Italian and German fascism—used much ink to describe groups and organizations that he deemed insig-nificant in the political upheaval of the mid-1930s. These, he said, were the "*farceurs*—the activists of American fascism." Among them were the "mostly local adventurers or fanatics hoping some-how to capitalize on anxiety and unrest" and who turned to the European dictators and their movements as models. Along with Pelley's Silver Shirts were the Khaki Shirts, some of whom came from the ranks of the veterans who made up the Bonus Marchers in 1932. The Khaki Shirts were typical of postwar veteran groups in the mold of the German Freikorps, which played a key role in the development of the fascist movement in Germany. Its leader was "General" Art J. Smith, who promoted a peculiar economic philosophy he called "manocracy." Smith demanded the abolition of Congress, revaluation of silver, and the building of the world's largest army and navy. Attempting to emulate Mussolini's 1922 March on Rome, Smith called on a million and a half veterans to march on Washington on Columbus Day 1933. But the event never came off, and Smith, who soon after was exposed as a con artist and convicted of perjury in a murder trial of one of his fol-lowers, served six years in prison and then disappeared.[30]

Of more substance was the Black Legion, which grew out of the so-called second Ku Klux Klan of the 1920s and had a highly visible presence in midwestern cities. The historian Peter Amaan locates its origins in the efforts of one man, William Jacob Shepard, a small-town doctor and Klan leader in Belaire, Ohio, who tried revitalizing his local Klan unit by getting rid of the white robes and replacing them with glamorous, red-trimmed black robes. The Black Guards, as they were initially called, also became known as the Black Night Riders—and eventually the Black Legion.[31]

According to Amaan, Shepard was a walking contradiction. The grandson of a Union soldier, he deified Confederate war heroes and talked endlessly about their southern gallantry and chivalry. But he was a born night rider who enjoyed flogging men who had run afoul of Klan scriptures. Known as "the little doctor of the poor," he was said to be the local abortionist as well "who took his fee in sexual favors." As the leader of two violently anti-Semitic organizations, the Klan and the Legion, Shepard was still named "Citizen of the Year" with support from the local chapter of B'nai B'rith. As a baptized Catholic, he often railed against Catholicism.[32] Amaan summed up the good doctor:

> He was the eternal joiner—Eagle, Moose, Thirty-second Degree Mason, luncheon club regular—and the everlasting outsider. He was a drunk who died cold sober. He was the town tough guy, the town comedian, the town saint, the town eccentric, who baffled his family, amused and irritated his contemporaries, and still defies attempts to draw up a final balance sheet.[33]

As an organization bent on terror, the Legion was a step up from the Klan. This was evident in the frightening initiation ceremony, itself an act of terror for prospective new members. Candidates swore allegiance to the organization on the basis of the Black Oath, which was derived from an oath written by a rogue Confederate officer to justify his criminal and terrorist acts against civilians. Recruits were taken to a secluded spot in the middle of the night where they swore to keep the secret of the ceremony and pledged to follow any order given by their superiors, including perjury when necessary. They agreed to uphold standard nativist, anti-immigrant, anti-Negro, and anti-Catholic positions and pledged to inflict violence against anyone who menaced native-born white Americans. A chaplain told them that the sole purpose of war was to kill and that the organization would "tear down, lay waste, despoil and kill our enemies." Then with a gun at their back and kneeling in front of their hooded officers, each recruit repeated the oath that ended in their solemn pledge "to exert every possible means in my power for the extermination of the anarchist, Communist, or Roman hierarchy and their abettors."[34]

Legionnaires saw nothing in the political system worth saving. Both parties were corrupt and dangerous to ordinary white Americans. Republicans only cared about the rich. The Democrats had succumbed to the alien forces of Catholicism and were tools of the papacy.[35] Shepard himself set a violent tone for the Legion. Night riding was vigilante justice and he believed he was born for it. The Legion became more violent in 1932 when leadership passed from Shepard to Virgil F. Effinger, a Grand Titan of the Klan in Lima, Ohio. Effinger had no interest in southern gallantry. Instead, he convinced Shepard that the Legion could grow nationally. Elevating Shepard to a ceremonial post, Effinger took the title of Major General and set out to reorganize the Legion on a military basis. Regiments formed in cities in Ohio, Michigan, Indiana, and Illinois. Thousands of men entered the Legion in 1934 and 1935.[36]

On the basis of his deep knowledge of European fascism, Amaan concludes, though not convincingly, that the Black Legion was not a fascist organization. For one thing, he argues that the Legion cannot be explained by occupation, income, or wealth, which immediately negates a class analysis of fascism. Instead, he tells us that Shepard "lived and died a poor man" and "a conjurer, not an ideologue, organizer, agitator or power wielder."[37] He then admits that Effinger was "the very prototype of the insecure lower middle-class individual who, we are told, flocked to the Nazis."[38] Yet he insists that the Legion was anything but middle class. Social composition and class consciousness were of no consequence. Instead, he proposes his own version of the fascist minimum. "If we translate a definition derived from European experience into the American idiom," he wrote, "the Black Legion certainly shared in the typical fascist hatreds." But when it came to their goals and objectives and their continual talk of staging an American version of Mussolini's March on Rome, Amaan sees in the Legion only "a very dim notion of the 'revolutionary' nationalist, authoritarian state dear to fascists" and "an even dimmer emphasis on the power of the will, and not a glimmer of a new 'corporate' economic order" that were clear features of European fascism. Thus, by comparison, the Black Legion met "some, but not all, of the fascist criteria." As he concludes, the "curiously primitive, underdeveloped, inarticulate sort of fascism" that the Black Legion exhibited made it not fascist but "fascisoid." For Amaan, the organization did not meet "fascist goals" because its nativist character fell short of the mark.[39]

Writing in 1983 and seemingly blind to class analysis, Amaan ignored a 1952 essay by sociologist Morris Janowitz, who focused on the class composition of the Legion. General membership consisted mainly of workers from Tennessee, Kentucky, and Mississippi who had migrated to the industrial centers of the Midwest. According to Janowitz, the typical member was a man from the South in his mid-thirties of Anglo-Saxon descent who had made the journey, usually with his family in tow, to live in some industrial suburb where he felt out of sorts. Getting a job and keeping it was the primary concern for these proud men who looked down on lazy people whose existence depended on government-supplied jobs. An avid churchgoer, the average legionnaire saw himself as the defender of True Americanism against Jews, communists, and Negroes. Based on police records, the evidence showed that many respectable middle-class individuals joined the Legion or were intimidated to do so. There were many cops in the ranks. Local politicians signed on to reap its political influence. "All available data," Janowitz wrote, "underline the middle-class origin of the top leaders."[40]

FATHER COUGHLIN: THE SONOROUS SOUNDS OF FASCISM

Much has been written about whether the Catholic radio priest Charles Edward Coughlin and Senator Huey P. Long of Louisiana were native-American fascists, and it warrants no repetition here. What is important is the extent to which some writers help us to understand what both men brought to the making of American fascism. Coughlin commanded a great following across much of America through his brilliant use of the radio. Long was already considered the "emperor of Louisiana in all but name" until the evening of September 8, 1935, when a local political rival mortally wounded him in the corridor of the state capitol.[41]

As reactionaries who have been categorized as fascist, quasi-fascists, or fascist forerunners, Long and Coughlin shaped a potent and infectious politics based on the meshing of nativism, anti-communism, and attacks on Roosevelt and the New Deal. Many recent writers tend to distinguish nativism from fascism as a political feature distinct to American society. Others have argued that the changing political character of nativism caused by economic dislocation in the early and mid-1920s, and the crisis decade of the thirties, generated political extremism that could turn fascist if and when merged with the interests of the most reactionary elements of the ruling capitalist class.

Coughlin's radio ministry began in 1926, only three years after he took his final vows in the diocese of Detroit. His superior, Bishop Michael Gallagher, had told him to build a church in the suburb of Royal Oak. There were few Catholic families in the parish, but Gallagher saw great potential in new parishioners from the auto industry. It was also a suburb heavily in the grips of the Ku Klux Klan. This was of little concern to Gallagher, who instructed his ambitious and determined young prelate to "build a church at the crossroads of faith and religious persecution," and "make it a missionary oasis in the desert of religious bigotry." Coughlin did just that. Even after the Klan burned a cross on the front lawn of his new church, the Shrine of the Little Flower, Coughlin's resolve to establish a Catholic presence in the community only strengthened. But this required financing beyond diocesan support. Recognizing the power of his oratory as a preacher, Coughlin approached the manager of a local radio station to propose a radio ministry. With Bishop Gallagher's blessing, and with the financial backing of the station owner, Coughlin went on the air for the first time on October 17, 1926, dressed in vestments and standing at the altar of his church.[42]

By generally avoiding controversial issues and instead focusing on Catholic teachings, Coughlin became increasingly popular in Detroit. While neutralizing the Klan threat, his radio ministry expanded to the rest of Michigan. Meanwhile, people flocked to his small church, prompting him to build a bigger church on the very spot where the Klan burned its cross. Rising from a large octagonal church and central altar, Coughlin imagined a "tower that would climb to the sky to the Virgin Mary's bosom." Though he claimed the sole purpose of building the church was to give people work, the construction company he hired used non-union labor at wages below the union level. As he preached to the suffering whose money was scarce, Coughlin spent over $800,000 to build the new church.[43]

Coughlin successfully tapped into the anxiety and fears of the middle and lower middle classes by explaining how they had been victimized by Big Business and the federal government. The year 1930 was a banner one for the radio priest as the nation fell deeper into the Depression. Christian civilization, he cried, was under attack from an international conspiracy that aimed to enslave them. He called on his radio audiences to choose "Christ or the Red Fog" and attacked the philosopher Bertrand Russell for his socialist and communist ideas. Testifying to a congressional committee investigating communist propaganda in the United States, Coughlin predicted a revolution by 1933. Meanwhile, he negotiated a deal with CBS radio, enabling him to reach an estimated 40 million listeners in twenty-three states. Coughlin quickly became a national figure. Tempering anti-communism with sermons on "bread and butter economic issues," he wrapped his solutions in Catholic social justice teachings, often citing Pope Leo's 1891 encyclical, *Rerum Novarum*, which emphasized the need for capital and labor to find common ground. Coughlin's sermons applied a moral imperative to relieve the mass suffering caused by the Depression. But he also affirmed the Church's position to find solutions within existing capitalist relations. Coughlin did not attack capitalism itself, but he strongly believed that the prime movers of the communist threat were international bankers, namely Jews, who were robbing the American people of their labor. Capitalism, he argued, when properly understood, meant that owners made acceptable profits and still treated workers justly. As his biographer Sheldon Marcus wrote, Coughlin spoke repeatedly about paying "a living wage for the sacred commodity they brought to the economic marketplace—their labor." For Coughlin, the usury of big bankers was instrumental in generating the global communist movement. But as Marcus noted, he created confusion when he attacked "the international bankers for helping to disseminate communism."[44]

According to historian Alan Brinkley, there is no way to know how many Americans Coughlin reached in his Sunday broadcasts. Brinkley estimates that it routinely amounted to 10 million listeners. Coughlin could boast of a national network of nearly thirty stations by 1934. This gave him a solid lock on audiences in the East and Midwest, but it wasn't until 1935 that his voice penetrated airwaves in the South or the West.[45] As Coughlin continued his assault on capitalist greed and the communist rejection of private property, he upheld the sanctity of the latter on the basis of entrenched Catholic teachings. The Catholic Church stands for private ownership, he told his listeners, and "will stand by it and die for it if necessary. But it will likewise proclaim that there is a limitation upon the use of hoarded wealth."[46]

Coughlin's hatred for big bankers extended to President Hoover and the Republican establishment. Like millions of other Americans, he became enraged by Hoover's insensitivity and his administration's sometimes brutal treatment of people merely trying to survive. He resented Hoover for repeatedly claiming that the crisis was ending, that recovery was around the corner, and that all public relief was the responsibility of local government and private charity. This only made Hoover a "tool" of international bankers now made richer from "torture more refined than was ever excogitated by the trickery of the Romans or the heartlessness of slave owners." Coughlin also castigated Hoover for pushing Congress to create the Reconstruction Finance Corporation (RFC). As a government entity, the RFC gave financial support to state and local governments for public works projects and also made loans to banks, railroads, and mortgage associations. For Coughlin, this was just another step toward "financial socialism." But nothing compared to Hoover's callousness and brutality when he unleashed the U.S. Army on thousands of American "heroes" who had marched to Washington in the summer of 1932 to claim the bonus they had been granted by Congress for their service in the Great War. Not only was it morally right for the government to give the vets their bonuses, Coughlin reasoned, the bonus would also enable them to put $2 billion of their purchasing power back into the economy.[47]

By the spring of 1932, Coughlin had already decided to support Franklin Roosevelt in the November election. From their first meeting, Coughlin was sure that his ideas would become integral to Roosevelt's plans for a new deal. His slogans of "Roosevelt or Ruin" and "The New Deal Is Christ's Deal" became familiar during the campaign. After the election, Roosevelt was grateful for Coughlin's support of his whirlwind legislative agenda during his first hundred days in office. Yet Roosevelt was always suspicious of Coughlin, though cordial whenever the priest sought a meeting. Roosevelt believed that Coughlin was an unpredictable and dangerous "demagogue" who should be tolerated and "tamed" but never trusted. His arrogance and presumptuousness were simply too much for the president.[48] Whatever unity the two men had shared dissolved when Coughlin realized that Roosevelt and his advisers would never accept his economic policies. At that point, Roosevelt became a bitter enemy.

Coughlin tapped into the growing anti–New Deal sentiment spreading across the nation in 1934. Among the discontented was a small group of businessmen, politicians from the farm states and a few economists who formed the Committee for the Nation to push for substantive changes in monetary policy as the main solution to end the Depression. The committee championed the remonetization of silver—making silver legal tender as redeemable in dollars just as was gold—by claiming that it would put more money into circulation, allowing the market to expand and thereby improving the economic position of the small farmer, merchant, manufacturer, and banker. Coughlin took up this theme in his radio broadcasts and writings in *Social Justice*, his personal newspaper. He made much of his own claim that remonetization would expand U.S. trade with China and other nations that operated on a silver standard, thus making it easier for them to buy goods made in America. Monetary policy was the key to recovery, something, he argued, Roosevelt did not understand. Remonetization would end unemployment since more labor could be bought to increase production. Advocating for a bimetallic base took Coughlin to his next step: nationalization of the whole banking system, which would empower the American people to decide how to control the flow of money to their advantage.[49]

By the end of 1934, the honeymoon with Roosevelt had ended and Coughlin entered the peak years of his popularity. Convinced that Roosevelt was not serious about ending the Depression, he called for the creation of a "new American dollar" that contained 25 cents in gold and 75 cents in silver. This, he argued, would stabilize the banking system and consequently end unemployment.[50] Coughlin also charged that Roosevelt's most significant New Deal agency, the NRA, had achieved the opposite of what it was intended to do. Instead of leveling the playing field between capital and labor, and also strengthening the position of the middle classes in relation to monopolies and big banks, it had fueled greater concentration of wealth and power. The AAA was even worse for destroying crops and livestock and limiting production to raise prices on farm commodities. Referring to Roosevelt's hold on power as a monopoly that resembled communism, Coughlin called on Congress to abandon the New Deal and create its own recovery program. Backed by powerful financial and political forces, especially the media empire of William Randolph Hearst, whose newspapers avidly promoted Coughlin's views, Coughlin charted his own path when he announced the creation of a new organization called the National Union for Social Justice (NSJU) in November 1934. The NSJU would act like a third political party, though Coughlin saw it mainly as an "articulate, organized lobby of the people" to pressure lawmakers in both parties to pass laws needed by the public.[51]

In a document called the "Sixteen Principles," Coughlin sought middle ground between the right of the individual to utilize natural resources by his own labor and the necessity of securing that right in fulfillment of a Christian society founded on social justice. To reach it required removing all wealth from the "harsh, cruel and grasping ways of wicked men who first concentrated wealth into the hands of a few." Here, Coughlin's economic views resembled those of other middle-class reformers who wanted to do away with the worst abuses of capitalism. Coughlin envisioned a society cleansed of big banking and finance and restored to a just capitalist order of small-scale production and exchange—operating on the basis of voluntary association between producers. At the same time, he was oblivious to fundamental capitalist contradictions that could neither be glossed over nor dismissed. He upheld the sanctity of property rights but called for the abolition of the Federal Reserve because it was "privately owned," insisting that it be replaced by a government-owned Central Bank that would "maintain the cost of living on an even keel and arrange for the repayment of dollar debts with equal value dollars."[52] The NSJU would promote these views as an independent political movement because the Republicans were totally bankrupt, while the

Democrats were "on trial" for upholding "one of the worst evils of decadent capitalism, namely, that production must be only at a profit for the owners, for the capitalist, and not for the laborer."[53]

In his unpublished 1954 doctoral dissertation in political science, Victor Ferkiss aptly concluded that Coughlin's thought, activities, and appeal "vividly illustrates the degeneration of a native American radicalism into fascism." Ferkiss regarded "Coughlinism" as a mix of central tenets that expressed Coughlin's complex and highly contradictory views on politics and economics—all a clear indication of an American fascism in the making. Coughlin claimed to represent the masses chopped up by liberal capitalist democracy and now being served on a platter to revolutionary socialism by the evils of big bankers. His egalitarian and democratic views wrapped in the language of True Americanism were clear. But his classical education and the hierarchical worldview of Catholic doctrine added a strange twist that undercut his version of the doctrine. Steeped in the theology and philosophy of medieval scholasticism and papal social teachings of the late nineteenth and early twentieth centuries, his training for the priesthood "emphasized the normative almost to the exclusion of the empirical." Moreover, he knew very little about America. His views on society were grounded in European thought and culture; his curriculum at St. Michael's College gave scant attention to U.S. history and its basic issues. Apart from his training in theology, his education was "roughly equivalent to that of the average American high school student" and "overlaid with a tightly defined series of propositions about society in the abstract" that "developed within a European milieu."[54]

Undoubtedly, Coughlin was a preeminent force of political reaction in the mid-1930s. The New Deal had saved Wall Street and the giant corporations but had left much of society behind. Ferkiss says Coughlin began to quote passages from *The Economic Consequences of the New Deal* by Benjamin Stolberg and Warren J. Vinton, whose statistical analysis demonstrated that the New Deal had made the rich richer and the poor poorer.[55] As the educator and author Sheldon Marcus has written, Coughlin skillfully captured the fears of middle-class people and workers whose political consciousness was not exactly proletarian:

> Among the lower and lower-middle classes—both rural and urban—Coughlin succeeded in galvanizing a feeling of class discrimination, which evolved into class and eventually religious hatred. His followers had become fed up with big business and its tool, the federal government. They wanted scapegoats for the Depression and solutions to bring them out of it, and many were convinced that Father Coughlin was providing these solutions. Regardless of prior ideological commitment, on the Left or on the Right, they were attracted by Coughlin's slashing attacks against the concentration of power in the hands of big business and the federal government's passivity in the face of crisis.[56]

For Coughlin, capitalism had degenerated from the simple and direct exchange of earlier times in a market that supposedly elevated principles over profits. This put him in the current of petty-bourgeois reformism of the 1930s that was steeped in late nineteenth- and early twentieth-century forms of agrarian and populist radicalism. But the forward-looking radicalism of his predecessors became in Coughlin's politics a wholesale reaction against capitalist modernization and all its political forms. The twin evils of the time threatening Christian civilization were the socialists whose atheism and materialism were anathema to Christianity and the Jewish international bankers who were guilty of draining wealth from its actual producers in society—both fueling the communist threat. The taking of interest was not only usurious but the first sin in a market society that should be operating on the basis of Christian principles. The coming of modern industry and finance made usury even more destructive. Private bankers with great fortunes manipulated the money supply for their own gain and at the expense of those who were indebted to them. Defending the principle of private ownership as God-given, Coughlin's ideal was small capitalist enterprise dominated by the merchant and farmer.

It was a vision with precedent. As noted above, his views were grounded in Catholic teachings that called on employers to pay fair wages and allow workers to unionize and defend their interests without fear or penalty. Capitalist plutocracy was the enemy, but the capitalist system was sacred if rooted in the ideal of small ownership. Coughlin generally favored a commercial society that operated on the basis of cooperation and specifically the formation of cooperatives that would trade with one another by means of prearranged agreements and notes of exchange. In this respect, his views of a new society flowed from earlier notions, including the nineteenth-century mutualism of Pierre-Joseph Proudhon. Production and exchange in a society grounded in small private ownership could be achieved fairly and justly by voluntary association and mutual respect for one another's needs. Like the Proudhonists, Coughlin and his followers embraced the idea that all economic activity was subordinate to life on spiritual, intellectual, and familial terms. And just like Proudhon's, Coughlin's new society would be based on a dominant, conservative middle class, and an idealist portrayal of the family farmer and the small merchant, manufacturer, and banker. For both men, the real struggle under capitalism was not between capital and labor but between the producer and the money changer.[57]

By the late 1930s, the contradictions of petty-bourgeois ideology with a specific Catholic twist in Coughlin's thought gave way to a rabid and systemic anti-Semitism. This was the only message he had left in 1938. Promoting himself as a principled independent opposed to Republicans and Democrats alike, he had supported a third-party candidate for president in 1936, William Lemke, a Republican congressman from North Dakota who became the standard bearer for the short-lived Union Party. Despite his disdain for Lemke, Coughlin promised to deliver nine million votes to the candidate on Election Day. This proved fatal to Coughlin's notoriety after Lemke polled less than 900,000 votes (2 percent). Shocked by his total lack of influence in the election, Coughlin bid a tearful goodbye to his listeners and signed off. Though he eventually returned to radio, his real power had dissolved. All he could do now was to press forward his conspiratorial views about Jewish bankers who doubled as communists. Here was Coughlin's unique contribution to fascist demagoguery in the United States in the late 1930s. The incoherence of his political economy plus his belief that real democracy was only possible in a Christian nation left him with only one evil to bellow about—the World Jewish Conspiracy.

Ferkiss explains how Coughlin's core anti-democratic thinking within an authoritarian Christian framework propelled him toward fascism. Coughlin's own writings in *Social Justice* in 1938 and afterward argue that real democracy requires its rulers to be good men, and the extent to which America is a Christian nation implies that only good Christian men fit the bill. As Coughlin wrote in 1940, obstruction of good rulers is not freedom but license. "Freedom must be distinguished from license," he wrote, and "discipline must be placed on the same plane as liberty." Moreover, "religion is more important than democracy"; and "Christ-less democracy has always failed and always will." This troubled Ferkiss. In Coughlinism, he writes, there occurs "a debasement of the language" similar to a typical leftist expression like "economic Democracy." Coughlin's use of the term "Christian democracy" represents the same thing, namely,

> the identification of democracy with the substantive end of governmental activity rather than with the process by which the community makes decisions. If one adopts this definition, it becomes possible for a Hitler to profess devotion to democracy. Such a definition provides an excuse for junking the process if one does not like the results achieved. . . . All governments are in some sense democratic; a good government is one which does its job well. Hence, fascism may be preferable to liberal constitutional democracy; it may even be more "democratic."[58]

The irony perhaps is that Coughlin's ideal democracy could only exist within the authoritarian structure and practice of the corporate state. This was a good thing because it institutionalized the natural unity and complementary function of capital and labor. In the pages of *Social Justice* and elsewhere in 1938, Coughlin wrote that the corporate state constitutes "representative democracy on an organic basis." All men play different roles according to their individual strengths and weaknesses. The organic unity of the corporate state is far superior to an atomized liberal democracy. "Rugged cooperation" replaced rugged individualism in American democracy. "In unity there is strength. In individualism there is weakness," Coughlin wrote. All functions within the corporate state guarantee equity and justice given that it is ruled by good Christian men. Coughlin saw no threat to the individual in this otherwise hierarchical and tightly controlled society guided by the formulation and implementation of a master plan. Oddly, he believed this was the true form of democracy. The main challenge was not in production of the things that were needed but in their distribution. This is where both capitalism and communism failed and the result in both was massive concentration of wealth and power in the hands of the few.[59]

By the late 1930s, Coughlin's earlier populist radicalism had run its course. With his economic theories discredited and his Catholic following dwindling, Coughlin had nowhere to go than deeper into the political thicket of his conjured anti-Semitic worldview. The Jews as international bankers had created liberal democracy and then communism when the former failed. "I am not against Jews as Jews," he clamored in self-defense, claiming that he was no anti-Semite. On the contrary, as he wrote in *Social Justice*: "As a rule, Jews are so far superior in intelligence, in initiative, and perseverance to Gentiles that they cannot help but rise to positions of power and thereby gain control over the arteries of commerce, education, and public life."[60] What he opposed is what Jews had created as an economic and political system. From Freemasonry to the French Revolution to the Bolshevik Revolution in Russia, and now the New Deal—all were products of Jewish zealots who had lost their faith in Jehovah and replaced it with an international scheme to control the world.[61] Faced with choosing between communism and fascism, Coughlin said he would accept the latter. Just like National Socialism, Ferkiss concluded, Coughlinism was "violently nationalist" but with an important difference. Coughlin justified his virulent nationalism on a Catholic basis, sweetened by a sonorous voice that contributed to a reactionary choir praising "America for the Americans."[62]

HUEY LONG: THE EMPEROR OF LOUISIANA WHO LONGED TO BE PRESIDENT

Huey Pierce Long's rise to power in his home state from governor and then to the Senate gave him the national platform on which he became, in the words of historian Arthur Schlesinger Jr., "The Messiah of the Rednecks." His campaign phrase "Every Man a King, ut No One Wears a Crown," which he took from the turn-of-century populist and presidential candidate William Jennings Bryan, got him elected to the governorship of Louisiana in 1928. First as governor and then as senator, Long tamed the oligarchy of big corporations who had come into Louisiana and established a virtual personal dictatorship. To his credit, he built roads, schools, and infrastructure, bringing the state into the twentieth century. He provided free textbooks to all students and guaranteed access to education as far as one desired. He transformed Louisiana State University into a first-rate institution of higher learning. In short, Huey Long managed to modernize the most underdeveloped and backward state in the nation in only a few years. Nevertheless, as Schlesinger wrote, he continued to "cajole, threaten, browbeat, and bribe" all who stood in his way to becoming a dictator. When an opponent put a volume of the state constitution in his face, Long replied. "I'm the Constitution around here now."[63]

Long forever claimed that he grew up in a modest log cabin, but that was far from the truth. His father overcame a dirt-poor existence to become a well-off landowner who moved his family into an "imposing colonial home" in the small town of Winnfield. Growing up in relative comfort, Huey was a bright student who read widely and was "outspoken, opinionated … and intensely, consumedly self-centered." As an adolescent, he knew that his family's middle-class prosperity was representative of the glaring inequalities in the town and its surroundings where most poor sharecroppers barely lived at subsistence levels, and not much above disenfranchised black folk. Yet he was more disturbed by the increasing encroachments of commercial interests such as the railroad and lumber industries that threatened the region's traditional economic and political life. Long's formal education ended when he left high school without a diploma. He traveled around the South and the Midwest working as a door-to-door salesman selling a variety of home products. After four years of such work, and now married, he enrolled in Tulane University law school as a part-time student, and quickly realized it would take forever to become a lawyer. With less than a year in the program, he petitioned for a special bar examination and passed. At age twenty-one, he and his wife, Rose, moved back to Winnfield where he began his practice, first with an older brother and then on his own. He made little headway as a town lawyer until he took what his peers considered a hopeless case—that of a woman who had sued the local bank over an insurance claim—and won. From the notoriety of winning the case, he represented other underdogs against powerful commercial interests. With success under his belt, Long and his wife moved to Shreveport to practice law and pursue his real love, politics.[64]

In a vivid account of Long's political career published in 1935, journalist and author Carleton Beals described Long's rule in Louisiana as "a personal dictatorship" based in part on his extraordinary powers to bind subordinates and supporters to "a pseudo-radical program" that masked his real drive for absolute control.[65] Having spent many years in Latin America observing and writing about its wily dictators, Beals recognized the distinct characteristics of Louisiana that made Long's demagoguery possible. He was a "buccaneer frontier individualist" whose political orientation and development was conditioned by an environment and political culture that was more like Cuba or Mexico than Connecticut. Given its semi-colonial, sharply racial, and still partly feudal character, Louisiana lacked the modern political traditions that had become firmly rooted in the United States. For one thing, the combination of Negro disenfranchisement and large-scale white illiteracy and poverty prevented true democratic practices. Government in Louisiana by "decent" men had always been "polite fiction," Beals wrote. Here was Long proclaiming himself a "decent" officeholder but showing himself to be more clever than his predecessors in successfully covering up corruption. Dictatorship had always ruled the state.[66] But Long took it to new levels:

> Colonialism, slavery, then feudalism—all were overwhelmed by Northern industrialism and now increasingly by monopoly and financial capitalism. In only the past five years the trapping industry—Louisiana produces more furs than all of Canada— has passed from a free individualist régime to one of ironclad monopoly with serf-like conditions comparable to those of the West Virginia coal industry. And just as a hierarchical state and religion are the proper expressions of a feudal economy, so the logical expression of monopoly capitalism is one-man dictatorship.[67]

Until his sudden and consequential assassination in 1935, Huey Long fit this bill perfectly. No one proved more capable of fulfilling dictatorial power in his own state, which might then open the door to the possibility of similar leadership on the national level. No one was more adept at expressing the hopes of poor people in the South, making them "feel as though they themselves were spitting in the face of the rich and powerful."[68] Yet for all his railing at the plutocrats, he also made them believe they had nothing to fear from his actions.

Beals was not alone in his assessment of Long's duplicitous relationship with Big Business. Presenting himself as a tribune of the middle class and the poor and disenfranchised people in the state, Long knew how to play his hand with the plutocrats to get what he needed. The journalist Raymond Gram Swing cites Long's estranged brother and former law partner, Julius, who told a Senate committee under oath that Long's first run for governor in 1924 was financed mainly by the Southern Gas and Electric Company. "They handed my brother a large roll of money, I think a couple of times, while I was there, which he tucked into one of the back pockets of his trousers. It looked like it would almost pull them off."[69] More exemplary of Long's duplicity was his relationship with the Standard Oil Company. Publicly, Long never ceased attacking the state's biggest employer for the way it exploited resources and labor in Louisiana. As governor in 1929 he had tried to force the state legislature into creating a processing tax on refined oil that would impose five cents on every barrel.[70] The effort failed and nearly got him impeached, though he finally succeeded in getting the tax in 1935. According to a more recent biographer, Richard White, Long held a secret meeting with the head of Standard Oil and agreed to rebate four of the five cents to the company in return for its Baton Rouge refinery using 80 percent of crude oil from Louisiana oil fields. The company agreed to rehire workers it had discharged, which also benefited several of Long's supporters who were independent oil drillers. Long also gave tax assessors a green light to devalue the property of the refinery by $10 million.[71]

Only in a state so backward could a petty-bourgeois upstart like Huey Long rise to power as the facilitator of capitalist modernization. "If he were to die today, and the fear and hatred of him died too, and an honest group of politicians came into control of Louisiana," Raymond Gram Swing wrote in 1935, "they would find a great deal to thank Huey Long for." First as governor and as a senator—he got a crony elected to the second seat in 1932—Long had transformed an archaic state government into a centralized and efficiently run operation. To build roads, schools, and badly needed infrastructure, he increased the state debt from $11 million to $150 million in the six years he was in power. While pushing higher taxes on those who could bear them, he got legislation passed that relieved the poorest in the state from many taxes, including exemption on property assessed at $2,000 or less. As Swing noted, this meant that most Negroes and more than half of the poor whites would be free of taxes except for what they paid in sales taxes on tobacco, liquor, and gasoline. Long stepped up efforts to stamp out illiteracy in a state that put it "near the bottom of America's disgrace list." As a result, more than 100,000 adults—white and black—had learned to read and write in a single year.[72]

Long had brought Louisiana into the twentieth century by breaking all the molds of American politics. He promised the world to poor people, white and black, while building a political machine on the basis of his core of middle-class landowners and merchants. His immense power operated on patronage, from the highest of officials to the lowliest of workers. Local political bosses who Long needed at one moment often found themselves out of work and blackballed for crossing the "Kingfish," as he was called. Long defended himself by railing against "lying newspapers" that criticized his every move. So Long created his own media. His circulars reached every part of the state in only a day. He published his own newspaper called *Louisiana Progress*. He made routine use of the radio and seemed to be constantly traversing the state in chauffeured automobiles, accompanied by numerous aides and bodyguards. Of course, as Alan Brinkley wrote, "Power of such magnitude required money," which the Long machine seldom lacked. Corruption had become a staple of government. When the U.S. Treasury Department sent agents to New Orleans, they reported that "Long and his gang are stealing everything in the state." Still, the main feature of the machine's corruption was not graft but "a brazenly open system of deductions from the salaries of state employees, deductions collected automatically every month and kept—in cash—under Long's personal control." According to sources cited by Brinkley, the "deduct box," as it was called, was rumored to contain a million dollars at a time.[73]

Beals saw something deeper in the structure of Long's regime. Long had become emperor of Louisiana in only six years by recognizing the increasing powers of capitalist modernization. But he did this on existing anachronistic social relations in the state. Regional and cultural differences rooted in its Spanish and French colonial past; the destruction of indigenous peoples followed by the enslavement of Africans; the essentially feudal relations imposed by large landowners on their tenants; the concentration of merchant and banking capital in New Orleans which was once the second-largest port in the nation; the dominant role of Standard Oil in exploiting the state's oil reserves and sites offshore—all made Louisiana ripe for Huey Long's unique brand of demagoguery in a sea of backwardness. "Obviously," Beals wrote as he sought to explain what was unique about Long's power,

> a single ruler cannot, beyond a certain point, run counter to the dominant economic forces of his community unless he smashes them. Louisiana is a monopoly capitalist and feudal enterprise. The standard of living there is approximately 60 percent lower than that in the Northern states; the percentage is perhaps even worse for the poorer wage levels. Culturally and economically, Louisiana is closer to Peru than to Wisconsin or Indiana. Its people live on a low Balkan standard, in some places are as badly off as Chinese coolies. Its population has never done anything important to emancipate itself.[74]

But the emperor did nothing to change the overall quality of life in Louisiana. Especially after the Depression hit, Long continued to think and function within the existing framework of capitalist relations in the state while prophesying to anyone who listened that a new and "unabated wave of prosperity" would soon occur and transform it. "Growth will be almost magic," he declared in 1930. To Beals this was just Long's contribution to "Hooveresque ballyhoo" since unemployment was swelling everywhere. "His personality shines out in showy undertakings," wrote Beals about Long's phantasmagoria of social progress, "but it cannot be said that he did anything whatsoever of a fundamental nature to improve, or attempt to improve, the general conditions of poverty and backwardness of the state." Louisiana was surely a great place for Long to share his doctrines of wealth redistribution where the growing concentration of monopoly brought declining living standards for workers. He made no effort to help the thousands who were starving, nor did he end the horrific regime of child labor in the state. Nonattendance of schoolchildren was the highest in the United States in 1932, the worst year of the Depression. Three years later, an investigation by a New York newspaper found that there were no limits on the hours worked by children during the picking season. He also ignored the exploitation of female workers and the ridiculously low wages they were paid. In the countryside, sharecroppers were just holding on. Various publications were replete with statistics and analyses of working conditions that were worsening across the board.[75]

Long's treatment of blacks was even worse. From his world-historical perspective, Beals was able to grasp the precise nature of Long's racist thinking and behavior. Given that black people always got "the raw deal in everything," Beals observed that conditions in Louisiana created "perfect tinder for a Southern Nazi or Fascist movement with its concomitants of race brutality, prejudice and violence." But he cautioned that such terminology was strained based on what he understood to be happening in Louisiana. Even before the Depression, "the traditional system" of race and class, as it was throughout much of the South, was more like Cuba. There, the "importation of blacks from Jamaica and Haiti was gradually pushing the native white Cuban worker out of the cane fields and out of jobs." A parallel course was developing in Louisiana where the Negro was used increasingly as a "social strike-breaker, a lowerer of wage scales and living standards." The state had plenty of black workers without need of importing more. Conditions in Cuba and Louisiana were variations of a similar process in capitalist political economy. "In a free labor market the cheapest labor wins. Bad money drives out good money," Beals wrote. With the backing of southern elites, the New Deal "temporarily halted this

process and buttressed up the neo-Confederate system," the existing regime of white labor in the service of white supremacy. "The
slight raising of wages in the South by the N.R.A. codes turned the
tide the other way. The poor whites, because of the arbitrary wage
scales, were everywhere favored . . . more than the blacks." In this
respect, the NRA enabled "the old cushion of black enslavement"
in southern states to withstand "shocks" from the crisis. For Beals,
this made "the depression, in its worst phases . . . a 'black' depression." Long's program countered the New Deal. His public works
projects gave more work to blacks than whites only because Long
ignored the codes on wages, lowering them as much as possible
on the basis of black labor. As a result, blacks got more jobs in
public works than whites and were paid less than whites. This was
a feature of Long's racist regime. "Huey, in order to carve his name
on bridges, roads and public buildings, and make his showing as
ostentatious as possible, exploited human labor to the ultimate;
he exploited the Negro to the ultimate, and thereby perhaps gave
the Negro in Louisiana an alternative to lying down and dying."
For Beals, Long "never used much white chauvinism and racial
hatreds to feather his political nest, because it was not necessary."[76]

Nevertheless, Long always showed a visceral if not virulent
racism in his routine affairs. He thought nothing of using the word
"niggah." Because Long did not grow up in the "Black Belt" of
Louisiana, Beals reasoned that he lacked the "passionate virulence
of certain white chauvinists" but not "certain typical poor-white
prejudices" that often resulted in "blunders on the national scene."
In an exchange with Heywood Broun, a seasoned journalist who
often wrote on social issues, Long went on about himself until
Broun interrupted and asked him to respond to a comment made
by a Negro waiter in a dining car of a train during one of Broun's
travels. "Don't you pay any attention to that Senator Long," the
waiter told Broun. "He is no radical; he is just a Fascist." According
to Broun, Long "sputtered for 30 seconds and grew profane, com-
menting on ignorant people who couldn't possibly understand
him." This prompted Broun to ask how the Negro fit into his plans

for wealth distribution. "Oh, he will get the minimum, all right," Long responded. Here Beals grasped the racial character of Long's feudal domain. It was the glue that kept his capitalist empire together. Confronted with economic and social oppression, of peonage in a black caste, of glaring warnings about what was "For Whites" and "For Colored" in all aspects of social, economic, and political life, of "racial discrimination and hatred overleaping all pathological bounds"—Long moved forward in his quest for capitalist modernization in a sea of racist backwardness. "Whenever the dreaded question of Negro rights arose," Beals wrote, "Huey Long and his followers were good pat Southerners."[77]

Until he met his end in September 1935, Long's influence had expanded greatly beyond Louisiana and the South. During the last two years of his life, he posed a serious threat to the status quo of both mainstream political parties, and especially frightened Roosevelt and the New Dealers with his own brand of populism. In January 1934, he founded a national political organization whose slogan, "Share Our Wealth," called for the liquidation of all personal fortunes over a certain amount that would then be redistributed to the general population. Long had paved the way two years earlier when he proposed a resolution on the floor of the U.S. Senate that the government take all personal income over a million dollars and all inheritances over five million by aggressive taxation. The revenue would be used to guarantee every American family with a "homestead allowance" of $5,000 and an annual income of $2,000. But that was not all. The working day would be limited while the government balanced production and consumption through storage and controls. All Americans over age sixty would receive pensions, while young men and women would get a college education at government expense—all thanks to heavy taxation of the country's richest people.[78] Long's organization had grown dramatically in a little more than a year, establishing 27,000 clubs across the country and compiling a massive mailing list of more than 7,500,000 persons throughout the North, Midwest, and much of the South. With it, he unleashed a full-scale attack on the New Deal.[79]

Long's redistributive schemes sounded good to people who were knocked to the ground by the Depression and knew little or nothing about how the economy really worked. As Carleton Beals made clear

> he forged his political strength with the ignorant and miserable whites of the backwoods, the dwellers in mud shacks and log cabins, the sufferers from pellagra, hookworm and malaria. His chosen were also the petty commercial class of the small interior towns whose little establishments long ago supplanted the commissaries of the large plantations.

Whatever power and importance these class elements had enjoyed in previous decades was now "being pushed back into economic misery" by the Depression.[80] These were Huey's people. He understood them because he grew up among them in Winn Parish and learned their ways. He impressed others as a voracious reader in his youth and then demonstrated a brilliant grasp of the law that he learned how to twist to his advantage as a politician. Otherwise, he showed no patience or willingness to engage in rigorous study and analysis. His approach to all important matters except for the intricacies of the legal system was folksy and anti-intellectual.

For Victor Ferkiss, this penchant for "simplicity itself" was a key characteristic of Long's fascist proclivities. He consistently reduced complex issues to the simplest terms and threw out easy solutions to problems created by irreconcilable contradictions. "Never explain, my boy, never explain! For explanation is the mother of sectarianism," he told Benjamin Stolberg in an interview for *The Nation* in 1935.[81] Long constantly said there was no real economic crisis because the problems were easily solved. "We have no Depression," he told the *American Progress* in 1934, a newspaper Long had founded four years earlier. "What we have is an oppression of the masses by a few people. Some few hold everything with the purchasing power to buy everything else."[82] His simple solution lay in the goodness in capitalism because its creation was an act of Providence. Good capitalism meant a society of small entrepreneurs and "molded in the image of the old middle class" that would bring an end to glaring inequalities of wealth. This was God's plan. "The husbandry of Cain and the flocks and land of Abraham," Long told the *New York Times* just before Roosevelt's inauguration on March 4, 1933, "represented capitalism in its first form, direct from the inspiration of the Creator." [83]

Yet all this reactionary, populist, and demagogic language that appealed to his base was only possible against the backdrop of an unprecedented and totalizing crisis in America that, for Victor Ferkiss, helped to make Huey Long "the first of the popular agitators who [could] be correctly classified under the generic term fascist."[84] By 1934, the New Deal had stalled and the political mood of the country had once again turned ugly. More than any other demagogue in the mid-1930s, Long capitalized on the general malaise in Louisiana by shaping an interpretation of the crisis and its solution that transformed populist, petty capitalist, and fundamentalist Christian ideas into a blend of proto-fascist politics.

Ferkiss is one of the few writers in the non-Marxist tradition to recognize the centrality of the economic crisis in the trajectory of Long's politics toward fascism. From a careful mining of sources, he tells us that Long held liberalism responsible for the economic troubles of the times. Moreover, the plutocrats who had created the laissez-faire practices of the New Era of the 1920s had made a mess of the economy they could not solve. Long had grasped the impact of liberal capitalist failure on the middle class, which now looked to alternatives like his Share the Wealth program. Of course, socialism was out of the question because it destroyed private property and traditional values. Long's populism appealed to the middle classes because he held up the virtues of the small businessman and local government. Yet he had certainly helped to cripple them all in his home state, a glaring contradiction between rhetoric and reality. Lacking any concrete plan for a decentralized, democratic alternative, Long could only promote a solution based on what Ferkiss described as an unchecked "collective action by an executive" that acted in accordance with "the general approval of the populace." Here was a huge contradiction for anyone who happened to notice it. That Long never worked it out explains partly why Ferkiss is correct when he says that Long was not "a completely developed fascist" at the time of his death, though it was crucial to recognize how his politics marked "a transitional stage in the breakdown of populism into fascism."[85]

HISTORIANS IN THE LIBERAL tradition have generally dismissed the idea that Coughlin and Long were fascists. Among the most notable is Alan Brinkley, whose 1983 book, *Voices of Protest*, is standard fare in liberal historiography. Brinkley admitted that both men might "have displayed fascist sympathies unwittingly." But that was as far as it went. There is little evidence, he claimed, to suggest that either man was sympathetic to fascism or even showed interest in it until 1938 when Coughlin's anti-Semitism was all that remained in his once formidable political arsenal. What is startling about Brinkley is that he literally takes both men at face value. Long always opposed "fascism or any other ism" and once told a reporter not to compare him to "that sonofabitch" Adolf Hitler. Like Coughlin, Long accused others of fascism if it served his purpose, even calling Roosevelt and the New Deal fascist shortly before his assassination. The more troubling thing about Brinkley's methodology, however, is his unwillingness to move beyond straightforward political and ideological comparisons. In fact, he is even defiant. Those who claim that both men held definite fascist sympathies, he writes, "have rested their arguments on casual statements" attributed to them that "are either apocryphal or subject to serious distortion." But then he argues that the real problem is the ambiguous character of fascism as a political term.[86] Not since the 1930s has there ever been "anything remotely approaching agreement" about its meaning among politicians and historians. "No commonly accepted body of literature articulates a theory of fascism," he wrote. "There is no single, coherent set of social or economic policies common to all so-called fascist regimes." Brinkley recognizes some utility in the approach of the fascist minimum but then says:

> If the term "fascism" is to have any meaning, it must define a particular kind of relationship between a leader and his followers. Or it must suggest a particular set of ideas and programs, a vision of society distinct from that of other political philosophies.[87]

In the end, Brinkley leaps over the difficulty with his own version of the fascist minimum. He acknowledges that the middle-class movements that formed around Long and Coughlin resembled those that catapulted Mussolini and Hitler into power. But they differed in one important respect. Though they promised to restore "a small man's paradise," European fascists sought to capture the state and create a new type of regime. What Coughlin and Long really wanted was a return to the era of small capitalism, and this required "a far more fundamental assault upon the 'plutocrats' and 'financial despots' than the European fascists ever attempted." In the end, this made both men populists for Brinkley, not fascists.[88]

Like all the small-fry fascisti, Coughlin and Long had roots in the petty bourgeoisie, the class that lost the most in the early days of the Great Depression. Angry at the ruling class for robbing it of livelihood and status, it also stood fast against the masses that they believed threatened them more. Amid the swirl of change, dislocation, and anxiety about the present and fears for the future, they made up the great wave of political reaction during the mid-1930s. Their world had been shaken by forces that seemed beyond their control. Even during the previous decade of prosperity, they had felt out of joint in the crowded streets and tall buildings that were so startling from their earlier rural and small-town existence. Now the Depression had thrown them to the ground. Not understanding how and why those above them were responsible for the crisis that threatened them, they blamed most of it on the enemies lurking below, the Negroes, Jews, Catholics, Mexicans, anarchists, socialists, and, of course, the communists—all enemies of True Americanism.

Unlike Brinkley, Victor Ferkiss examined Huey Long's political career against the backdrop of capitalist crisis and saw in it the transition from populism to fascism. In the case of Louisiana, Carleton Beals observed how Long had taken command of the state by tapping into the fears of the middle classes when liberal capitalist democracy had undermined their economic and social position in a time of crisis. In following Long, they gave up the last vestiges of their petty-bourgeois liberalism to follow a demagogue. In Long's political trajectory are the first hints of a break between liberal capitalist democracy and American fascism. Long might have become the demagogue the ruling class needed if the general crisis of American capitalism deepened and became a crisis of class rule—and if his assassin had failed.

10—The Class Character of Embryonic American Fascism

IN HIS 1933 BOOK, *Seeds of Revolt*, Mauritz Hallgren became one of the first American writers to focus on the plausibility of fascism in America. "What is fascism?" asked Hallgren, a veteran journalist and regular contributor to *The Nation* magazine:

There has been much confusion of thought and opinion concerning the meaning of this term. Radical students have applied it to the growing economic power of the monopolists. Others, with Mussolini and Hitler in mind, identify fascism with dictatorship. Still others look upon fascism as a popular political movement, as revolutionary or even socialistic. The growth of monopoly capitalism is, of course, the principal element in the making of fascism. And there can be little doubt that the fascist State is a dictatorial State. Fascism may appear to be the outgrowth of a popular movement, for under some circumstances the support of the people is necessary to its proper development—it was so in Germany, for example, though not in Italy. Nor can fascism be considered either revolutionary or socialistic, though it apparently contains a few elements of both. For, accurately speaking, fascism is a political philosophy based upon the need of capitalism to employ the power of the State to protect the institution of production for private profit.[1]

Hallgren recognized the genesis of fascism in the workings of U.S. monopoly-finance capitalism. Long ignored by contemporary U.S. historians and political commentators, his analysis of the class character of embryonic fascism in America is striking for its pith and relevance. Writing in the aftermath of Roosevelt's inauguration in March 1933, Hallgren explained how the sequence of the booming 1920s and the Depression that followed had made the contradictions between the middle class and the ruling capitalist class irreconcilable. Historically, the middle class had always sought security from the rising power of monopoly by supporting progressive reforms that were taken up by presidents Theodore Roosevelt and Woodrow Wilson. Ironically, these efforts only strengthened the power of the state, which had become the domain of capitalist elites.

The contradiction between the middle class and Big Business had sharpened during the prosperous 1920s. With labor vanquished and middle-class progressives in disarray, small manufacturers, merchants, salaried employees, mid-level professionals, and artisans clung to the doctrine of economic liberalism trumpeted by capitalist elites and their political servants in the White House and Congress. Once the crisis hit in 1929 and the Depression deepened, the middle class looked to the federal government for relief and recovery but made no headway with Hoover and his circle of elites, who refused to "interfere with the operation of the *laissez-faire* economy upon which modern or monopoly capitalism was founded."[2] Roosevelt managed to calm the storm with his promise of a new deal and indeed responded with pushing Congress toward dazzling innovations in government power during the first hundred days of his presidency. But they did little to quell grave concerns about the future. For one thing, the New Deal gave even greater power to monopolies and financial capitalists in the hope that they would work in good faith to establish equilibrium between capital and labor. But its hallmark creation, the National Recovery Administration, was quickly recognized as something other than what the people, especially the middle class, needed.

By spring 1934, there was clear evidence of a rising tide of public opinion about the prospects of America going fascist. Even committed New Dealers seemed to agree. Only two weeks into a national fact-finding tour of the nation for the Federal Emergency Relief Administration (FERA), Lorena Hickok reported to her boss Harry Hopkins that she was greatly discouraged by what she had observed and was "almost forced to agree" with a business-man who told her he favored fascism as a solution to the economic crisis. "If I were 20 years younger and weighed 75 pounds less, I think I'd start out to be the Joan of Arc of the Fascist movement in the United States." Hickok, who submitted a summary of her find-ings to Hopkins on January 1, 1935, after eighteen months on the road, described a "stranded generation" of middle-aged men with no jobs and half-grown families, a growing class of "unemploy-ables" whose skills and mental aptitudes had declined and were kept alive thanks only to government relief. "And so they go on," she wrote, "the gaunt, ragged legion of the industrially damned."[3]

Hickok believed she had accurately taken America's pulse and assumed that the country was moving toward fascism, though she offered no detailed assessment of what she meant by the term. What would a fascist solution mean for the "ragged legion" of "unemployables" other than an authoritarian political regime? Why did the Texas businessman favor fascism? Who were the fas-cists and what did they want for America? Would fascism mean the dictatorship of an American Duce or Fuehrer? These ques-tions were central to the larger one. How did one define fascism in America? Would it look like Italy and Germany in the 1930s? If not, how would it differ? Based on what Hickok and many of her contemporaries described at the time, fascism was an alternative to constitutional democracy. But what did it mean in this particular context, and what form would it take in the United States?

During the next two years, a few astute observers addressed these questions and concluded that big business and financial capital were driving America toward fascism. Generally, their examinations were based on what Marxists call class analysis— in other words, determining which social class, or classes, were responsible for the genesis of fascism in the United States. Four studies from this period stand out, all written by Marxists or influenced by Marxism: *Do We Want Fascism?* by Carmen Haider, *The Crisis of the Middle Class* by Lewis Corey, *Forerunners of American Fascism* by Raymond Gram Swing, and an essay by Harry F. Ward in the *Annals of the American Academy of Political and Social Science* titled "The Development of Fascism in the United States." All four works, long buried by liberal historiography, resonate in the current moment. Each argued that the United States would go fascist if the capitalist class continued to amass wealth and power over the rest of society. Their positions also accorded with that of the Communist International, as articulated in 1935 by General Secretary Georgi Dimitroff in his report to the Seventh Congress, defining fascism as "the power of finance capital itself."[4]

Carmen Haider: Fascism Emerging in the Two-Party System

Perhaps the most intriguing of these forgotten works is by Carmen Haider. A Columbia University–educated historian, Haider traveled to Italy in the 1920s to study the structure of Mussolini's corporatist state, documenting her findings in one of the earliest academic studies of European fascism.[5] On returning to the United States, she conducted a similarly rigorous investigation of the nascent fascism in her own country. In *Do We Want Fascism?* Haider argued that the rise of American fascism would not require a distinct party, as in Italy and Germany. Rather, fascism could penetrate the two-party system and lead to a fascist state, which Haider defined as "a dictatorial form of government exercised in the interests of capitalists."[6]

Though not a Marxist, Haider drew on Marxian concepts to argue that the New Deal had saved the capitalist order, but only temporarily. She focused on the National Recovery Administration, established by Congress in June 1933, and charged with reviving American industry. Though it stabilized the economy for a time, the NRA's attempts at economic planning only sharpened contradictions between capital and labor. Although the agency mandated production quotas and commodity price controls, it surrendered most of the power to set and implement these requirements to Big Business. At the same time, as a concession to labor, workers were guaranteed the right to collective bargaining and unionization. Designed to restore equilibrium between production and consumption, the NRA did little to reform the system of monopolies already in control of the productive sectors of the economy. Without a significant increase in mass purchasing power, recovery stalled in 1934 as anxiety spread across the class spectrum. Capitalists grew increasingly resentful of government intrusion and sought a return to laissez-faire policies. Meanwhile, millions of workers who had weathered the worst years of the Depression, only to be frustrated by a slow and uneven recovery, began to ponder political alternatives to the status quo.

This much Haider understood. Even if the NRA had restored prosperity, it would not last. Capitalists would demand a return to laissez-faire, which, for Haider, could only mean that "the forces which brought about the crisis of 1929 would continue to be at work in the future."[7] Either way, she foresaw an even greater crisis in the immediate future, one that would intensify the contradictions between capital and labor. The NRA had shown that the state could be used to reorganize industry in capital's own interests, thus lessening the distaste among employers for permanent state intervention in the economy. As for labor, President Roosevelt's decision to give power to industrial capitalists meant that the promise of collective bargaining and unionization, though not insubstantial victories, posed no immediate threat to capital. Roosevelt had pinned his hopes on cajoling capitalists into dealing with labor in good faith. But labor remained wholly subject to capital. These considerations prompted Haider to raise some key questions. Where was the NRA heading if it survived rising opposition from Big Business? Or, what would be different if it failed and some new iteration took its place?

As Haider explained, the NRA's survival would depend on public works to increase employment and boost consumption. But these would require higher taxes on the rich, thus sharpening the contradiction between capital and labor. New industrial growth would be thwarted by attempts to restore purchasing power to workers. Although this was expected to counter rising unrest among the unemployed, more permanent public works would compel additional taxation on the middle class. As was evident in several states, new sales taxes had already taken the place of increased income taxes. But the whole arrangement "would substantially amount to a redistribution of funds among the masses rather than the creation of new purchasing power."[8] And though industry's domination over government would ensure wage suppression, the expansion of public works could also bring greater hardship for workers in the form of inflation. Whatever the scenario, the end would be the same, a "system of outright self-control by industry" with only one plausible outcome:

> Such a turn to the Right would essentially amount to Fascism, since it would be an attempt to introduce a collective form of capitalism in the place of individualism. Violence might accompany it only in the form of state force against the workers if they should rebel against what must become an oppressive system for them. While thus the essence of Fascism would be present, the secondary aspects, particularly the seizure of power through middle class support, would be missing.[9]

Here was a crucial point. The middle class would always play a subordinate role to Big Business and finance in the making of American fascism. To be sure, Haider did not dismiss the growing distress and increasing militancy among all sections of the middle class. Resentment and anger toward big capital among small business owners, as well as salaried white-collar employees, was already fueling a reactionary politics. She saw this in groups ranging from the grandiose aspirations of the Silver Shirts, Khaki Shirts, and other such exotic groups to the more grounded nativism and racism of the Ku Klux Klan and the American Legion. For Haider, however, no organization was more significant than the Farm-Labor Federation (FLF), with its contradictory petty-bourgeois politics. Vehemently opposed to socialism, the FLF also proclaimed that capitalism was dead. Opposed to monopoly and banking capital, it was nevertheless firmly committed to the principle of private ownership. Such contradictions only weakened the FLF's political posture, making it easier for Big Business to gain control of the FLF and other middle-class movements.

Noting that leading U.S. capitalists were already aware that middle-class discontent had fueled fascist movements in Italy and Germany, Haider predicted that they might decide that the best course of action would be to take charge and redirect this discontent toward their own ends. To Haider, this would not in itself be a problem:

> To grow, every movement needs financial assistance, and if such assistance should be forthcoming at the right moment from the industrial and banking group of this country, they would have a good chance of getting a hold on the situation. It is obvious that such an arrangement would take place behind the scenes, and that, for the purposes of popular appeal, pronouncements against the bankers would continue and the promises would be reiterated that, once the new party comes to power, their influence will be destroyed.
>
> Such declarations might be expected to be instrumental in drawing other dissatisfied groups in the country into the

movement, since they would be given a tangible enemy on whom to blame their troubles, but this by no means implies that these threats will ever find realization through party action.[10]

For these reasons, a coming American fascism did not require a third, fascist party. It could emerge from political realignments within the two-party system, transformed by a social, economic, and political crisis. Haider contended that with the Democrats in power, Republicans, who already included "several of our foremost financiers and industrial leaders," knew what they had to do. "It would be an insult to their ability to think that they could not take care of a movement of discontent and direct it into party channels," she wrote, "even though, possibly, this would imply a recasting of the party."[11] In that sense the Republicans would also pull in reactionary Democratic elites and reshape their party to oppose Roosevelt and the New Deal coalition. Given this political realignment, fascism could take root without disturbing the two-party system.

Here again, the NRA played a major role. A new "conservative Right" led by bankers and big businessmen opposed to New Deal labor provisions "might be expected to give impetus to a Fascist movement directed against the present administration," which Haider saw as the core of a "new Center group" that included progressive Republicans and even many socialists. In Haider's predicted realignment, a third group would form, "an ultra-Left party," made up primarily of communists, who were approaching the height of their influence in the United States. Under fascism, this party would be outlawed, "in accordance with the totalitarian idea of the Fascists." At the same time, the fascists would also move to reduce the center party to impotency, if not destroy it outright.[12]

The main actors in this realignment were reactionary industrialists and bankers, whose drive for economic dominance pitted them against more reform-minded elements of the ruling class. Out of this political deadlock, Haider said, the reactionary wing of the capitalist class would take over the Republican Party and wage political warfare against Roosevelt and the New Deal. Then, if the latter failed,

> Congress could be captured from within, since a powerful Fascist movement caught in Republican Party channels would send its own representatives to Congress. The opposition might be negligible.
>
> Moreover, a national economic council might be established and the Fascist group, in endorsing economic planning, would probably also approve of occupational representation. Determination of the economic aspects of national life might be turned over to this council as was done in Italy, whereby the power of Congress would be substantially reduced.[13]

For Haider, the Roosevelt administration's attempt to end the capitalist crisis on its own terms had only heightened class conflict within the ruling class, and the split between reactionaries and reformers could only be resolved at the expense of the rest of society.

LEWIS COREY: THE ROLE OF THE MIDDLE CLASS

The following year, the Marxist economist Lewis Corey also argued that any middle-class movement toward fascism would in the end be absorbed by Big Business and finance capital. In his second major work, *The Crisis of the Middle Class*, Corey argued that the New Deal's prioritization of big capital and monopolistic firms had deepened the distress of America's petty bourgeoisie. By limiting abundance in order to raise prices and boost economic growth, New Deal reformers were compelled to destroy existing capital and curtail production. Aligned with the NRA's effort to restrict production and achieve equilibrium in the supply and demand of industrial goods, the Agricultural Adjustment Administration (AAA) limited farm production to reduce inventories, raise prices, and restore purchasing power to farmers and rural workers. Both hurt small business owners, who struggled to make a profit as prices rose. Limiting production also meant that salaried members of the "new" middle class—office clerks, managers, accountants, lawyers, teachers, engineers, public officials, and others—were thrown into chronic unemployment. This, Corey wrote, drove the middle class toward new ideas and forms of action:

> What shall they be? If they are still conditioned by the illusion that the class crisis can be solved within the relations of capitalist property, the middle class completely abandons its old democratic ideals and mobilizes against labor, whose struggle for the new socialist order becomes ever more conscious and aggressive. By that act the middle class throws itself into the consuming fires of fascism.[14]

The middle class could not unite its economically antagonistic factions to form an independent political program. All of its elements, old and new, were committed to saving capitalism from the threat of socialism. But the consensus ended there. While the "old" middle class of small merchants and farmers sought to limit the power of monopoly, the new class of well-paid managers and supervisors, employed by large-scale industry and finance, wanted just the opposite. For Corey, this made both groups susceptible to reactionary demagoguery. Yet the independent strata would only go so far in opposing monopoly, fearing that the continued struggle would heighten existing instability and create an opening for the revolutionary aims of socialists and radical labor unions. As Corey noted:

> Hence security and the crushing of labor become the new ideals. The old middle class of independent enterprisers gives up its fight against monopoly, limiting itself to a struggle for mere survival within the relations of monopoly capitalism, in a new set-up of caste and rigid class stratification enforced by the repressive might of the state. This meets the approval of the higher salaried

employees, who are accustomed to the hierarchical relations of corporate industry and are not averse to imposing them on the whole social and political life of the nation.[15]

This ultimately turned the middle class, once the flagbearer for liberty, individualism, and bourgeois democratic ideals, toward the opposite extreme. Now, Corey wrote, "the struggle to save such property as still survives from the all-consuming maw of monopoly capitalism drives the class to reaction, to negation of the ideals for which it fought in its youth."[16] Its desperation only drove it into the willing arms of authoritarian state capitalism, which could be relied on to restrict labor radicalism.

The perceived threat of a left-labor alliance also drove the "new" middle class toward reaction. For example, managers and supervisors would become more authoritarian in their treatment of workers as dictated by their corporate owners and bosses. Thus, the reactionary consciousness of the middle class as a whole only strengthened as it clung desperately to any hope for a secure caste position in a declining capitalism, which only sharpened class conflict and political instability. Trapped in the vise between monopoly-finance capital and the specter of socialist revolution, the middle class embraced fascist politics just as it had in Europe. As Corey wrote, "out of the middle class leaps the monster of fascism: the class that once waged revolutionary war on authoritarianism now provides, in a final desperate struggle for survival, the ideology and mass support for a new authoritarianism determined to destroy all the remnants, and the very concepts, of liberty, equality and democracy." Yet the middle class by itself could not bring about fascism:

> The reaction of the middle class becomes fascism when it merges with the reaction of the big bourgeoisie, of the magnates of finance capital. A part, even if only a minor part, of all the capitalist relations of production, the middle class is incapable of independent class action: its apparently independent struggle

for survival and caste privileges becomes an expression of the needs of dominant capitalism.[17]

Raymond Gram Swing: Those Who Paved the Fascist Road

In his 1935 work, *Forerunners of American Fascism*, Raymond Gram Swing profiled several fascist demagogues in the making, among them Huey Long, Father Coughlin, and William Randolph Hearst. But Swing stood firm that American fascism would not rest primarily on their political influence. Instead, he defined fascism in systemic terms as a "reorganization of society to maintain an unequal distribution of economic power by undemocratic means." The NRA had given power to the nation's biggest employers without any real leverage by employees or consumers. There was much in the New Deal that Swing considered fascist despite its claim to bring about democratic reform. Though the United States differed from fascist Germany in its "democratic technique of operating the country," the distinction was only temporary and superficial. America would go fascist when "enough people" in positions of power decided to prolong the maldistribution of economic power to the point that they would then "be willing to scrap democratic machinery and democratic privileges to maintain it." When and if that occurred—Swing did not believe fascism in the United States was inevitable—America would move in the same direction as fascist countries by, among other things, suppressing personal liberties and oppressing minorities. The structure of the capitalist economic system remained, though democracy would be sacrificed.[18]

Swing discounted the reactionary character of fascism, seeing in it instead a radical attempt to maintain the maldistribution of economic labor that favored finance capital. Though Swing saw the structure of fascism in the New Deal, he was not willing to call it fascist per se. The New Deal could only be considered symptomatic of American fascism if Roosevelt had appealed "to passion and prejudice for his authority" and implemented it by force. While Roosevelt was "being pressed in a fascist direction by the consequences of economic maldistribution in America" his was not an example of "conscious fascist leadership." All Roosevelt had shown was that he was "weaker than the forces of finance capitalism."[19] What Swing saw was a more complex process at work:

> We have in America the organism of finance capitalism with its relentless expansion, stronger than the forces of democratic control. We have a social passion, too, rising to resist it. Fascism would be the combination of these dual forces into a single movement united in the determination to maintain the chief (the "best") elements of capitalism. If this is a paradox it is none the less true. Fascism swallows up the social conflict and promises to digest it.[20]

Swing recognized that the United States had its share of powerful demagogues. Whether they would ally with Big Business was still "a matter of prophecy." Yet Swing felt certain this was the trajectory:

> They are capitalist demagogues, and they are trying to establish no new economic order. They believe passionately in the rights of private property and in the profit system. So far they are radical, just as Hitler and Mussolini began as radicals. But when Hitler and Mussolini became threatening and strong, big business made friends with the future and poured funds into their coffers. And in this country, unless there is a recovery, I should expect to see our demagogues receiving funds from Wall Street just as soon as Wall Street sees that the future is theirs.[21]

In the end, fascism would emerge as a radical coalition between the popular movements shaped by the demagogues into a new nationalism but all serving Big Business. Such a recovery would not necessarily "avert fascism." Big Business had already made the necessary adjustments to the Depression. Dividends were 50 percent higher than they were in 1926. The future of Big Business was not on the line, but rather the rest of American society struggling to survive the crisis. For Swing, increasing class conflict was more likely than a recovery, one Swing doubted democratic government could achieve, even one as progressive as the Roosevelt administration. "The limit of democratic salvation is the New Deal," Swing wrote. But it had failed in two main areas: the redistribution of wealth based on "social taxation" and the whittling down of Section 7(a) in the NRA to the point where the commitment to collective bargaining was more about rhetoric than reality. Roosevelt's record with labor proved "disheartening and ominous." Instead of firming up the rights of organized labor to engage in collective bargaining, the NRA had "vastly increased the organized power of employers."[22] Suspension of the antitrust laws made it easier for monopolies to organize at even greater levels while labor languished amid provisions that were never enforced. In short, the New Deal did not accomplish what it promised and the result was growing popular unrest and dissatisfaction. This would necessarily give rise to the demagogues who in short order would be recognized by those who held economic power. At that point, Swing asserted, the United States would go down the same road as Germany and Italy in creating a "coalition between the radicals and the conservatives in the name of national unity."[23] Once this happened, the American public would be told:

> The trouble with America is that we have too much liberty, too much individualism, too much of everybody trying to outdo everybody else, and that our salvation lies in all pulling together, and particularly in bending our wills to the will of the leader. And a good many people will be ready to throw away their liberties as they toss up their hats. We shall be told then that it is un-American to oppose and to criticize. We shall be told that the unequal distribution of economic power is part of the American

tradition, just as we already are told that it is against the spirit of
the constitution to advocate economic democracy.[24]

HARRY F. WARD: ANTI-FASCIST CHRISTIAN AND "FELLOW TRAVELER"

Another contribution to class analysis of American fascism is
found in the writings of Harry F. Ward, a Methodist minister who
taught Christian ethics at Union Theological Seminary, held a law
degree from the University of Wisconsin, and was the first chairman of the American Civil Liberties Union (ACLU). In 1934,
Ward became chairman of the American League Against War and
Fascism, a mass organization created by the Communist Party
later renamed the American League for Peace and Democracy.
Ward remained chair in the new organization and served in that
capacity until 1940, when he wrote one of the clearest exposi-
tions about the threat of American fascism, *Democracy and Social
Change*. Ward had already staked out his position five years earlier in a succinct essay in which he argued that the policies of the
Roosevelt administration had established the economic basis of
fascism in the United States.

Like Haider and Corey, Ward saw the driving force of American
fascism coming from the top of the economic and political order.
He dismissed small fascist groups that imitated larger European
movements, as well as "indigenous" types in the "pattern of the
Ku Klux Klan," as insignificant forces in the making of American
fascism. Nor did he put stock in the "high-brow, dress-shirt type
of fascism" of reactionary intellectuals who rejected democracy
outright and saw the best form of government in the rule of "the
allegedly efficient and cultivated few." As a Christian socialist
who understood the class character of fascism from a Marxist
perspective, Ward criticized liberals for promoting various ideas
of a "planned capitalism, controlled by experts" to replace "the
economic chaos that uncontrolled profit seeking had produced."
In these ideas, Ward observed "one of the essential aspects of

fascism—the attempt to preserve the present class-controlled society." The only thing delaying the drive toward full-blown American fascism was the absence of a "popular base" similar to the European movements.[25]

Ward also minimized the role of conspiratorial politics that drew some media attention in 1934, specifically an alleged plot by Wall Street magnates to overthrow Roosevelt. According to retired Marine Corps general Smedley Butler, representatives of the DuPont financial empire and other reactionary Big Business leaders opposed to the New Deal had asked him to lead an army of 500,000 veterans on Washington to either assist Roosevelt in ending the Depression or replace him if necessary. While the plot was something of a sensation—Butler made the public aware of most of what he knew—Ward reduced its significance as nothing "but a juvenile parroting of European precedent" and "quite removed from present realities" in the United States. Americans needed to understand that the real fascist forces were already established and there was no groundswell of mass consciousness to oppose it. "The political form of American fascism had already been set in another direction by the present administration," he argued. This explained why a congressional committee and most of the major newspapers reduced the so-called Wall Street plot to a non-story. Ward conceded that the allegations made by Butler revealed "the temper of these forces" and showed they were prepared to "act outside the limitations of constitutional procedure." But the real significance of the alleged plot was its premature timing. The willingness of the plotters to even consider "unconstitutional action" was itself a clear sign of another "essential and universal" characteristic of an American fascism in the making. For the time being, no such actions were required. The "form" of an embryonic fascism in the United States was developing within a "supposedly democratic state" that continued to serve "the dominant economic forces," as the Roosevelt administration had done. Make promises to the majority to end the Depression while protecting the "few who live by property." For Ward, the Roosevelt administration had advanced the power of the state to preserve the existing economic order and protect the interests of the ruling capitalist class.[26]

Just as Lewis Corey had argued the year before in *The Decline of American Capitalism*, Ward interpreted the movement toward state capitalism as a symptom of a moribund economic system—parts had already turned fascist within the framework of traditional forms of authoritarian capitalist rule. Up until the twentieth century, capitalism had functioned within the liberal-democratic state to secure and protect capitalist interests on a national scale. But the rise of monopoly within the most advanced capitalist nations—especially the United States after the First World War—had fueled the need for expanding markets and opportunities for new productive investment. Simply put, the coming of the American Empire had required a corresponding advance in state power to manage it. Here, for Ward, was the turn from state capitalism toward fascism. "Since its own nature has become monopoly, not freedom," Ward wrote, "capitalism finds democratic machinery unsuited to its purpose. It needs rigid and centralized controls. Above all, it needs repression of the forces that could resist its continued garnering of profits at the expense of lives." The fundamental contradiction between monopoly capitalism and the democratic state was now exacerbated by the Great Depression that had begun in the United States and spread quickly to the world capitalist system. To survive the crisis required a powerful centralized state unprecedented in history. Such power could hold the working class in check by smashing trade unions and destroying revolutionary political parties. This was precisely what the fascist regimes in Italy and Germany had accomplished to preserve the profit system. Similar conditions, Ward said, were now developing in the United States but only more slowly. "In the countries where democratic procedure is more deeply rooted and democratic tradition longer established," fascism "proceeds more gradually, by the whittling away of representative controls and guarantees of freedom. These aspects of fascism are steadily developing in the United States."[27]

Ward believed the United States had moved toward fascism before Roosevelt and the New Deal. The first turn had come in 1932 when President Hoover pushed Congress to create the Reconstruction Finance Corporation, a government corporate entity empowered to provide financial assistance to banks, mortgage associations, railroads, and other businesses. The RFC also provided subsidies to state and local governments for direct relief and public works. Hoover's halfhearted effort to extend state power to management of the economy was trumped by Roosevelt who, immediately upon entering the White House, unleashed a sweeping agenda for Congress that saved the economic system from collapse. Capitalist necessity catapulted the executive branch of government beyond the balance of powers afforded by the Constitution. The New Deal revealed as never before how "the consolidation of political power followed the concentration of economic power." The Roosevelt administration had superseded Congress in wielding the power of the purse, and this ran counter to one of "the initial processes in the development of democracy." Given its "vast powers over the lives and liberties of the American people," the New Deal stood as "a serious abrogation of the principle of 'government of the people, by the people, and for the people.'" The real power of the state lay in its service to "the most powerful monopolistic groups of financiers and industrialists."[28]

For these reasons, Ward saw fascism developing in the United States without a Mussolini or a Hitler and their respective movements. "The economic aspect of fascism" had "clearly developed" but had not "yet taken the sharply repressive political form" as in Italy and Germany. Ward proposed two reasons for its delay in the United States. First, the strength of long-established democratic forms of government still enabled the purely economic purpose of fascism to preserve monopoly-capitalist development, at least in the short term. Second, there was an absence of any clear revolutionary threat to the established order. Yet, political fascism was plausible because the "inner necessities of a declining economic system" were moving in a fascist direction. This was clear in the

intent of the "capitalist order . . . in its extremity . . . to attempt to
abrogate all democratic rights" at the federal level and get the states
to follow suit by passage of sedition laws that made it impossible
for any political organization to seek radical change of the economic system through electoral politics. If such laws were passed,
it would not be necessary "to spend any money in support of Nazi
Storm Troops." Such repression could be had by "due process of
law, under the form of an allegedly democratic state." Then again,
the United States had its own tradition of "lawless violence." The
Depression made it clear that brutal, home-grown vigilantes had
"nothing to learn from Mussolini's Black Shirts or Hitler's Storm
Troops."[29]

Ward's analysis of fascism is significant. As a leftist Christian
minister and anti-fascist activist, he shared common ground with
Marxists who made the historical antagonism between capitalism and democracy central to their arguments. The concentration
of capital and the centralization of economic and political power
by the ruling capitalist class made it impossible to deliver what
modern democracy had always promised. Ward tracked the genesis of American fascism on the basis of class analysis informed
by his Christian values. In many ways, he was a harbinger of the
Christian-Marxist dialogue that emerged among revolutionary-
minded people in the 1960s and 1970s. His working relationship
with the Communist Party to build a united front of all democratic
forces in the United States against fascism at home and abroad
made him the most prominent of "fellow travelers"—not official
members of the Party but acting as though they were. His accord
with the basic tenets of Marxist political economy in the mid-
1930s only deepened his opposition to fascism as a Christian.

LIBERALISM AT THE CROSSROADS—AGAIN

Unlike Ward, the majority of left-liberals were staunchly anti-
communist and incapable of asking as Marxists did why the germ
of fascism inhered in monopoly capitalism. Instead, most believed

the solution to the crisis required drastic reform of the existing capitalist order by means of a planned economy, which could extend the life of American democracy and save it from communism and fascism alike. Moreover, as the liberals believed, if fascism came to power in the United States, it would be primarily from a revolt of the middle class. Implicitly, their definition of fascism was a consequence of their abiding commitment to capitalism. Unlike Haider, Corey, Swing, and Ward, most left liberals worked themselves into deeper contradictions by failing to recognize that the very idea of a planned economy within capitalism was contradictory.

Frank A. Warren, a U.S. historian, gave full treatment to the matter in his 1966 book, *Liberals and Communism*. The Depression had shaken the faith of the majority of left-liberal intellectuals in capitalism and fueled "a type of anticapitalism among liberals that had not been present in earlier liberal reform movements."[30] On the other hand, they could not transcend their belief that capitalism could still work. As Warren tells us, the Great Depression had spurred the return of liberals to political life after their retreat during the 1920s. Their disappointments about the Progressive era and feelings of betrayal toward President Wilson for failing to extend reforms aimed at the greater democratization of American society had brought their despair and political withdrawal. For much of the 1920s, liberal intellectuals acted mainly as media and literary critics of the rampant political corruption during the Harding-Coolidge-Hoover years of Republican rule in the White House, as well as the general "vulgarity of the capitalist culture."[31] But the Depression ushered their return to the political arena as erstwhile reformers. Many saw real progress in the efforts of communist planning in the Soviet Union. Compared to the miseries of the capitalist crisis in the United States, the Soviets were meeting the basic needs of their people. Economic planning became the clarion call of American liberals. George Soule, a left-liberal and borderline socialist, captured this viewpoint in 1931 when he wrote that capitalism's "chief fault" was its "lack of planning and control in the general interest."[32]

But a Gordian knot tied up all their proposals. Left liberals could not break with capitalism given their vision of what it still could be. Their revolt against the failures of capitalism became a mission still stamped with the "chief psychological effect" of their withdrawal from politics during the previous decade, namely, a deep sense of powerlessness. Now, once again moved to action by the Depression, left liberals were driven by "an image of the power they wished they had had during the twenties." Rejecting the abuses of capitalist power made them more bent on seeking power themselves. "They clung to certain modes of thought characteristic of capitalist society; they had the American penchant for 'getting things done' regardless of the cost, and accepted the old argument that though the means involve hardship and suffering, the ends are necessary and worthwhile."[33] Meanwhile, their failure to make a clean break from the system they were taking to task brought mockery from those outside their ranks. Communists charged that liberals were simply wrong and delusional in trying to save a system that was already dead. Warren cites an article in the *New Masses*, the leading periodical of the Communist Party, castigating the editorial stance of *The Nation*, one of the most prominent of its left-liberal counterparts, for its dead-end politics. Liberals cared little how "the putrid corpse of capitalism . . . is perfumed and tidied up, so long as the cadaver is preserved."[34]

According to Warren, left liberals proposed various plans either aimed at a wholesale reform of the capitalist system or some intriguing though hazy alternative to it. Despite their differences, all shared common ground in believing that "collective planning" did not require "a sharp break with the past." Planning held them together. Most left-liberal intellectuals wanted to extend the reformism of the earlier Progressive era on a larger national scale. Planning involved a pragmatic approach by government to apply science and technology toward a resolution of the crisis. As Warren put it, left liberals were convinced that "social engineering" could achieve "humane ends." Any alternative to laissez-faire capitalism would have to deliver greater distribution of wealth in society and must be forged along democratic lines. To this end, planning would be more geared toward the economic rationale of production for *use* rather than the existing priorities of *exchange*. From Warren's spirited perspective in the mid-1960s, this "reinterpretation of liberalism" by left liberals three decades earlier created a new problem. "Clearly left behind," he wrote, "were the moral absolutes of the Progressive age." Pragmatism had won out over idealism. "Liberalism in the 1930s clearly accepted historical relativity, the industrial complex, and was clearly associated with collectivism." Though they differed in key respects on approach and method, all shared the belief in a planned economy designed "for communal ends." The goal was a "socialized collectivism."[35]

But it would not be a socialist or communist one! Apart from Ward who combined Christian faith and Marxist political economy, left-liberal intellectuals were anti-communist to the core. Among the most prominent were John Dewey, America's leading philosopher of the interwar period; Stuart Chase, the labor economist and social critic whose 1932 book, *A New Deal*, was a seminal contribution to Roosevelt's political orientation during his first presidential campaign; George Soule, longtime editor of the left-liberal periodical *The New Republic*; and Alfred Bingham, the well-educated and worldly son of a Yale historian who discovered the Inca ruins at Machu Picchu in Peru in 1911, and who became co-editor of the radical, independent journal *Common Sense*. Among them, Dewey and Bingham were the most hostile toward a socialist or communist alternative to capitalism in the mid-1930s. But both offered different versions of socialized planning.

For Dewey, corporate capitalism in the United States remained a given. Indeed, one had to recognize that it was the historic outcome of an earlier period when the "isolated individual" in the era of small production had succeeded in establishing the foundation of the American capitalist order. The challenge now lay in replacing the old individualism associated with laissez-faire economics and classical liberalism. Dewey had gone to the Soviet Union to observe its efforts to establish a planned economy while completely rejecting Karl Marx's theory of the class struggle. Instead, Americans must cultivate a real spirit of mutual coöperation in building "a coöperative industrial order . . . consonant with the realities of production enforced by an era of machinery and power." To do this required what he called in his 1935 book, *Liberalism and Social Action*, a "renascent liberalism" grounded in education, which, for Dewey, was constantly building its capacity to influence all walks of life by the growth of science and the application of its experimental method to solve social problems. The challenge for liberals was to recapture the classical liberal ideal to bring about "the habits of mind and character, the intellectual and moral patterns, that are somewhere near even with the actual movements of events." To do this liberalism had to become "radical" and, as such, a guide for all who would attempt to generate this mental transformation. Dewey recognized the gulf between actually existing conditions and the possibilities that people could now ponder for the future. The necessary changes could be brought about by "gradual" reform with a "social goal based upon an inclusive plan" aimed not at piecemeal efforts to end abuse but to change "the institutional scheme of things." Dewey called for harmony through cooperation to replace the violence of the past generated by the belief in class struggle and a communist alternative to capitalism.[36] Even the "objective clash of interests between finance-capitalism that controls the means of production and whose profit is served by maintaining relative scarcity, and idle workers and hungry consumers" could be overcome by efforts to "bring the conflict into the light of intelligence where the conflicting interests can be adjudicated in behalf of the interest of the great majority." For Dewey, renascent liberalism was the philosophic guide necessary for a radical turn toward the democratization of capitalism. But as gradual reform, Dewey did not seek a radical break with capitalism.[37]

ALFRED BINGHAM'S COOPERATIVE COMMONWEALTH: MIDDLE-CLASS PHANTASMAGORIA

Going beyond Dewey's ideal of an enlightened, democratic capitalism within the existing structure of capitalist concentration and centralization, Alfred M. Bingham called on the revolutionary middle class in America to form a third party to win power through the ballot and then begin constructing a "*Cooperative Commonwealth*" to replace capitalism.[38] Bingham was staunchly anti-communist like Dewey but retained the Marxist theory of the class struggle, though with a decidedly anti-Marxist twist. Karl Marx was simply wrong to claim that the industrial working class was the only truly revolutionary class capable of liberating the whole society from capitalist exploitation and oppression. Instead, Bingham assigned this role to the middle class, specifically, in the United States. As he argued in his 1935 book, *Insurgent America,* Marxists had completely dismissed the middle class as a revolutionary force in its own right. As the subtitle of Bingham's book made clear, the middle class was now in revolt: "A scientific revolutionist must recognize that there is a tremendous social force inherent in the middle-classes in every advanced capitalist country, but particularly in this country." Marxist theorists had committed a "most egregious error" in "misunderstanding and under-rating this force," which, he added, was "*the chief reason for their failure*" to make the revolution on their own historic terms.[39]

The source of the problem was the communist misunderstanding of the middle class based on its narrow definition of the petty-bourgeois shopkeeper, artisan, and town dweller. It was far too narrow to encompass the totality and substance of the American middle class during the 1920s and 1930s. Bingham echoed other writers—the Marxist economist Lewis Corey among them—by identifying the middle class not as a class in itself but rather "innumerable social classifications and groupings, merging into each other with bewildering complexity."[40] Generally, occupation helped to determine its composition, at least discernable in two large groups: the "old" middle class composed of small businessmen and farmers, skilled artisans, teachers, and low-level public officials; and the various business types, professionals, and salaried employees who made up the rising "new" middle classes. For Bingham, the latter constituted a dynamic force for change and progress in American society. Its "new and different psychology, a new and different class-consciousness" set it apart from the influence of the working class and control of the labor movement.[41] Workers, whether "organized or unorganized," had become thoroughly "bourgeoisified" in their outlook and behavior.[42] Class lines had become so thoroughly blurred that one could not easily find any clear division between the middle and working classes. Bingham was sure that a middle-class consciousness in the broadest possible sense now pervaded U.S. society. A whole range of Americans who considered themselves middle class all tended to "wear similar clothes, drive the same kind of car, eat the same kind of food, have similar mental and physical habits—quite irrespective of vast differences in income."[43] For Bingham, the psychology of the middle classes shaped the essence of its mass consciousness.

Precisely on this basis, Bingham attempted to explain where the wide swath of the middle classes stood in relation to capitalism itself, and it is here where he parted company with Dewey and other left liberals. As the driving force of potential progress in America, the middle class's *"craving for security"* was "probably the best criterion for measuring the middle-class stake in capitalism." In that sense security depended on several factors, among them a "stock of worldly goods" and "possessions, such as clothing and shelter and tools," as well as "an assured income, to replenish these stocks as they are exhausted, and to supply the daily requirements of food, fuel and other necessities and comforts."[44] Bingham could not be more sweeping in his assessment of middle-class consciousness under capitalism—but with a caveat. The middle class was not capitalist in its orientation, at least as defined by the system that now prevailed. Instead, it adhered to the principle of ownership in terms of "ordinary possessions" rather than its class relations with the "ownership of the means of production" as the communists claimed. Whether it was a home, piece of land, household goods, savings, or financial interests, property was understood mainly as possession.[45]

For Bingham, the middle-class attitude of property as possession was the linchpin in determining what it wanted and the political turn it would take when it reached "the point of desperation in the crisis of capitalism." This was a decisive moment for the middle class. Either it moved toward an alternative to capitalism or resorted to creating fascism to save it. On this Bingham could not be clearer. Even when "capitalist interests" employ the ranks of the middle class in violent attacks on the labor movement, "the fact remains that *in origin, in mass support, and in emotional and intellectual attitudes, Fascism is essentially a middle-class movement.*"[46] This was something the Marxists could not grasp. Fascism was not the result of class struggle between capitalists and workers and, therefore, the "last stand of capitalism" by its ruling class in the form of a violent dictatorship. The Marxists were also wrong to deem the middle class as mere pawns of the capitalists and "incapable of playing an independent role" in pursuit of their own class interests, instead of falling prey to "the wiles of a demagogue, and use it as a bludgeon to beat back the threatening revolution of the proletariat."[47] On the other hand, the middle class could indeed go down the fascist road unless its leaders recognized that a viable alternative was possible. As Bingham wrote:

> Fascism may be "the last stand of capitalism"; but it would be more true to say that it is the last stand of the middle-classes for capitalism, than that it is the last stand of the capitalist class for capitalism.[48]

Bingham had no doubt in 1935 that events in the United States were trending toward fascism. Like Haider, Swing, and Ward, he identified "certain features" of the New Deal as fascist, especially in the NRA as a "parallel" to the "corporative system" of Italian fascism that would result in a "rubber-stamp Congress." Certainly, the success of the New Deal was sufficient to prevent a movement led by a fascist demagogue from getting off the ground. Nevertheless, the New Deal had "prepared the way for Fascism" and might even take it there if it could be done without "a disciplined party organization" like the ones that brought it to power in Italy and Germany. No, fascism in America would develop in its own particular, national form. Like most other serious observers, Bingham dismissed the "shirt-movements" as "too obvious imitations of European Fascism to be genuine." As he wrote, "American Fascism will unquestionably be so indigenous as not even to call itself Fascist or recognize itself as Fascism."[49] What mattered to Bingham was that it would be a middle-class revolt. No matter how much the capitalists relied on middle-class vigilantes against labor to defend its own class interests, the mass movement would rely on its own agenda and not a defense of the status quo.

In 1935, Bingham recognized that "the only genuine threat of an American form of fascism" was coming from Senator Huey Long, the virtual dictator in Louisiana who was looking ahead at the presidency. Long's program was not necessarily fascist. But the way he wrapped his attacks "against the *status quo*, against the power of Big Business and the Bankers" and his demands for "a sharing of the wealth" across the nation came close. His slogan of "Every Man a King" tapped into the mentality of the majority of Americans who wanted greater security, higher living standards, and more opportunities in education. Unlike Mussolini or Hitler, Long lacked a "shirted legion" behind him.[50] But he did have his own armed guard and use of the state militia at his will. Bingham claimed that Long may have benefited from the support of powerful business groups but wrote that "they do not appear to be well authenticated, and so far Long's career to power seems to be financed in ways best known to himself." Historically, we know this was far from the truth. Capitalist elites were just as "horrified" as the communists with Long's dramatic rise to national prominence. For Bingham, this was critical. The point had not yet been reached for the capitalist class to use Long as "a counter-foil to a radical movement"; besides, the capitalists still did not recognize "the desperateness of their own position." Thus, for the time being, there was only "a radical revolt of the un-class-conscious Americans" who were swept up by Long's bold and thunderous attacks on the status quo. Bingham thought this situation could prevail indefinitely, in which case it would "serve only to perpetuate capitalism as Fascism [had] done in Europe." This was precisely what made fascism a middle-class revolt against capital and labor that was not "sponsored or financed" by the capitalists. "It is not now, and it may never become so." Rather, Bingham insisted, the road to fascism was being paved by an "untutored" middle class "committed to the perpetuation of the open-market system."[51]

The only viable alternative to fascism for the middle class was to form a third political party and win power. Only then could it create what Bingham called a Cooperative Commonwealth in the United States. The time had come to do this, given the extraordinary capacity of modern production to create an ever-rising abundance of goods. This, in turn, infused a corresponding psychology of "abundance" into middle-class consciousness. Bingham cited the technocrats, whose ideas about making production more rational by putting engineers and scientists in charge of the economy supported his view that America was ready for a new economic system based on production for use and not for profit.[52] People were learning about capitalism and its pitfalls firsthand, even if only in simplest terms. They were begging to understand that poverty and misery caused by a capitalist crisis was unnecessary:

It is a hopeful sign, perhaps as hopeful as any, because if the practical-minded American people ever become convinced that there is no shred of excuse for poverty and insecurity, nothing can force them so relentlessly to recognize that it is private ownership of the means of production which necessitates scarcity.

And *they may come to demand the abolition of capitalism before they have even begun to be truly class-conscious.*[53]

Bingham called for immediate action. But it had to begin by recognizing what the middle class craved the most psychologically. At the top of the list, of course, was the constant desire for greater security and higher living standards. The architects of the Cooperative Commonwealth also needed to respect basic "*American characteristics of optimism, sentimentality, patriotism, and Puritanism*" based on a "*constructive, practical plan for thorough-going change.*" This required "ultimate" objectives instead of "immediate" demands. One could now demonstrate that "the capitalist system itself is at fault and that a new system based on a different principle must be built." All efforts toward this end had to minimize disturbances during the transition. Americans would not leap blindly into possible chaos and just hope for the best. They were far too practical and needed to be shown how it could be done. In the process, "they may get into a revolution, and they may accept a dictatorship." But they would do so "only in the name of peaceful, constitutional, democratic processes."[54]

The plan was published in *Common Sense* in May 1935 and included in Bingham's book. It called for a "gradual and peaceful transition with a minimum of disruption" to maintain "law and order and the continued functioning of the capitalist system" until the new, planned economy replaced it. Still, it was likely that chaos would arise as the old system disintegrated, requiring the president to "declare a *national emergency* comparable to a state of war." By law he could exercise executive power "to assure domestic tranquility" and possibly to gain "sufficient control of the organs of public opinion" to quell opposition. No matter. Members of the commonwealth would accept these measures if it meant building "democratic *economic* institutions to fulfill the promise of liberty contained in the Declaration of Independence." Consistent with these values, membership would be "*voluntary and open to all producers and consumers,*" though the first admitted would be those millions of unemployed who would return to work on the farms and in the factories to produce goods that were deemed essential. The Industrial Authority would lease vacant plants or those operating below capacity from private corporations and transform them into cooperatives. Workers would be paid in scrip issued by the Commonwealth Bank for use in Cooperative stores. Most important in Bingham's plan, production would be carefully calculated to make the total amount of purchasing power equal to the amount of goods available in the stores. To build a new economy based on large-scale cooperative farms and processing plants, the government would also buy land to build 750,000 homes, half of which would be made available to Commonwealth members.[55] As for industry:

> The properties of all corporations which operate public utilities and services, transportation and communication, extraction of minerals and other natural resources, and basic or monopolistic industries, may be acquired by the Federal Government, on payment of an annual rent of 5 percent of the assessed valuation, and declared a Public Enterprise. The corporations owning these properties would no longer operate them, but could continue to distribute the income received from rentals or otherwise to their stockholders, bondholders and officers.[56]

The plan emphasized that Commonwealth membership was voluntary. Total freedom of choice extended to the consumer and to choice of occupation. Democratic control would be assured as well as principles of local and functioning autonomy. Genuine cooperative stores would be run by consumers and all cooperative enterprises self-governed and self-disciplined. The Cooperative Commonwealth would prove so efficient and successful that it would take no more than ten years for "the great bulk of economic activity in the United States" to be operating within it. All financing aimed at sustaining the capitalist system until replaced by the Commonwealth required "*public ownership of the banking system;*

public control over the creation of currency and credit; high income
and inheritance taxes; a graduated capital levy on all fortunes of
over $100,000." The whole banking system would be "acquired
and unified," with each bank functioning as a branch of the
Commonwealth or National Bank.[57] Ideally, the whole transition
period would be smooth and tranquil:

> Private enterprise will only be discontinued as cooperative
> public enterprise proves its superiority in terms of the welfare of
> those engaged in it. During the transition period it will be neces-
> sary to maintain production for profit, until production for use
> can take its place.[58]

For Bingham, the main outlines of the plan were so clear that
the new party could easily succeed if it took on the likes of "a crusade."[59] Still, the plan itself was the main instrument of change and
had to be "drawn in sufficient detail and made sufficiently fool-
proof." Only then could the new party build a movement and win
elections. As soon as it assumed power, the party had quickly to
begin building the new Cooperative Commonwealth to ease the
transition from a disintegrating capitalist economy. Bingham reasoned that disruptions would be minimal. But if the new regime
faced chaos from any number of sources, it would take a hard
line against all who opposed it. Conditions might even require "a
certain measure of dictatorship." This would only be temporary.
The main outlines of the plan would remain, but "the tempo of
its introduction might change, and whatever the degree of democratic procedure that could be maintained during the early stages
of its introduction."[60]

AS LEFT LIBERALS, John Dewey and Alfred Bingham give us
much to ponder about the role of the middle class in the making
of American fascism. As the most independent-minded of its
intellectual representatives, Bingham proposed a planned economy based on voluntary association and cooperation between all

members of a Cooperative Commonwealth to replace the existing capitalist order. But to get there might also require them to accept some form of dictatorship in its early stages of development. Bingham did not blink at the apparent contradiction because he was quite sure the end justified the means. The proposed "Plan of Transition" originally published in *Common Sense*, a periodical well-known for contributions from social critics and theorists who tended toward liberalism and radicalism, offered a daring alternative between communism and capitalism powered by a revolutionary middle class. Yet left to its own "unconscious" state of thinking, Bingham was equally certain that the middle class also carried the potential as the ultimate force for counterrevolution and fascism as the product of a middle-class revolt. For Bingham, it was the psychological makeup and not the class structure that mattered.

Dewey, who was a psychologist, did not see the same thing occurring in the United States. Renascent liberalism, as opposed to socialism or fascism, offered what he considered a scientifically based radicalism that would enable the United States to emerge from the crisis of the Depression stronger than ever. Though he acknowledged that "our institutions, democratic in form, tend to favor in substance a privileged plutocracy," he was certain that the cooperative intelligence of educated people who were engaged pragmatically and in the spirit of ongoing experimentation toward solving all social problems would prove decisive in preserving and strengthening democracy. For Dewey, it was "sheer defeatism to assume in advance of actual trial that democratic political institutions are incapable either of further development or of constructive social application." He had no doubt that even in the midst of a profound crisis, "the forms of representative government" remained "potentially capable of expressing the public will when that assumes anything like unification." Moreover, "there is nothing inherent in them" that would prevent further "supplementation by political agencies" designed to represent "definitely economic social interests, like those of producers and consumers."

Here was the ultimate philosophic justification, and for Dewey an utterly pragmatic one at that, for the idea of American exceptionalism in the world:

> To profess democracy as an ultimate ideal and the suppression of democracy as a means to the ideal may be possible in a country that has never known even rudimentary democracy, but when professed in a country that has anything of a genuine democratic spirit in its traditions, it signifies desire for possession and retention of power by a class, whether that class be called Fascist or Proletarian.[61]

As events unfolded in the late 1930s, Dewey's push for an enlightened democratic government corresponded to the logic of monopoly-finance capitalism. On the other hand, Bingham's vision of a Cooperative Commonwealth to replace American capitalism, the epicenter of the world-capitalist system, was mere fantasy, though indicative of a deeper and complex phantasmagoria that glossed over irreconcilable contradictions of political economy. From a practical standpoint, however, there were obvious reasons why Bingham's ideas failed to gain traction among the various strata of the middle class. For one thing, Roosevelt's second New Deal in 1935 had delivered what was absent in the first—Social Security, unemployment insurance, and a far stronger commitment to labor for the right to organize and bargain collectively. Roosevelt had finally afforded some comfort to the middle class, which in Bingham's own terms addressed its psychological needs. More to the point, all proposals for a planned economy by left-liberals to the right of Bingham were subsumed by the New Deal. This applied to Dewey more than to any of the others since his brand of pragmatism became even more fixed to the dictates of capital in its higher, corporate form.

By the end of 1935, left-liberal opposition to the New Deal and claims that it was in some way fascist had dissolved. Roosevelt's campaign for reelection in 1936 turned into a landslide win as a result of the coalition of labor and progressive groups that had ral-lied behind his efforts to satisfy those left behind in the recovery. Just as Bingham had figured, the middle class was satisfied—at least for the moment.

The progressive character of the second New Deal and the easing of class tensions, if only temporary, also blunted efforts of analysts like Haider, Corey, Swing, and Ward to press for a greater understanding about what they deemed the real fascist threat still gaining force but even more disguised as capitalist reform. As the American Behemoth loomed on the horizon, all agreed that it was fed primarily by the power of capital. Big Business, not the middle class in rebellion against it, was the driving force of fascism in the United States in the 1930s. All agreed in principle that the fascist bent of the ruling capitalist class—considering parts of the New Deal as fascist or indicative of a transition to fascism—would only drive the middle class further toward reaction and plausibly into the hands of a waiting demagogue.

Even Alfred Bingham could agree with Lewis Corey that if Huey Long had lived and successfully challenged Roosevelt's liberal coalition, he might have been the demagogue needed to facilitate the merger of middle-class reaction with the reactionary finance capitalists, thereby taking America into full-blown fascism—if the general crisis had deepened.

11—Roosevelt on Fascism and the False Dichotomy of Good vs. Bad Capitalism

IN APRIL 1938, the vicissitudes of monopoly-finance capitalism brought Franklin Delano Roosevelt to another critical juncture in his presidency. After five years of steady recovery, a devastating recession seemed to take the nation back to the winter of 1932–1933, the worst months of the Great Depression. True, it was not as calamitous as when Roosevelt took office a few months later and pledged to deliver the nation from the throes of the crisis. This time there was no run on the banks, nor were there calls to suspend the Constitution and create what a *New York Times* editorial called an emergency Council of State to resolve the crisis and save the whole economic and political system from the abyss.[1] Roosevelt had now to decide whether to restore deficit spending after cutting the budget the previous fiscal year or to listen to those in his administration who insisted he must balance the budget so business would regain confidence in the economy and invest further in productive enterprise.

Big Business had welcomed the New Deal in the spring and summer of 1933 but soon opposed it as an unwarranted obstacle and alien to the spirit of American free enterprise and democracy. Reactionaries in Roosevelt's own party had played a leading role in the formation of the American Liberty League in 1934. In the final speech of his bid for reelection two years later, Roosevelt called out "the old enemies of peace—business and financial monopoly, speculation, reckless banking, class antagonism, sectionalism, war profiteering." As Roosevelt said:

> They had begun to consider the Government of the United States as a mere appendage to their own affairs. We know now that Government by organized money is just as dangerous as Government by organized mob.

They had become his enemies as well:

> Never before in all of our history have these forces been so united against one candidate as they stand today. They are unanimous in their hate for me—and I welcome their hatred.[2]

Now, almost two years later, as the nation endured a crushing recession that once again brought unemployment, misery, and starvation, Roosevelt had to decide whether to restore the federal spending he had cut the previous fiscal year, or yield to the one man in his cabinet, and close personal friend, Treasury Secretary Henry Morgenthau, who badgered him constantly that he must satisfy business leaders and balance the budget.

For Roosevelt, it was indeed another decisive moment, and perhaps more significant than most historians have determined. He could give in to monopolists and finance capitalists—Big Business—and facilitate the triumph of the most reactionary elements of the capitalist ruling class. Or he could reaffirm the New Deal as the great promise of liberal reform by committing the federal government to permanent deficit spending while curbing and ultimately reversing the growing concentration of wealth and power in the United States. Failing to do the latter would mean the coming of American fascism.

The "Roosevelt Recession" of 1937–1938

Plummeting stock prices in the fall of 1937 triggered a recession that confirmed the warnings of Leon Henderson, an astute economist who served in the Works Progress Administration, the largest New Deal agency created in 1935. In a memo to Roosevelt in March 1937 titled "Booms and Busts," Henderson predicted a major downturn within six months due to rapidly increasing prices on consumer goods during an economic upswing in the second half of 1936 that had caused consumption to lag. As demand for goods declined, big businesses held on to profits because they saw little or nothing to gain from new investments in production. For Henderson, the problem was that decisions were being made by larger and fewer monopolies. Here were the makings of renewed crisis. Though he saw all this clearly, Henderson was "a voice crying in the wilderness."[3] True to his warning, a deep recession did set in by October 1937, and much to the president's chagrin his political enemies took delight in calling it the "Roosevelt recession."[4]

Blaming Roosevelt resonated among a suddenly dispirited public and not without some justification. In January 1937, the president had declared that the nation had made it through the worst of the Depression and government had done its part to end the emergency. Now, he said, it was time for business to assume responsibility for leading the nation toward complete recovery and renewed prosperity. Indeed, a gradual and substantial improvement made possible by extraordinary federal expenditures had been underway since Roosevelt's first hundred days in office in the spring and early summer of 1933. Throughout 1936 and into the first nine months of 1937, the pace of recovery appeared steady. Business had rebounded, corporate profits and wages were up, and national income had risen dramatically. Government spending in the billions had helped to revive consumption and lift corporate profits. Yet much of the business world disliked Roosevelt. According to a report in *Kiplinger's Washington Newsletter* in the spring of 1935, 80 percent of American businessmen opposed the New Deal.[5]

Since the so-called second New Deal in 1935, working people, mainly white, had much reason to champion the president. As historian Ira Katznelson has written, the Roosevelt administration took "giant steps" in its domestic policy agenda "to reshape capitalism" during the New Deal's most radical year. Two key pieces of legislation had helped to raise living standards for millions of Americans who could feel more confident in the government's commitment to human welfare as part of its overall effort to end the Depression. The reemergence of a potent labor militancy the previous year had compelled Congress to pass the National Labor Relations Act on July 5, known also as the Wagner Act by virtue of its resolute sponsor, Sen. Robert Wagner of New York, which affirmed the rights of labor to organize and bargain collectively within a legal framework. Passage of the Social Security Act came a month later. The federal government would now provide old-age pensions and unemployment insurance in the form of grants to the states, as well as give assistance to the indigent elderly and aid to dependent children. But millions were denied these benefits along occupational lines that were de facto racist. Social Security did not include farmworkers, which in the South was the largest single occupation and much of it African American, or maids who served the wealthy in both the North and South. This was similarly true for the Wagner Act. Neither agricultural laborers nor domestics were covered under the term "employee."[6] Nevertheless, these measures helped to boost morale and fuel even greater approval for Roosevelt, whose landslide reelection in 1936 only seemed to confirm that the New Deal was surely working, though as Roosevelt told the nation in his second inaugural address on January 20, 1937, there was still "one third of a nation ill-housed, ill-clad, ill-nourished."[7]

Still, full recovery was seemingly at hand and Roosevelt believed he could now look to balance the budget in the next fiscal year. On April 20, he instructed departments and federal agencies to eliminate all unnecessary expenditures and seven days later called for curtailment of all federal government expenditures. "I propose to use every means at my command to eliminate this deficit during the coming fiscal year." He would withhold expenditures as much as possible by eliminating "a substantial percentage of the funds available for that year" and seek to raise "receipts of the Treasury through the liquidation of assets of certain of the emergency agencies" that the New Deal had created. It was "extremely important" to "achieve a balance of actual income and outgo" in the new fiscal year.[8] By reining in deficit spending, his administration was returning to the time-honored orthodoxy of a balanced federal budget. Expenditures for recovery and relief were cut by a third, about $2 billion.[9]

It was a terrible mistake. A few months later the recession hit, opening deep cracks in the broad coalition of workers, farmers, and small businessmen who had supported Roosevelt's sweeping reelection victory in 1936. Once again, middle-class longing for security was stymied, the second time their president had let them down. Big Business smelled Roosevelt's blood. As conditions worsened in late 1937, Republicans and conservative Democrats declared that Roosevelt was "solely responsible" for a government-made depression.[10] As Roosevelt biographer Kenneth Davis has written, Roosevelt had "lost control over his own party" by December 1937.[11] A resurgent working-class militancy made big business hostility to labor and the New Deal stronger than ever and bore more and more, in Roosevelt's eyes, "the earmarks of a developing American Fascism." He added:

> For large corporations now made war, increasingly bloody war, upon their workers. . . . They employed labor espionage and subversion; they stockpiled arms and munitions; they allied themselves with organized crime as they recruited strike-

breaking gangs of thugs—private armies whose only allegiance was to those who paid them. The possibility, the threat, of a Fascist coup appeared to Roosevelt not only real but growing as the economic recession continued with no end in sight.[12]

A year later, A. B. Magil and Henry Stevens provided numerous examples in a chapter of their book, *The Peril of Fascism*, which they titled "Terror, Incorporated."[13]

The Problematic Character of the New Deal Recovery

Apart from Leon Henderson and a few others, most economists had tended to avoid questions that might cast doubt on the future of the recovery. An exception was Alvin Hansen, an adviser to the Roosevelt administration. Hansen was initially skeptical of the views of the British economist John Maynard Keynes, who in his 1936 book *The General Theory of Employment, Interest and Money* argued for the necessity of government intervention in the economy during periods of crisis. By early 1938, Hansen was completely won over to Keynesian economics and had become its major proponent in the United States. In his own widely read book published that year, *Full Recovery or Stagnation?*, Hansen explained why the recession was so sudden and devastating: "The fragile and uncertain recovery from the Great Depression in the United States stopped dead in its tracks in 1937 and quickly began to slide back toward the deplorable depth from which it had started."[14] The main problem with the recovery was that it had been driven by consumption rather than investment. Since the start of the New Deal, and particularly from 1935 to the fall of 1937, income, employment, and output had expanded from two main sources: (1) a rising demand for durable goods, especially automobiles, that was made possible by a $5 billion expansion in installment credit, and (2) the income-stimulating expenditures of the federal government amounting to some $14 billion that had propped up employment on public works; provided relief to the unemployable; and infused capital into cities, towns, and communities across the nation. But the gains were short-lived because all aimed at increasing purchasing power rather than expanding production and overall economic growth. As Hansen viewed matters, the extent to which recovery was sustained on this limited basis required renewals and replacements of consumer goods, which had surely spurred capital expenditures, but only to the extent that the goods were purchased.[15]

Here, Hansen contended, was the structural flaw in the recovery from the second New Deal to the renewal of crisis conditions. Rising consumption did stimulate real investment, which brought growth in employment and payrolls and, consequently, higher levels of purchasing power. But the latter depended on increasing federal spending to inflate the economy to boost consumption. According to Hansen, government net contributions in the 1937 budget put about $3 billion into the hands of consumers.[16] Then Roosevelt decided to balance the budget in the 1938–1939 fiscal year. Even to that point, a consumption-based recovery meant that the economy had failed to produce sufficient levels of new capital formation necessary for sustainable economic growth. Instead of an upswing driven by capital expenditures, which, Hansen argued, typically brought technological innovation, new product development, and the need for additional resources and materials, the recovery between 1935 and the fall of 1937 was driven by increases mainly in purchasing power. In turn, businessmen made capital commitments that were immediate to their needs. Here was the structural flaw—a recovery driven by consumption rather than production, which resulted in an "inventory crisis" that had become ruinous due to four "accidents" that had hit by early 1937: inflated prices in raw materials caused by British rearmament; the horrific drought in the Midwest that drove up the prices of agricultural commodities; alarmist talk of inflation despite persistent deflationary realities; and steep hourly wage increases won by labor in late 1936.[17] General instability, Hansen wrote, created an unfortunate "conjuncture of circumstances" that brought on a collapse of stock prices in October 1937 and the onset of a deep and painful recession.[18]

There was a solution. As a convinced convert to Keynesianism, Hansen argued that federal expenditures were indispensable for continued recovery. Without it, the economy would operate on the basis of its normal tendency, which meant stagnation (slow or no growth)—and eventual crisis. As he wrote:

> A recovery resting almost exclusively on a rising tide of consumption can go forward only so long as the consumption stimulus is applied. Worse yet, it cannot even maintain the level reached once new funds are no longer poured into consumers' markets. For it is a peculiarity of business activity, geared closely to consumption demands, that once consumption ceases to rise, there are forces at work causing contraction. . . . In a peculiar sense a recovery based on consumption cannot stand still.[19]

Once the federal government withdrew spending, the dramatic turn from expansion to contraction in the fall of 1937 was rapid and devastating. A spike in unemployment pushed down demand for consumer goods. Inventories flooded over, putting a halt to the production of consumer goods and, more critically, further net investment in capital goods. "This is the dilemma which confronts a recovery reared on the stimulus to consumption," Hansen wrote. "Such a recovery can proceed no farther than it is pushed. It has no momentum of its own. It has no inner power to complete its own development."[20]

Capitalism appeared to require sustained, and perhaps permanent, deficit spending by government to spur new investment in productive enterprise. Hansen's conclusions in 1938 were not without precedent. In 1935, Lauchlin Currie, a Harvard economist then working at the Federal Reserve, had calculated that the federal government would have to spend $5 bilion to $6 billion for the next three years in order to achieve full recovery, much larger than the $3.6 billion that had been approved in the previous year's budget.[21]

Even more insistent about the necessity of permanent government deficit spending was chairman of the Federal Reserve Marriner Eccles, who had Roosevelt's ear in the winter of 1937–1938. Well before Hansen, Eccles had anticipated Keynes. He was one of the first big American bankers to insist that the federal government had to spend more than it collected in revenue to stimulate consumer demand to match the productive capacity of the economy. "In this conception," he wrote in his 1951 memoir,

> the government is the compensatory agent for an economy based on principles of private enterprise. It does not compete with private enterprise. But it consciously uses its system of taxation and expenditures, supplemented by monetary and credit policies, for the purpose of maintaining economic stability through maximum production and employment.[22]

Echoing Hansen for the most part, Eccles argued that the primary cause of the 1937–1938 recession was "a rapid and speculative building up of business inventories at a time when government spending was drastically curtailed." National income from 1933 to late 1936 had increased in "an orderly and stable fashion." Bank credit and private expenditures were also rising steadily. This proved that government borrowing for relief and public works and other programs was working. The long-awaited bonus of $1.7 billion to veterans of the Great War contributed to mass purchasing power.[23]

But government stimulus created contradictions in the private economy that led to the 1937 recession and, once pulled from the next budget, would turn a convergence of contradictory forces at work into a recession. Still expecting that the government would continue to spend and maintain cheap credit policies, businesses feared they could not meet rising demand without increased costs. To counter these trends, corporations embarked on "a major inventory boom" in 1936 by converting "money into things." Orders for new goods rose mainly on the basis of this speculation, which drove up the value of inventories by $4 billion in 1937. Then Roosevelt's balanced budget for 1937–1938 pulled the rug from the government's compensatory spending. Here was the root cause of the recession though there were other contributory elements. The collection of $2 billion in Social Security taxes in 1937 and the absence of the $1.7 billion bonus to veterans paid the year before created a major reversal in purchasing power. Eccles saw the recession as a conjuncture of declining purchasing power and the speculative policies of business, creating "a drastic deflation" in the economy.[24]

In his memoir, Eccles mentions a personal meeting with Roosevelt in March 1937. He pressed Roosevelt to consider that a sustained recovery could only be achieved by government exercising proper use and coordination of all major activities involving business conditions. "Unless this is done," he told Roosevelt,

> there is a grave danger that the recovery movement will get out of hand, excessive rises in prices encouraging inventory speculation will occur, excessive growth in profits and a boom in the stock market will arise, and the cost of living will mount rapidly. If such conditions are permitted to develop, another drastic slump will be inevitable.

Six months later, when Eccles visited Roosevelt at his family home in Hyde Park, he found the president unable to explain the recession and wondering how he could win back public trust.[25]

While Eccles pleaded with Roosevelt, and Hansen made himself the chief American popularizer of Keynesianism, Harvard economist Sumner H. Slichter took issue with Hansen's conviction. Slichter did not agree that better planning could end the Depression and counter the inherent tendency in monopoly-finance capitalism to stagnate without deficit government spending. Slichter saw the key cause of the recession closer to a

Marxist critique. It was the result of the enduring problem of low profitability for capitalists, whose avenues for further productive investment were restricted. Despite the rise in industrial production since the onset of the recovery in the summer of 1933, profits had remained low by pre-1929 standards, even in 1936 when recovery had peaked. Hansen had deliberately downplayed this fact. For Slichter, persistent low profits had restricted investment on new capital goods to short-run considerations, that is, either replacing or adding what was necessary to maintain existing processes, or some innovation aimed at capitalizing on quick returns. Viewing recovery as a matter of increasing consumption, Hansen failed to see that it generated a budding crisis of profitability based on rising inventories. As Slichter duly noted, inventories were not necessarily excessive in relation to production before April 1937. After that, they became excessively large in relation to new orders, which involved the further expansion of capital goods. Consequently, a protracted problem had become acute as a result of a convergence of circumstances. The failure to find new outlets for investment in the production of capital goods—a persistent problem in the ongoing efforts to transcend deflationary forces at work since the beginning of the recovery—proved decisive in the sudden downturn in the fall of 1937. When the stock market nosedived, production quickly followed. Like Hansen, Slichter saw "a conjunction of events in the critical period from April to September 1937."[26]

Regardless of whose case was more sound about the causes of the 1937 recession, Roosevelt had made a terrible mistake and the nation was paying dearly for it.

Concentrated Wealth Breeds Bad Citizens

By the end of 1937, the U.S. economy was in acute crisis. Huge sell-offs in the stock market were accompanied by business failures across the board, from auto dealerships to nightclubs. Between September and December, two million people were thrown out of work. During the winter months of 1938, many more Americans feared they would starve. "In Chicago," writes historian William Leuchtenburg, "children salvaged food from garbage cans; in Cleveland, families scrambled for spoiled produce dumped in the streets when the market closed. During the first six days of 1938, sixty-five thousand Clevelanders on the relief rolls went without food or clothing orders." Thousands of newly unemployed workers in the automobile towns of the Midwest swelled government relief rolls. In the poverty-stricken South, an untold number in seventeen states went hungry amid other longstanding deprivations.[27]

Throughout the winter and early spring of 1938, Roosevelt's handling of domestic policy was "wavering, uncertain, and ineffectual." In his State of the Union Address on January 3, Roosevelt affirmed the New Deal in the face of renewed crisis at home and what he described as "a world of high tension and disorder." He assured that his administration remained firmly committed to provide work for every willing and able American, relief to those who were unemployable, and support for legislative efforts aimed at increasing wages and reducing the workday. As for leading businessmen, he was "as anxious as any banker or industrialist" to bring the budget of the U.S. government "into balance as quickly as possible."[28] Roosevelt deliberately minimized the sharp and punishing recession as an aberration and temporary. "All we need today," he told Congress, "is to look upon the fundamental, sound economic conditions to know that this business recession causes more perplexity than fear on the part of most people and to contrast our prevailing mental attitude with the terror and despair of five years ago."[29] On the other hand, Roosevelt recognized a deep structural problem, namely, "the concentration of economic control [in the hands of big business] to the detriment of the body politic—control of other people's money, other people's labor, other people's lives." Such concentrations could not "be justified on the ground of operating efficiency, but have been created for the sake of securities profits, financial control, the suppression of competition and the ambition for power over others." Roosevelt seemed intent to hit Big Business with new anti-monopoly legislation.[30]

For Roosevelt, everything turned on a sound relationship between government and business. Firmly opposed to the laissez-faire Big Business practices of the 1920s that caused the Depression, he would not allow the restoration of "abuses already terminated or to shift a greater burden to the less fortunate." Instead, there must be more discussion about the "wider field of the public attitude toward business" and an understanding that greater purchasing power for the majority of Americans "presupposes the cooperation of what we call capital and labor," though he made clear which was primary:

> Capital is essential; reasonable earnings on capital are essential; but misuse of the powers of capital or selfish suspension of the employment of capital must be ended, or the capitalistic system will destroy itself through its own abuses.

Roosevelt connected the misuse of capital and the abuses of capitalists to bad citizenship. "The overwhelming majority of business men and bankers intend to be good citizens," he insisted. Only "a small minority" were to blame. Moreover, their response to exposure and attacks for "specific misuses of capital" had created an even bigger problem: "a deliberate purpose on the part of the condemned minority to distort the criticism into an attack on all capital." Any attack "on certain wrongful business practices" brought forth eager voices to claim that it was "an attack on all business." It was all a matter of "willful deception" by the minority.[31]

He claimed that most Americans now believed that certain business practices must end:

> tax avoidance through corporate and other methods ... excessive capitalization, investment write-ups and security manipulations; price rigging and collusive bidding in defiance of the spirit of the antitrust laws by methods which baffle prosecution under

the present statutes. They include high-pressure salesmanship which creates cycles of overproduction within given industries and consequent recessions in production until such time as the surplus is consumed; the use of patent laws to enable larger corporations to maintain high prices and withhold from the public the advantages of the progress of science; unfair competition which drives the smaller producer out of business locally, regionally or even on a national scale; intimidation of local or state government to prevent the enactment of laws for the protection of labor by threatening to move elsewhere; the shifting of actual production from one locality or region to another in pursuit of the cheapest wage scale.[32]

Roosevelt reminded Congress that "a permanent correction of grave weaknesses in our economic system" had been done by making "new applications of old democratic processes." Unlike other nations faced with economic crisis, Americans had "rejected any radical revolutionary program." The federal government had achieved much by "preserving the homes and livelihood of millions of workers on farms and in cities, in reconstructing a sound banking and credit system, in reviving trade and industry" and making other great strides in guiding the nation to recovery. Now it was necessary to confront the main problem that still remained, which, however, did not threaten the economic system.

Unlike the spring of 1933 when Roosevelt declared that emergency measures were necessary to save the economic system, he now insisted that "a new moral climate in America" required "business and finance to recognize that fact" and, accordingly,

cure such inequalities as they can cure without legislation but to join their government in the enactment of legislation where the ending of abuses and the steady functioning of our economic system calls for government assistance. The Nation has no obligation to make America safe either for incompetent business men or for business men who fail to note the trend of the times and continue the use of machinery of economics and practices of finance as outworn as the cotton spindle of 1870.[33]

Roosevelt had wavered on policy-making decisions, but he made up for it in his unique way of inspiring people. He had serious help. As president, he was surrounded by individuals who had clearly and forcefully identified Big Business as the main fascist threat in America. None worked harder at this than the pugnacious Secretary of the Interior, Harold Ickes, a Republican whose support for the New Deal was uncompromising. Ickes was one of the first New Deal heavyweights to call out the fascist threat in public. In a 1935 speech in Altoona, Pennsylvania, Ickes had referred to "a sinister movement" in America that sought "to super-impose on our free American institutions a system of hateful fascism." Ickes said the movement was "composed of, or at least has the active support of, those who have grown tremendously rich and powerful through the exploitation not only of natural resources, but of men, women and children of America." These people "will stop at nothing to hold on to that wealth." Ickes blamed the American Liberty League for riling up "patriotic fervor" by "pretending that a Communist uprising threatens in this country," thereby "attempting to line us up in support of a fascist coup d'état." [34]

Two years later, as America reeled from the recession, Ickes and others around Roosevelt, especially Assistant Attorney General Robert Jackson, stepped up the offensive against Big Business, pushing the president to do so himself. In a speech to the American Civil Liberties Union in New York and broadcast over national radio, Ickes attacked corporate America and the "fascist-minded men" who were "the real enemies of our institutions," men who had

a common interest in seizing more power and greater riches for themselves, and ability and willingness to turn the concentrated wealth of America against the welfare of America. It is these men who, pretending that they would save us from dreadful communism, would superimpose upon America an equally dreadful fascism.[35]

Jackson joined the assault throughout the month of December. Addressing the American Political Science Association in Philadelphia on December 29, Jackson pointed out that unlike democratic forms of government, which were subject to periodic checks and changes through elections,

> there is no practical way on earth to regulate the economic oligarchy of autocratic, self-constituted and self-perpetuating groups. With all their resources of interlocking directors, interlocking bankers, and interlocking lawyers, with all their power to hire thousands of employees and service workers throughout the country, with all their power to give or withhold millions of dollars worth of business, with all their power to contribute to campaign funds, they are so dangerous a menace to political as well as to economic freedom. Modern European history teaches us that free enterprise cannot exist alongside monopolies and cartels.[36]

Ickes put an exclamation point to the month-long attack the following night in another national radio broadcast speech titled "It Is Happening Here," his take on the satirical 1935 novel *It Can't Happen Here*, by Sinclair Lewis, which depicted the rise of a Huey Long–type populist getting elected president with the help of an utterly fraudulent media tycoon and then turning America into a fascist dictatorship. In his diary, Ickes reveals that others had assisted him toward completion of a final draft, which he called "an attack on great agglomerations of capital." He added: "I raised the monopoly issue [in the speech], pointing out that the struggle in this country was now, as it had been in the past, one between democracy and monopoly. I pointed out that if the latter won, it meant a fascist state with an end to our liberties."[37]

Roosevelt entered the first months of 1938 carrying all this on his shoulders. By all accounts, he was beleaguered and caught between fiscal conservatives led by Morgenthau who pushed for an end to deficit spending for fiscal year 1938–1939 and a growing number of advisers and confidants urging him to restore the spending he had cut the previous year. These included Eccles, Ickes, Jackson, and Works Progress Administration director Harry Hopkins. There was also the battery of administration economists and economic advisers, including Leon Henderson, Lauchlin Currie, and Alvin Hansen. All advised Roosevelt that the only way to overcome the immediate crisis of the recession and finally end the Depression was permanent deficit spending, what Eccles before all the others had called a compensatory economy. Yet Roosevelt was still incapable of resolving basic contradictions, as his biographer Kenneth Davis believes:

> He was acutely aware of the threat. He did not know what to do about it. If he saw merit in each of the two broad and widely divergent courses of action that were pressed upon him by advisers, courses determined by radically different conceptions of what had gone wrong, he also saw grave hazards. Balanced against each other, the alternatives canceled each other out: He was unable to think his way through either of them to a conclusion that felt "definitely" more "right" than the conclusion reached when he considered the other. And so he continued to drift on a sea of troubles, tossed this way and that by waves of contradictory advice, as the long winter wore itself away.[38]

Roosevelt's inability to make a decision left Eccles angry and bewildered. In an early March memorandum to Roosevelt, he reminded the president of his visit to Hyde Park the previous October when he had warned of ominous times ahead:

> We appear to be launched on a severe depression of considerable duration. If this is allowed to happen, the New Deal and all it stands for is in danger of being discredited. Alibis will

not be accepted. . . . The conciliatory attitude adopted by the Administration has borne no fruits either in dollar terms or in goodwill. By the nature of the case, leadership can come neither from business nor from the Congress. It is the responsibility of the Administration.

The greatest threat to democracy today lies in the growing conviction that it cannot work. . . . I urge you to provide the democratic leadership that will make our system function. Only in that way can the growing threat of Fascism be overcome.

Congress should be provided with a reflation program *now*. To permit it to adjourn without adopting vigorous remedial measures is to waste precious time and to court the danger of a 1931–32 winter. The stresses and strains, frictions and conflict that would result from another year of deepening depression would make our system even more difficult to work in the future.[39]

By month's end, Roosevelt was moving in this direction. During a five-day visit to his summer cottage in Warm Springs, Georgia, he gave a speech in the city of Gainesville where he told his audience that the nation "will never permanently get on the road to recovery if we leave the methods and the processes . . . to those who owned the Government of the United States from 1921 to 1933."[40]

Soon after, Harry Hopkins arrived in Warm Springs "well armed with facts and figures about the economic situation, and with policy arguments written and oral" to convince Roosevelt that he needed to renew deficit spending in the coming fiscal year. As one of Roosevelt's closest advisers and himself an architect of the New Deal, Hopkins was determined to get Roosevelt on board with Eccles and others who argued that government compensatory spending and curbing the power of monopolies were intertwined. According to Kenneth Davis, Hopkins was delighted to find Roosevelt "already well headed in that direction." Both men recognized that a temporary return to laissez-faire economic policies in the previous budget "must be abandoned." Roosevelt offered no resistance to any of the main arguments made by Hopkins. According to Davis, he and Hopkins were joined the next day by Jackson and Ben Cohen, a speechwriter and adviser to Roosevelt, as they all rode back to Washington together on the president's special train. Jackson and Cohen reinforced what Hopkins had stressed about the necessity of linking deficit spending with the restoration of a competitive market economy and flexible prices—which was only achievable through government action against monopolies. By the time the train arrived in the capital, Roosevelt had agreed that Congress should investigate the problem of concentrated wealth and the power of monopolies.[41]

Morgenthau, who had also been vacationing in Georgia, learned of Roosevelt's intentions but did not return to Washington until April 10, whereupon he went straight to the White House with a memorandum on "fiscal responsibility" that he dutifully read to the president, pleading with him to at least "sleep on it." Morgenthau tried again during the next two days but to no avail. Claiming that the spenders had "stampeded him like cattle," Morgenthau wrote that Roosevelt "has lost all sense of proportion" and threatened the president with his resignation.[42]

On April 14, Roosevelt sent a budget message to Congress titled "Recommendations to the Congress Designed to Stimulate Further Recovery." After weeks of riding the fence between two camps of his closest advisers, Roosevelt acted decisively by asking Congress to restore funding for government agencies and programs for the purpose of creating an "upward spiral" that would end the recession and then build on what the New Deal had achieved since its inception in March 1933. Accordingly, Roosevelt requested additional appropriations and loans totaling $3.6 billion for relief, public works projects, and other government employment programs, as well as desterilizing $1.4 billion in gold reserves that would pump more money into the economy.[43]

ROOSEVELT DEFINES FASCISM IN ITS AMERICAN FORM

Two weeks later, on April 29, Roosevelt sent another message to Congress asking that it appropriate $500,000 for specified government agencies to conduct a "thorough study of the concentration of economic power in American industry and the effect of that concentration upon the decline of competition."[44] If Roosevelt viewed his April 14 request for fiscal stimulus as a remedy for the ailing economy, this one took aim at the source. To sustain recovery as the basis for a return to prosperity, it was necessary to restore competition in the marketplace for capital and labor alike. But this could only be done by contesting the steady march of corporate power over the rest of the economy. For Roosevelt, the consequences were ominous. Monopolies and the power of financial capital had delivered serious blows to competitive enterprise, which he considered the backbone of American democracy. To make his point, Roosevelt opened his request with language that is startling today. "Unhappy events abroad," Roosevelt began, brought home "two simple truths":

The first truth is that the liberty of a democracy is not safe if the people tolerate the growth of private power to a point where it becomes stronger than their democratic state itself. That, in its essence, is Fascism—ownership of Government by an individual, by a group, or by any other controlling private power.

The second truth is that the liberty of a democracy is not safe if its business system does not provide employment and produce and distribute goods in such a way as to sustain an acceptable standard of living.

Both lessons hit home.

Among us today a concentration of private power without equal in history is growing. This concentration is seriously impairing

the economic effectiveness of private enterprise as a way of providing employment for labor and capital and as a way of assuring
a more equitable distribution of income and earnings among the
people of the nation as a whole.[45]

To make his case to Congress, Roosevelt cited statistics from
the Bureau of Internal Revenue for 1935 and a report from the
National Resources Committee (NRC). According to the IRS,
one-tenth of 1 percent of all reporting corporations owned 52 percent of combined corporate assets; 5 percent owned 87 percent of
total assets. The same lopsidedness applied to corporate profits.
Less than 4 percent of reporting corporations took in 84 percent
of all net corporate profits. Roosevelt also connected these dis
parities to the economic crisis: "The statistical history of modern
times," he wrote, "proves that in times of depression concentration of business speeds up." Big business had grown even bigger
"at the expense of smaller competitors who are weakened by financial adversity." Moreover, the growing concentration of corporate
wealth also fueled a sharp upward distribution of income. Based
on the NRC report for 1935–1936,

> forty-seven percent of all American families and single individ-
> uals living alone had incomes of less than $1,000 for the year;
> and at the other end of the ladder a little less than 1½ per cent
> of the nation's families received incomes which in dollars and
> cents reached the same total as the incomes of the 47 per cent at
> the bottom.

Still, statistics alone were insufficient to "measure the actual
degree of concentration of control over American industry." It was
necessary to grasp how "holding companies" and reliance on "stra-
tegic minority interests" by skilled managers facilitated the growth
of financial control over industry "through interlocking spheres of
influence over channels of investment"—yet publicly "masquerade
as independent units."[46]

For Roosevelt, the steady integration of financial and management control within the largest American companies had given them dominance over the marketplace, driving out smaller, independent businesses. Monopolization was stifling the productive capacity of the entire U.S. economy. "Private enterprise is ceasing to be free enterprise," Roosevelt declared, and is becoming a cluster of private collectivisms; masking itself as a system of free enterprise after the American model, it is in fact becoming a concealed cartel system after the European model." The promise of efficiency in the potential of modern capitalism had turned into "banker control of industry." In the process, monopolies created rigid and tightly managed prices that made it difficult for smaller, competitive companies to buy what they needed. The result was the decline of competition, job loss, and the destruction of buying power across the board, from the average American businessman to the individual consumer.[47]

An examination of all extant drafts of the message indicates that the earliest one did not include the word *fascism*. Nor did a revised draft made in Roosevelt's own hand. The word appears in what is supposedly the fourth draft, but it is misspelled as "facism."[48] Amusingly, the misspelling is corrected in the next revision but then misspelled again in the one that followed. Further inquiry into the private papers of Ben Cohen, Robert Jackson, and another key Roosevelt adviser and speechwriter, Thomas Corcoran, may shed light on the mystery of whose idea it was to include the word *fascism* in the message. All three huddled with Roosevelt and two secretaries on April 28 to construct a final draft, which the president sent to Congress the next morning. Whoever had proposed the word, Roosevelt certainly agreed.[49]

Whatever Roosevelt thought about fascism is interesting to ponder. At a press conference in Washington a little more than a week before he sent the anti-monopoly message to Congress, he offered a rambling response to a specific question about the danger of fascism in the United States. He began by noting the threat to society when a breakdown or failure of a long-standing process results in a small group taking control of it. He made them laugh when he said he would not engage in a discussion of America's "sixty or eighty families," referring to a widely read book published the previous year by the journalist and writer Ferdinand Lundberg. Instead, Roosevelt pointed to the power of finance capital centered in New York and how that power had prevented economic development in the southern states. He gave two examples. First, the New York ownership of the Georgia Power Company had kept it from expanding throughout the state of Georgia because the owners in New York controlled the money. Second, lumber companies in several southern states wanted to begin making print paper from the yellow pine that dominated their forests. But all the profits were going north where the company owners were. If only profits had remained in the South, Roosevelt said, the lumber companies could invest in production and increase employment in the pulp mills of Mississippi, Georgia, and the Carolinas. Wages and living standards would rise. "I am greatly in favor of decentralization," he finally concluded, "and yet the tendency is, every time we have trouble in private industry, to concentrate it all the more in New York. Now that is, ultimately, fascism."[50]

Certainly there is nothing in his April 29 message to suggest that he believed fascism in the United States would come with the triumph of a populist demagogue, even if the latter had support from elements of Big Business. America got a glimpse at the possibility in Louisiana Senator Huey Long, whose populist rhetoric and growing opposition to the New Deal had swept him to rising national influence. Roosevelt feared Long. No doubt he felt some relief when Long's political trajectory ended abruptly in September 1935, when Long fell mortally wounded to the floor of the state capitol, after being shot by a relative of a long-standing political enemy, and there were no worthy successors in the wings. But the fascist enemy was more than one man's threat to the status quo. Roosevelt now declared that fascism in the United States was present in something far greater, Big Business, and it had become increasingly dangerous. This same political force that sought to own the democratic state was responsible for failing to meet the material needs and necessary employment for Americans to sustain decent living standards. This was implicit in Roosevelt's definition of fascism in its specific U.S. form. American fascism meant business dictatorship and the end of democracy. Roosevelt sounded no different from the Marxists who defined fascism as the rule of finance capital. He and the communists shared much common ground. But Roosevelt actually said more about American fascism when he identified the *business system* as fascist in its aim to destroy democracy.

After several weeks of deliberation, Congress consented to Roosevelt's request and created the Temporary National Economic Committee (TNEC) on June 16, 1938. For the next two years, the committee held hearings and called hundreds of witnesses whose testimony amounted to thirty-one published volumes. It commissioned scores of government economists to study economic data and record their findings in forty-three monographs.[51] To date, the collected works of the TNEC remain the most comprehensive and thorough study of American business enterprise ever attempted by the federal government. In March 1941, its work completed and funding exhausted, the committee issued a two-volume final report, its findings and recommendations only to be pushed aside as Roosevelt and his advisers went from attacking fascist Big Business to harnessing its powers to prepare for a global war against fascism elsewhere.

FRANKLIN DELANO ROOSEVELT was a man at odds with himself in the winter and early spring of 1938. Stunned by the recession that bore his name and seemed destined to kill the New Deal, he remained in the wings while Ickes and Jackson went public about the looming danger of Big Business fascism—until he could no longer do so. When he finally rose to the occasion, he made contradictory statements and offered unworkable solutions under capitalism. In his April 1938 request to Congress to investigate the power of monopolies, Roosevelt assured American businessmen that the effort was in their best interests and, consequently, for American democracy. "No man of good faith will misinterpret these proposals," he wrote. "They derive from the oldest American traditions. Concentration of economic power in the few and the resulting unemployment of labor and capital are inescapable problems for a modern 'private enterprise' democracy." For Roosevelt, nothing could be clearer: American capitalism was *good* in itself because it was competitive and democratic. It became *bad* capitalism when ruled by monopolies and the business system. Accordingly, he claimed, his proposals "should appeal to the honest common sense of every independent business man interested primarily in running his own business at a profit rather than in controlling the business of other men." Nor was this an indiscriminate program of "trust-busting." Instead, it aimed

> to preserve private enterprise for profit by keeping it free enough to be able to utilize all our resources of capital and labor at a profit.
>
> It is a program whose basic purpose is to stop the progress of collectivism in business and turn business back to the democratic competitive order.
>
> It is a program whose basic thesis is not that the system of free private enterprise for profit has failed in this generation, but that it has not yet been tried.

Roosevelt's utopian vision of a fully democratized, competitive capitalism was unmistakable. There were no permanent contradictions in capitalism, only temporary abuses that were rectifiable:

> Once it is realized that business monopoly in America paralyzes the system of free enterprise on which it is grafted, and is as fatal to those who manipulate it as to the people who suffer beneath its impositions, action by the government to eliminate these artificial restraints will be welcomed by industry throughout the nation.[52]

Here was the classic middle-class utopia now raised to what could only be a moral platitude in the era of monopoly-finance capital. The authors of the final report of the TNEC followed Roosevelt closely in this regard by concluding in March 1941 that "America must find the way to bring about a permanent decentralization if the ideals of a democratic social and economic structure for all our people are to be achieved." But only after the global war on fascism was won. As the TNEC findings showed, the concentration of wealth and power was fueled even more by war preparations.[53] Amazingly—or not—Roosevelt and the TNEC still clung to the principle of laissez-faire despite acknowledging that it now belonged to the monopolists who had destroyed it.

By the late 1930s, Roosevelt had seemingly become trapped by his own pragmatic thinking. Ever since he became president, he seemed forever caught between serving the capitalist order and believing that the New Deal would create a new morality in government that would fulfill the hopes of the "forgotten man," a term Roosevelt employed as a presidential candidate in 1932 to describe the ordinary American worker savaged by the Depression. If not sufficiently aware of this irreconcilable contradiction, he never retreated from his defense of democracy as he understood it. Roosevelt was ever fearful of Big Business, which he considered the source of American fascism. He chose to run for an unprecedented third term because he viewed the Republican nominee, Wendell Willkie, as the personification of such a threat. During his first cabinet meeting after the Republican convention, Roosevelt said that Willkie represented "a new concept in American politics—the concept of the 'corporate state.'" As Richard Moe has written, Roosevelt "knew that it was a huge stretch to try to connect Willkie with fascism," yet he was certain that Willkie would become "a front for big business interests" and agreed with Harold Ickes who declared that "Willkie means fascism and appeasement."[54] In his message to party leaders in Chicago after the start of the Democratic Party convention, Roosevelt made clear that the party could not "straddle ideals" in the face of this looming threat:

In these days of danger when democracy must be more than vigilant, there can be no connivance with the kind of politics which has internally weakened nations abroad before the enemy has struck from without.

It is best for America to have the fight out here and now.

I wish to give the Democratic Party the opportunity to make its historic decision clearly and without equivocation. The party must go wholly one way or wholly the other. It cannot face in both directions at the same time.[55]

After his reelection Roosevelt recognized that liberalism's defense of the capitalist system still required fulfilling the basic needs of Americans. This was his motive for a "second bill of rights" which became increasingly important to him in his final years as president. It was present in his State of the Union message in 1944, in an "Economic Bill of Rights" that would make employment, housing, educational opportunities, and other benefits essential for human well-being as a right of citizenship.

At the time of his death, Roosevelt had taken the social-democratic impulse as far as possible within the framework of monopoly-finance capital. He seemed always on the fence between serving capital on the one hand and human needs on the other. An eternal pragmatist in defense of capitalism, he was in some sense its most significant victim. His utopian vision of a triumphant good capitalism could only be saved by eliminating bad monopoly capitalism.

While the United States did not go fascist, the threat still remained since the power of fascist monopolies and financial institutions was growing, just as the TNEC final report stated. That America escaped fascism to become in Roosevelt's own words the "Arsenal of Democracy" in the global struggle against fascism elsewhere is something to ponder. Is it perhaps a supreme irony of contemporary world history that the germ of fascism inhered in the heart of capitalist modernization in a nation renowned in the world as the beacon of democracy?

12—The Seminal Work of Robert A. Brady on Fascism in the Business System

IN HIS REQUEST to Congress on April 29, 1938, for an inquiry into the concentration of economic power in the United States, President Franklin Delano Roosevelt defined fascism as "ownership of Government by an individual, by a group, or by any other controlling power." This was the first of "two simple truths" now evident to Americans as the result of "unhappy events abroad," namely, the rise of fascism in Europe and Japanese militarism in East Asia. The second truth for Roosevelt was that "the liberty of a democracy is not safe if its business system does not provide employment and produce and distribute goods in such a way as to sustain an acceptable standard of living." Both truths, Roosevelt declared, pointed to the genesis of American fascism. Concentrated wealth and economic power in the United States—monopoly—was now "without equal in history." Roosevelt blamed the business system for "seriously impairing the economic effectiveness of private enterprise" and failing to provide "employment for labor and capital" to assure "a more equitable distribution of income and earnings" for all Americans."[1]

Big Business was taking the nation toward fascism by seeking more and more control, and eventual ownership, of the democratic state. This was hardly a surprise to millions of Americans. They had heard it for the first time in the early, frightful years of the Depression when some of the titans of Big Business and their servants in government ignored mass suffering and audaciously called for an American-style Mussolini to save the capitalist economy—that is, their wealth and power. By the late 1930s, Americans, educated or not, were not blind to fascism. Distinct if not always coherent discussions about an internal fascist threat had risen from the streets, union halls, police stations, universities, and other quarters of American society. Several astute writers had argued that Big Business fascism was destroying American democracy. Some argued that it would even come in the name of anti-fascism and would emerge within the framework of constitutional democracy and the two-party system. By 1935, a discourse had developed from reports and exchanges in newspapers, magazines, literary and academic journals, and books. Some questioned whether the New Deal itself was fascist or a transition to fascism. When a deep recession in 1937 threw millions out of work yet again and left children starving in the streets, it fueled a crescendo of attacks against Big Business, including by some of Roosevelt's closest advisers and committed New Dealers. A year later, A. B Magil and Henry Stevens wrote that the masquerade of fascism in America had concealed its real genesis in monopoly capitalism and its "fountainhead," Wall Street.[2] If there was anything new about all the talk about fascism in the spring of 1938, it was that the president himself was warning that the country would go fascist unless the people and their government came to the defense of its great democracy and against the imminent fascist threat.

At that point an economist and economic historian, Robert A. Brady, was arguing that the business system itself was a totalizing power in its own right, and that made it fascist. Writing in the spring issue of the Marxist journal *Science & Society*, Brady said that the fascist threat to democracy was possible in all capitalist nations. Consequently, as a global form of politics, it had to be grasped from the standpoint of its class composition and particular national formation. Only then was it possible to penetrate the "seeming paradox" and "endless confusion" created by those who saw fascism mainly in its outward appearances, from "swashbuckling militarism" to the "decimation of the middle classes" and its "entire prolix, iridescent, contradictory and fanatical propaganda for the masses." All such approaches defied "summary analysis in terms of a struggle to the death along an ever-widening 'fault' of class cleavage."[3]

Based on his analysis presented a year earlier in *The Structure and Spirit of German Fascism*, Brady asserted that fascist ideas and processes in all capitalist nations were products of monopoly capitalism and the emerging business systems in each. This was true for the United States as well:

> Just as the business community in America lobbies through most of the effective economic legislation while complaining about governmental interference in business, so German and Italian big business support the government which they bought and paid for while complaining about the incidence of certain burdens it necessitates.

For Brady, fascism was already apparent in the United States, where

> many persons strategically placed in American business confidentially argue that it is already here in both spirit and intent. Business is going political as it never has before, and it has learned to funnel its funds and pressures through highly centralized, interest-conscious, informed and exceedingly well-manned, united front organizations.[4]

In Germany's case, Brady argued that it was misleading to dwell on fascism as reactionary. Looking carefully at the role of the Junkers—the landed aristocracy of blood—in Hitler's rise to power, Brady contended that their wealth had become intertwined with the industrial and financial ruling class. As the major political force behind the rise of modern Germany, the Junkers had helped make it the most powerful nation-state on the European continent. Stalwarts of feudal and monarchical power, their "fusion" with the modern industrialists and business magnates, now the dominant partners in the German ruling class, belied their claims as anti-capitalists. Any real power the Junkers now had was subject to the industrialists and bankers, whose portfolios of concentrated wealth increasingly included their interests as well. Once the economic crisis deepened after 1930, the Junkers took their place in a "united front of the right" controlled by great commercial, industrial, and financial forces. Despite their differences and priorities, all these components of the German ruling class aimed not at "the abolition of capitalism, but the riveting of the social class relationships peculiar to its monopoly phase of capitalist development."[5] For Brady, this was the key to understanding fascism as a function of monopoly-capitalist enterprise:

> Though the formula varies to some degree or other from country to country, this picture holds for every country fully oriented to, or rapidly shaping up its policies in accordance with Fascist practice. . . . Yet a little reflection will show that the formula is neither new nor the outlook fundamentally different from that common to wide-ranging and monopoly-oriented business enterprise. What is new is the thoroughgoing rationalization of pattern and doctrine, and the coordination of all ways and means to realization of the full implications of such class control. This is what we know as Fascism.[6]

Put another way, the business systems in all advanced capitalist nations were intrinsically fascist because they subordinated all other reactionary and anti-democratic forces to their imperatives. As Brady saw the connection between capitalism and the rise of fascism in Germany, the "evolution of capitalistic organization" had always been the product of a growing relationship between all elements of the ruling class. "The key feature in this evolution has been the tendency toward monopoly supported by the centralization of business policy-forming power," Brady wrote. Within the business world, such "banding together" of ruling-class interests would be determined by the particular needs of organizations acting in concert to defend and promote mutual interests. And within each business, it meant a unidirectional movement toward organization for the purpose of achieving political objectives. This tendency was emerging in every capitalist nation to a greater or lesser degree. In the most advanced capitalist nations, cartels in heavy and light manufacturing were increasing, as were mergers of ever bigger corporations. Controls on prices, production, and marketing followed the same pattern. How were people to interpret these developments? First, he said, the entire trend was "cumulative, relentless and uni-directional." There was no rolling back to an earlier point in history. Operating at such increasingly high levels of organization as ever-centralizing monopolies, business organization "inevitably takes on a political cast and begins to reach for political power. Every attempt to do so calls for increased unity of policy, program and general outlook—leads, in short, to growing centralization of the power to determine policy."[7]

In the United States, Brady singled out the National Association of Manufacturers (NAM) as one of the most powerful of these "central policy-forming bodies," given its affiliation with over three hundred other national trade associations and more on the state level. The NAM was joined by the American Retail Federation, which coordinated policy for all retailers and along all product lines. This same structure and purpose was true for banking and other fields of production, distribution, and the rising service economy. Simultaneously, "parallel bodies" had emerged in "every major industrial country." Brady was unrelenting in emphasizing the global character of these central business organizations and their common objectives of achieving "full political, social and economic coordination on behalf of the interests of business in general" in each of their national economies. All of it required "an agreed-upon line of tactics."[8]

These tactics were necessary in the United States. The growing power of a resurgent labor movement in the mid-1930s had driven the business system to push for greater political power and influence. The imperatives of monopoly capitalism left "no alternative but to meet political measure with political measure." Labor militancy had struck "at the very heart of the sanctions and the philosophy on which the capitalistic system rests." This fueled class consciousness among businessmen who believed they were the true leaders of American society. Their top-down authority was not to be questioned. Their outlook was utterly authoritarian and undemocratic. Even the Roosevelt administration had succumbed to the miasma of Big Business philosophy, when the National Recovery Administration (NRA) handed power to the magnates of capital who were convinced they knew how to run the economy better than anyone. Given the main hand in creating codes on prices, quotas, and wages, industry representatives from the trade associations resisted organized labor, which was supposed to share in the decision making. Cooperation was nonexistent. The unflinching belief of American businessmen in their model of "self-government," now willingly adopted by the NRA, made it fascist. As Brady explained, the program American businessmen had been pushing was the same one the fascists in Italy and Germany had already created. "Given legal sanctions," he wrote, "'self-government' in business becomes overnight a 'corporative' system." There was no conceptual difference between the American business system and the corporatist systems operating under European fascist regimes. The only real difference was that organized labor had been totally subjected to fascist rule in Italy and Germany, while American labor leaders were labeled as "racketeers."[9]

The business system relied on the "ambidextrous advertising agent" to generate its version of the truth. In return, the consumer was expected to have faith that business had "his interest at heart, no matter how high the prices or how shoddy the goods." The laborer must always be taught that a businessman is his "natural leader." This is what the NAM leaders preached. As Brady wrote:

> There is nothing in the attitude of the industrial or public rela-tions counselors of giant American enterprise or its various trade associations which is at odds with the whole mood and outlook of Fascist propagandists along these lines. Nor is there general disagreement in the tactic which is to use the schools, the churches, the Press, the radio and all other means to put the message across: to work especially hard on the women and the children, and to operate as if the masses were stupid and dumb, cared only for baubles and not for realities, and could be satis-fied with bread and circuses. The assumptions are that the only realities are symbols, that democracy "is a white lie," that all talk of "equality" involves a fundamental falsification of nature, that it is force veneered over with a pale cast of mystic doggerel con-cerning divine or racial mission which regiments the mind and guides the otherwise aimless footstep.[10]

In the spring of 1938, Brady believed that fascism was certainly possible in the United States. So did American businessmen.

"THE LOOMING SHADOW OF FASCISM OVER THE WORLD"

Much of the material in Brady's *Science & Society* article came from the first of his two seminal works, *The Spirit and Structure of German Fascism*. From the standpoint of the present, the breadth and depth of his thinking in 1937 about the fascist char-acter of organized business is remarkable, and especially evident in the last chapter of his book, aptly titled "The Looming Shadow of Fascism Over the World." Brady captures the essence of fas-cism as a global feature rooted in the unidirectional movement of monopoly-finance capitalism. Fascism was clearly evident in the business systems in all advanced capitalist nations that sought total control over their respective governments. For all his training in economics and his knowledge of history, Brady revealed the sensitivities of a man who grew up in a poor farming family in the Pacific Northwest. He opens the chapter by recognizing that the existence of fascism throughout much of the world was "a matter of common knowledge" in the United States and a matter of profound political importance:

> Every man on the street has some familiarity with its insignia and phrases. Every daily paper carries news of its successes or failures abroad, of its newly won adherents or opponents at home. A rapid succession of dramatic events—the persecution of the German Jews, the Italian conquest of Abyssinia, the bitter and fratricidal civil war in Spain—has served to pose its programs to both the humble and the proud. In millionaires' drawing-rooms and wretched tenements its slogans are being discussed. In academic halls and on the public forum its progress is being charted, and its issues analyzed.

Brady eloquently described the defining feature of the times, a civil war between the right and the left with the new element of fascism added to the old mix:

> As a flame or time separates chemicals in a retort, so some major divisive forces in modern society seem to be slowly separating the people of every nation into warring camps. Left and right, Popular Front and Fascist, red and reactionary, capital and labor—the terms vary with time and circumstance, but the cleavage remains the same. Remains the same, but forever widens, forever deepens, forever sharpens the edge of hatred and brings nearer the threat of war, civil and international. However the divisive forces may be analyzed; the fact that this cleavage runs, like a widening geological fault, through all the layers of society is beyond question.[11]

The global fault line ran deep "through the social structures of every people and every nation" where fascism was on the rise and being contested, or had already taken power. Italy and Germany were its "major exponents." But its ideas, processes, and personalities were surely present or developing in other countries, the United States among them. What did it all mean? he asked.

Brady pointed to Spain, where civil war was then brewing and where the fault line in society appeared the sharpest and epitomized the class struggle. Brady, a great believer in democracy, saw it clearly:

> For what reason should the events in Spain seem no more than tragic episodes fitted into a long chain of events which appear to lead up to an impending struggle that may engulf the world—a struggle which may, as many experts believe, succeed in destroying much, if not all, of what we term "modern civilization"? What lies behind? Why does the issue turn on "fascism," and not on something else? Or, does the issue really turn on "fascism" at all?

These were real questions to consider about the emergence of fascism in Spain—or wherever it threatened democracy. His answer was direct: "Knowledge of the facts and a little reflection," showed that it was not about

> fascism *per se*, but on that form of capitalism of which it is no more than the politically conscious phase. For better or worse, the deeper issue now being squarely faced is whether *capitalism as a coercive political and economic system* should be allowed any longer to survive.[12]

The civil war in Spain was part of a wider struggle in global capitalist society that occurred "almost daily between massed employer and labor groups elsewhere." What distinguished Spain was that the warring parties had moved from the "'peaceable' to the overtly warlike plane." All parties knew the end result: "the triumph of reaction and a new lease on life for monopoly capitalism, or else a victory for socialism and the extermination of the rich and powerful of bank, factory, bivouac, and cloister." That both sides in the civil war were so "*politically conscious*" made the struggle in Spain "*a war to the death between fascism and people's rights.*"[13]

Yet fascism was still considered in words rather than "actualities." In Italy, mass poverty and privation that fueled revolutionary action by the oppressed majority was met by "Italian financial and industrial interests" that became the underwriters of "Mussolini's bought-and-paid-for Fascism." Capitalist crisis and the revolutionary movement of the German left also "caused German capital to strike its bargain with Hitler." It had the same effect in Spain, forging a unity of the right that was fascist. It was the challenge of "poverty-stricken laborers and farmers" in England, France, and the United States to confront the growing consolidation of fascist forces within their borders.[14]

Indeed, the tenor of revolt was rising in the advanced capitalist nations that were still democratic, especially the United States at the height of the Depression. While Brady was speaking for conditions in general terms, he certainly had his own nation in mind and in the forefront of his thinking. Mass unemployment meant that those still employed would, "in the absence of effective organization," see wages driven down to the point where their living standards were little or no different from the unemployed. The ruinous effects on life in general added to what Brady keenly observed to be "the psychological malaise so characteristic of modern times." Still, the whole system was going down because the "markets on which capitalism feeds for the gathering of profits" were being destroyed and so were the profits without which the system could not exist. Brady saw the genesis of fascism in the cycle of production and consumption, especially now that it was breaking down. As markets collapsed, so did "purchasing power at the source," then the inevitable curtailment of production in order to achieve the desirable balance between supply and demand. These conditions raised the level of protest to which the responses were immediate relief and public works, or full recovery on the basis of restoring competition and democracy to the economic system. This was not possible under monopoly capitalism, however, which prevented "the full restoration of the international division of labor" or "the free and unhampered expansion of activity at home." Under these conditions, "economic recovery" became "primarily *business* recovery" and not "the reabsorption of any considerable percentage of the unemployed."[15] Full recovery was nothing but a dream under monopoly capitalism.

Neither the dole nor public works provided by the New Deal offered a permanent solution. The accumulation of debts for both would have to be paid, and the latter required shifting the means of payment from taxes on income to those who held government bonds. Here, Brady saw that the contradiction between production and consumption would remain unless an economic recovery was powerful enough to increase the purchasing power of the general population. Without this

> the revolution-charged situation is temporarily relieved by a leveling down of real income through disbursement of borrowed money to the out-of-work as a condition to a later scaling up by way of tax levies upon the whole community in order to secure funds with which to pay off the rich who bought the bonds. The crisis which will then ensue is bound to be much more serious than the present one unless new borrowing possibilities are opened up at that time. And, if these are discovered, the issue is only delayed one point further. Sooner or later the economic system must give permanent work to the growing army of unemployed or it will collapse.[16]

The fact that business could offer nothing more only fueled rising unrest. But it was now more purposeful, direct, and organized. Workers understood better than ever that industry could indeed deliver the goods but not the system of delivery determined by the capitalists. Brady said it made no difference how the case was stated or by whom, "whether the charges take the emotional form of hatred of 'Wall Street' or the 'money trust,' or the calculated argument of left-wing and Marxian writers." The crisis had raised public understanding that there was something quite "fundamentally wrong" with the economic system and businessmen could be held accountable. In so doing, workers ran "full tilt into a fact of enormous portent for the 'shape of things to come'—that *business itself is organized and politically conscious.*" Business had become a system of power in its own right:

> Business already possesses predominant influence in the councils of every capitalistically organized state. If the challenge of the forces arrayed against it prove sufficiently serious, capital will no longer remain a "silent partner" to government. Rather than surrender power it will resort to the *coup d'état* and reach out for the mantle of sovereign power. It will seek, in short, to establish a fascist regime.[17]

The resources of organized business were vast and flowed downward to the most basic levels of modern capitalist society. An organized network committed solely to "promotion of the interests of business enterprise" and its "prime beneficiaries" ranged from top to bottom, from the trusts and combines themselves to "the looser federations of business such as trade associations and the Chamber of Commerce" whose purpose above all is "*to formulate and direct business policy.*" As Brady then wrote, this "*very centralization of policy-forming power*" had "*turned these central coordinating bodies into politically active and fascist-inclined agents.*"[18]

Brady recognized that the growth of monopolies and their influence since the 1880s, and from which the genesis of business organization had occurred, meant "a steady erosion of the necessary conditions for the maintenance of *free competition* and laissez-faire" in the capitalist nations. Cartels, trusts, trade associations, and other organizations that made up the network of organized business were increasing in number and expanding "the range of business activity over which they exercise some form of control." In the process, they became "more *politically conscious* of the powers for coercion which lie within their grasp." Their growing control over all aspects of life relating to business enterprise and the market reached down into almost all aspects of civic life. "Today scarcely a field of business activity in any capitalistic country is without its central business association," he wrote. "All lines of manufacturing, of wholesale and retail trade, of domestic and foreign shipping, of finance and banking, possess their own trade associations, cartels, syndicates, pools, or other alliances."[19] Once again, the top-bottom relationship reinforced an understanding of common interests:

> It makes no difference which way the process runs—whether local organizations are brought together on a regional and finally on a national basis, or whether a skeleton national organization is first set up and then local and regional subdivisions organized and attached thereto. In all cases the tendency is for centralization of power to form policies with regard to prices, wages, labor unions, markets, imports and exports, and other matters to be uniform and national in scope.[20]

Brady estimated that the number of trade associations in the United States at that time could be anywhere between 3,000 and 5,000 and tended to be of two types. The first represented a particular line of business, whether in manufacturing, distribution, transportation, or finance. The NAM wielded the greatest clout. The second type tended to include all business enterprise within a state, city, or town. Here the dominant force was the local Chamber of Commerce. Thousands like it formed the base of the great "pyramids" of the U.S. Chamber of Commerce. This was true of every capitalist country, each with its own "vast network of business organization" that comprised "layer after layer of these webs of control" being continuously spun and in step with the march of monopoly capitalism. Since the 1880s, they were becoming progressively "knitted into the national economic framework" of every capitalist country.[21]

Again, what all this meant on a world-historical level to Brady in 1937 was this:

> *Laissez-faire capitalism*, in other words, *has been giving way to control capitalism*, with the clear and unmistakable implication of ultimate exercise of deliberate, formal, and all-inclusive monopoly powers. *Power to control policy* relative to wages, unions, prices, markets, production, investment, and other features of business strategy *has been, is being, and gives every indication of continuing to be centralized throughout the entire business world, and in every capitalist country. The tendency is to all intents and purposes well-nigh universal, unidirectional, and quite irresistible.*[22]

In the United States, government had not done enough to stem the tide of organized business. "Oriented as they were against the superficial facts of formal business combination, America's trust-busting tactics had little more effect than to compel either more rational or more subtle forms of control." The National Recovery Administration was a case in point. Despite its program of "regulating free competition" it had actually served as "a partial catalyst" toward further centralization. The same was true of all other industrial nations, whether Britain or Germany, democratic or fascist. While they differed as nations "in tradition, general economic organization, and types of political machinery," their governments contributed greatly to the centralization of the business system. "In one form or another—ranging from the closed and rigidly organized combinations to the looser forms of cartels—this process was practically complete in Germany before the advent of the Hitler regime." Prior to that, the extent to which democratic government had developed in Germany did nothing to halt the march. Centralization had already made the qualitative leap to the hegemony of monopoly where one or a handful of the greatest of business combinations controlled various parts of the economy.[23]

Something "analogous" was also happening in the United States: Far more important than the mere fact of centralization, however, is the truism that *control over business policy means central command, and central command means massed strength*. It matters little whether the controls exercised relate to mere formation and focusing of opinion, or to the enforcement of decisions as though they had the effect of law. The principle is the same. And the principle is that *massed strength is political strength. Power to influence legislation is political power; power to coerce trade unions is political power; power to enforce price policies is political power; power to command more or less exclusive use of media for manipulating public opinion is political power.*[24]

The business system was growing "persistently and cumulatively" and flowing "into more and more fields" while increasing its sense of "singleness and directness of purpose." Brady was unrelenting as he wound his way toward a conclusion:

This coagulation of *business sentiment* and this *mobilization of the arrayed resources* of the business community involve directly, inevitably, and inescapably a reaching out for control over the effective and organized powers of the state. The big combines are already *states within states*, and all the facts of modern history, even without any direct threat or challenge to the capitalistic system, are operating to stimulate continued federation, with the only possible ultimate result being an attempt to take over direct control of the government itself.[25]

And so the class struggle had widened and Brady described it all as passionately as any communist would:

Like organized capital, organized labor is engaged in the struggle for power, and its political consciousness grows in direct proportion as it acquires strength, confidence, and centralized *interest-oriented* authority. And it grows steadily more militant as it becomes aware of the full implications of the system with which it is face to face: as it becomes aware of the prodigal wastage of the people's natural resources, of the vast armies of rootless millions sinking down into the wretched misery of slum and dump-heap and looking hungrily for any snatch at a job however poorly paid, of the loss of security to job, family, and home, of the lack of futures for the children and the yet unborn, of the crushing and all-destroying black madness of endlessly impending wars.[26]

This highly charged and volatile political moment of labor militancy and "its stated or implied thrust" was central to the capitalist system. In response, what kind of "politico-economic system" could businessmen be "expected to promote" except fascism given the "inescapable" logic of the past quarter-century? For Brady, fascism was the "wedding of a *condition* and a *myth*." As he wrote:

The *condition* represents no more than formal extension, through the employment of the machinery of the state, of the leading principles of business-as-usual to encompass the entire population. And the *myth* is that interpretation of the business case which is designed to gain popular support. With regard to this latter, it may be laid down as an indispensable condition that, without some measure of popular support, fascism—even with the aid of the military—becomes next to impossible to put across at the beginning.[27]

Here Brady pointed to his own conclusions on how fascism is ultimately achieved with the aid if not full support of the population. It is precisely in the hierarchical, authoritarian, and autocratic character of organized business. This was true for every nation whose business system operated on "principles" dictated by monopoly capitalism as a rising totalitarian force in society:

Every business practices toward its own staff the "leader" and the "authority" principles, and it undeviatingly aspires toward the "total" principle. That is to say, all officers and staff members are appointed and removed from on top entirely at the discretion of management (*leader* principle), and authority is from the top down, responsibility from the bottom up (*authority* principle). And every employer attempts to control so far as humanly possible the attitudes, beliefs, and points of view (*Weltanschauung*) of his employees and every section of the public with which he comes in contact (*total* principle).[28]

Every business establishment is, in other words, completely autocratic and completely undemocratic in structure, ideology, and procedure. It is, by the same token, completely intolerant of all opposition within or without, or of any criticism which does not redound to the advantage of the profit-making possibilities of the enterprise. The enterprise may be compelled, it is true, to make important concessions on all points, but it should not be forgotten that these are *concessions, not departures from principle.*[29]

This is more or less how businessmen would rule. Moreover, it was entirely "*natural to them*" given their "good breeding and respectable station." It also made them akin to that other singular, anti-democratic force in modern capitalist society, the military, which also "holds the key to political power."[30] If the rank and file eagerly follows the generals, then fascism occurs immediately. If not, there is still another road no matter the delay.

With the aid of the officer corps the conditions of business may be maintained as valid for all members of society (fascism) provided some way can be found for neutralizing or completely eliminating organized opposition. It is here that business forces attempt to build up a *myth*. The myth is designed purely and simply as a means for circumventing opposition, and its propositions are regarded as equivalent to "true" and undeniable facts if they can be successfully put across, since, as is usual in business, success is the measure of "truth" as well as of ability.[31]

Myth is central to the making of organized business, and this makes it fascist. Its "business evangelism," Brady writes, "has two faces, an inner and outer," both about power. The first is about what businessmen, especially the captains of industry and finance, think about themselves in relation to the rest of society, which they consider inferior. The second is what they want their inferiors to believe about them as part of the "the business-military hierarchy—'leaders'" who instruct them to know their place in the world and to appreciate what is being offered to them.[32] "Both these propaganda faces," Brady wrote, "is the same in all nations ordered on a capitalist basis."

Brady affirmed this in his study of German fascism, with parallels to a nascent American counterpart:

> Almost the entirety of the German Nazi program and line of argumentation is identical in content and point of view with that of the American business community. Such elements as the persecution of the Jews is different, not in *intent*, but only in the fact that such persecution could serve Nazi ends in Germany in the particular circumstances of the years 1933–36. When the American situation has ripened to that of Germany in 1933, there will be race terror in the United States as well, and it will be anti-Negro, anti-Jew, anti-Mexican, and anti-Japanese.[33]

If these were the outer faces of terrorist-fascist processes, they were products of an "inner face of fascism" that looked upon man as essentially "a beast of prey." Here was the general philosophic outlook of fascism, the war of all against all that necessitated a social and political doctrine of "might makes right" and which, for Brady, made pirate and stockbroker one and the same. What the outlaw pirate did on the high seas was no different from "a legitimate game in which each man is pitted against every other man" for as many of the prizes as he can get.[34] This was the mentality of the businessman that contributed to the making of American fascism:

That business men in the United States hold this view is beyond question. They hold it to be axiomatic in describing the character of their own kind, and they hold it to be valid for the human race at large. Anyone who has taken the trouble to interview stockbrokers, captains of industry and finance, advertisers, public relations counselors, or other participants in, and apologists for, the business system will soon learn that this view of human nature governs their actions and their behavior in practically all things, and that it is regarded as so obviously true as to require no comment, explanation, or justification.

The ideological justification for such power over any nation was logically extended outward as it intensified at home. Businessmen showed "not the slightest objection to using all the armed forces of the state in a war on India, on Morocco, on Manchuria, on Abyssinia, on Nicaragua, Spain, or Mexico. If you are big enough, strong enough to take it, the rule is: take it." Likewise there was no objection to

> using the troops against strikers, hunger-marchers, sharecroppers, or any other group which for any reason whatsoever wants a little of what the insiders may have. All the emphasis on war, all the promotion of the army and the navy, of "national defense," of that curiously bellicose frame of mind commonly known by the euphemistic term "patriotism," is born of the same view of life, of human nature, of civilization and culture.[35]

If fascist ideology and the terror it justified is one face of fascism, the other "is that which it presents to the public" in the form of a program guided by the "'ethic' of the advertising 'profession'— *suppressio veri, suggestio falsi*," that is, either suppress the truth or suggest that the false can be proved:

> What is effective? What will succeed? What will suppress, or deflect, or undermine opposition? What will create a favorable

attitude? If this means to suppress the truth and suggest the false, the same will be done. If it means, however, to tell some portion, or on occasion all, of the truth, this in turn will be done. And if it means so to redefine the meaning of "truth" that it becomes whatever is told by those able to enforce compliance with doctrine, then "truth" will become, *ipso facto*, whatever is told the people.

Propaganda—meaning the *propagation of doctrine*—which supports the business system, is the mental-emotional diet which must be ladled out to the public. This propaganda is based upon the *conquest of attitude, of belief, of point of view*, and it proceeds on two levels. The first might be called the *persuasive*, or educational, level; the second is the *coercive* level. The second does not dispense with persuasion, but it adds thereto the compulsion to conform.

On both levels it seeks to instill in the popular mind belief that the "leaders" of economic and political affairs are endowed with inspired vision, wide humanitarian interests, and the highest type of acceptable social ethics. On both levels, business propaganda attempts to inculcate in the public the attitude it expects from paid employees: (1) belief in the "rights" of those in possession to own, to enjoy superior emoluments, and to command in all things; (2) unquestioning obedience, respect, and a proper degree of servility and abnegation; (3) belief that each has his allotted function, graded to his talents, which he must perform, and from which alone he may obtain his due meed. The first promotes the need for myths of leadership, of authority, and the nature of life values. The second promotes emphasis on discipline and loyalty. The third promotes the formation of a class or caste hierarchy. The first is theological in stamp, the second military, the third medieval or caste.[36]

In the 1930s, what separated non-fascist capitalist states and the fascist regimes was not in the content "*but in the level* on which the propaganda is promoted." The non-fascist state, as in England and the United States, the Argentine, Belgium, etc., are still "*mainly on the persuasive level*, while the fascist, as in Italy and Germany, are fully oriented *on the coercive level.*" In the United States, business was still trying to sell itself to the public while in Germany it no longer had to.[37]

BUSINESS AS A SYSTEM OF POWER: TRADE ASSOCIATIONS AND THE NAM

Brady built on this concept of the fascist business system in his second great work, published in 1943, *Business as a System of Power*. His global focus revealed shared features of business systems in six advanced capitalist countries, three of them still under constitutional and democratic forms of government (France, Great Britain, and the United States) and the other three operating under fascist regimes (Italy, Germany, and Japan). Brady argued that all six had undergone significant changes in their respective industrial systems that were "unidirectional, additive, [and] cumulative" and could not be rolled back to some earlier forms, especially since all six had now to meet the demands of a new "total war."[38] Even before the coming of a second world war in 1939, Brady saw "parallel webs of control" being spun by Big Business in all six nations during the interwar period. By the mid-1930s all had reached a point where "separate strands" developing spontaneously had come to the point where businessmen were compelled to choose between democracy and fascism. In Italy, Japan, and Germany, they had chosen "the totalitarian road" by giving themselves over to a politics that could as easily

> demolish as resurrect any given structure of preexisting special-interest controls, including—through the precarious fortunes of subsequent wars, revolutions, or internal paralysis—those of the business interests which fathered, with money, ideas, and leaders, the original *coup d'état*.

On the other hand, businessmen in France, Great Britain, and the

United States had chosen with varying success to widen "the lati-tude for direct public participation in the formulation of economic policies affecting the public interests" and thus remained operat-ing in "the orbit of the liberal-capitalistic system." For Brady, organized business had two alternatives: engage the public in fur-thering democratic controls over it or succumb to inherent trends in its structure that led to fascism.[39]

While the fascist road had led to successive disasters and war, the democratic alternative necessarily challenged the growing central-ized machinery and political power of organized business, forcing it to find common ground in what Brady called a "collective mind." This was a challenge given the range of differences, including those between big and small businesses, those who sought contraction while others wanted to expand, or the size of the market—local, national, or international—that determined the extent of its opera-tions. At all levels, the problem was competition versus monopoly. "For widely varying reasons," Brady wrote, "some favor dictator-ships, while others—particularly small businesses—can survive only in a democratic world." Finding a collective mind was even more difficult given the need for

> a collective will, in focusing effort on the articulation of an inter-nally coherent business program, in giving membership a sense of direction through promotion of a common social-psycholog-ical outlook, and in formulating for the doubtful a common set of simple and realizable goals.

The challenge was to do this at a time when the world econ-omy was in crisis and the rejection of the democratic choice by organized business was seriously restricted. Its inherent drive toward centralization and power might be quite incapable of even "halfhearted compromises urged upon it," removing even the "the time-honored principles of 'muddling through.'" For Brady, that time had passed. Certainly, the one constant in this central-izing trend of business meant that the small owner was "losing out," while competition among the giants had them engaged in ruthless methods that would lead to a purge. Brady pointed to the larger and more dangerous struggle, "that organized business in one national system will show no mercy to organized business in another national system, once conflicts of interest have forced matters to the arbitraments of war."[40]

Brady compared the business systems of the six nations in question and their respective approaches to the expansion of business controls, observing four dominant trends common to each. First, the transformations in each of the three totalitarian countries were "fully consonant with" and "the logical outgrowths of, previous trends in structure, policies, and controls within the business world itself." Put another way, the move from liberal-capitalist democracy to fascism meant no rupture with the existing business system. Second, "parallelisms" detected in "the evolution of business centralization" made them "appear the common product of a single plan." Third, all policies of each faced "widespread—in many respects very highly organized and always potentially threatening—popular opposition," forcing each beyond traditional policies and practices. This established new benchmarks for business leadership. Finally, such opposition necessarily challenged business leaders to recognize that "all economic issues" took on "a political meaning," thereby compelling government "to grow in importance in a sort of geometric ratio." The more business centralized and extended its political control over the economy, the more government needed to do the same. In the end, all their efforts proved fundamentally incompatible with democratic institutions.[41] In the mediating role were the trade associations whose activities helped to develop these trends. Growth in the "concentration of economic power" and defined by the word "trustification" required the "unification" or "synchronization" of its policies and practices. If the former dictated a "growing resort to monopoly practices," the latter compelled greater "political and social awareness." In short, Big Business had moved directly into politics.[42]

To understand how these forces materialized in the United States, Brady examined the NAM for the role it played in the synchronization of American capitalist enterprise. In it was the same unidirectional movement that Roosevelt saw in the business system as undemocratic and ultimately fascist. Since the late nineteenth century, the NAM had come to wield power in connecting the spheres of a developing business system while establishing reciprocity with government that benefitted both. The First World War marked the pivotal moment. Production for total wartime and related goods—indeed, the entire industrial sector of the economy—fueled the concentration of wealth and centralization of power among the biggest corporations and cartels, some already giants. The NAM had come a long way in a very short time, indeed, a reflection of the quick rise of the United States as a capitalist empire—Pax Americana. Its leaders considered it the "mother of associations" from which "all American industry might be organized." The NAM became even more central to American capitalism during the Great Boom of the 1920s. Pamphlets on "Unit Thinking and Unit Acting on the Part of American Industry," "The Nation's Industry—Organized," "The Nation's Industry Synchronized," and many other like them reflected the view of its patrician leaders who, Brady wrote, "think of control of property as it relates to all things and with respect to all men, classes, interests, and principles." The NAM accomplished its ends by various means, from "direct pressure of organized lobbies, sometimes by the aid of propaganda, and sometimes by the further organization of business interests along special trade, regional, or industrial lines."[43]

Blossoming in the New Era, the NAM broadened and deepened within the march of monopoly capital. It proved a leading force in the growing powers of organized business to address the "national economic picture" at many levels, a by-product of wartime production and planning. "As in all belligerent countries, war control in the United States was exercised primarily through the intermediation of businessmen and business organization." Businessmen connected to the NAM made major decisions in economic affairs, "naturally and habitually" relying on their organizations "for the instrumentation of policies—policies which combined, so happily, patriotic performance of a critical 'public duty' with lucrative gains to the trades and industries which the businessmen represented." In the process "two leading ideas" among businessmen flourished during the booming 1920s. One was "the conception of universal organization of all business enterprise into all-inclusive and appropriate trade and industrial associations." The other was the idea of "'self-government in industry,' meaning specifically that any such organization of trade, commerce, and industry should be autonomous, interdependent, self-regulating."[44]

As the NAM grew, so did its political efforts to suppress labor in the early 1920s. Its introduction of the American Plan, which promoted the "open shop" and company unions or some similar approach in the name of management, industrial, or personnel "relations," sought "industrial peace" and "harmony between labor and capital" as its main objectives. But the rosy "dream world" of the New Era came to "a rude close" with the Wall Street crash and the onset of the Depression. Roosevelt's New Deal creation, the NRA, sought to reconcile capital and labor once again, this time only clarifying that the interests of both "proved to be at bottom irreconcilable." The attempt to wed the principle of industrial self-government with "Roosevelt's Jeffersonian conception of a felicitous economic paradise—an honest competitive system"— could not possibly work.[45]

For Brady, nothing was more exemplary of business as a system of power than the NAM's organization and the trends that characterized its development. Both mirrored the evolution of the corporation itself. As he wrote:

> Just as the giant corporation takes on as an incident to its growth a definite political significance as a wielder of power over increasing numbers of people and their interests, so it is inevitable that the NAM should in its much larger sphere be transformed, as it

grows and expands, into a community force ever more politically potent and politically conscious. . . . All economic issues are transmuted into terms of social and cultural issues, increasingly, as the political implications and the military possibilities of cumulated economic power are realized. Propaganda then becomes a matter of converting the public, or all special divisions of the public—small businessmen, consumers, labor, farmers, housewives—to the point of view of the control pyramid.[46]

As a power in its own right, Big Business threatened to destroy democracy. Its spell over society grew stronger through war and then peace—and a driving force toward another global war.

A View of Fascism Once Lost, Now Recovered

Robert Brady was an exceptional social scientist and an intellectual whose writings revealed a deep sensitivity to the ordeals of whole populations during the Great Depression. He knew what fascism was and feared it. It meant another world war, international as well as civil: left vs. right, socialism vs. fascism. Just as the Marxist writers Magil and Stevens had written in *The Peril of Fascism*, Brady detected the genesis or germ of fascism in monopoly capitalism. While Magil and Stevens emphasized the terrorist aspects in the making of American fascism, Brady focused on the non-terrorist mechanisms and mentalities generated within the business system, what he called "the other side of fascism." He demonstrated that the tendency toward centralization and monopoly in its mode of operation—the business system with sufficient power to challenge the democratic state—made it fascist. Brady's examination of the spirit and structure of capitalist enterprise in Germany, and then later of the role of trade associations in the economic systems of six nations, three liberal democracies and three fascist regimes, revealed a common path toward the synchronization of business enterprise required to perpetuate capitalist accumulation at levels sufficient to sustain the rate of profit and the reproduction of capital.

For Brady, the capitalist system was dying and this compelled the monopolists to go fascist. Lewis Corey had made a similar if not exact argument in *The Decline of American Capitalism* (1934). Corey and Brady are parallel figures in the emerging discourse on American fascism. Corey's analysis of the system of production and exchange showed how the fundamental contradiction between capital and labor led to crisis, depression, fascism, and war. Brady's work focused on the concrete operations of the business system itself. For Brady, business was going fascist because its essentially authoritarian and anti-democratic character flowed from the unidirectional and irreversible development of its organization and systemic efforts to dominate society. In *Business as a System of Power*, Brady deepened his analysis by focusing specifically on the role of trade associations. That his test case consisted of three capitalist countries that had gone fascist did nothing to invalidate his findings. In all six countries, organized business as a system of power sought absolute control over political life and the democratic state, its proponents always believing that they could manage it better than elected officials who supposedly represented the will of the majority.

Brady was not a Marxist, though he saw the same dangers in monopoly-finance capitalism as did Marxists like Corey, Magil, and Stevens, and in generally the same terms. Fascism was inherent in the movement of capital toward centralization and against democracy. Brady was fiercely anti-capitalist. Some view him as a radical populist, though it might be better to understand him as a radical republican and fierce proponent of democracy. In other words, he believed deeply in the democratic spirit and saw the evils of capitalism but could not reconcile the contradiction between the two. Yet his work contributes to an understanding of the transition from capitalism to fascism, what two eminent

Marxist political economists, Paul Baran and Paul Sweezy, were to discuss in the 1950s about the "jumping place from quantity of class domination to the quality of fascism."[47]

To date, there is no evidence that historians, Marxist or otherwise, have extended the seminal work of an exceptional social scientist who, with knowledge and courage, pointed to the business system as the real germ of fascism in American monopoly-finance capitalism.

"The Looming Shadow of Fascism" indeed.

Conclusion: Fascism and the Problem of American Exceptionalism

WHAT CAN WE say about the coming of the American Behemoth in the 1920s and 1930s now that it is fully grown? How is it that we never saw the fascist monster growing within and above us to the point where it threatens the entire world? Who is responsible for this debacle in the making? Why all the evidence for its genesis and still no history of it?

These are the questions that arise in light of the evidence I present in this book. The extent that it appears in a basic chronological form is designed only to create entry points for further discussion. This is possible thanks to those writers in the 1930s and early 1940s who recognized the genesis of American fascism in monopoly-finance capitalism, that is, Big Business. My attempt to focus on the capital-labor relationship comes from their observations, analysis, and commentary.

Yet these writers are wholly absent in mainstream U.S. history. There is no mention of Lewis Corey's great work on the structural contradictions of American capitalism that located the seeds of the Great Depression in the Great Boom. It is startling to learn how Americans have been denied Corey's work given the attention it once received. When *The Decline of American Capitalism* was published in 1934, even the *Wall Street Journal* reported that Corey "has undertaken what is perhaps the most complete statistical and factual study made to date of the underlying disharmonies of our economic system" and "is almost monumental in its scope and wealth of factual detail." In short, it was not a book to ignore. "Mr. Corey sees a trend toward state capitalism and then on to Fascism in the attempt of the propertied classes to save themselves from the consequences of capitalist decline." Naturally, the reviewer was not sympathetic to Corey's communist alternative. "But as a comprehensive study of class, labor and political conditions" he concluded:

> *The Decline of American Capitalism* should stand out as an important reference work. Some of the questions it poses will be very hard for business and political leaders of the present order to solve. Whether or not one concurs in Mr. Corey's findings, he can hardly fail to discover pertinent sidelights on today's national hodge-podge.[1]

One would think such praise coming from finance capital's main media advocate would have prompted serious attention. Instead, liberal historians in the 1950s and 1960s, adamant in their Cold War hostility toward Marxism, ignored or trivialized Corey's book and other valuable studies that shed light on the *bust* in the *boom*. Among the earliest of these notable, liberal Cold War historians is William Leuchtenburg, whose highly acclaimed *The Perils of Prosperity* appeared in 1958. Leuchtenburg argued that the prosperous 1920s had changed the United States in significant yet problematic ways. Chief among them was the failure by businessmen to act responsibly given the enormous political and social power that prosperity had provided. For Leuchtenburg, the general crisis of the U.S. economy was explicable mainly for the cultural and moral failings of business elites; it was a crisis of leadership and character. Leuchtenburg extended his thesis of moral failure to the masses, whose collective mindset had shifted away from "facets of the American character that had developed under an economy of scarcity."[2] The promise of a universal abundance that assured everyone they had the power to become wealthy made money the full measure of a man's worth. Capitalist tenets had found their way into a fundamentalist Christianity devoid of spirituality and godly virtues. There was no room for Corey's analysis of capitalism's structural contradictions as the cause of a general crisis of U.S. capitalism in decline and decay, which could open the door to fascism.

Less than a decade later, Arthur Schlesinger Jr. ridiculed Corey's book in *The Politics of Upheaval*, the third volume in his *Age of Roosevelt*, a triumph of Cold War liberal historiography and the politics of liberalism. "The *Decline* was a long-winded and pretentious book, turgid in style, abstract and pedantic in its approach, filled with irrelevant learning," Schlesinger wrote. "Corey detested the notion that the American experience might compel the slightest modification in Marxist theory." Schlesinger noted that American communists liked the book until "headquarters began to perceive in Corey a possible threat to the Party pundits. Nearly everybody else was unmoved."[3] Schlesinger could not have been more wrong. Admittedly, *The Decline of American Capitalism* is repetitive and challenges the reader's ability to engage the text. But Schlesinger's shoddy dismissal is telling; his explanation of the economic causes of the Great Depression are severely lacking without Corey's Marxist analysis.

In his biography of Corey, Paul Buhle writes that *Decline* "was hailed by radical and conservative critics alike as a powerful treatise against the existing order" when it appeared. Buhle cited a review by Louis Hacker, a Columbia University economics historian and one of the many "independent-minded Marxist academics." His review "overflowed with praise" for Corey's book, proclaiming it to be "Radicalism's Complete Handbook" and "an amazing economic, historical and ideological exposition of the communist position in the United States." For Hacker, Corey's book was "an indispensable prolegomenon to capitalist economics" and "a brilliant appendix, drawn entirely from American experience, to Marx's *Capital*."[4]

In the end, *The Decline of American Capitalism* has mattered little to the architects of liberal historiography, from Schlesinger to Ira Katznelson. There is no mention of Corey in Katznelson's recent book, *Fear Itself!*, about the New Deal and its legacy in our times. To my knowledge, the best of non-Marxist historiography still perpetuates a learned ignorance about Lewis Corey or others who wrote about the Great Depression and the threat of American fascism from a Marxist standpoint, or were in some way informed by the Marxist worldview and method. There are exceptions. Alan Dawley, one of the few American historians during the last two decades to recognize the significance of *The Decline of American Capitalism*, recalled that Corey and a few other Marxists in the early and mid-1930s had not been surprised when the stock market crashed in 1929. Only Marxists, Dawley wrote, understood that crisis was inevitable in the processes of capitalist accumulation, the product of "inner contradictions" that arose and became a crisis when "capitalists could no longer squeeze more surplus value (profits) out of wage labor." With the exception of some attention given to *Decline* by the late Chris Harman in his impressive 2009 work, *Zombie Capitalism*, there is little recognition of its significance in contemporary U.S. historiography or political commentary.[5]

All the more reason why reading these works of the 1930s and early 1940s by Corey, Carmen Haider, Robert Brady, and others helps us to recover an important and highly relevant chapter of American history, omitted or marginalized in mainstream historiography. We would be better off today if their seminal contributions to the study of American fascism had not run dry in the erudite works of eminent liberal historians. Then again, some were victims of political circumstances independent of their will. Always confronting great personal difficulties as a dissident Marxist economist, Corey died in despair from the twists and turns of the Communist Party. Perhaps we can reason that Corey died on the slaughterhouse floor of history, a Marxist intellectual wrecked by forces he once so completely understood only to wind up bewildered by them in the end. Within only a few years after *Decline* was published, Corey had turned away from communism as vigorously as he had forged it in the formative days of Communist Party–building in the United States in the immediate aftermath of the First World War.

We know very little about most of the others whose works are so instrumental in making my case. Carmen Haider virtually disappeared from the political scene after her prescient book *Do We Want Fascism?* came out in 1934. I found only a few reviews; the best one paid short shrift of its seminal argument and contents. Robert Brady published three more books on industrial organization, technology, and labor after his great work, *Business as a System of Power*, appeared in 1943. Clinging to his belief that democratic decision making was the key to rational planning under capitalism—one commentator said he looked vaguely toward a guild socialism—Brady could never make the leap to socialism despite what his own dedicated study had revealed. He was a professor of economics for thirty years at UC Berkeley until a series of strokes in the 1950s left him an invalid. Brady died in 1963. Haider and Corey are just two of the many writers whose contributions to our knowledge of embryonic American fascism have disappeared from the pages of later histories.

THE FORGOTTEN VOICES RESTORED

Whatever their individual shortcomings, these early writers provided the foundation for our understanding of the conditions that led to the emergence of fascism in the United States. Collectively, they point to monopoly-finance capitalism as the seedbed. They agreed on other key points. Our fascism would not look like Italy and Germany. It would not arise from a mass movement led by a demagogue who eventually seized state power and became a dictator. The obverse was true in the United States. Here, it was quite literally the growing power of finance capital over all aspects of American life. This is what A. B Magil and Henry Stevens meant when they pointed to Wall Street as the "fountainhead" of American fascism.

Like Magil and Stevens, all of these writers were internationalists to varying degrees. Their understanding of fascism as a nascent global phenomenon distinct to the contemporary world, synonymous with the epoch of monopoly-finance capitalism and imperialism, enabled them to locate its genesis in the advanced capitalist nations after the First World War. Its national forms varied according to political institutions, traditions, and other cultural characteristics. But the one thing all national forms had in common was that they emerged in a moment of capitalist crisis and came to power when the rule of the capitalist class was in jeopardy. It was like this for Mussolini's meteoric rise to power in Italy in 1922, as well as the protracted yet mightier affair managed by Hitler and the National Socialists a decade later that created the most powerful and destructive capitalist dictatorship in history.

Though it would take a more grounded understanding of fascism as a function of the contemporary world-capitalist system—the sociologist Walter Goldfrank indicated as much in 1978—these writers, whether Marxists or radical Republicans like Brady and George Seldes, understood that Big Business in America meant the expansion of imperialist reach.

They had pointed to the biggest bankers and financiers who were the real policymakers at home and abroad. During the 1920s, Andrew Mellon used the Treasury Department to set things right for the plutocrats whose loans had propped up the fascist regime in Italy because Mussolini was their man in Europe. Franklin Roosevelt would do the same as president when he called a Central American dictator "*our* son-of-a-bitch." Herbert Hoover, from the time he became the commerce secretary in 1920 until his election to the presidency eight years later, had turned the Commerce Department into an advertising arm and public relations clearing house for Big Business and Wall Street. As the epicenter of the world capitalist system—in all respects unique in its history as perhaps the first and only core of the world capitalist system—fascist processes inhered in the rise of Pax Americana in all their terrorist and non-terrorist forms.

The hidden powers of capital in the epicenter of the world system also explain another important characteristic of embryonic American fascism—its disguises. When the drunkard and alleged dullard Warren Harding took up the slogan "America First" to rally the small capitalist behind flag and country, he knew which Americans he was serving. As a businessman in the White House, Harding made it clear a month after his inauguration that he had always called for "less of government in business as well as more business in government." In fulfilling this objective, Harding embodied the nativist, racist impulses of the white middle classes now being swept up by the forces of capitalist modernization and controlled by the plutocracy of Big Business. This more than anything—grasped within the paradigm of political culture shaped by monopoly-finance capitalism and imperialism—explains why the disguises of American fascism made up the greatest of masquerades. The line usually attributed to Huey Long that fascism would come in the name of anti-fascism is the most practical expression of a deeply complex political phenomenon. The utterly paradoxical form of American fascism as the ideology of corporate capitalism, its spell so powerful as to create a phantasmagoria—an exhibition of shadows created by the magic lantern of commodification and reification—corresponded to the paradox of capitalist progress during the booming 1920s: growing poverty in a rising sea of prosperity. Though fascism everywhere showed two faces, terrorist and non-terrorist, the role of the latter was greatest in the United States where the powers of capital were most highly developed.

FASCIST PROCESSES IN CAPITALIST MODERNIZATION

In the capitalist epicenter, fascist processes inhered in capitalist modernization itself, in the imperatives of monopoly-finance capitalism and Big Business now steadily acquiring political power in its own right.[6] The forces of production governed by the general law of capitalist accumulation, as explicated by Marx in *Capital* and applied by Corey in *The Decline of American Capitalism*, demonstrated how capital bound labor more tightly to its dictates. This was all due to the concentrated wealth and centralizing powers of Big Business, the collective face of America's most powerful corporations as revealed in a landmark study by Adolf A. Berle and Gardiner C. Means, *The Modern Corporation and Private Property*, published in 1932. In the preface, Berle wrote that "American industrial property, through the corporate device, was being thrown into a collective hopper wherein the individual owner was steadily being lost in the creation of a series of huge industrial oligarchies."[7] Capitalism was becoming more collective in its organization and function.

In chapter 3, "The Concentration of Economic Power," Berle and Means explained how the corporate system functioned and its inherent trajectory. "Within it," they wrote, "there exists a centripetal attraction which draws wealth together into aggregations of constantly increasing size, at the same time throwing control into the hands of fewer and fewer men. The trend is apparent; and no limit is as yet in sight." What they found was astonishing. As of 1930, the 200 largest non-banking corporations had combined assets that amounted to nearly half of all the corporate wealth in the United States. Throughout American society, every individual, directly or indirectly, was in some way impacted by the growing concentration of wealth and economic power. Financially, these largest of the non-banking corporations also dominated the New York Stock Exchange, the nerve center of U.S. finance capital. According to weekly reports, 130 out of the 573 independent American corporations engaged in a typical week of activity were "huge companies" with gross assets over $100 million in each. Below them were 71 corporations with between $50 million and $100 million, and then 372 corporations with assets of under $50 million. Put another way, the top 130 corporations held

81.7 percent of the total assets represented on the exchange while the 372 at the bottom tier held only 10.9 percent of the total. The "small corporations" had no importance in the daily operations of the stock market. The dominant role of the largest non-banking corporations was also evident in relation to the total number operating in the country. At the beginning of 1930, these 200 largest companies—42 railroads, 52 public utilities, and 106 industrials—had combined assets of over $81 billion, which from a total of $165 billion meant that they controlled nearly half of all non-banking corporate wealth. According to their research, Berle and Means estimated that the roughly 300,000 smaller companies that made up business enterprise owned the other half.[8]

Almost a decade later, in its final report to President Roosevelt on March 31, 1941, the summarized findings of the Temporary National Economic Committee (TNEC) showed an even greater concentration and centralization of wealth. The committee affirmed the intent and purpose of Roosevelt's request to find a way to curb the power of monopolies. But it exceeded Roosevelt's expectations and may have caused him discomfort. He realized that what he had deemed the rising, internal fascist menace—monopoly—was now needed to prepare the United States for entry into the widening global war. Against fascism!

The final report makes clear that the president and the committee were of one mind. It was now necessary "to marshal the resources of America in defense of democracy" and organize them in a way for the United States to meet the threat of totalitarian aggression that threatened all democratic nations in the world. But in so doing, it fueled the very thing that had brought the committee into existence—the fear that monopoly would take America toward its own fascism. War preparation fueled the massive defense contracts by the War and Navy Departments that between June 1, 1940, and March 1, 1941, amounted to some $12.7 billion, a sum "more than half of all the value added by manufacture in all the industrial plants of America for all industrial commodities during the year 1939" and also one that "exceeds the total assessed

valuation of all the real and personal property within the boundaries of 21 States." Moreover, the distribution among the states
confirmed "most dramatically the degree to which the concentration of economic power and wealth has proceeded in America."
Here the investigation saw distinct features that were alarming to
anyone who equated capitalist competition with democracy. Most
states had barely gotten more than a small percentage of these
defense contracts, while four—California, Pennsylvania, New
Jersey, and New York—received almost 40 percent of the total.
Given all the evidence on the distribution of these contracts, just
over 82 percent of the total went to only fifteen of the forty-eight
states. What troubled the committee was that the defense contracts had gone to those states where industry and its organization
was already the most advanced. This was the one great imbalance
in the U.S. economy that had to be corrected after the war. "This
committee recites the facts only for the purpose of demonstrating that concentration does exist and that America must find the
way to bring about a permanent decentralization if the ideals of a
democratic social and economic structure for all our people are to
be achieved."[9]

The work of the TNEC was unprecedented for its comprehensive investigation that led to thirty-two published volumes of
material and forty-three monographs. The investigation that was
supposed to curb the problem of monopolies became a forum for
determining how they could instead be directed toward greater
responsibility in creating a balanced economy and more equitable
economic growth in the future. The opening pages of the final
report affirmed Roosevelt's commitment to preserve the free-
enterprise system against the abuses of concentrated wealth and
monopoly. The central task of the TNEC was to assemble information that when "eventually properly analyzed and disseminated"
would enable the American people to preserve free-enterprise and
competition in the economy as the bedrock of American democracy.[10] To that end, one of the monographs focused on economic
power and its political arm made up of various organizations

and groups that worked as an invisible force to influence public opinion. Pressure groups such as major trade associations like the U.S. Chamber of Commerce and the National Association of Manufacturers (NAM), as well as other organizations less directly involved in the forging of corporate and banking economic policies, effectively promoted the political agenda of the "business community."[11]

Here was the real story behind the familiar face of Big Business, in essence, a *business system* driven by the need *to go political* as Robert Brady had written in 1943. And it could be heavy-handed. The interwar period is replete with examples of Big Business employment of vigilantes, cops, private security firms, hooligans, and at times the "small-fry fascisti" groups like the Silver Shirts as George Seldes called them. According to historian Frederick Rudolph in 1950, it had taken less than a year into the New Deal for many prominent members of the ruling class, "whose gods were Adam Smith and Herbert Spencer," to determine that their future was highly uncertain. "Correspondence, reflecting despair and anger, flowed from one citadel of economic power to another," Rudolph wrote. Though much of it remained in private hands and unknown to the public, some evidence of the frustration did come to light. One example was an exchange in March 1934 between R. R. M. Carpenter, a retired DuPont vice president, and John J. Raskob, retired chair of the Democratic Party, former head of General Motors, and still a vice president with DuPont. "Five Negroes on my place in South Carolina refused work this spring," Carpenter complained to Raskob, adding that "a cook on my houseboat in Fort Myers quit because the government was paying him a dollar an hour as a painter." Knowing that Raskob had access to Roosevelt, would he please ask the president where the country was going. It all seemed to be the opposite of what America had always promised to its people. Raskob urged Carpenter to "take the lead in trying to induce the DuPont and General Motors groups, followed by other big industries, to definitely organize to protect society from the sufferings which it is bound to endure if we allow communistic elements to lead the people to believe that all businessmen are crooks." To this end, Raskob saw the need for "some very definite organization that would come out openly with some plan for educating the people to the value of encouraging people to work; encouraging people to get rich." No one was in a better position to do this than Carpenter, who, along with friends in high places, controlled the largest share of American industry.[12]

Carpenter did just that, and the result was the creation of the American Liberty League on August 15, 1934. Charging itself with instilling "respect for the rights of persons and property" in American society, it also called on government "to protect individual and group initiative and enterprise, to foster the right to work, earn, save, and acquire property, and to preserve the ownership and lawful use of property when acquired." The Liberty League, Rudolph wrote, was "as indigenously American as the New Deal which it was determined to destroy." Merging long-standing American traditions with the new realities of contemporary economic, social, and political life, the League dedicated itself to a broad defense of the Constitution against a host of alleged enemies, from the so-called socialist New Deal and various small political groups on the left and right, as well as demagogues like Senator Huey Long and Father Charles Coughlin. Its *Statement of Principles and Purposes* complained that business, which bore the responsibility of employment and wages in the national economy, had little voice in government. Once again, businessmen must be enabled to do the business of America just as it had under Roosevelt's three Republican predecessors, Harding, Coolidge, and Hoover. With the Republican Party now weakened, the Liberty League took up the mantle of defending civilization on the basis of enabling the "uncommon man," who, standing at the "pinnacle" of society, must once more be free "to follow the bent of his natural talents, unfettered by government regulation and control."[13]

At the top of its founders' list were the DuPont brothers (Irénée, Pierre, and Lamont), whose vast industrial empire produced everything from plastic to paint to munitions. Other representatives of Big Business included leaders of America's largest companies, including Alfred P. Sloan of General Motors, Edward F. Hutton of General Foods, J. Howard Pew of Sun Oil, Sewell L. Avery of Montgomery Ward, and Ernest T. Wier of National Steel. The rest of its membership was filled out by financiers and financial officers, corporation lawyers, politicians, and some academicians. All were grounded to a greater or lesser degree in the racist thinking of Social Darwinism. Its leading political spokesman was Roosevelt's former mentor and now bitter rival, Al Smith, the former Democratic governor of New York. Until 1936, much of its membership came from the upper echelons of the Democratic Party. Rudolph pointed to "the cloak" of an organization whose program was made up of "respectable generalities, partial self-delusion, intense sincerity, and frequently embarrassing hypocrisy." Its most effective cover was the Constitution, held up as the ultimate guarantor of the right of the individual to engage freely in whatever rightful activity he chose—in this case the right to pursue wealth and become rich at the expense of others—without impediment by government bureaucracy.[14] Presenting itself as a nonpartisan educational group whose aim was to combat radicalism and preserve property rights, it sometimes used the Constitution to promote its ideals among unsavory associations. Irénée DuPont hoped the League would form alliances with other groups that he believed aimed to defend the Constitution in perilous times, including the American Legion and "even the Ku Klux Klan."[15]

For Grace Hutchins, a communist and radical labor historian, it was critical for Americans to grasp the League's true motives. Writing in 1936 on the eve of the General Election and Roosevelt's bid for a second term, Hutchins contended that its defense of the Constitution, which protected the rights and privileges of Big Business, was a cover for the real intent of its members, which was to do as their predecessors had done so successfully before the Depression—get rich. But this went hand-in-hand with the defense of the ruling class by government. Raskob said as much in a letter penned on his personal stationery encouraging capitalist elites to become members of the League, "*which is doing everything possible to root out the vicious radical element that threatens the destruction of our government.*"[16] The League's support for the Republican candidate, Alf Landon, showed its resolve to oppose every progressive measure in the interest of workers and labor organizations.

According to Hutchins, this gave the League a primary role in the trajectory toward fascism. To protect society from "communistic elements" required it to defend big businessmen who were, in fact, the biggest crooks in America. Its defense of the Constitution was nothing more than a platform to oppose organized labor's ongoing struggle for higher wages and better working conditions. And by stressing nonpartisanship, the League showed that it represented the common interests of capitalists, Democrats and Republicans alike. It had opposed the National Labor Relations Act because it guaranteed the right to collective bargaining and the right of workers to choose their own unions. This, the League said in one of its pamphlets, dealt "an unjust blow at company unions which have been highly successful in the establishment of mutually satisfactory relations between employees and the management in many large industries." It opposed other New Deal measures and agencies that provided relief to the unemployed millions, calling it "wasteful [and] inefficient" and "boondoggling." It demanded that the Roosevelt administration abolish all federal government relief and return the responsibility to state and local agencies, only "contributing temporarily such amounts as are necessary for direct relief and subsequently assisting with loans" to states to do so on their own. The League opposed the Social Security Act because unemployment and old age insurance "should be dealt with entirely under state laws" and because the act "imposes a heavy financial burden upon industry." It blasted the Roosevelt administration for its use of taxation "to accomplish social objectives." It called for broadening the tax base while cutting taxes on the rich. "The purpose of the Congress should be to ease rather than to increase the tax burden upon business, upon the home and upon the individual." It even called for "civil liberties" for corporations.[17]

To demonstrate the fascist intent of the Liberty League, Hutchins focused on who paid for all its propaganda by drawing on the findings of a Special Senate Committee to Investigate Lobbying Activities. The investigation examined the books of the League as well as other related organizations like the Crusaders, the Sentinels of the Republic, and the Southern Committee to Uphold the Constitution that together contributed significant amounts of money to other right-wing extremist organizations and white supremacist groups.[18]

Finally, one of the largest contributing members to the League and a member of its national executive committee was Grayson M. P. Murphy, director of Guaranty Trust and the Bethlehem Steel Corporation. Murphy was the individual identified by retired Marine Corps General Smedley Darlington Butler, recipient of two Medals of Honor and an iconic figure in the American military, who tried recruiting him to lead a private army against the White House. Butler subsequently told congressional members of a Special Committee on Un-American Activities in a secret session that he had been approached by Murphy, as a representative of finance capitalists, to organize 500,000 veterans to march on the capital and install extraordinary executive power to co-run the federal government with the president—or simply remove Roosevelt if he refused to go along with the program. Butler was reporting a plot aimed at a fascist coup planned by members of the American Liberty League.[19]

THE MIDDLE-CLASS REACTION

And what can we say of the middle class? To begin, I prefer "middling men," as Nancy MacLean so astutely observed from its wide social composition, thus freeing us from the notion that the lower middle class alone drives American fascism from below. Regardless of differing strata and respective peculiarities, the middle-class outlook had become increasingly pervasive in American society during the Great Boom of the 1920s. Many millions of middling men and women, mostly white, were swept up in the spectacle and bustle of urban life, ever listening to the ballyhoo about continued prosperity and uninterrupted social progress. The spell cast upon society by the gurus of advertising, public relations, and propaganda pulled their minds into the force field of capital. Modernization meant the steady bourgeoisification of society aimed at turning the entire public into a commodity. Ballyhoo was thoroughly middle class in design and purpose. What to wear? What to drive? How to avoid halitosis so the man or woman of your dreams does not turn away and then disappear?

But middle-class consciousness was by nature reactionary, as the writers included in these chapters have shown. Perhaps the one true revolutionary moment in the contemporary epoch came during the worst years of the Depression when the middle class looked to the progressive Roosevelt as someone who would use state power to its benefit, only to be left behind as the New Deal propped up the capitalist order under the aegis of Big Business. Now it was laissez-faire for the top 200 non-financial corporations and the Wall Street fountainhead that pumped capital into productive and then into speculative, unproductive enterprise. Only the second New Deal kept the middle class loyal to Roosevelt, and that was the product of renewed labor militancy that could not be bottled up. But renewed crisis in 1937—the recession within the Depression—forced Roosevelt into a Keynesian turn, which restored confidence to the business system. It could now prepare for a new round of capitalist accumulation in preparing industry for war. Then war came, and profitability was fully restored. Keynesianism was in fact military Keynesianism and the beginning of a permanent war economy in the United States.

Nancy MacLean's exceptional class analysis of the middling men of the Klan allows us to ponder their mental outlook during the Great Boom of the 1920s. From Albram Lipsky, the author of the 1925 book *Man the Puppet*, comes an introduction to the methods of mind control in capitalist America. Here was irony. As advertisers tapped into the realm of individual desire to sell a product, public opinion makers sought to create a "crowd-mind" mentality that lowered the "sense of personal responsibility" required "for the correctness of one's thinking." Ideas were peddled not for their soundness but for acceptability by the crowd. "With the surrender of responsibility," Lipsky wrote, "there comes an intoxication, a feeling of irresistibility."[20] It all depended on the work of the public relations gurus:

> Everywhere in business we see individuals engaged in laboring to influence the minds of others, sometimes by means of logical argument, but more often by indirect appeals to the subconscious, to masked instincts, and to that curious susceptibility to mob contagion that is just beginning to be understood. The bulls try to communicate their bullishness; the bears their bearishness. Business is the sum total of this bluffing and higgling, this cajolery, deception, intimidation, propaganda and persuasion.[21]

To wander further into the mentality of the American middle classes during the 1920s and 1930s requires a study all its own. Yet, it is tempting to speculate on the split personality of the middling men in the 1920s, personalities whose internal cracks would deepen in the crisis decade that followed, and with political consequences throughout the period. Unlike the big capitalist, his middle-class counterpart perhaps can be understood as Dr. Jekyll and Mr. Hyde. The good doctor resents the big capitalist for his excesses, but the evil man longs to have it all himself—maybe not all, but comfortable enough. Jekyll embraces the principles of democratic capitalism—Everyman a capitalist!—while his evil other shouts "only for 100 percent Americans!" As small capitalists, salaried employees, or teachers and lawyers whose oath is to serve others, they always perform at a disadvantage to the elites they serve, forever hoping they could coexist, even if not entirely as equals. As for the small merchant, the backbone of an earlier American capitalism, he must sell the product knowing that his profit can never match the department store chain. By day he endures the unfair competition with a smiling face just as Babbitt did, praising the virtues of his product as the advertisers urged. That night, he attends a Klan meeting and is compelled to consider that all these modern products he is laboring to sell are directly or indirectly immoral and even sinful. Anything to do with enhancing the look or scent of a cosmopolitan woman could be nothing else. In most cases, he is a True Christian who really worships the market; his faith is in the hustle as well as in Jesus.

LIBERALISM AND THE PERSISTENT MYTH OF AMERICAN EXCEPTIONALISM

When in 1935 the political scientist Arthur Steiner arrived at his "minimum doctrinal standards" to determine whether America would or could go fascist, he gave license to a conviction that fascism was primarily a European political affliction from which America was immune. Herein was another important contribution to the myth of American exceptionalism, perhaps the most fatal. We see this in a book by Stephen Raushenbush, *The March of Fascism*, published by Yale University Press in 1939. Raushenbush believed in the possibility of an American-style fascism based on standard comparisons with Italy and Germany. Yet there were mitigating factors. The "great dissimilarities" that existed in the United States "should not be forgotten." For one thing, democratic tradition and loyalties were far stronger in America than in Italy or Germany. Raushenbush made his case for American exceptionalism based on liberal-democratic assumptions, some quite dubious:

> We are a people of sections, stubborn to resist sectional prejudices and habits other than our own. We have no overwhelming racial majority. We have no tradition of being regimented, no conscript army to teach us an unconditional obedience to superiors in office. . . . Our religious divisions are less strong than theirs were. Our major political parties have not been entirely discredited by their failure to give security. We have not, like

Germany, been defeated, nor, like Italy, frustrated in war. We are not confined to an area too small for us to expand our economic possibilities to the full. No strong leader of a Fascistic movement has as yet arisen to challenge us, talking American to us. We have no tradition of absolutism. These are strong but not insurmountable barriers to Fascism in the United States.[22]

Raushenbush presupposed a unique American character on a historic path in order to suggest that simple comparisons between fascist developments in the United States and those in Italy and Germany were misleading. He warned that America could very well pave its own fascist road if citizens remained ignorant or dismissive of conditions that had caused Italy and Germany, their own democratic weaknesses notwithstanding, to go fascist. Americans needed quickly to learn how unemployment, insecurity, instability, and anxiety proved fertile ground for fascist development. This applied especially to middle-class businessmen and professionals who felt squeezed by the concentrated wealth and power above them and the frustration over a perceived lack of purchasing power they believed they deserved as members of a rising productive class.

Raushenbush pointed to the desperation felt by millions of young people, especially those in the hardest-hit regions, who worked for beggar's wages even if employed and who were vulnerable to a Hitler promising any kind of future. There were also the farmers, whose long-standing suspicions of urban workers drove them into alliances with industrialists. Given these conditions, fascism would come to America if neither of the major political parties took sufficient heed of history and read the warning signs, which were similar to Italy and Germany in their respective pre-fascist years. "To stay democratic," Raushenbush advised, "a state must meet adequately certain fundamental demands of its people." If not:

Fascism comes by default. While it can be aided by members of the wealthier groups of society, its driving force comes from the lower middle classes who feel insecure, disinherited, abandoned by the state. When the state stops moving, stops giving its citizens a sense of motion, of endeavor, when it accepts a huge unemployment as normal, for example, the people start deserting it. The man who comes along with a promise of a future for youth, jobs and security for the older people, can then secure their assent to his destruction of liberty. Fascism is not simply dictatorship, it is dictatorship with mass support.[23]

For Raushenbush, the world had not yet created a "successful defense against Fascism." Democracy had come to depend on a "thin liberalism" that was no longer working. Leaders of these "liberal nations" were necessarily drifting toward conservative and reactionary positions because there was no other alternative.[24] Here was fascism by default for most of Europe, and the same was possible for the United States. Americans could be drawn into a movement led by a demagogue. Democracy was not a given in any nation, even in the United States—where democratic traditions were considered the strongest anywhere—if government failed to offer livelihoods and security for basic needs. People would give up their freedoms to halt "an endless prolongation of misery or humiliation."[25] After almost four years of New Deal recovery, the recession of 1937 had made this obvious. So much of the New Deal had failed to alleviate the insecurity of the people. Moreover, parts of it, such as the National Recovery Administration, were undemocratic, granting all the power to industrialists.[26] The American people were "not participating in many of the significant decisions of their lives." Democracy at the local level was beaten down by the "chain belts of our factories to the national arena." People could still decide what was best for their communities in matters of schooling and policing. "But whether the community can afford good schooling, or whether children can afford to continue in school, are matters determined by factors beyond local control. Even the functions of the local police are more and more affected by national developments."[27]

The solution to the nation's ills—and halt of the march toward fascism—was to create a "bridge from local to national democracy" to save the "liberal state," especially "when another depression comes." The response would have to surpass New Deal efforts:

> Attempts to increase the national income by collaboration between industry, labor, and government will again be made. If they are to succeed in a democratic way there will have to be democratic controls from the bottom up. Otherwise great and dangerous power may be given to industry or government or a combination of the two. The N.R.A. indicated this to us clearly.[28]

Raushenbush pointed to the deeper danger to democracy, one that was "growing formalistic and empty of living content." Americans knew little how to vote on national issues except increasingly "in fear, either of Fascism or of radicalism." Conservatives and liberals alike understood that changes requiring more democratic controls of the economy needed to be made. But they were paralyzed. So were their political parties. To prevent American fascism required a "strong state, carefully guarded by the democratization of its controls."[29] Even this was not enough. It all depended on Americans rediscovering their

> sense of values about life, human personality, and dignity. Only a profound conviction and determination to give reality to equality and fraternity as well as liberty will give us immunity to the values of the totalitarian states.[30]

Raushenbush made clear that if any nation in the world could successfully defend itself from fascism, it was the United States. This is what made it exceptional. Americans must "recapture the world for our way of life" so they could "realize the American Dream in our time and set the nation in full motion again."[31]

Today, we are being treated to more sophisticated arguments about why America is immune from fascism. All boil down to perpetuating the myth of American exceptionalism. A good example is Ira Katznelson, who, in his 2013 book *Fear Itself!*, deftly explains how responses by U.S. leaders to the Depression resembled those in fascist Italy and Germany. Katznelson mentions how powerful people called for some form of dictatorship immediately preceding and following Roosevelt's election in 1932. He also focuses on the commentary about resemblances between the New Deal and fascist corporatism in Italy; indeed, these discussions are prominent in his book. Katznelson even challenges the usual liberal narrative of the New Deal by pointing to the role played by southern Democrats. While the latter were critical in helping Roosevelt to create the New Deal and lead the crusade against fascism abroad, they did so in return for a pass by Roosevelt allowing them to buttress white supremacy and institutionalized racism.

In this respect, Katznelson's important contribution to the historiography of the New Deal also brings to light the contradictory and paradoxical course of American liberalism. Yet his failure to consider how these developments unfolded within the broader framework of political economy is glaring. He shows little interest in analyzing how capitalist imperatives bound ownership and management to the politics of white supremacy in the South other than to see the matter in the usual terms of cheap labor and racism, and he never mentions the earlier, liberal critique of monopoly capitalism that viewed racism as a contingent form of American fascism. For that matter, none of the individuals whose works are central to this study are to be found in Katznelson's 700-page tome. Instead, he seemingly breaks with the logic of his own case, which points to the same indigenous fascist processes his predecessors saw clearly, and resorts to an eloquent defense of American exceptionalism:

> During the Roosevelt and Truman years, Washington successfully wrestled with the problem of how to find a durable and democratic role for Congress in the face of crises characterized by fear and an urgent need for action. The breakdown of so many democracies between the two world wars was marked by

the failure to find productive answers to this challenge. Indeed, the very triumphant assertiveness of the dictatorships was rooted in their rejection of the need to find an answer, since they totally discarded the eighteenth- and nineteenth-century liberal idea of a separation of powers and promoted the utter collapse of a parliamentary system. The United States, by contrast, stood for the ways in which American democracy secured the capacities of Congress to make laws and oversee their consequences. Congress did not become obsolete or irrelevant. It was not an anachronism. To the contrary, it kept and utilized the authority that liberal principles and democratic practices required that it not cede to others.[32]

The perpetuation of such liberal historiography flies in the face of contemporary Marxist analysis and historical method, which is grounded in the concept of *totality*—all relations in capitalist society are interconnected within the whole of capitalist society. This concept is evident in Marx's understanding of "real, profane history," the history that presents "men as the actors and authors of their own history," which for Marx is "the real starting point" in the approach to writing history.[33] Perhaps only a revolutionary impulse from society that views its *profane history* from the standpoint of class, gender, race, religion, and other cultural forms of differentiation within the totality of capitalist relations—always subject to the fundamental contradiction between capital and labor—will spark such writing about American fascism.

Good vs. Bad Capitalism: The False Dichotomy in Liberalism that Leads to Fascism

In its final report to Roosevelt, the TNEC affirmed the intent and purpose of his request to examine the problem of monopoly. But he also made clear he meant no harm to solid and principled businessmen. In his April 29, 1938, request to Congress for the inquiry into monopoly, Roosevelt opposed "any ill-considered 'trust-busting' activity which lacks proper consideration for economic results." Instead, he insisted:

> It is a program to preserve private enterprise for profit by keeping it free enough to be able to utilize all our resources of capital and labor at a profit.
>
> It is a program whose basic purpose is to stop the progress of collectivism in business and turn business back to the democratic competitive order.
>
> It is a program whose basic thesis is not that the system of free private enterprise for profit has failed in this generation, but that it has not yet been tried.

Roosevelt was resolute. Once Americans "realized that business monopoly in America paralyzes the system of free enterprise on which it is grafted, and is as fatal to those who manipulate it as to the people who suffer beneath its impositions, action by the government to eliminate these artificial restraints will be welcomed by industry throughout the nation."[34]

In its report to Roosevelt three years later, the Temporary National Economic Committee recommended that the government seek to reverse the trajectory toward greater monopolization of the economy and instead move toward its "reconstruction" based on "permanent decentralization," creating more ownership across the board and less control by giants at the top. It is jarring, however, to learn how the committee viewed its findings in the context of world events. Europe was already at war, and the conflict would soon expand to Eurasia with the German invasion of the Soviet Union in June and the Japanese attack on Pearl Harbor in December. Thus, a solution to the current problem of concentrated wealth and the power of monopoly would have to be addressed in the future. "In submitting its recommendations," the report began,

> the Temporary National Economic Committee is conscious that with democracy engaged in a world-wide struggle for its very

life, public attention has been diverted momentarily from the study of the problems of economic concentration for which the committee was brought into existence. Far from detracting from the importance of economic reconstruction, however, the events of the past year have served only to emphasize the need for read-justments after the present crisis is over. It is quite conceivable that the democracies might attain a military victory over the aggressors only to find themselves under the domination of eco-nomic authority far more concentrated and influential than that which existed prior to the war.[35]

Roosevelt and the Committee typified the liberal belief that capitalism was essentially good because it was competitive and therefore democratic. But to preserve *good capitalism* required the elimination of its abuses, *bad capitalism*—which meant monopoly-finance capital and fascism. Roosevelt was the beacon of such thought in 1930s America. Attacking monopoly as the driving force of American fascism, he wrongly believed that it could be controlled. We know from the arguments presented in this book, however, that this has not been the case, nor will it ever be. As Marx proved and Corey affirmed, the general law of capitalist accumulation only widened the fundamental divide between capital and labor during the 1920s and 1930s. All prog-ress under capitalism was a paradox. The widening gap between wealth and poverty led to a general crisis of American capitalism and with it the plausibility of fascism. The liberal perpetuation of a false dichotomy of good vs. bad capitalism wrapped in the ide-ology of American exceptionalism does much to explain how we got to where we are today.

The recovery of forgotten voices that have spoken once again in this text can help us to establish a critical framework for the study of American fascism. More important, they provide us with the knowledge and insight of people who feared its rise in their time—knowledge and insight we must possess as we fight its much greater strength today. As we go to press, the fascist reordering of government is underway under Trump, one that replicates what the Germans called *Gleichschaltung* under Hitler—a fascist dictatorship in the making. We now have the gangster state that Franz Neumann saw in Hitler's regime.

Epilogue

ONCE THE DRAFT of this book was done, my friend Al Brilliant suggested that I write an essay about how it came to fruition. I thought about this for a few weeks. Everything that came to mind was anchored to my life in Greensboro, North Carolina, my home for the last forty years.

I arrived not long after the 1979 murders of five members of the Communist Workers Party by the Klan and local Nazis and became a comrade to the survivors. I bumbled from one odd job to another until I was hired as a staff writer by the black-owned weekly paper, the *Carolina Peacemaker*. In graduate school I had read a famous essay about the "historian as detective" and reasoned I could do the work of a journalist because it was essentially no different from the work of a historian.

After two years of writing, shooting photos, and putting the paper together every Wednesday night so it would hit the street on Thursday—all for six bucks an hour and no overtime—I moved to the Greensboro daily paper, the *News & Record*, where I hoped after a six-week paid internship—the oldest in the lot by a dozen years—I would be hired as a reporter. Instead, I was offered a position on the copy desk, despite having co-written a front-page story on my first day as an intern. Later, I found out why. The executive editor thought I was a communist, though he actually didn't know the real story. It was enough for this genteel southern gentleman that my last name was Roberto and that I had come over from the *Peacemaker* and was a radical who could not be trusted to report the news objectively. Still, I did the drill on the copy desk in news and features and wrote many book reviews, and even occasionally was allowed to write a news story or a piece for the commentary section of the Sunday paper.

Meanwhile, I became immersed in the study of the Iran-Contra scandal, especially the role played by former CIA chief and then sitting vice president, George H. W Bush, in the illegal Contra resupply network. The managing editor of the *News & Record*, at the time part of the arch-conservative Landmark chain, told me to drop my inquiry, which I pursued on my own time, and focus on copyediting or face firing. After failing to convince the *Boston Globe* and the *Washington Post* to publish my investigative work, some of it eventually appeared in a lengthy piece in, of all places, Landmark's flagship paper, the *Virginian-Pilot*. In retrospect, Iran-Contra was my first real introduction to the genesis of American fascism. I consider it a pivotal moment in the leap from liberal-capitalist democracy that occurred in 2016 with the election of Donald Trump. The proto-fascism of the Reagan-Bush presiden-cies survived a violation of the Constitution by establishing an "off the shelf" government to direct a terrorist, imperialist war on Nicaragua and its people. We can now see the fascist trajectory from Reagan-Bush to Trump as the outcome of the second general crisis of Pax Americana—the capitalist imperatives of an empire in decline that brought the Reagan-Bush Washington consensus to become firmly rooted in the neoliberalism of Clinton, then to the neoconservative George W. Bush, followed by Obama's vapid recovery program in the face of an acute crisis that enabled Trump's entry into the White House as a bona fide American fascist.

In between then and now, I finished my Ph.D. with a disserta-tion on Marx's concept of progress, thanks to Paul Breines, the late Roberta Manning, and other supportive faculty in the history department at Boston College. This ended five years as a full-time part-timer in the history department at North Carolina Agricultural and Technical State University, where I finally got a real position in 2003 and earned tenure and promotion in 2009 at age sixty-one. As the contemporary world historian among a small faculty, I occasionally taught courses on socialism, fascism, and environmentalism. Along the way, I began my rewarding collaboration with Gregory Meyerson about the crisis of the American Empire and the plausibility of fascism. Since 2011, it has been a whirlwind of study and activism aimed to make it all count for the people in Greensboro.

The young Marx once wrote that truth is the path to it. The totality of study and activism rooted in a Marxist understanding of the dialectical relationship between theory and practice is a compelling idea to anyone who opposes what is now occurring in America, which is our own *Gleichschaltung*. This march toward fascism, however, is more protracted and unique in its barbarisms than its German predecessor. We live in a moment of profound crisis, of politics, and of the mind and soul, the state of alienation in myriad forms all derived from a totalizing force—capital. I do not believe that historians who write for the public can feel its beat unless they are rooted in a critical understanding of its movements, and that requires engagement. This, I believe, is what the young Marx meant by "profane history" in *The Poverty of Philosophy* in 1847, which he wrote while fully engaged in the revolutionary politics of the proletarian struggles in Brussels, from which came the first attempt to organize European workers in the nascence of a united front. This is what shapes *my* thinking.

One of my heroes in this book, Harry F. Ward, believed he knew what it meant to be a Christian *and* a communist. Here was a thoughtful man whose religious calling was to care for the flock while recognizing that the concrete form of evil that endangered it was the capitalist system. In the nineteenth century and within the European context, Marx was right when he called religion the

opiate of the masses. It is fair to say that Ward saw this too. But as
a Christian a century later, he recognized in the epoch of monopoly-capitalist crisis and the coming of fascism that the ideological
mystifications of organized religion had been subsumed by a more
powerful drug—the barbarous and alienating powers of capital
itself. It is likely for this reason that his biographer, David Nelson
Duke, wrote that Ward always believed in a "historic dynamic that
impelled humanity toward its full realization." While some called
this dynamic God, the communists in the Soviet Union denied
it and said it was man alone. Ward asked, who cares? "They do
what they do, as they do, because for them the world is young; the
former things are passing away, all things are becoming new." This
made me think about the Sandinista revolution and the struggle of
the Nicaraguan people against the American Empire in the 1980s,
as they fought against the naked and brutal methods of imperialist
aggression that many on the U.S. left called Third World fascism.
It was a moment when the old Marxist revolutionary Tomás Borge
Martinez said that the Nicaraguan revolution would be made by
revolutionary Christians and non-Christian revolutionaries. A
united front indeed.

Carmen Haider, who helped me understand how American fascism would arise within the framework of the two-party system,
talked about the "possibilities of resistance" against it. Though not
a Marxist—or at least the extent one can say given her virtual disappearance from public discourse—Haider was certain that only
a working-class movement could prevent it. She recognized that
the farmers and the middle class were on the other side; that is,
they were fighting *for* fascism but not conscious of it. It would
not be enough to win them over to the workers' movement; their
permanent allegiance could only be won if they were made to
understand the difference between appearance and essence. This
would take education in an ongoing struggle against complacency.
The whole revolutionary process for a rising class consciousness,
she believed, could be "accelerated by the leadership of any group
which will make it its task to explain the situation."

Haider might have been a closet communist for all we know. She made no bones that those responsible for creating class consciousness had to understand the simple fact that the "poorest paid workers and unemployed" were the "revolutionary vanguard" that, as Marx once wrote, had nothing to lose but their chains. While the better-paid workers would come around slowly, Haider warned that the middle class showed reluctance even in crisis times "to consider its interests as synonymous with those of the working class," preferring instead to identify itself in in its outlook and aspirations with the dominant group in society—the capitalist class. When Haider looked at the whole political landscape in America in 1934, all she could say was this:

> Under these circumstances it will require brilliant leadership to increase the class-consciousness of the American masses to such a point as to make them engage in an active opposition to Fascism. Moreover, a remarkable rise of such class-consciousness would itself stimulate the counter-attack, since under present conditions in the United States the employers must be regarded as more fully class conscious than the workers.

This was the revolutionary challenge when the American Behemoth was rising in the 1920s and 1930s; and so today it is greater, now that the beast is at full strength.

Notes

Introduction: Fascism as the Dictatorship of Capital

1. Historicus, "Fascism in America," *Monthly Review* 4/6 (October 1952): 181.

2. Daniel Guerin, *Fascism & Big Business*, trans. Frances and Mason Merrill (New York: Pioneer Publishers, 1939), introduction by Dwight McDonald, xi.

3. Mathew Feldman, ed., *A Fascist Century: Essays by Roger Griffin* (London and New York: Palgrave Macmillan, 2008), 49.

4. Walter L. Goldfrank, "Fascism and World Economy," in *Social Change in the Capitalist World Economy*, ed. Barbara Hockey Kaplan (Beverly Hills, CA, and London: Sage Publications, 1978), 75–120.

5. R. Palme Dutt, *Fascism and Social Revolution: How and Why Fascism Came to Power in Europe* (Chicago: Proletarian Publishers, 1974), 47.

6. Frank Costigliola, *Awkward Dominion: American Political, Economic, and Cultural Relations with Europe, 1919–1933* (Ithaca and London: Cornell University Press, 1984), 124.

7. Goldfrank, "Fascism and World Economy," 101.

8. Gregory Meyerson and Michael Joseph Roberto, "Fascism and the Crisis of Pax Americana," *Socialism and Democracy* 22/2 (July 2008): 157–91.

9. I am indebted to Joel Kovel, who has brilliantly demonstrated that the efficient cause of the global ecological crisis that threatens our very existence in these times is the constant necessity of capital to reproduce itself for the sake of profit. See Kovel, *The Enemy of Nature: The End of*

Capitalism or the End of the World? (London and New York: Zed Books, 2007).

10. Paul M. Sweezy, *The Theory of Capitalist Development: Principles of Marxian Political Economy* (New York: Monthly Review Press, 1970), 346.

11. A. B. Magil and Henry Stevens, *The Peril of Fascism: The Crisis of American Democracy* (New York: International Publishers, 1938), 60.

12. Mauritz A. Hallgren, *Seeds of Revolt: A Study of American Life and the Temper of the American People during the Depression* (New York: Alfred A. Knopf, 1933), 264.

13. Georgi Dimitroff, *The United Front: Problems of Working-Class Unity and the People's Front in the Struggle Against Fascism and War* (New York: International Publishers, 1938), 11.

14. Herbert Marcuse, *One-Dimensional Man: Studies in the Ideology of Advanced Industrial Society* (Boston: Beacon Press, 1964), 3.

15. George Seldes, *Facts and Fascism* (New York: In Fact, Inc., 1943), 69.

16. Franz Neumann, *Behemoth: The Structure and Practice of National Socialism, 1933–1944* (Chicago: Ivan R. Dee, 2009), 459.

17. Ibid., 463.

18. Ibid., 464.

19. Ibid., 465.

20. Ibid., 470–71.

1. The Wonders of American Capitalism in the New Era

1. Ronald Allen Goldberg, *America in the Twenties* (Syracuse, NY: Syracuse University Press, 2003), 26–27.

2. Lucia Pradella, "Crisis, Revolution and Hegemonic Transition: The American Civil War and Emancipation in Marx's *Capital*," *Science & Society* 80/4 (October 2016): 460. Pradella also cites a letter from Marx to Nokolai Danielson in 1879, in which Marx wrote that the United States had "much overtaken England in the rapidity of economical progress, though they lag still behind in the extent of acquired wealth."

3. Karl Marx and Frederick Engels, "Preface to the Second Russian Edition of the *Manifesto of the Communist Party*," in *Karl Marx Frederick Engels Collected Works*, vol. 24 (New York: International Publishers, 1989), 425–26.

4. Engels to August Bebel, December 22, 1882, *Collected Works*, vol. 46 (New York: International Publishers, 1992), 415.

5. Anna Rochester, *Rulers of America: A Study of Finance Capital* (New York: International Publishers, 1936), 26–28. Rochester was also a labor activist and advocate for the rights of children and longtime companion of Grace Hutchins, whose political activism and journalism was done as a lifelong member of the Communist Party USA.

6. Lenin, *Imperialism, The Highest Stage of Capitalism, Collected Works*, vol. 22 (Moscow: Progress Publishers, 1964), 197, 202–3, 227, 229, 236–37.

7. Rochester, *Rulers of America*, 29–30.

8. George Soule, *Prosperity Decade, From War to Depression: 1917–1929* (New York: Harper & Row, 1968), 7. Soule's book appeared originally as volume 8 of *The Economic History of the United States* published in 1947 by Holt, Rinehart and Winston.

9. Adolf A. Berle and Gardiner C. Means, *The Modern Corporation and Private Property* (New Brunswick, NJ: Transaction Publishers, 2007), 14. Originally published by Harcourt, Brace, and World in 1932.

10. Bruce Minton and John Stuart, *The Fat Years and the Lean* (New York: International Publishers, 1940), 7. With very few exceptions, this valuable study of the interwar period is not found in recent U.S. historiography and commentary, primarily because it is the only sweeping but credible history of the 1920s and 1930s written from a communist point of view and aimed at the public.

11. Ibid., 20–21.

12. Stephen C. Mason, "Revitalize the Nation's Industries!," *American Industries* 20 (March 1920): 8, quoted in James Warren Prothro, *The Dollar Decade: Business Ideas in the 1920s* (Baton Rouge: Louisiana State University Press, 1954), 102.

13. Elbert H. Gary, "The Menace of the Closed Shop," *American Industries* 20 (January 1920): 31–32, quoted in Prothro, *Dollar Decade*, 101–2.

14. Minton and Stuart. *Fat Years and the Lean*, 18–19.

15. Ronald Radosh, "The Corporate Ideology of American Labor Leaders," in *The Twenties: The Critical Issues*, ed. Joan Hoff (Boston: Little, Brown, 1972), 75–77.

16. William Pencak, *For God & Country: The American Legion, 1919–1941* (Boston: Northeastern University Press, 1989), 3–23. Pencak provides surprising and disturbing examples of its members in their commitment to "Americanism."

17. Nancy MacLean, *Behind the Mask of Chivalry: The Making of the Second Ku Klux Klan* (New York and Oxford: Oxford University Press, 1994), 9–10.

18. Niall Palmer, *The Twenties in America: Politics and History* ((Edinburgh: Edinburgh University Press, 2006), 44.

19. Barbara Foley, *Spectres of 1919: Class and Nation in the Making of the New Negro* (Urbana and Chicago: University of Illinois Press, 2003), 12–13.

20. Goldberg, *America in the Twenties*, 22.

21. Robert K. Murray, *The Politics of Normalcy: Governmental Theory and*

Practice in the Harding-Coolidge Era (New York: W. W. Norton, 1973), 15.

22.   Goldberg, *America in the Twenties*, 26.

23.   Sean Dennis Cashman, *America in the Twenties and Thirties: The Olympian Age of Franklin Delano Roosevelt* (New York and London: New York University Press, 1989), 84, 87.

24.   David Burner, "1919: Prelude to Normalcy," in *Change and Continuity in Twentieth-Century America: The 1920s*, ed. John Braeman, Richard H. Bremmer, David Brody (Ohio State University Press, 1968), 13.

25.   Address of Warren G. Harding, President of the United States to the Joint Session of Congress, April 21, 1921, https://babel.hathitrust.org/cgi/pt?id=hvd.32044032157059;view=1up;seq=3.

26.   Goldberg, *America in the Twenties*, 24.

27.   Richard Frankin Pettigrew, *Imperial Washington: The Story of American Public Life from 1870 to 1920* (Chicago: Charles H. Kerr & Company, 1922), 399–400. Pettigrew is an amazing source who is not recognized for his role in making history. According to a 1949 report by George Novack to the Fourth International, Pettigrew was one of the many anti-monopolists apart from Marxists who deemed plutocracy as the deadliest enemy of the rights of the people and, as such, of American democracy. One will find no mention of Pettigrew in the best-known liberal histories of the period. Though he lacked insight into the laws of capitalist development, he had learned much from his decades-long struggle against his own bourgeoisie and considered capital to be "stolen labor," and its only function "to steal more labor." Novack also recalls how Lenin knew of Pettigrew's book. A year before it was reprinted by Charles Kerr, Pettigrew had published the book under a different title, *Triumphant Plutocracy*. When Lenin sat for the American artist Oscar Cesare in October 1922, Cesare saw Lenin reading a "red-bound copy" of the earlier version, who then told the artist, "It's a very fine book." See Novack, under the pseudonym William F. Warde, "A Forgotten Fighter Against Plutocracy," *Fourth International* 10/2 (February 1949): 53–57.

28.   Ferdinand Lundberg, *America's 60 Families* (New York: Citadel Press, 1946), 218–19. Even Harding's cronies in the cabinet contributed to this formula, unless they dragged him into scandals. The worst of them was his old poker-playing and drinking buddy, Interior Secretary Albert Fall, who went to prison for accepting payoffs in return for signing over leases of government oil reserves at Teapot Dome, Wyoming, to private companies. Harding appointed another one of his buddies, D. R. Crissinger, as governor of the Federal Reserve. The ignorant and "impressionable" Crissinger, a small businessman with no expertise in finance capital, was manipulated by Benjamin Strong, then a member

of the House of Morgan, to turn the Fed toward buying up government securities in large quantities. The result was that banks were flooded with liquid capital that required profitable investment.

29.   Cashman, *America in the Twenties and Thirties*, 89.

30.   Frederick Lewis Allen, *Only Yesterday: An Informal History of the 1920's* (New York: HarperCollins, 2000), 78. The book was first published by Harper & Row in 1931.

31.   Karl Marx and Frederick Engels, *The Manifesto of the Communist Party*, *Collected Works*, vol 6. (Moscow: Progress Publishers, 1976), 487.

32.   Geoffrey Perrett, *America in the Twenties: A History* (New York: Simon & Schuster, 1982), 297–98.

33.   Michael E. Parrish, *Anxious Decades: America in Prosperity and Depression, 1920–1941* (New York and London: W. W. Norton, 1992), 39.

34.   Perrett, *America in the Twenties*, 254–60, 297–99.

35.   My use of the two forms of capital's totalizing powers as terrorist and non-terrorist is derived from Herbert Marcuse's critique of advanced industrial society. In *One–Dimensional Man: Studies in the Ideology of Advanced Industrial Society* (Boston: Beacon Press, 1964), 3, Marcuse states: "By virtue of the way it has organized its technological base, contemporary industrial society tends to be totalitarian. For 'totalitarian' is not only a terroristic political coordination of society, but also a non-terroristic economic-technical coordination which operates through the manipulation of needs by vested interests. It thus precludes the emergence of an effective opposition against the whole. Not only a specific form of government or party rule makes for totalitarianism, but also a specific system of production and distribution which may well be compatible with a 'pluralism' of parties, newspapers, 'countervailing powers', etc." Marcuse's critique of industrial society also included the Soviet Union. This leads to many questions regarding Marcuse's view of existing socialism at the time, though it does not preclude an implicit understanding that Marcuse is still describing what he understands to be the totalizing power of capital.

36.   Silas Bent, *Ballyhoo: The Voice of the Press* (New York: Boni and Liveright, 1927), 223.

37.   Ibid., 199.

38.   Stuart Ewen, *PR! A Social History of Spin* (New York: Basic Books, 1996), 147. I am indebted to Ewen for his tremendously important study of the many works of the 1920s and 1930s.

39.   Bent, *Ballyhoo*, 223.

40.   Ewen, *PR!*, 183–86.

41.   Marx and Engels, *Manifesto of the Communist Party*, *Collected Works*, 6; 483.

42. Cashman, *America in the Twenties and Thirties*, 46–47.
43. Gerald Horne, *Blows Against the Empire: U.S. Imperialism in Crisis* (New York: International Publishers, 2008), 66. For Horne, the concept of white supremacy is integral to U.S. imperialism.
44. Karl Marx, *Capital*, vol. 1 (Moscow: Progress Publishers, 1978), 189.

2. Fascist Processes in Capitalist Accumulation

1. A. B. Magil and Henry Stevens, *The Peril of Fascism: The Crisis of American Democracy* (New York: International Publishers, 1938), 60. Magil was a seasoned journalist who wrote extensively for the Party. My search for information on Stevens came up empty, as did my attempt to find his name on Party rolls, suggesting that Stevens was most likely a *nom de plume*.
2. Ibid., 60.
3. Ibid., 36.
4. Ibid., 36–37.
5. Ibid., 22.
6. Ibid., 118.
7. Ibid., 56.
8. Ibid.
9. Ibid., 23.
10. Volker Ullrich, *Hitler: Ascent, 1889–1939*, trans. Jefferson Chase (New York: Alfred A. Knopf, 2016), 419–20. In this recent and quite revealing biography of Hitler, Ullrich recounts a critical moment just after Hitler was named chancellor on January 30, 1933. Hitler still needed new elections for the Reichstag, counting on the National Socialists to claim a clear majority, who would then call for passage of what became known as the Enabling Act, giving Hitler complete control of the state. With the Nazi Party coffers empty, Herman Göring hosted a reception on February 20 of twenty-seven leading industrialists and Germany's preeminent banker Hjalmar Schacht, who listened to Hitler affirm his belief in private property and also declare that the National Socialists alone offered "salvation from the Communist danger." As a result, Göring reported the next day that the desired donation in the amount of 3 million reichsmarks had been delivered to the party.
11. Magil and Stevens, *Peril of Fascism*, 29.
12. Ibid., 30.
13. Ibid., 32.
14. Ibid., 56.
15. David Harvey, *A Companion to Marx's* Capital (London & New York: Verso, 2010), 7.
16. Ibid., 8.

17. For a historical context to Marx's writing of *Capital*, see the acclaimed overview by the Marxist historian Eric Hobsbawm, *The Age of Capital: 1848–1875* (New York: Vintage, 1996). Originally published in 1975, Hobsbawm's book remains central for those who wish to reap benefits from a compelling work of modern world history.

18. Karl Marx, *Capital*, vol. 1 (Moscow: Progress Publishers, 1978), 574.

19. Harry Braverman, *Labor and Monopoly Capital: The Degradation of Work in the Twentieth Century* (New York and London: Monthly Review Press, 1974), 377.

20. Marx, *Capital*, 575. "If we suppose that, all other circumstances remaining the same, the composition of capital also remains constant (*i.e.*, that a definite mass of means of production constantly needs the same mass of labour-power to set it in motion), then the demand for labour and the subsistence-fund of the labourers clearly increase in the same proportion as the capital, and the more rapidly, the more rapidly the capital increases. Since the capital produces yearly a surplus-value, of which one part is yearly added to the original capital; since this increment itself grows yearly along with the augmentation of the capital already functioning; since lastly, under special stimulus to enrichment, such as the opening of new markets, or of new spheres for the outlay of capital in consequence of newly developed social wants . . . the scale of accumulation may be suddenly extended . . . the requirements of accumulating capital may exceed the increase of labour-power or of the number of labourers."

21. Ibid., 575–76. As Marx states: "As simple reproduction constantly reproduces the capital-relation itself, *i.e.*, the relation of capitalists on the one hand, and wage-workers on the other, so reproduction on a progressive scale, *i.e.*, accumulation, reproduces the capital-relation on a progressive scale, more capitalists or larger capitalists at this pole, more wage-workers at that. The reproduction of a mass of labour-power, which must incessantly re-incorporate itself with capital for that capital's self-expansion; which cannot get free from capital, and whose enslavement to capital is only concealed by the variety of individual capitalists to whom it sells itself, this reproduction of labour-power forms, in fact, an essential of the reproduction of capital itself. Accumulation of capital is, therefore, increase of the proletariat."

22. Ibid., 580.

23. Ibid., 582.

24. Ibid., 587–88. Marx observed this in England in the 1860s as he was writing *Capital*. The magnitude of total social capital amassed by the winners had brought centralization to new heights. All the surviving and larger capitalist enterprises were driven toward more

organized production and greater productiveness. As he concluded: "Centralisation completes the work of accumulation by enabling industrial capitalists to extend the scale of their operations. … Everywhere the increased scale of industrial establishments is the starting-point for a more comprehensive organisation of the collective work of many, for a wider development of their material motive forces—in other words, for the progressive transformation of isolated processes of production, carried on by customary methods, into processes of production socially combined and scientifically arranged."

25. Ibid., 588.
26. Ibid., 590–93.
27. Ibid., 591–92.
28. Ibid., 592–93.
29. Ibid., 595.
30. Ibid., 600–2.
31. Ibid., 602–3.
32. Ibid., 603.
33. Lewis Corey, *The Decline of American Capitalism* (New York: Covici Friede Publishers, 1934), 113. Corey was originally Louis C. Fraina, an Italian immigrant intellectual who was one of the founders of the communist movement in the United States. Accused of spying by the Communist International, Fraina disappeared from sight to live a quiet and impoverished life of study in New York City. He reemerged as Lewis Corey, a serious writer in the Marxist tradition, in the early years of the Depression. Still an outsider to the Communist Party in the United States, he remained a committed Marxist. In a note in *The Decline of American Capitalism*, Corey wrote: "It is one of the tasks of this book, using the American statistical material, the most abundant in the world, to make a quantitative, as well as qualitative, demonstration of the Marxist conception of the fundamental aspects of capitalism—and this despite the tendency, on the part of bourgeois economists, to sneer at 'Das Kapital' as an 'outworn economic textbook.' Marx, in fundamental theory and analysis, is more contemporary than contemporary bourgeois economists."
34. Ibid., 114–16.
35. Ibid., 116–17.
36. Ibid., 117.
37. Ibid., 223.
38. Ibid., 225.
39. Ibid., 225–26.
40. Ibid., 226–28.
41. Ibid., 228–32.

42. Michael Roberts, *The Long Depression: How It Happened, Why It Happened, and What Happens Next* (Chicago: Haymarket Books, 2016), 53–54.
43. Marx, *Capital*, 555.
44. Corey, *Decline of American Capitalism*, 44–45.
45. Ibid., 45.
46. Ibid., 46.

3. The Spectacle of Prosperity and the Necessity of Spin

1. Marx and Engels, *Collected Works*, 6:489.
2. Jonathan Norton Leonard, *Three Years Down* (New York: Carrick & Evans, 1939), 18.
3. Harold Underwood Faulkner, *American Political and Social History* (New York: Appleton-Century-Crofts, 1957), 757.
4. William E. Leuchtenburg, *The Perils of Prosperity, 1914–1932* (Chicago and London: University of Chicago Press, 1993), 108. The book was first published in 1958.
5. Ibid., 15.
6. Richard B. DuBoff, *Accumulation and Power: An Economic History of the United States* (Armonk, NY, and London: M. E. Sharpe, 1989), 72.
7. George Soule, *Prosperity Decade, From War to Depression: 1917–1929* (New York: Harper & Row, 1968), 78.
8. Michel Beaud, *A History of Capitalism, 1500–2000*. trans. Tom Dickman and Anny Lefebre (New York: Monthly Review Press, 2001), 177.
9. Lewis Corey, *The Decline of American Capitalism* (New York: Covici Friede Publishers, 1934) 63.
10. Leuchtenburg, *Perils of Prosperity*, 108.
11. Ibid., 104.
12. Ronald Radosh, "The Corporate Ideology of American Labor Leaders," in *The Twenties: The Critical Issues*, ed. Joan Hoff (Boston: Little, Brown, 1972), 75–77.
13. Warren I. Cohen, *Empire Without Tears: America's Foreign Relations, 1921–1933* (New York: Alfred A. Knopf, 1987), 3–4.
14. Harry Magdoff, *The Age of Imperialism: The Economics of U.S. Foreign Policy* (New York and London: Monthly Review Press, 1969), 70–84.
15. Benjamin M. Friedman, *The Moral Consequences of Economic Growth* (New York: Alfred A. Knopf, 2005), 145.
16. Corey, *Decline of American Capitalism*, 63–64.
17. Alan Lawson, *A Commonwealth of Hope: The New Deal Response to Crisis* (Baltimore: Johns Hopkins University Press, 2006), 10.
18. Soule, *Prosperity Decade*, 146.
19. Leuchtenburg, *Perils of Prosperity*, 179.

20. DuBoff, *Accumulation and Power*, 83–84.
21. Sean Dennis Cashman, *America in the Twenties and Thirties: The Olympian Age of Franklin Delano Roosevelt* (New York and London: New York University Press, 1989), 42.
22. Soule, *Prosperity Decade*, 318.
23. Corey, *Decline of American Capitalism*, 65–66.
24. Tom Kemp, *The Climax of Capitalism: The U.S. Economy in the Twentieth Century* (London and New York: Longman, 1990), 49–50.
25. Beaud, *History of Capitalism*, 180–82.
26. Kemp, *Climax of Capitalism*, 49–50. The term "Taylorism" is derived from its founder, Frederick W. Taylor, who sought to challenge and mitigate workers' control over the workplace, as well as to blunt the power of unions.
27. Soule, *Prosperity Decade*, 325, 327.
28. Lawson, *Commonwealth of Hope,* 10.
29. Donald R. McCoy, *Coming of Age: The United States during the 1920s and 1930s* (Harmondsworth, UK: Penguin, 1973), 63.
30. Frederick Lewis Allen, *Only Yesterday: An Informal History of the 1920's* (New York: HarperCollins, 2000), 145–46.
31. Sinclair Lewis, *Babbitt* (New York: New American Library, 1980), 7, 37. The book was first published by Harcourt Brace Jovanovich in 1922.
32. Ibid., 38.
33. Stuart Ewen, *PR! A Social History of Spin* (New York: Basic Books, 1996), 221.
34. Lewis, *Babbitt*, 80–81.
35. Allen, *Only Yesterday*, 153–54.
36. Ibid., 145.
37. Bruce Barton, *The Man Nobody Knows: A Discovery of the Real Jesus* (Chicago: Ivan R. Dee, 2000), 4, 44. The book was first published by Bobbs-Merrill in 1925.
38. Ibid., 50–51.
39. Ibid., 52.
40. Ibid., 4.
41. Ibid., 77–78, 83.
42. Roland Marchand, *Advertising the American Dream: Making Way for Modernity, 1920–1940* (Berkeley, Los Angeles, and London: University of California Press, 1985), 8.
43. Richard M. Fried, *The Man Everybody Knew: Bruce Barton and the Making of Modern America* (Chicago: Ivan R. Dee, 2005), 101–2.
44. Ibid., 98.
45. Piers Brendon, *The Dark Valley: A Panorama of the 1930s* (New York: Vintage Books, 2002), 66–67.

46. John M. Blair, *Seeds of Destruction: A Study in the Functional Weaknesses of Capitalism* (New York: Covici Freide Publishers, 1938), 214–17.

47. Ibid., 214.

48. Ewen, *PR!*, 174–75.

49. Ibid., 182.

50. Ibid., 190.

51. Blair, *Seeds of Destruction*, 215.

52. George Duhamel, *America the Menace: Scenes from the Life of the Future* (New York: Arno Press, 1974), 128. This is a reprint of the 1931 edition originally published by Houghton Mifflin. I am indebted to Stuart Ewen who in *PR!* brings Duhamel's compelling but forgotten text to light.

53. Ibid., 128, 133.

54. Ibid., 24–27.

55. Ibid., 210–11.

56. Marchand, *Advertising the American Dream*, 206–7.

57. Ibid., 165–66, 217.

58. Ibid., 218.

59. Ibid.

60. Ibid., 220–22.

61. Barton, *The Man Nobody Knows*, 47; Marchand, *Advertising the American Dream*, 8–9.

62. Corey, *Decline of American Capitalism*, 15–17.

63. Michael E. Parrish, *Anxious Decades: America in Prosperity and Depression, 1920–1941* (New York and London: W. W. Norton, 1992), 8.

64. Ferdinand Lundberg, *America's 60 Families* (New York: Citadel Press, 1946), 150.

65. Parrish, *Anxious Decades*, 48–49.

66. McCoy, *Coming of Age*, 100.

67. Silas Bent, *Ballyhoo: The Voice of the Press* (New York: Boni and Liveright, 1927), 224.

68. Ewen, *PR!*, 224–25.

69. Parrish, *Anxious Decades*, 48–50.

70. Lawson, *Commonwealth of Hope*, 11.

71. Keith L. Bryant Jr. and Henry C. Dethloff, *A History of American Business*, (Upper Saddle River, NJ: Prentice-Hall, 1990), 193.

4. Every Man a Capitalist? Fascist Ideology of Businessmen in 1920s America

1. Thomas Nixon Carver, *The Present Economic Revolution in the United States* (Boston: Little, Brown, 1925), 9–10.

2.   Ibid., 10–11.
3.   Ibid., 12.
4.   Ibid., 28.
5.   Ibid., 88.
6.   Ibid., 89.
7.   Ibid., 90–92.
8.   Ibid., 113–18.
9.   Ibid., 209. Carver also believed that the capitalist revolution in America was proving itself as a great victory in the struggle over ideas. For Carver, Marx and his followers were simply wrong when they promulgated a materialist interpretation of history— this was simply rubbish. Idealism liberated men and women, not a materialist worldview.
10. Ibid., 233–35.
11. Ibid., 209.
12. Ibid., 210–11.
13. Ibid., 211–12.
14. Ibid., 218.
15. Ibid., 220.
16. Ibid., 165–66.
17. James Warren Prothro, *The Dollar Decade: Business Ideas in the 1920s* (Baton Rouge: Louisiana State University Press, 1954), xiii.
18. Charles Norman Fay, *Business in Politics: Suggestions for Leaders in American Business* (Cambridge, MA: Cosmos Press, 1926), vii–x.
19. Ibid., x.
20. Ibid., xi.
21. Ibid., 10–11.
22. Ibid., 11–12.
23. Ibid., 12.
24. Ibid., 13–14.
25. Ibid., 14.
26. Ibid., 166–67.
27. Ibid., 23–24.
28. Ibid., 26.
29. Ibid., 26–27.
30. Ibid., 29–30.
31. Ibid., 32.
32. Ibid., 39.
33. Ibid., 47.
34. Ibid., 48.
35. Ibid., 49.
36. Ibid., 55.
37. Ibid., 56.

38. Ibid., 56–58.
39. Edward Bernays, *Propaganda*, Introduction by Mark Crispin Miller (Brooklyn, NY: Ig Publishing, 2005), 37. The book was first published in 1928.
40. Ibid., 37–38.
41. Ibid., 47–48.
42. Ibid., 48.
43. Ibid., 52.
44. Ibid., 54–55.
45. Ibid., 60.
46. Ibid., 63.
47. Ibid., 84.
48. Ibid., 85–87.
49. Ibid., 110–11.
50. Ibid., 112–15.
51. Marx used the word phantasmagoria in 1847 to describe the worldview of Pierre-Joseph Proudhon, who attempted to establish a new political economy to guide producers acting in harmony toward the creation of a balanced and just system. Marx considered it sheer fantasy that Proudhon wanted a true capitalist world without capitalist contradictions. Michael Joseph Roberto, "Crisis, Revolution, and the Meaning of Progress: The Poverty of Philosophy and Its Contemporary Relevance," *Cultural Logic* (2010) http://clogic.eserver.org/2009/roberto.pdf.

5. The Paradox of Capitalist Progress, 1922–1929

1. Lewis Corey, *The Decline of American Capitalism* (New York: Covici Friede Publishers, 1934), 18–19.
2. Irving Bernstein, *The Lean Years: A History of the American Worker, 1920–1933* (Boston: Houghton Miflin Company, 1960), 47.
3. Ibid., 48.
4. Louis M. Hacker, *American Problems of Today* (New York: F. S. Crofts & Co., 1939), 115–16. Hacker was one of the few writers of the 1930s who recognized the crucial role played by the agricultural depression of the 1920s in the making of the general crisis that followed. It was one of "four outstanding problems" that had threatened the well-being of the nation. Full treatment of the four outstanding problems can be found on pages 99–145.
5. Bernstein, *Lean Years*, 51–55, 58–59.
6. Mauritz A. Hallgren, *Seeds of Revolt: A Study of American Life and the Temper of the American People during the Depression* (New York: Alfred A. Knopf, 1933), 15, 26–27. Hallgren cites an earlier 1929 study by Paul H. Nystrom, *Economic Principles of Consumption*, which revealed

that about 47 million of the 119 million people in the United States in 1929 were living at a level of "Comfort" or above. There were 20 million at the Comfort level itself; 15 million Moderately Well-to-Do; 10 million Well-to-Do; and 2 million who enjoyed "Liberal Standards of Living."

7.   Ibid., 16–17.
8.   Ibid., 19–20.
9.   Ibid., 23.
10. Ibid., 23–24.
11. Ibid., 24–25.
12. Ibid., 21–23.
13. Ibid., 27–28.
14. The paradox of capitalist progress had always been integral to world capitalist development. From its genesis in Western Europe in the sixteenth century, the Atlantic economy was built on the horrors of slavery and wage labor. From that time capitalist contradictions intensified quantitatively and qualitatively as industrialization developed in the core capitalist countries of the world system. By 1850, England ushered in what historian Eric Hobsbawm called the "Age of Capital." Once again, Marx saw these developments more clearly than others, if only in their embryonic stages. In his inaugural address to the International Working Men's Association in London in 1864, which came from material he would include in the publication of *Capital* three years later, Marx established the paradox of capitalist progress as a theoretical tenet of his materialist interpretation of history and his contributions to political economy: capitalist accumulation necessarily widened the gap between wealth and poverty which, in turn, intensified existing contradictions that if not resolved would produce a crisis of the whole system, *a general crisis*. Michael Joseph Roberto, "Capitalist Crisis, Cooperative Labor, and the Conquest of Political Power: Marx's 'Inaugural Address' (1864) and Its Relevance in the Current Moment," *Socialism and Democracy* 28/2 (July 2014): 82–106.
15. Hallgren, *Seeds of Revolt*, 30–31.
16. Ibid., 229–30.
17. Ibid., 95.
18. Ibid., 30.
19. Robert Moats Miller, "The Ku Klux Klan," in *Change and Continuity in Twentieth-Century America: The 1920s (Modern America)*, ed. John Braeman, Robert H. Bremner, and David Brody (Columbus: Ohio State University Press, 1968), 216
20. The oath is taken from a booklet titled *Ku Klux Klan Secrets Exposed: Attitudes Toward Jews, Catholics, Foreigners and Masons. Fraudulent*

Methods Used. Atrocities Committed in Name and Order (Chicago: Ezra A. Cook, 1922), 58.

21. Miller, "The Ku Klux Klan," 216.
22. Seymour Martin Lipset and Earl Raab, *Politics of Unreason: Right-Wing Extremism in America, 1790–1970* (New York: Harper & Row, 1970), 111.
23. Nancy MacLean, *Behind the Mask of Chivalry: The Making of the Second Ku Klux Klan* (New York and Oxford: Oxford University Press, 1994), 8.
24. Ibid., xiii.
25. Ibid., 4–5.
26. Miller, "The Ku Klux Klan," 240.
27. Sean Dennis Cashman, *America in the Twenties and Thirties: The Olympian Age of Franklin Delano Roosevelt* (New York and London: New York University Press, 1989), 75.
28. MacLean, *Behind the Mask of Chivalry*, 5, 7–8.
29. Roland G. Fryer Jr. and Steven D. Levitt, "Hatred and Profits: Under the Hood of the Ku Klux Klan," February 2011, 3–4, 11. https://scholar.harvard.edu/files/fryer/files/hatred_and_profits_under_the_hood_of_the_ku_klux_klan.pdf.
30. MacLean, *Behind the Mask of Chivalry*, 65.
31. Ibid., 67.
32. Ibid., 78.
33. Ibid., 65.
34. Ibid., 65–66.
35. Ibid., 66.
36. Ibid., 66–67.
37. Alan Lawson, *A Commonwealth of Hope: The New Deal Response to Crisis* (Baltimore: Johns Hopkins University Press, 2006), 10–11.
38. V. G. Kiernan, *America: The New Imperialism: From White Settlement to World Hegemony*, 2nd ed. (London and New York: Verso, 2005), 218.
39. Donald R. McCoy, *Coming of Age: The United States during the 1920s and 1930s* (Harmondsworth, UK: Penguin, 1973), 63.
40. Kiernan, *New Imperialism*, 218.
41. Sidney Lens, *The Forging of the American Empire* (New York: Thomas Y. Crowell Company, 1971), 269.
42. McCoy, *Coming of Age*, 53.
43. Frank Costigliola, *Awkward Dominion: American Political, Economic, and Cultural Relations with Europe, 1919–1933* (Ithaca and London: Cornell University Press, 1984), 124.
44. Lens, *Forging of the American Empire*, 269–70.
45. Hacker, *American Problems of Today*, 127.
46. Ibid., 127–35.
47. Ibid., 135.

48. Bruce Minton and John Stuart, *The Fat Years and The Lean* (New York: International Publishers, 1940), 78.

49. Ibid., 79–80.

50. James A. Emery, "Address of Mr. James A. Emery," *Proceedings*, N.A.M. (1923), 289, quoted in James Warren Prothro, *The Dollar Decade: Business Ideas in the 1920s* (Baton Rouge: Louisiana State University Press, 1954), 204.

51. John P. Diggins, *Mussolini and Fascism: The View from America* (Princeton: Princeton University Press, 1972), 144–45.

52. Ibid., 146–47.

53. Ibid., 147.

54. Ibid., 146–48.

55. Ibid., 60.

56. Merle Thorpe, "That Man Mussolini!," *Nation's Business* 15 (December 1927): 62, quoted in Prothro, *Dollar Decade*, 205.

57. Diggins, *Mussolini and Fascism*, 24–27.

58. Gian Giacomo Migone, *The United States and Fascist Italy: The Rise of American Finance in Europe*, trans. Molly Tambor (New York: Cambridge University Press, 2015), 56.

59. Ibid., 47–48.

6. Onset of the 1929 Crisis and the Pivot toward Fascism

1. Jonathan Norton Leonard, *Three Years Down* (New York: Carrick & Evans, 1939), 16–17

2. George Soule, *Prosperity Decade, From War to Depression: 1917–1929* (New York: Harper & Row, 1968), 290–91.

3. Chris Harman, *Zombie Capitalism: Global Crisis and the Relevance of Marx* (Chicago: Haymarket Books, 2009), 144.

4. Lewis Corey, *The Decline of American Capitalism* (New York: Covici Friede Publishers, 1934), 163.

5. Ronald E. Seavoy, *An Economic History of the United States: From 1607 to the Present* (New York: Routledge, 2006), 280.

6. Donald R. McCoy, *Coming of Age: The United States during the 1920s and 1930s* (Harmondsworth, UK: Penguin, 1973), 170.

7. Corey, *Decline of American Capitalism*, 429.

8. William E. Leuchtenburg, *The Perils of Prosperity, 1914–1932* (Chicago and London: University of Chicago Press, 1993), 109; Seavoy, *Economic History of the United States*, 280.

9. David M. Kennedy, *Freedom from Fear: The American People in Depression and War, 1929–1945* (New York and Oxford: Oxford University Press, 1999), 16–17.

10. Kennedy, *Freedom from Fear*, 17.

11.   Leuchtenburg, *Perils of Prosperity*, 100.

12.   Ibid., 101.

13.   Alan Lawson, *A Commonwealth of Hope: The New Deal Response to Crisis* (Baltimore: Johns Hopkins University Press, 2006), 22.

14.   Leuchtenburg, *Perils of Prosperity*, 101.

15.   Corey, *Decline of American Capitalism*, 154.

16.   Richard B. Duboff, *Accumulation and Power: An Economic History of the United States* (Armonk, NY, and London: M.E. Sharpe, 1989), 89.

17.   Kennedy, *Freedom from Fear*, 35.

18.   Soule, *Prosperity Decade*, 286.

19.   Robert S. McElvaine, *The Great Depression: America, 1929–1941* (New York: Three Rivers Press, 1993), 41.

20.   Soule, *Prosperity Decade,* 172.

21.   Corey, *Decline of American Capitalism*, 163.

22.   Soule, *Prosperity Decade*, 287.

23.   Corey, *Decline of American Capitalism*, 65–72.

24.   Lawson, *Commonwealth of Hope*, 21.

25.   McElvaine, *Great Depression*, 38.

26.   DuBoff, *Accumulation and Power*, 87.

27.   Ibid., 88.

28.   Corey, *Decline of American Capitalism*, 67.

29.   A. B. Magil and Henry Stevens, *The Peril of Fascism: The Crisis of American Democracy* (New York: International Publishers, 1938), 62.

30.   Lawson, *Commonwealth of Hope*, 10.

31.   Alan Dawley, *Struggles for Justice: Social Responsibility and the Liberal State* (Cambridge, MA, and London: Harvard University Press, 1991), 300.

32.   Lawson, *Commonwealth of Hope*, 21.

33.   McCoy, *Coming of Age*, 120.

34.   Corey, *Decline of American Capitalism*, 72–73.

35.   Leuchtenburg, *Perils of Prosperity*, 189.

36.   DuBoff, *Accumulation of Power*, 80.

37.   Leuchtenburg, *Perils of Prosperity*, 190–92.

38.   Soule, *Prosperity Decade*, 279–80, 284.

39.   McElvaine, *Great Depression*, 43–44.

40.   Corey, *Decline of American Capitalism*, 114.

41.   Ibid., 116.

42.   Ibid., 73.

43.   Ibid., 170–71.

44.   Historicus, "Fascism in America," *Monthly Review* 4/6 (October 1952): 181–82.

45.   Ibid., 182.

46.   Magil and Stevens, *Peril of Fascism*, 60.

47.	Ibid., 56.
48.	Ibid., 11, 148.

7. "Years of the Locust" and the Call for a Mussolini

1.	Gilbert Seldes, *The Years of the Locust: America, 1929–1932* (Boston: Little, Brown, 1933), 3, 256.
2.	Jonathan Norton Leonard, *Three Years Down* (New York: Carrick & Evans, 1939), 113.
3.	Ibid., 113–14.
4.	Edmund Wilson, *The American Jitters: A Year of the Slump* (Freeport, NY: Books For Libraries Press, 1932), 1–3.
5.	Edward Robb Ellis, *A Nation in Torment: The Great American Depression, 1929–1939* (New York: Coward-McCann, 1970), 230.
6.	David M. Kennedy, *Freedom from Fear: The American People in Depression and War, 1929–1945* (New York and Oxford: Oxford University Press, 1999), 89.
7.	Matthew Josephson, *Infidel in the Temple: A Memoir of the Nineteen-Thirties* (New York: Alfred A. Knopf, 1967), 95–96.
8.	Kennedy, *Freedom from Fear*, 88.
9.	Robert S. McElvaine, *The Great Depression: America, 1929–1941* (New York: Three Rivers Press, 1993), 91.
10.	Leonard, *Three Years Down*, 188.
11.	Seldes, *Years of the Locust*, 294–95.
12.	Ibid., 281–82.
13.	Wilson, *American Jitters*, 298.
14.	Ibid., 302–3.
15.	Ibid., 303–4.
16.	Ibid., 304.
17.	Fraser M. Ottanelli, *The Communist Party of the United States: From the Depression to World War II* (New Brunswick, NJ, and London: Rutgers University Press, 1991), 35. A good local example of much of this evidence appears in a recent study of the Communist Party in North Carolina by Gregory S. Taylor, *The History of the North Carolina Communist Party* (Columbia: University of South Carolina Press, 2009).
18.	Wilson, *American Jitters*, 11–12.
19.	Richard B. Duboff, *Accumulation and Power: An Economic History of the United States* (Armonk, NY, and London: M.E. Sharpe, 1989), 89.
20.	Chris Harman, *Zombie Capitalism: Global Crisis and the Relevance of Marx* (Chicago: Haymarket Books, 2009), 148.
21.	Broadus Mitchell, *Depression Decade: From New Era through New Deal, 1929–1941* (New York and Toronto: Rinehart & Company, 1947), 59–60.

22. McElvaine, *Great Depression*, 74–75.

23. Charles P. Kindleberger, *The World in Depression, 1929–1939*, 2nd ed. (Berkeley, Los Angeles, and London: University of California Press, 1986), 112.

24. Mitchell, *Depression Decade*, 68.

25. Ibid., 357.

26. Sidney Lens, *The Forging of the American Empire* (New York: Thomas Y. Crowell Company, 1971), 288.

27. Kindleberger, *World in Depression*, 114–16.

28. Mitchell, *Depression Decade*, 60–62.

29. McElvaine, *Great Depression*, 75.

30. Mitchell, *Depression Decade*, 91–92.

31. Ibid., 98.

32. Piers Brendon, *The Dark Valley: A Panorama of the 1930s* (New York: Vintage Books, 2002), 86–87.

33. Ibid., 87–88.

34. Mitchell, *Depression Decade*, 104.

35. Mauritz A. Hallgren, *Seeds of Revolt: A Study of American Life and the Temper of the American People during the Depression* (New York: Alfred A. Knopf, 1933), 232.

36. Ibid., 233.

37. Herbert Stein, *The Fiscal Revolution in America* (Chicago and London: University of Chicago Press, 1969), 20–22.

38. Brendon, *Dark Valley*, 69.

39. Stein, *Fiscal Revolution*, 8–9.

40. McElvaine, *Great Depression*, 77.

41. Mitchell, *Depression Decade*, 64; McElvaine, *Great Depression*, 77.

42. Ronald E. Seavoy, *An Economic History of the United States: From 1607 to the Present* (New York: Routledge, 2006), 276.

43. John A. Garraty, *The Great Depression* (Garden City, NY: Anchor Books, 1987), 34–35; Albert U. Romasco, *The Poverty of Abundance: Hoover, the Nation, the Depression* (London, Oxford, and New York: Oxford University Press, 1965), 93–94.

44. Stein, *Fiscal Revolution*, 28.

45. McElvaine, *Great Depression*, 89.

46. Elliot A. Rosen, *Roosevelt, The Great Depression, and the Economics of Recovery* (Charlottesville, VA, and London: University of Virginia Press, 2005), 8.

47. Alan Lawson, *A Commonwealth of Hope: The New Deal Response to Crisis* (Baltimore: Johns Hopkins University Press, 2006), 27.

48. Kennedy, *Freedom from Fear*, 79.

49. Stein, *Fiscal Revolution*, 20–27.

50. Leonard, *Three Years Down*, 243–44.
51. Ibid., 245–51.
52. Ibid., 250–55.
53. Ibid., 255–57.
54. A. B. Magil and Henry Stevens, *The Peril of Fascism: The Crisis of American Democracy* (New York: International Publishers, 1938), 76–78.
55. Ibid., 78–79.
56. Hallgren, *Seeds of Revolt*, 226.
57. Ibid., 231–33.
58. Ibid., 233–35.
59. Ibid., 240–41.
60. Ibid., 244–45.
61. Ibid., 245.
62. Ibid., 278–79.
63. Ibid., 280.

8. The New Deal as a Transition to Fascism

1. Bruce Minton and John Stuart, *The Fat Years and the Lean* (New York: International Publishers, 1940), 291.
2. Ira Katznelson, *Fear Itself: The New Deal and the Origins of Our Time* (New York and London: Liveright, 2013), 118–19.
3. Ibid., 121–22.
4. The highly regarded historian Willian Leuchtenburg describes how the Brain Trust came together in 1932 as Roosevelt positioned himself for the presidential race. As governor of New York, Roosevelt "consulted frequently with college professors on legislative policy." One of them, Raymond Moley, quickly became the leader of an impressive group of academics whose concerted effort and planning materialized in the New Deal legislation immediately after Roosevelt stepped into the White House as president on March 4, 1933. Leuchtenburg says that the Brain Trust, as it had become known, actually disbanded after the election. *Franklin D. Roosevelt and the New Deal, 1932–1940* (New York: Harper & Row, 1963), 32–33.
5. The term "state capitalism" is a loaded and highly debated term and, in my view, applies here. That fascism became a distinct feature of the world capitalist system in the 1920s and 1930s, primarily in Italy and Germany, occurred in the general framework of state control over the economy, though the latter meant a profitable if not entirely free hand for big monopoly-finance capital in both fascist states. Thus Lenin's statement in his seminal work of 1917, *The State and Revolution*: "Imperialism—the era of bank capital, the era of gigantic

capitalist monopolies, of the development of monopoly capitalism into state-monopoly capitalism—has clearly shown an extraordinary strengthening of the 'state machine' and an unprecedented growth in its bureaucratic and military apparatus in connection with the intensification of repressive measures against the proletariat both in the monarchical and in the freest republican countries." *V. I. Lenin, Collected Works*, vol. 25 (Moscow: Progress Publishers, 1964), 410.

6. David M. Kennedy, *Freedom from Fear: The American People in Depression and War, 1929–1945* (New York and Oxford: Oxford University Press, 1999), 132–33.

7. Ronald E. Seavoy, *An Economic History of the United States: From 1607 to the Present* (New York: Routledge, 2006), 283–84.

8. Broadus Mitchell, *Depression Decade: From New Era through New Deal, 1929–1941* (New York and Toronto: Rinehart & Company, 1947), 135–36.

9. Ibid., 180.

10. Alan Lawson, *A Commonwealth of Hope: The New Deal Response to Crisis* (Baltimore: Johns Hopkins University Press, 2006), 84–85.

11. Katznelson, *Fear Itself*, 229.

12. For the earliest and most comprehensive treatment of the NRA, see Leverett S. Lyon, Paul T. Homan, Lewis Lorwin, George Terbough, Charles L. Dearing, and Leon C. Marshall, *The National Recovery Administration: An Analysis and Appraisal* (Washington, D.C.: Brookings Institution, 1935). The fine work of Ellis W. Hawley, *The New Deal and the Problem of Monopoly: A Study in Economic Ambivalence* (Princeton: Princeton University Press, 1966), is extremely thorough for its detailed assessment of the motives and major issues surrounding discussions and implementation of the NRA. There is also the more critical assessment by Bernard Bellush, *The Failure of the NRA* (New York: W. W. Norton, 1975).

13. Lawson, *Commonwealth of Hope*, 87.

14. Robert S. McElvaine, *The Great Depression: America, 1929–1941* (New York: Three Rivers Press, 1993), 160.

15. Lewis Corey, *The Decline of American Capitalism* (New York: Covici Friede Publishers, 1934), 96.

16. McElvaine, *Great Depression*, 160.

17. Corey, *Decline of American Capitalism*, 96–97, 463.

18. Ibid., 61.

19. McElvaine, *Great Depression*, 161.

20. Mitchell, *Depression Decade*, 180–185.

21. Benjamin Stolberg and Warren Jay Vinton, *The Economic Consequences of the New Deal* (New York: Harcourt, Brace and Company, 1935), 4–5, 8.

22. Ibid., 6–8.

23. Ibid., 81.

24. Ibid., 24–26.

25. Ibid., 35–36.

26. Ibid., 37–38.

27. Ibid., 41.

28. Ibid., 43–45.

29. Ibid., 48.

30. Ibid., 49–52.

31. Ibid., 52.

32. Ibid., 64–65.

33. Ibid., 66.

34. Ibid., 85.

35. E. Francis Brown, "The American Road to Fascism," *Current History* 38 (July 1, 1933): 398.

36. John P. Diggins, *Mussolini and Fascism: The View from America* (Princeton: Princeton University Press, 1972), 279.

37. J. B. Matthews and R. E. Shallcross, "Must America Go Fascist?," *Harper's Magazine* 169 (June 1934): 2.

38. Ibid., 4.

39. Ibid., 4–5.

40. Ibid., 5.

41. Ibid.

42. Ibid., 6.

43. Ibid.

44. Ibid., 9.

45. Ibid., 10.

46. Ibid.

47. Ibid., 10–11.

48. Ibid., 11.

49. Ibid.

50. Ibid., 12.

51. Ibid.

52. Ibid., 12–13.

53. George E. Sokolsky, "America Drifts toward Fascism," *American Mercury* 32/127 (July 1934): 259.

54. Ibid., 258.

55. Ibid., 259.

56. Ibid.

57. Ibid., 262.

58. Ibid.

59. V. F. Calverton, "Will Fascism Come to America? A Symposium,"

Modern Monthly 8/8 (September 1934): 469. Other contributors included Stuart Chase, Charles A. Beard, Theodore Dreiser, Norman Thomas, Waldo Frank, and Horace M. Kallen.

60. Ibid., 471–72.
61. Corey, *Decline of American Capitalism*, 494, 498.
62. Ibid., 502, 505.
63. Ibid., 511.
64. R. Palme Dutt, *Fascism and Social Revolution: How and Why Fascism Came to Power in Europe* (Chicago: Proletarian Publishers, 1974), 271.
65. Georgi Dimitroff, *The United Front: Problems of Working-Class Unity and the People's Front in the Struggle Against Fascism and War* (New York: International Publishers, 1938), 9.
66. Ibid., 10–11.
67. Ibid., 41–42.
68. Richard B. DuBoff, *Accumulation and Power: An Economic History of the United States* (Armonk, NY, and London: M. E. Sharpe, 1989), 91.

9. "A Smokescreen over America"

1.   George Seldes, *Facts and Fascism* (New York: In Fact, Inc., 1943), 69.
2.   H. Arthur Steiner, "Fascism in America?," *American Political Science Review* 29/5 (October 1935): 821–30.
3.   A. B. Magil and Henry Stevens, *The Peril of Fascism: The Crisis of American Democracy* (New York: International Publishers, 1938), 11, 60.
4.   Leo P. Ribuffo, *The Old Christian Right: The Protestant Far Right from the Great Depression to the Cold War* (Philadelphia: Temple University Press, 1983). For Pelley and Winrod, I rely on Ribuffo's stellar framework and analysis; his interpretation of these two early Christian fascists remains unsurpassed. Many of his major findings are salient to the making of American fascism as presented in this book.
5.   Ibid., 25, 27, 29.
6.   Ibid., 32–35.
7.   Ibid., 36.
8.   Ibid., 43.
9.   Ibid., 43–44.
10. Ibid., 44–49.
11. Ibid., 49.
12. Ibid., 52–54.
13. Ibid., 57.
14. Ibid.
15. Ibid., 59.
16. Ibid., 59–60.

17. Ibid., 63–65.
18. Victor Ferkiss, "The Political and Economic Philosophy of American Fascism" (PhD diss., University of Chicago, June 1954), 273–74.
19. Ribuffo, *Old Christian Right*, 91.
20. Ibid., 81.
21. Ibid., 83.
22. Ibid., 89–92.
23. Ibid., 99–100.
24. Ibid., 102.
25. Ibid., 103.
26. Ibid., 104–5.
27. Ibid., 109–10.
28. Ibid., 118.
29. Ibid., 119–27.
30. Arthur M. Schlesinger, Jr., *The Politics of Upheaval, 1935–1936* (Boston & New York: Houghton Mifflin Company, 1960), 78–80.
31. Peter H. Amaan, "Vigilante Fascism: The Black Legion as an American Hybrid," *Comparative Studies in Society and History* 25/3 (July 1983): 493–94.
32. Ibid., 494–95.
33. Ibid., 495.
34. Ibid., 496–97.
35. Ibid., 497.
36. Ibid., 505–6.
37. Ibid., 499, 501.
38. Ibid., 508.
39. Ibid., 522–23.
40. Morris Janowitz, "Black Legions on the March," in *America in Crisis: Fourteen Crucial Episodes in American History*, ed. Daniel Aaron (New York: Alfred A. Knopf, 1952), 305–8.
41. Carleton Beals, *The Story of Huey P. Long* (Philadelphia: J. B. Lippincott Company, 1935), 12.
42. Sheldon Marcus, *Father Coughlin: The Tumultuous Life of the Priest of the Little Flower* (Boston and Toronto: Little, Brown, 1973), 21–27.
43. Ibid., 29–30.
44. Ibid., 31–34.
45. Alan Brinkley, *Voices of Protest: Huey Long, Father Coughlin, and the Great Depression* (New York: Vintage Books, 1983), 119.
46. Charles E. Coughlin, *Father Coughlin's Radio Discourses* (Royal Oak, MI: Radio League of the Little Flower, 1932), 27.
47. Marcus, *Father Coughlin*, 38–40.
48. Brinkley, *Voices of Protest*, 107–9.

49. Ferkiss, "Philosophy of American Fascism," 171–73, 178.

50. Brinkley, *Voices of Protest*, 112.

51. Ibid., 126, 133–34. In 1937, Ferdinand Lundberg was among the first writers to draw attention to the support that Hearst gave to Coughlin and how the latter willingly followed his lead. See Lundberg, *Imperial Hearst: A Social Biography* (New York: The Modern Library, 1937), 277–78.

52. Marcus, *Father Coughlin*, 71–73.

53. Brinkley, *Voices of Protest*, 126.

54. Ferkiss, "Philosophy of American Fascism," 166–68.

55. Ibid., 171.

56. Marcus, *Father Coughlin*, 37.

57. Ferkiss, "Philosophy of American Fascism," 195.

58. Ibid., 208.

59. Ibid., 215.

60. Ibid., 223.

61. Ibid., 229.

62. Ibid., 242.

63. Schlesinger, *Politics of Upheaval*, 42–47.

64. Brinkley, *Voices of Protest*, 11–14.

65. Beals, *Story of Huey Long*, 364, 366.

66. Ibid., 14–15.

67. Ibid., 15.

68. Ibid., 366.

69. Raymond Gram Swing, *Forerunners of American Fascism* (Montauk, NY: Julian Messner, Inc., 1935), 104–5.

70. Richard D. White, Jr., *Kingfish: The Reign of Huey P. Long* (New York: Random House, 2006), 61–63.

71. Ibid., 235.

72. Swing, *Forerunners of Fascism*, 75–77.

73. Brinkley, *Voices of Protest*, 26–27.

74. Beals, *Story of Huey Long*, 340.

75. Ibid., 340–43.

76. Ibid., 350–51.

77. Ibid., 351–53.

78. Schlesinger, *Politics of Upheaval*, 62–64.

79. William Leuchtenburg, *Franklin D. Roosevelt and the New Deal, 1932–1940* (New York: Harper & Row, 1963), 99.

80. Beals, *Story of Huey Long*, 18–19.

81. Ferkiss, "Philosophy of American Fascism," 132, 156.

82. Ibid., 133.

83. Ibid., 151.

84. Ibid., 126.
85. Ibid., 133.
86. Brinkley, *Voices of Protest*, 273–74.
87. Ibid., 276–77.
88. Ibid., 281–82.

10. The Class Character of Embryonic American Fascism

1. Mauritz A. Hallgren, *Seeds of Revolt: A Study of American Life and the Temper of the American People during the Depression* (New York: Alfred A. Knopf, 1933), 264.
2. Ibid., 265.
3. David M. Kennedy, *Freedom from Fear: The American People in Depression and War, 1929–1945* (New York and Oxford: Oxford University Press, 1999), 214–15.
4. Georgi Dimitroff, *The United Front: Problems of Working–Class Unity and the People's Front in the Struggle Against Fascism and War* (New York: International Publishers, 1938), 9–11. Dimitroff reported that "in a more or less developed form, fascist tendencies and the germs of a fascist movement are to be found almost everywhere." At the same time, he carefully defined fascism as "the open terrorist dictatorship of the most reactionary, most chauvinistic and most imperialist elements of finance capital," a designation he applied only to those capitalist states where fascism had come to power. For Dimitroff, the "German type" set the benchmark: Hitler's regime exhibited "bestial chauvinism" and "a government system of political gangsterism," making it "*the spearhead of international counter-revolution*" and the "*chief instigator of imperialist war*." Thus fascism should be considered neither a form of state power "standing above" the bourgeoisie and the proletariat, nor "the revolt of the petty bourgeoisie which has captured the machinery of the state."
5. Haider's book, *Capital and Labor Under Fascism*, was published by Columbia University Press in 1930.
6. Carmen Haider, *Do We Want Fascism?* (New York: John Jay Company, 1934), 123.
7. Ibid., 222.
8. Ibid., 227.
9. Ibid., 228.
10. Ibid., 243.
11. Ibid., 244–45.
12. Ibid., 245–46.
13. Ibid., 247.
14. Lewis Corey, *The Crisis of the Middle Class* (New York: Covici Friede Publishers, 1935), 279–80.

15. Ibid., 281.
16. Ibid., 282.
17. Ibid., 283.
18. Raymond Gram Swing, *Forerunners of American Fascism* (Montauk, NY: Julian Messner, Inc., 1935), 14.
19. Ibid., 17.
20. Ibid., 18.
21. Ibid., 21–22.
22. Ibid., 24–25
23. Ibid., 28–29.
24. Ibid., 29.
25. Harry F. Ward, "The Development of Fascism in the United States," *Annals of the American Academy of Political and Social Science* 180 (July 1935): 55.
26. Ibid., 56.
27. Ibid., 57.
28. Ibid.
29. Ibid., 59–60.
30. Frank A. Warren III, *Liberals and Communism: The "Red Decade" Revisited* (Bloomington and London: Indiana University Press, 1966), 8.
31. Ibid., 9.
32. Ibid., 8.
33. Ibid., 9.
34. Ibid., 12.
35. Ibid., 32–33.
36. John Dewey, "Renascent Liberalism," in *The Philosophy of John Dewey: The Lived Experience*, vol. 2, ed. John J. McDermott (New York: G. P. Putnam's Sons, 1973), 647.
37. Ibid., 657.
38. Alfred M. Bingham, *Insurgent America: Revolt of the Middle-Classes* (New York and London: Harper & Brothers Publishers, 1935), 238.
39. Ibid., 47.
40. Ibid., 48.
41. Ibid., 51.
42. Ibid., 63.
43. Ibid., 65.
44. Ibid., 78–79.
45. Ibid., 79.
46. Ibid., 104.
47. Ibid., 104–5.
48. Ibid., 111.
49. Ibid., 185–86.

50. Ibid., 187.
51. Ibid., 188.
52. Ibid., 191.
53. Ibid., 192.
54. Ibid., 197.
55. Ibid., 237–40.
56. Ibid., 241.
57. Ibid., 243.
58. Ibid., 244.
59. Ibid., 200.
60. Ibid., 210.
61. Dewey, "Renascent Liberalism," 661.

**11. Roosevelt on Fascism and the False Dichotomy of
Good vs. Bad Capitalism**

1. *New York Times*, February 5, 1933, cited in A. B. Magil and Henry Stevens, *The Peril of Fascism: The Crisis of American Democracy* (New York: International Publishers, 1938), 79.

2. "We Have Only Just Begun to Fight," Campaign Address at Madison Square Garden, New York City, *The Public Papers and Addresses of Franklin D. Roosevelt, 1936*, vol. 5: *The People Approve*, ed. Samuel I. Rosenman (New York: Random House, 1938), 568.

3. David Lynch, *The Concentration of Economic Power* (New York: Columbia University Press, 1946), 18–19.

4. Alan Brinkley, *The End of Reform: New Deal Liberalism in Recession and War* (New York: Alfred A. Knopf, 1995), 98. "A series of public opinion polls conducted in March 1938 showed a steady rise in the number of respondents who blamed the 'present decline in business' on the administration, and agreed that it deserved the label the 'Roosevelt recession.'" One of Roosevelt's most vocal critics at the time, John T. Flynn, called it the "Roosevelt Depression." See Flynn, *The Roosevelt Myth* (Garden City, NY: Garden City Publishing, 1948), 116.

5. Albert E. Kahn, *High Treason: The Plot Against the People* (New York: Hour Publishers, 1950), 129.

6. Ira Katznelson, *Fear Itself: The New Deal and the Origins of Our Time* (New York and London: Liveright, 2013), 257–60.

7. "I See One-Third of the Nation Ill-Housed, Ill-Clad, Ill-Nourished," Second Inaugural Address. January 20, 1937, in Rosenman, *The Public Papers and Addresses of Franklin Delano Roosevelt, 1937 Volume: The Constitution Prevails* (London: Macmillan and Co., 1941), 5. The papers in this volume will be hereinafter referred to as *Public Papers and Addresses, 1937*.

8.   "A Recommendation for the Appropriation for Work Relief for 1938, and for Curtailment of Certain Other Expenditures, April 20, 1937," *Public Papers and Addresses, 1937*, 165.

9.   Broadus Mitchell, *Depression Decade: From New Era through New Deal, 1929–1941* (New York and Toronto: Rinehart & Company, 1947), 42–43.

10. Ellis W. Hawley, *The New Deal and the Problem of Monopoly: A Study in Economic Ambivalence* (Princeton: Princeton University Press, 1966), 388.

11. Kenneth S. Davis, *FDR: Into the Storm, 1937–1940* (New York: Random House, 1993), 158.

12. Ibid., 159.

13. A. B. Magil and Henry Stevens, *The Peril of Fascism: The Crisis of American Democracy* (New York: International Publishers, 1938), 197–232.

14. Alvin Harvey Hansen, *Full Recovery or Stagnation?* (New York: W. W. Norton, 1938), 7–8.

15. Ibid., 273–74.

16. Ibid., 282.

17. Ibid., 268–70.

18. Ibid., 274.

19. Ibid., 280–81.

20. Ibid., 282.

21. Michael Hiltzik, *The New Deal: A Modern History* (New York: Free Press, 2011), 380.

22. Marriner S. Eccles, *Beckoning Frontiers: Public and Personal Recollections*, ed. Sidney Hyman (New York: Alfred A. Knopf, 1951), 393.

23. Ibid., 294.

24. Ibid., 294–95.

25. Ibid., 296, 301.

26. Sumner H. Slichter, "The Downturn of 1937," *Review of Economic Statistics* 30/3 (August 1938): 107–10. As Slichter wrote: "An unwillingness of enterprises to put more working capital into industrial equipment, consumer resistance to higher prices, decline in the government's contribution to incomes, all coming at a time when inventories were large, profits were dangerously low, and when the demand for goods based upon long-term planning was small."

27. William Leuchtenburg, *Franklin D. Roosevelt and the New Deal, 1932–1940* (New York: Harper & Row, 1963), 249.

28. Davis, *FDR*, 200.

29. "Annual Message to the Congress, January 3, 1938," *The Public Papers*

and Addresses of Franklin D. Roosevelt, 1938 Volume: The Continuing Struggle of Liberalism, ed. Samuel I. Rosenman (London: Macmillan and Co., 1941), 12. The papers in this volume will be hereinafter referred to as *Public Papers and Addresses, 1938*.

30. Davis, *FDR,* 200–201.
31. Annual Message to the Congress, January 3, 1938, *Public Papers and Addresses, 1938,* 9–10.
32. Ibid., 10–11.
33. Ibid., 12.
34. Kahn, *High Treason,* 192–93.
35. Jeanne Nienaber Clarke, *Roosevelt's Warrior: Harold L. Ickes and the New Deal* (Baltimore and London: Johns Hopkins University Press, 1996), 250.
36. See http://www.roberthjackson.org/files/thecenter/files/bibliography/the-menace-to-free-enterprise.pdf.
37. Harold L. Ickes, *The Secret Diary of Harold L. Ickes,* vol. 2: *The Inside Struggle, 1936–1939* (New York: Simon and Schuster, 1954), 282–83.
38. Davis, *FDR,* 205–6.
39. Sidney Hyman, *Marriner S. Eccles: Private Entrepreneur and Public Servant* (Stanford, CA: Stanford University Graduate School of Business, 1976), 245.
40. Davis, *FDR,* 215.
41. Ibid., 219–22.
42. Brinkley, *End of Reform,* 99–100.
43. "Recommendations to the Congress Designed to Stimulate Further Recovery, April 14, 1938," *Public Papers and Addresses, 1938,* 226–30.
44. "Recommendations to the Congress to Curb Monopolies and the Concentration of Economic Power, April 29, 1938," *Public Papers and Addresses, 1938,* 315.
45. Ibid., 305–6.
46. Ibid., 306–8.
47. Ibid., 308–9.
48. Master Speech Files (Microfilm), Series 2, File no. 1133, Franklin Delano Roosevelt Presidential Library, Hyde Park, NY.
49. Brinkley, *End of Reform,* 101–2.
50. A Special Press Conference with Members of the Associated Church Press, Washington, D.C., April 20, 1938. *Public Papers and Addresses,1938,* 254–55.
51. A summary of its findings and recommendations appears in the *Final Report and Recommendations of the Temporary National Economic Committee*, Public Resolution No. 113 (Washington, D.C.: Government Printing Office, 1941).

52. "Recommendations to the Congress to Curb Monopolies and the Concentration of Economic Power," *Public Papers and Addresses, 1938,* 320.

53. *Final Report and Recommendations of the Temporary National Economic Committee,* 4.

54. Richard Moe, *Roosevelt's Second Act: The Election of 1940 and the Politics of War* (New York: Oxford University Press, 2013), 171, 218.

55. Ibid., 238.

12. The Seminal Work of Robert A. Brady on Fascism in the Business System

1. "Recommendations to the Congress to Curb Monopolies and the Concentration of Economic Power," *The Public Papers and Addresses of Franklin D. Roosevelt, 1938 Volume: The Continuing Struggle of Liberalism,* ed. Sameul I. Rosenman (London: Macmillan and Co., 1941), 305-6.

2. A. B. Magil and Henry Stevens, The *Peril of Fascism: The Crisis of American Democracy* (New York: International Publishers, 1938), 118, 148.

3. Robert A. Brady, "The Fascist Threat to Democracy," *Science & Society* 2/2 (Spring 1938): 147–48.

4. Ibid., 164.

5. Ibid., 151–52.

6. Ibid., 152.

7. Ibid., 154–56.

8. Ibid., 156–57.

9. Ibid., 157–60.

10. Ibid., 162.

11. Robert A. Brady, *The Spirit and Structure of German Fascism* (New York: Viking Press, 1971), 361. The book was first published in 1937 by the Citadel Press.

12. Ibid., 362.

13. Ibid., 363.

14. Ibid., 363–64.

15. Ibid., 366.

16. Ibid., 367.

17. Ibid., 368.

18. Ibid., 368–69.

19. Ibid., 369–70.

20. Ibid., 371.

21. Ibid., 371–72.

22. Ibid., 372.

23. Ibid., 373–74.

24. Ibid., 374–75.
25. Ibid., 375.
26. Ibid., 375–76.
27. Ibid., 376.
28. Ibid.
29. Ibid., 377.
30. Ibid., 377–78.
31. Ibid., 378–79.
32. Ibid., 379–80.
33. Ibid., 380.
34. Ibid., 380–81.
35. Ibid., 382.
36. Ibid., 382–84.
37. Ibid., 384.
38. Robert A. Brady, *Business as a System of Power* (New Brunswick, NJ, and London: Transaction Publishers, 2001), 1. Brady's book was originally published by Columbia University Press in 1943.
39. Ibid., 1–2.
40. Ibid., 3–5.
41. Ibid., 5–6.
42. Ibid., 8.
43. Ibid., 193.
44. Ibid., 194–95.
45. Ibid., 196.
46. Ibid., 217.
47. Nicholas Baran and John Bellamy Foster, eds., *The Age of Monopoly Capital: The Selected Correspondence of Paul A. Baran and Paul M. Sweezy, 1949–1964* (New York: Monthly Review Press, 2017), 93.

Conclusion: Fascism and the Problem of American Exceptionalism

1. *Wall Street Journal*, October 16, 1934.
2. William E. Leuchtenburg, *The Perils of Prosperity, 1914–1932* (Chicago and London: University of Chicago Press, 1993), 8.
3. Arthur M. Schlesinger, *The Politics of Upheaval, 1935–1936* (Boston and New York: Houghton-Mifflin Company, 1960), 167–70.
4. Paul M. Buhle, *A Dreamer's Paradise Lost: Louis C. Fraina/Lewis Corey (1892–1953) and the Decline of Radicalism in the United States* (Atlantic Highlands, NJ: Humanities Press, 1995), 118.
5. Alan Dawley, *Struggles for Justice: Social Responsibility and the Liberal State* (Cambridge, MA, and London: Harvard University Press, 1991), 336, 342; Chris Harman, *Zombie Capitalism: Global Crisis and the Relevance of Marx* (Chicago: Haymarket Books, 2009), 146–47. Harman

emphasized Corey's analysis on the role of "luxury consumption, unproductive expenditures and credit" in the 1920s that helped to sow the seeds of the coming crisis, perhaps at the expense of Corey's larger analytical framework.

6.   The position taken here reflects a world-system approach based on the Marxist definition of fascism as the power of finance capital—the dictatorship of capital—over society and its institutions. It differs, but is not antagonistic to, the approach taken by Roger Griffin, who defines fascism as an "an alternative modernity" to the decadence of the contemporary world. Griffin's studies of European fascism do much to bring out what he calls the "modernist dynamics" of European fascist movements and their leaders. But he chooses not to view fascism as a functional property of monopoly-capitalism in crisis. For Griffin, capitalist crisis is a necessary condition but not a main cause of fascism. On this basis, he defines fascism as "a revolutionary species of political modernism originating in the early twentieth century whose mission is to combat the allegedly degenerative forces of contemporary history (decadence) by bringing about an alternative modernity and temporality (a 'new order' and a 'new era') based on the rebirth, or palingenesis, of the nation." For Griffin fascism emerges from "acute crisis conditions" as a nationalist movement led by a charismatic leader "performing the role of a modern prophet" who offers his followers "a new 'mazeway' (worldview) to redeem the nation from chaos and lead it into a new era, one that drew on a mythicized past to regenerate the future." Thus, "fascism is a form of programmatic modernism that seeks to conquer political power in order to realize a totalizing vision of national or ethnic rebirth. Its ultimate end is to overcome the decadence that has destroyed a sense of communal belonging and drained modernity of meaning and transcendence and usher in a new era of cultural homogeneity and health." None of this really applies to the genesis of American fascism in the 1920s and 1930s, and it ironically gives more weight to those writers at the time who said that it would not look anything like Italy or Germany. See Griffin, *Modernism and Fascism: The Sense of a Beginning Under Mussolini and Hitler* (New York: Palgrave Macmillan, 2007), 181–82.

7.   Adolf A. Berle and Gardiner C. Means, *The Modern Corporation and Private Property* (New Brunswick, NJ: Transaction Publishers, 2007), li.

8.   Ibid., 18–30.

9.   *Final Report and Recommendations of the Temporary National Economic Committee*, Public Resolution No. 113 (Washington , D.C.: Government Printing Office, 1941), 3–4.

10.   Ibid., 4.

11. "Economic Power and Political Pressures," *Investigation of Concentration of Economic Power*, Monograph No. 26 (Washington, D.C.: U.S. Government Printing Office, 1941), 2.

12. Frederick Rudolph, "The American Liberty League, 1934–1940," *American Historical Review* 56/1 (October 1950): 19–20.

13. Ibid., 20–21.

14. Ibid., 21–22.

15. Kim Phillips-Fein, *Invisible Hands: The Businessmen's Crusade Against the New Deal* (New York and London: W. W. Norton, 2009), 10.

16. Grace Hutchins, "The Truth About the Liberty League," *International Pamphlets* No. 50 (1936): 6.

17. Ibid., 5–13.

18. Ibid., 14.

19. For the best summary of the Butler plot, see Sally Denton, *The Plots Against the President: FDR, A Nation in Crisis, and the Rise of the American Right* (New York: Bloomsbury Press, 2012).

20. Albram Lipsky, *Man the Puppet: The Art of Controlling Minds* (Mansfield Centre, CT: Martino Publishing, 2014), 58. The book was first published in 1925 by Frank-Maurice, Inc.

21. Ibid., 122–23.

22. Stephen Raushenbush, *The March of Fascism* (New Haven: Yale University Press, 1939), 2–3.

23. Ibid., 24.

24. Ibid., 314.

25. Ibid., 317.

26. Ibid., 339.

27. Ibid., 340–41.

28. Ibid., 341.

29. Ibid., 341–42.

30. Ibid., 345.

31. Ibid., 346.

32. Ira Katznelson, *Fear Itself: The New Deal and the Origins of Our Time* (New York and London: Liveright, 2013), 126.

33. Karl Marx and Frederick Engels, *The Manifesto of the Communist Party, Collected Works*, vol. 6 (Moscow: Progress Publishers, 1976), 170.

34. "Recommendations to the Congress to Curb Monopolies and the Concentration of Economic Power," *The Public Papers and Addresses of Franklin D. Roosevelt, 1938 Volume: The Continuing Struggle Against Liberalism*, ed., Samuel I. Rosenman (London: Macmillan and Co., 1941), 320.

35. *Final Report and Recommendations of the Temporary National Economic Committee*, 3.

Index